The Priesthood of Industry

THE PRIESTHOOD
OF INDUSTRY

*The Rise of the Professional Accountant in
British Management*

DEREK MATTHEWS, MALCOLM ANDERSON,
and JOHN RICHARD EDWARDS

OXFORD UNIVERSITY PRESS
1998

Oxford University Press, Great Clarendon Street, Oxford OX2 6DP

Oxford New York

Athens Auckland Bangkok Bogota Bombay
Buenos Aires Calcutta Cape Town Dar es Salaam
Delhi Florence Hong Kong Istanbul Karachi
Kuala Lumpur Madras Madrid Melbourne
Mexico City Nairobi Paris Singapore
Taipei Tokyo Toronto Warsaw

and associated companies in
Berlin Ibadan

Oxford is a trade mark of Oxford University Press

Published in the United States
by Oxford University Press Inc., New York

British Library Cataloguing in Publication Data
Data available

Library of Congress Cataloging in Publication Data
Matthews, Derek.
The priesthood of industry: the rise of the professional accountant in business
management / derek Matthews, Malcolm Anderson, and John Richard Edwards.
p. cm.
Includes bibliographical references and index.
1. Accounting—Great Britain—History. 2. Accounting firms—Great Britain.
3. Accountants—Great Britain—History. I. Anderson, Malcolm.
II. Edwards, J. R. III. Title.
HF5616.G7M38 1998
657'.0941—dc21
97-33637
CIP
ISBN 0-19-828960-X

1 3 5 7 9 10 8 6 4 2

Typeset by Best-set Typesetter Ltd., Hong Kong
Printed in Great Britain
on acid-free paper by
Biddles Ltd,
Guildford and King's Lynn

PREFACE

> Our experts describe you as an appallingly dull fellow, unimagina-
> tive, timid, spineless, easily dominated, no sense of humour, tedious
> company and irrepressibly drab and awful. And whereas in most
> professions these would be considered drawbacks, in accountancy,
> they're a positive boon.
>
> (Monty Python, *And Now for Something Completely Different*,
> quoted in Bougen, 1994: 320)

Thus, twenty years ago, Monty Python mercilessly lampooned the professional accountant, and there is little doubt that their assessment (with
relatively minor variation) was, and still is, shared by many. It is nevertheless the case that accountants are, today, by far the most prominent professionals active in British management. They have been remarkably
successful in establishing their craft as the leading management qualification. This is not the case in many other countries and it was not always so
in Britain.

There has been much discussion as to the possible effects of this increased role of accountants in the management of British industry. Early
writers such as Stacey (1954) saw the trend as beneficial, but more have
argued the reverse. It has been suggested that the participation of accountants in management has led to a 'penny-pinching negative approach', to
excessive caution and an unwillingness to take risks, to too great an
emphasis on 'the bottom line', and to the need for investment to show a
profit in the short term (Armstrong, 1985: 129; 1987: 416, 425; Earl, 1983:
99–142). In America too, the rise of the accountant, as part of the
professionalization of management, is seen by some as responsible for
a deterioration in its economic performance (Hayes and Abernathy,
1980: 74).

The role of the accountant as manager has recently been questioned in
the political arena. Michael Heseltine (who accountants like to point out
failed his final accountancy examinations as a young man, but who jok-
ingly ripostes by describing himself as an 'unqualified success' since he
left the profession) suggested that, in comparison with Germany and
Japan, accountants play too prominent a role in British management
(Heseltine, 1993: 8; *Financial Times*, 11 Mar. 1994). 'I am not suggesting that
accountants are unnecessary', he said, 'but I do want to suggest that
there is more to life than financial accountants' (*Accountancy Age*, 6
Jan. 1994). There is nothing new in this argument. Indeed, as early as 1926,
the *Daily Express* argued that there were too many accountants in business

(quoted in *Accountant*, 6 Nov. 1926: 635). Remarkably little is known, however, about when, let alone why, the accountant has risen to such prominence.

There was little more than a handful of accountants listed in the trade directories of Britain's major cities in the late eighteenth century, whereas the major professional accounting bodies today boast approximately a quarter of a million qualified members. It was during the second half of the nineteenth century that British accountants began to show a determination to acquire professional status, with a key feature in this process being the establishment of professional organizations, starting with the Edinburgh Society and Glasgow Institute in 1853. During the inter-war period accountants moved from public practice into industry in large numbers. This trend continued post-Second World War, with accountants increasingly dominating appointments as finance director and becoming more prominent in general management positions, including that of chief executive. Indeed, professional accountants are comfortably the leading professional grouping in British business management today. Underpinning this process has been the public accounting practice as the supplier of managerial talent, with the audit function providing opportunities for trainees to develop a thorough understanding of the business environment, while taxation and consultancy work have opened up opportunities for some to develop the range of skills valued by industry and commerce.

This book focuses on the individual—the professional accountant. By combining an array of secondary material with our own original statistical analyses and interpretations, we aim to offer a comprehensive history of the multi-faceted role of the professional accountant in British business development from the pre-professionalization era down to the present day. Given that we define a professional as a member of a professional body, Chapter 1 outlines some of the main theoretical explanations that have been developed to explain the professionalization process. This enables us to locate, for the reader, our own predilection which is that of the economic determinist. We argue that public accounting practices, which were the bedrock for the formation of the professional bodies, developed in response to demand within the economy for the services that they could supply. We recognize the existence of evidence to suggest that accountants benefited from insolvency legislation, and that some early statutes also gave recognition to the role of the public accountant, but, overwhelmingly, growth was spurred on by the market. In Chapter 2, we focus principally on the pre-professionalization period and show how the 'public accountant' was gradually delineated, in response to market pressures, from undefined groups of individuals offering the diverse range of services that found favour within the increasingly industrialized British economy.

In Chapter 3, we focus on five areas which serve, to a greater or lesser degree, as underpinning themes which we pursue throughout the rest of the book. These are the nature and growth of the accountancy firms, the role of the accounting societies, a longitudinal study of the numbers of professional accountants in Britain, the gender issue, and an indication of their social and financial backgrounds. The major emphasis of this book is on the movement of professional accountants from public practice to industry and the main societies of interest for this purpose are the Institute of Chartered Accountants of Scotland (and predecessor bodies), the Institute of Chartered Accountants in England and Wales, the Institute of Chartered Accountants of Ireland, the Society of Incorporated Accountants and Auditors, and the Association of Chartered Certified Accountants (together with its predecessor bodies). Members of the Chartered Institute of Management Accountants also receive some attention as relevant in measuring the involvement of professional accountants in top management, but they are not central to the story in the sense that their members qualify within industry, as do some certified accountants. Unqualified accountants are outside the scope of this study.

Chapters 4–6 contain a chronological study of the rise of the accountant in management, dealing separately with the Victorian and Edwardian era, the inter-war period, and the period since the Second World War. In the final chapter, we explore some explanations for the findings which we present. Specifically, we look to explain the vast growth in the number of professionally qualified accountants, and why so many transferred to business and succeeded in obtaining positions in top management. We pursue our economic determinist line of argument by analysing explanations for the move into industry into demand- and supply-side factors. Significant on the demand side were the growing scale and structure of corporations, financial distress, the financial environment, and the sheer number of companies requiring accounting expertise. On the supply side we find that the education and training obtained in a public practice has proved superior to all other methods of preparation for a business career. This last chapter also considers, in detail, the extent to which the professional accountants' hegemony may be attributed to their initial education and training and the subsequent experience that they accumulate when carrying out their job. In undertaking this final exercise, we will see that thinly veiled versions of Monty Python's characterization of the accountant play a part in the debate.

D. M.
M. A.
J. R. E.

Cardiff Business School

ACKNOWLEDGEMENTS

We wish to thank the Research Board of the Institute of Chartered Accountants in England and Wales for financial support, and David Musson of Oxford University Press for his patience and encouragement. We wish to express our gratitude to Peter Boys for much of the contents of the Appendix and to *Accountancy* for permission to reproduce these items.

We are grateful to Trevor Boyns for advice and comments on an earlier draft, Paul Turk for assistance with data collection, the participants at various conferences and seminars for comments on presentations based on material contained in this book, and Barry Morse, Ian Kirkpatrick, Keith Macdonald, R. H (Bob) Parker, Stephen Walker, and Hugh Willmott for reading and commenting on earlier drafts of selected chapters. We thank Lesley Plowman and Sandie Edwards for so ably preparing much of the typescript for this book. Any errors and omissions of fact or interpretation are of course our responsibility.

Finally, we are grateful to the *Economic History Review* for permission to reproduce passages from 'The Rise of the Professional Accountant in British Management' (1997), in Chapter 7.

CONTENTS

LIST OF FIGURES

LIST OF TABLES

ABBREVIATIONS

ACCA	Association of Certified and Corporate Accountants/Chartered Association of Certified Accountants/Association of Chartered Certified Accountants
CA	Corporation of Accountants
CAA	Central Association of Accountants
CIMA	Chartered Institute of Management Accountants
CIPFA	Chartered Institute of Public Finance and Accountancy
Edinburgh Society	Society of Accountants in Edinburgh
Glasgow Institute	Institute of Accountants and Actuaries in Glasgow
ICAEW	Institute of Chartered Accountants in England and Wales
ICAI	Institute of Chartered Accountants in Ireland
ICAS	Institute of Chartered Accountants of Scotland
ICMA	Institute of Cost and Management Accountants
ICSA	Institute of Chartered Secretaries and Administrators
ICWA	Institute of Cost and Works Accountants
IMTA	Institute of Municipal Treasurers and Accountants
LAA	London Association of Accountants/London Association of Certified Accountants
SAA	Society of Accountants and Auditors
SIAA	Society of Incorporated Accountants and Auditors
WW	*Who's Who*
WWW	*Who Was Who*

References in this book to the 'original chartered bodies' are to the ICAS and its predecessors, the ICAEW, and the ICAI.

1

Introduction

THE PROFESSIONALIZATION PROCESS

The rise of the professional in Britain is a topic that has received close attention in the literature. The issues debated include fundamental questions such as what constitutes a profession and the mechanism through which professional status is achieved (Carr-Saunders and Wilson, 1933; Elliott, 1972; Esland, 1980; Flexner, 1915; HMSO, 1949; Johnson, 1972; Larson, 1977; Lewis and Maude, 1952; McKinlay, 1973; Millerson, 1964; Perkin, 1989; Wilensky, 1964). This book deals with the rise of the professional accountant in British management, and we define a professional accountant (see Chapter 3) as a member of a professional accounting body. It is therefore necessary, as a methodological background to this study, to set out our assumptions concerning the achievement of this position of prominence.

The debate about the way in which the professions have achieved their present position has developed markedly over time, partly reflecting differing ideological standpoints. Until the 1960s, the prevailing school of thought among sociologists studying the professions, and indeed other subjects, was that of the functionalists or the structural functionalists. They, heavily influenced by the writings of Emile Durkheim (1857–1917; see also Perkin, 1989: 9), sought to examine the contribution made by selected phenomena to social and cultural life and, in this way, explain their existence. According to this view, the emergence of institutions generally was a natural consequence of the fact that they fulfilled useful roles within society. This logic, when applied to the study of the professions, entailed looking at the range of functions performed by professionals and, almost inevitably, led to a supportive and uncritical traits-based approach to the subject.

The formation of a professional association was, from the 'traits' viewpoint, seen to be a natural, and unproblematic, progression designed to provide practitioners with the training necessary to enable them to perform important roles within society. The fact that the designation 'profession' was largely restricted to the Church, medicine, and law, up to the beginning of the nineteenth century, may well have been a driving factor in this characterization of professions as valuable, altruistic, institutions. With the emergence of Britain as the first industrial economy, however, many new techniques in the sciences and administration developed and brought into being groups of expert practitioners such as engineers, architects, pharmacists, veterinary surgeons, dentists, actuaries, and accountants (Parker, 1986: 13). As their numbers increased, these practitioners joined forces to form societies, often modelling themselves on the ancient professions. The formation of these new professional associations was seen 'to provide a functionally appropriate means of regulating the competence and conduct of those possessing the talent to undertake such socially essential and beneficial activities' (Willmott, 1986: 557; see also Carr-Saunders and Wilson, 1933: 286).

The professions have always had their critics, of course, and even proponents of the traits-based approach were not entirely uncritical with Millerson, for example, convinced that the traditional virtuous image of the professional was not universally appropriate (1964: 6). A more concerted critical approach to the professions emerged in the 1960s, however, concurrent with a 'mounting public scepticism regarding the benefits of professionalism' (Johnson, 1993: 146). The theoretical underpinning of this change of direction was the decline of functionalism as the dominant paradigm in sociology, and the rise of 'symbolic interactionism' emanating largely from the Chicago School led by Everett C. Hughes (1963).

The interactionist sees knowledge as an active process in which people, their understanding, and worldly phenomena are bound together. According to Macdonald, one of the leading British sociologists writing in this area, with the 'shift in emphasis from structure to action the sociological question changed from: "What part do professions play in the established order of society?" to "How do such occupations manage to persuade society to grant them a privileged position?"' (1995: p. xii). Or as Hughes put it, writing in 1963, 'I passed from the false question "is this occupation a profession" to the more fundamental one "what are the circumstances in which people in an occupation attempted to turn it into a profession"' (quoted in Macdonald, 1995: 6). Interactionists, therefore, analyse a profession as an interest group. For them, members of the profession constantly strive to maintain and justify their professional standing in order to cling to the rewards that such status brings.

The re-examinations of the role of the professions have been based principally on the inspirational writings of Max Weber (1864–1920) and Karl Marx (1818–83). These revisionist analyses focus on the actions of professional bodies in the wider structural and institutional context. In Weber's view, society is made up of individuals pursuing selfish interests which, in turn, generate collectively conscious groups who strive for economic, social, and political power in conflict with other groups, including the State (1968: 342). To Weber, the specific attributes possessed by a group (for example, race, age, sex, religion, language) may be used for the 'monopolization of specific, usually economic opportunities. This monopolization is directed against competitors who share some positive or negative characteristics; its purpose is always the closure of social and economic opportunities to outsiders' (1968: 342). Following Weber, therefore, the interactionists were concerned with 'action' or how things get done and with the social construction of reality.

The implications of Weber's ideas for the treatment of the professions have been further explored by Larson (1977). She conceived the concept of 'the professional project', by which she meant 'an attempt to translate one order of scarce resources—special knowledge and skills—into another—social and economic rewards' (Larson, 1977: p. xvii). The specific aims of the professional project are seen to be, therefore, income security and social respectability (Larson, 1977: 81). Linkage with the class struggle is also made explicit, with the professional project designed to achieve a 'monopoly of status in a system of stratification . . . or collective social mobility' (Larson, 1977: p. xvii). Success in each of these endeavours is not merely a reflection of skill, expertise, or ethical standards, but the outcome of an active political campaign and a fierce power struggle.

Larson's work on the professional project concept has been taken up and extended by sociologists in Britain such as Macdonald, according to whom: 'In the economic order, to use Weber's term, the professional project is pursued in two main areas: the legal closure and monopolisation of the market and the occupation; and the exclusive acquisition of the knowledge and education on which the profession is based' (1995: 31). Once command of the market has been acquired, exclusionary closure is achieved through another concept fashioned by Weber, namely credentialism: 'a credential is some formal measure of competence such as a professional qualification which is accepted as being the basis for performing certain sorts of work' (Roslender, 1992: 23).

Proponents of a Marxist-based analysis of the professionalization process consider Weberian explanations neglectful of concepts such as class conflict. For Marxists, the professions are bound up in the social stratification based on: the means and, therefore, the relations of production; the appropriation of surplus value from labour and, therefore, the class struggle; and ultimately the role of the State (Macdonald, 1995: 41). Willmott agrees that '[t]he presence of specific skills, their changing valuation and the ability to gain recognition for "professional" claims is . . . conditioned less by the traits of professionalism and more by developments within the capitalist totality in which the professions themselves play a significant part' (Willmott, 1986: 558). All of this is clearly far removed from the cosy image of the worthy professional propagated by the functionalists.

THE ACCOUNTANCY PROFESSION

The way in which the accountancy profession has achieved its present position of prominence is also the subject of eager debate (West, 1996).

Many of the oft-cited histories of accountancy fall, if only implicitly, within the functionalist tradition. Loft has shown that the histories of leading professional accountancy associations, namely the Institute of Chartered Accountants in England and Wales (ICAEW) (Howitt, 1966), the Institute of Cost and Works Accountants (ICWA, 1969), and the Society of Incorporated Accountants and Auditors (Garrett, 1961), 'tend to assume not only that accountants are supremely necessary to society but also that the major factor enabling their current success has been their form of professional association' (Loft, 1986: 138). Moreover, Stacey, in the first history of the accountancy profession in Britain, saw accountancy as axiomatically 'an indispensable tool for ensuring the optimum output in any economic society' (1954: p. xiv).

The leading historian of accountancy firms, Edgar Jones, has also taken a generally uncritical view of the profession. His 1981 history of the firm Whinney, Smith & Whinney quotes, with approval, Millerson's analysis of the role of the professional, and continues:

despite the growing thicket of regulations, personal probity remains the elemental basis of the accountant's role. For instance, the English Institute's regulations which limit the size of clients in relation to the size of the accountancy practice (no firm should have a client that contributes more than 15% of its total fee income) were designed to avoid the possibility of such a company exercising undue pressure on an auditor concerned not to lose a substantial part of his business. In the nineteenth century unscrupulous accountants (particularly those not members of the professional bodies) doubtless gave in to such suggestions, while the majority, guided by a strong code of ethics, resisted temptation. (Jones, 1981: 249–50)

Jones's more recent history of Price Waterhouse gives prominence to the following statement made by the leading professional accountant of the post-war period, the late Lord Benson: 'I have noticed that the basic professional principles which were laid down by the Cooper Brothers in 1854 have remained unchanged all through my lifetime, and I do not think they will alter much in the years to come. It is only the outward trappings that change' (Benson, 1989: foreword). With concerns regarding the performance of Price Waterhouse as auditors of BCCI before him (*Accountancy Age*, 17 Mar. 1994: 3, 12 May 1994: 11; *Accountancy*, Aug. 1983: 19), Jones still asserts that 'most would agree that standards of professional conduct should have an enduring quality and that those promulgated by the Victorians largely pertain today' (1995: 24).

In a more critical vein, Macdonald has applied the concept of the professional project to British accountancy. He focuses particularly on the 'long battle to obtain state registration of accountants, by introducing legislation in Parliament'. The battle is judged to have been lost, however, because of 'the internecine quarrels' between the large number of accountancy societies that had grown up over the years, reflecting the wide range of the accountants' work, level of skill, and type of client (Macdonald, 1995: 199; Macdonald, 1985: 546; see also Walker and Shackleton, 1995: 499). Macdonald argues that accountants instead achieved market control by carefully building professional organizations with reputations for 'competence, probity and respectability', through the partial amalgamation of these organizations, and 'by obtaining the statutory restriction of accountancy functions to members of the senior professional bodies' (Macdonald, 1985: 554). He believes that the actions of accountants fit well the professional project model because they sought, not just economic gain, but social status and respectability. Through these latter two mechanisms the laity could be induced to trust the expert. As an example, Macdonald cites 'Scottish accountants, whose (successful) petitions to the Privy Council for Royal Charters emphasize their *respectability* far more than their education, training or usefulness to society, thus relying on an appeal to traditional, status values, rather than "modern" criteria' (1995: 60).

Macdonald believes that, over the years, accountants have successfully shifted the basis for their claim to professional status. In their infancy, professional bodies emphasized respectability and their 'gentlemanly' character. For accountants, this involved the insistence that they were not engaged in the provision of commercial services, such as those of auctioneers. Instead, as 'high status persons they could be trusted to charge a fair price and could not be expected to engage in cut-throat commercial competition' (Macdonald, 1995: 117). Once this starting point had been established, the focus switched towards 'high educational attainment and technical expertise' (Macdonald, 1995: 117). When the market had become convinced of the validity of this new test of a professional, accountants 'ventured back towards entrepreneurialism' (Macdonald, 1995: 117). This has manifested itself in the increasing extent to which, in recent years, accountants have engaged in a wide range of consultancy work; a move that has increasingly involved diversification into non-accounting areas (Jones, 1995: 295). Certainly, the leading firms now generate enormous incomes from consultancy. The 1995 'fee income split' showed that the 'big six' generated £763.9 million from that source, second only to audit/accountancy. Indeed, for Arthur Andersen, consultancy was comfortably the main source of income, accounting for 52.6% of all fees (*Accountancy*, July 1995: 19). Macdonald has noted how, in the late twentieth century, '[p]rofessionals have modified their position so as to fit in with the increased emphasis on commercialism as a social value' (1995: 118). For example, accountants have been permitted to advertise since 1984—a practice anathema to the profession in its infancy.

Linda Kirkham and Anne Loft also advocate the professional project model and argue that the various accounting societies engaged in 'usurpationary closure', when attempting to 'bite into the resources and benefits accruing to the dominant group' (Kirkham and Loft, 1992: 5). They also accuse Macdonald, and others, of being blind to the fundamental role of gender in the closure process (Kirkham and Loft, 1992: 6), and argue that he neglects the discursive strategies employed by accountants to achieve closure through constructing their own definition of accountants, thereby distinguishing themselves from clerks and bookkeepers (Kirkham and Loft, 1993).

Hugh Willmott also sees accountants as undertaking the professional project through their emphasis on 'socially valued traits of trustworthiness, independence and dependability' (1986: 559). Willmott argues that, by restricting the supply of labour through credentialism, associations are able to raise the market value of a professional's labour. This strategy is seen to rely on the client's ignorance and on the ability of the seller to '*socially construct* and negotiate the reality and value of the commodity (labour) to be supplied' (Willmott, 1986: 562). This mystique is defended through a monopoly created by restricted entry and training made 'all the more effective for being hidden by a cloak of gentlemanly conduct, specialist expertise and state legitimisation' (Willmott, 1986: 563). Professional bodies, according to Willmott, are able to influence both the demand and supply sides of the market for their labour. On the supply side, credentialism restricts the supply of labour, thus raising its quality and price. On the demand side, the establishment of associations can provide 'a powerful lobby for determining the nature and range of the services to be demanded' from the accountant (Willmott, 1986: 560).

Another of the leading Marxist writers in Britain, Terry Johnson, frequently refers to the accountancy profession in his empirical examples. He criticizes the Weberian tradition for failing to offer an explanation of why some occupations fail to be accepted as professions, whilst other strategies succeed. He cites television and washing-machine maintenance men and garage mechanics as evidence of other occupational groups who 'provide services generally associated with client ignorance and the application of complex bodies of knowledge, yet they are not accorded professional status' (1980: 341). For Johnson, it is neither the degree of complexity of the knowledge nor the significance which society places upon the particular function performed which differentiates success from failure in the transition from occupation to profession.

Rather, the very complexity of knowledge, the extent to which it remains 'esoteric', is determined by the degree to which it functions to promote and maintain capital in the course of its appropriation and expansionary dynamics, including realization. The 'ideology of professionalism' will be an effective strategy only when its claims coincide with and draw upon the dominant ideological processes of capital. (1980: 359)

Johnson continues: 'Modern accountancy is the creature of corporate business. First as a form of internal company control and then as an agency controlling transfers of value following the rise of the joint-stock company' (Johnson, 1980: 356). In more recent times, he sees accountancy as having 'become a significant mechanism of control in the armoury of the State in, for example, stimulating market conditions as a form of legitimisation for the allocation of capital' (Johnson, 1980: 356). The proactive role of the State in the professionalization process is also acknowledged by Johnson, in that 'such market monopolies were increasingly underwritten by government in the form of official recognition or license . . . linking the process of professionalisation directly to the process of state formation' (Johnson, 1993: 144).

Another writer on accounting history taking his precepts from Marxism, Peter Armstrong, also attributes the rise of accountants in Britain to their role in the 'global function of capital' (Armstrong, 1987: 417). He has 'tried to show that accountants and other organisational professions can be visualised as in group-level competition for access to key positions of command within the global function of capital and that from this base they then promulgate their own characteristic approaches to the problem of extracting surplus value' (1987: 417). Armstrong rejects what he sees as the essentially functionalist approach of two leading accounting theorists of the last twenty years, Watts and Zimmerman (1983). The argument that audits and accountants came about because they were a desirable outcome of the separation of the providers and users of finance is fundamentally flawed, according to Armstrong, in that 'desirable states of affairs do not, of themselves, always come about. The facts remain that audit requirements *were* imposed upon directors by law and that accountants *did* campaign to exclude the unqualified from auditing' (1987: 422). Further, Armstrong notes how 'accountants sometimes played a very active role indeed in creating a demand for their services as auditors', through persuading late nineteenth-century industrialists to adopt the public company form of business organization, 'with the bonus to themselves that they often retained the audits of the newly formed companies' (1987: 422).

DEMAND AND RESPONSE

These various analyses of the development of professional groupings, starting from a range of different standpoints, do much to explain the creation and role of professional bodies. We take the view that the accountant is an enthusiastic income maximizer, who pursues self-interest at the expense of other groups, and welcomes the enhanced social status conferred by society. It might also be argued that the accountant pursues these outcomes more vigorously than certain other professional groupings, though this is probably only a matter of degree. Indeed it is possible that, in recent years, the emphasis on income maximization has impacted on the quality of the service supplied and, in turn, on the accountant's standing within society. It is of course part of the role of the professional bodies to be aware of these tensions and to protect their members, sometimes by discouraging them from pursuing income opportunities that might damage the profession's image. It is equally clear that such organizations, in the endeavour to further the interest of their members, practise closure through restricting entry on the basis of wealth and examinations, acting as a pressure group within society, developing and protecting the value of designatory letters, and encouraging the acquisition of exclusive (arguably esoteric) knowledge. At the same time, the evidence presented in the following chapters demonstrate the view that the rise of accountants in Britain is principally attributable to the demand placed by society on the value of the services that they supply. It would seem to follow from this line of argument, therefore, that widespread criticism of accountants in recent years could result in their replacement by other groups capable of providing business with the required services. The fact is, however, that accountants have now achieved such an extremely powerful position within society that it would not be easy to shift them from that pedestal, even were this a desirable outcome.

Before returning to our main theme, we also acknowledge the fact that the formation of professional bodies and the rise of the professional accountant may have proceeded quite differently in other times and places and, consequently, one or other of the theoretical standpoints discussed above may provide the more persuasive framework within which to view developments. Even within Britain, we find the existence of different motivations for the formation of professional bodies. The formation of the Institute of Accountants in Edinburgh in 1853 (renamed the Society of Accountants in Edinburgh (Edinburgh Society) in 1854), for example, was principally motivated by the threatened loss of bankruptcy work to lawyers through legislation (Kedslie, 1990*b*: 8–9; Boys, 1990*a*: 110; Macdonald, 1995: 191; Walker, 1995). The Society of Accountants and Auditors (SAA) (renamed the Society of Incorporated Accountants and Auditors (SIAA) in 1908 and the Society of Incorporated Accountants in 1954) was formed because of the level of closure that the ICAEW had already put in place, while legislation—the Finance Act 1903 (see below)—led to the immediate formation of new bodies to achieve statutory recognition. These possibilities, and others, do not detract from our main thesis, which we set out below.

Accountants should be seen as income maximizers, rather than a group which, applying an 'altruistic' analysis (Edwards, 1989*a*: 276), charges a fair price for services rendered. Even friends of the professions, such as Tawney, have drawn our attention to the fact that fees charged by the eminent professionals could be excessive (1921: 107), and Millerson realized that 'a false impression is given of professional remuneration. While lawyers, doctors and surgeons have traditionally accepted fees, these charges have never been uniform. Practitioner's status mainly determined the size of fee' (Millerson, 1964: 7). Accountancy was no different. Edwin Waterhouse, writing in his diary in 1884, made it clear that there were no fixed rates for accountants' fees: 'some charge £3 3s a day for a principal's time and £1 11s 6d or £1 1s for clerks . . . £3 3s is of course much less than I estimate my own time as worth and get for it' (Jones, 1995: 59).

Edgar Jones's history of Price Waterhouse proves to be a source of illuminating information regarding the profitability of this firm. In 1866, the first full year of the practice, Price, Holyland & Waterhouse's fee income totalled £9,251, of which some 80% (£7,440) was profit. Whilst such margins have not been maintained due to 'the problem of rising overheads as the firm grew in size and widened the scope of its practise', considerable profits accrued to the partners over the years (Jones, 1995: 223). The position remains unchanged. Accountancy practices have historically been extremely coy about disclosing the profits that they earn, and probably for very good reasons. Arthur Andersen published figures in the USA in 1977, but this practice was not repeated until KPMG produced more detailed information than hitherto in the run-up to incorporating the auditing arm of its business in 1996. Its published accounts then revealed a pre-tax profit of £17.9 million, showed partners' salaries averaging £189,000 per annum, and a top payout of £740,000 to the firm's senior partner, Colin Sharman (Bassirian, 1996: 23). Accounts subsequently published by Ernst & Young show Nick Land's remuneration package as £326,701, while those for Pannell Kerr Forster show John Wosner to be one of five partners earning between £300,000 and £350,000. The Pannell Kerr Forster partners' salaries averaged £108,000, while those at Ernst & Young did rather better than even their counterparts at KPMG, at £200,000 a head (*Accountancy*, Jan. 1997: 13).

Accountants in industry also do extraordinarily well. A survey of the FTSE 100 finance directors—80% of whom are professional accountants—revealed a typical salary of £300,000. The top-paid chartered accountants were David Reid of Tesco and John Coombe at Glaxo Wellcome who received payments, respectively, of £680,000 and £666,333. The top-paid finance director was the certified accountant Ian Duncan, of Tomkins, who received £704,000, while Brian Walsh of the TI group led the management accountants with a package worth £457,000. Among the two women finance directors, Kathleen O'Donovan, ACA, of BTR, at £288,300 earned just over £65,000 more than Rosemary Thorne, FCMA, at Sainsbury (*Accountancy*, Dec. 1996: 20–1).

The high salaries and fees earned by accountants, however, have not been amassed in an uncompetitive market. Although, within the audit market, 'lowballing'—the practice of tendering a low figure for audit work to obtain access to more lucrative consultancy engagements—appears to be a relatively recent phenomenon, there has undoubtedly always been a market for the accountant's services, firms have always competed with one another, and do on occasions tout for business. And although Victorian accountants—certainly the City elite—endeavoured to promote an image of the superior, independent, detached professional who hardly liked to mention the subject of the fee, in reality firms chased business. As the official history of Grace, Derbyshire and Todd puts it: 'We threw our net for business wherever we thought it would catch fish, or I should say make money' (Grace et al., 1957: ch. 2). Moreover, we detail in Chapters 2 and 4 the fact that from the earliest times accountants personally acted as company chairmen, set up and ran companies, and in certain instances were highly successful entrepreneurs.

The accountant's high income, however, owes nothing, and probably could or should owe nothing, to monopolistic rights, such as those granted to doctors and barristers. From the pre-professional days, accountants' work included, albeit in differing levels of importance, book-keeping, the installation of accounting systems, management accounting, insolvency, management consultancy, tax advice, auditing, and fraud detection. It would not have been feasible to corner the market in any or all of these. As Macdonald has put it: ' "esoteric" knowledge was less than esoteric on the face of it, because there was scarcely an aspect that they did not share with some other occupation. Bookkeeping, company law, insolvency, taxation, trust accounts—lawyers, company secretaries and a host of bookkeepers and clerks with modest qualifications could be found to deal with each of these' (Macdonald, 1995: 201).

Hard economic reality underpinned demand for the accountant's work, which clearly involved a degree of difficulty requiring training and experience. Winding up a company, accurately valuing assets, installing costing systems, rooting out fraud, auditing company accounts, reconstructing companies, and arranging amalgamations were not the domain of the bookkeeper, as Kirkham and Loft (1993) and Willmott (1986) imply. Whilst each of these services can be performed badly, and has been on numerous occasions, executed competently they require skills way beyond those of a bookkeeper. We argue that, in the main, the history of the professional accountant should be analysed as a provider of financial services in the market place, and therefore take the economic (even technological) determinist viewpoint as the basis for our study. The material surveyed and presented in this history contains little evidence to suggest that accountants were able to construct their own reality or manufacture a status or demand for their services not justified by the economic imperatives of the market.

This line of argument is not meant to imply the absence of legislation beneficial to the profession—the Companies Act 1862 has been referred to as the 'accountants' friend', and the support provided by statute law for the accountant as either company liquidator or administrator of a bankrupt's estate is discussed in Chapter 2. In more recent years, the Finance Act 1965, through the introduction of corporation tax and capital gains tax, provided an enormous boost for the tax departments of many firms, and was in many cases instrumental in their formation. However, it is possible to use the single aspect of the accountant's work which comes within calling distance of being granted a monopoly by the State, namely auditing, to demonstrate the fact that the dominant position achieved by the professional accountant was, nevertheless, principally market driven.

The Friendly Societies Act 1875 (s. 14 (1) (c)), the Industrial and Provident Societies Act 1876 (s. 21), and the Friendly Societies Act 1896 (s. 26 (1)) provided some encouragement for the appointment of public accountants as auditors, while the Building Societies Act 1894 (s. 3) and the Industrial and Provident Societies Act 1913 (s. 2 (1)) made their engagement compulsory (see Chapter 4). The list of eligible auditors was restricted to chartered and incorporated accountants from 1920 because '[e]xperience showed that the work performed by lay auditors and by members of minor associations of accountants was often unsatisfactory' (quoted in Parker, 1986: 47). Whether these statutes had much impact on the decision to appoint professionals to undertake the audit function has not been the subject of detailed research, but the provisions clearly applied to only a small proportion of total economic activity, and developments elsewhere would suggest that their effect is unlikely to have been significant. The Municipal Corporation (Audit) Act 1933 permitted municipal corporations to adopt, instead of the elective audit, either the district audit or a professional audit undertaken by a member of an accounting body listed in a schedule to the Act. Coombs and Edwards (1996: ch. 7), however, have shown that professionally qualified accountants were already engaged by most if not all large corporations by 1914. The principal effect of the Finance Act 1903, which made provision for an accountant to appear before the revenue commissioners, and for this purpose defined him as a member of an incorporated society of accountants, was merely to encourage the formation of new accounting societies (Stacey, 1954: 70–1).

At the more general level, of course, the Companies Act 1947 conferred a legal monopoly of the audit of limited companies upon chartered, certified, and incorporated accountants. This again did little more than confirm what had already been established in the market place. Indeed, as early as 1886, of 943 British and Irish quoted companies known to be audited (admittedly a sub-section of the total corporate audit market), 725 (76.9%) were audited by professional accountants, of whom 719 (99.2%) were chartered (Anderson et al., 1996: 366). Parker acknowledges the fact that it has been their ability to establish themselves 'in the eyes of the business community . . . as possessing, as nobody else did, the requisite independence and competence', which explains the importance of audit to late nineteenth- and twentieth-century professional accountancy firms (1986: 39). It was not the product of a State-backed monopoly; indeed, 'it is doubtful whether the law caused a single change of auditor' (Parker, 1986: 39).

This does not mean that accountants were uninterested in State protection. Indeed, prior to the formation of the ICAEW in 1880, 'accountants at first attempted to obtain a Registration Act but were dissuaded by politicians and obtained a Royal Charter instead' (Macdonald, 1985: 548). There have over the years been recurrent attempts to achieve legal closure in one way or another. In 1891, the ICAEW introduced a bill to prohibit anyone else from using the designation chartered accountant. It was resisted by the SAA which, two years later, devised a bill designed to regularize the profession by providing for 'the registration and control of persons acting as public accountants' (quoted in Stacey, 1954: 34) This was in turn blocked by the ICAEW, and Stacey records further attempts to achieve closure in the last decade of the nineteenth century and the first two decades of the twentieth century (1954: 34–6, 83–90). The Departmental Committee appointed by the Board of Trade on the Registration of Accountants, under Viscount Goschen, reported in 1930 on the desirability of restricting the profession of accountancy to registered accountants. Conflicting evidence was presented by the accountancy bodies, and the Committee reported negatively on grounds which included: lack of public demand; the difficulty of defining a public accountant; uncertainty whether it would be in the public interest; and the fact that there were non-practising accountants who had a vested interest in accountancy work. Further initiatives in the direction of some form of closure based on qualifications, in the 1940s and 1950s, are recorded in the official history of the ICAEW (Howitt, 1966: 155–9).

Most recently, Walker and Shackleton (1995, 1996) have shown that the leading professional accountancy bodies retained a keen interest in this matter at least up to 1970. In 1939, the Accountants Advisory Selection Panel, consisting of leading practitioners, was set up to recommend professional accountants to the various ministries who needed to boost their administrative personnel. The development of close working relations with the government was seen as 'an opportunistic moment for addressing the problem of the organization of the accountancy profession' (Walker and Shackleton, 1995: 499). In 1942, the ICAEW resolved to discuss 'matters generally affecting the Profession' (quoted in Walker and Shackleton, 1995: 479), and the president of the ICAEW was instrumental in setting up an informal Co-ordinating Committee of the leading professional bodies 'to consider the co-ordination of the profession when approaching government departments' (Walker and Shackleton, 1995: 479). The aim was 'to secure a legal monopoly of public practice', with 'non public' and 'junior' organizations excluded from the arrangement (Walker and Shackleton, 1995: 467, 488). The initiative failed due to 'internecine conflict among some of the participants' and the fact that the closure move was 'alien to the prevailing consensus and collectivist politics' (Walker and Shackleton, 1995: 499).

CONCLUDING COMMENTS

The evidence presented in this history suggests that the degree of monopoly power achieved by accountants in public practice was not the product of State conferment, nor does it appear to have been principally driven by the professional bodies' endeavour to raise the status of the accountant in the public's esteem. At the same time, it is acknowledged that it is part of the purpose of professional associations to satisfy a public interest. In modern times, they have expressed this concern, and combined it with their responsibility to represent the interest of their members, in the following manner. In 1983, the ICAEW's president recounted how the council 'Felt it to be important that we should all take stock of the needs and aspirations of the members and how these can best be met, at the same time recognising that we are, and must remain, a profession, with a duty to serve the public interest' (quoted in Willmott et al., 1993: 76).

Efforts have undoubtedly been made to obtain a monopoly of the work undertaken by a public practice, but all have failed. Fundamentally, therefore, accountancy's place in the market is seen, in this book, to have been achieved in response to a real demand for its services. The whole process was driven by technological change and the chronology is of paramount importance to this analysis. The crucial and dynamic area of work for the British public practitioner, for much of the period covered by this book, was the corporate audit. This function did not become important, however, until after the successful application of steam technology to transport. Construction of the railways demanded huge investments of capital which, in Britain, were provided by the formation of joint-stock companies and the sale of shares to a wide range of investors, shares which were eventually bought and sold on a rapidly growing stock market. These 'blind' investors needed to monitor the operations and performance of their investments, particularly as they became more aware of the risks associated with the possibility of inefficient and fraudulent management. This divorce between ownership and control called forth the expert services of the accountant. As technology advanced, the steel industry, shipbuilding, chemicals, and an increasing number of new industries in turn gave rise to increased demands for capital and therefore for accountants.

We note, in Chapters 2 and 4, how an elite group of City accountants, including such people as William Quilter and William Welch Deloitte, established their reputations for skill and probity so that, following the scandals of the railway mania of the 1840s, they were drafted in to sort matters out and subsequently to provide professional audit services. City firms had established a significant influence in the audit of quoted companies as early as the 1860s—a position which they have never subsequently relinquished. In the 1870s, relatively small groups of accountants in the City of London and several major provincial cities that had already achieved a significant share of work in insolvency and audit formed five separate professional bodies. In 1880, these combined to form the ICAEW. This move served to establish the name, south of the border, by which they could be identified in the market place for financial services, and enabled them to control entry and thereby the quality of the product they had to offer, and in turn, enhance the value of their name. This was the aim in 1880 and remains so to this day, as evidenced by the following pronouncement of the 1994 council of the ICAEW:

Our activities in 1994 have focused on strengthening the value of the qualification 'chartered accountant'. That is not, however, a new objective . . . It is a shared interest in the value of the title that has always united all members . . . For the qualification chartered accountant to maintain its status as a premium brand it must continue to be seen as combining the higher standards of professional education and training with technical excellence. (ICAEW, 1994*a*: 4)

The market success enjoyed by accountants, therefore, preceded and indeed provided the bedrock for the subsequent formation of professional bodies, south of the border, rather than the other way around. It therefore seems reasonable to accept the traditional explanation for the formation of such bodies, namely as a mechanism for protecting their reputations (quite literally their good name) from being tarnished by disreputable characters.

We take the view that much of the subsequent history of accountants can be best understood by seeing accountants as agents operating within their economic context. Developments within the profession can be explained by accountants responding to economic signals in a quest for increased income. We have noted the response of accountants to the separation of corporate ownership and control in the provision of auditing services. As more companies were formed, accountants drew up their prospectuses. When companies faltered and needed reconstruction or amalgamation, members of the profession took on this work. They wound up companies that could not be rescued. When British capital went abroad, British accountants followed. As governments increased the burden of taxation through the twentieth century, the provision of tax advice became an important fee-earning activity for accountants. When companies wanted to employ their own accountants, professional accountants increasingly left practice and followed these job opportunities. Throughout the history that follows, therefore, we will see the activities of accountants responding to market opportunities in turn both created and changed by fundamental movements within the British and world economies.

The thesis that the rise of the accountancy profession has been driven primarily by the market is, in fact, almost self-evident in the case of accountants working in industry. We will see below (Chapter 3) that the formation of the Institute of Cost and Works Accountants in 1919 was mainly a consequence of the failure of the established bodies to make provision for accountants working in industry, and it was around this time that the members of the established bodies began to transfer their expertise from public practice to industry in greater numbers (Chapter 5). The concern of chartered accountants in industry with the lack of support from their professional organization has continued through the post-war period and led to the establishment of the Board for Chartered Accountants in Business in 1990 (see Chapter 7) in the endeavour to help address continuing tensions. It is in the absence of support from their professional bodies, therefore, that chartered accountants have nevertheless achieved a position of dominance both within the financial functions of industry and in top management positions, and this is despite the best efforts of the bespoke organization representing the interests of most accountants training in industry, now called the Chartered Institute of Management Accountants, to further the interests of its own members. We chart the rise to prominence of the professional accountant in business management in Chapters 4–6 and explore explanations in Chapter 7. First, however, we set the scene by examining how public accountants obtained a foothold as servants to business in the pre-professional days (pre-1853 in Scotland and pre-1870 in England and Wales) and then (Chapter 3) track a number of key developments during the post-professional period to help contextualize the study which follows.

2

Roots of the Profession

Account keeping pre-dates writing, of course, with the use of clay counters, for example, seen to constitute an accounting system in the Near East from about 8,000 BC to 3,000 BC (Mattessich, 1994; Schmandt-Besserat, 1992). It is well known that the Greeks and Romans kept detailed accounts in written form (de Ste Croix, 1956; Macve, 1986), and the earliest known fully articulated system of double-entry bookkeeping is contained in the account books of Giovanni Farolfi (1299–1300; Lee, 1977). Turning to Britain, an Italian firm of merchants—the Gallerani company of Siena—employed double-entry bookkeeping at their London branch between 1305 and 1308 (Nobes, 1994), while the first English text dealing with this technique, by Hugh Oldcastle, was published in 1543. Its widespread adoption, in Britain, in place of existing systems of single-entry bookkeeping occurred, of course, much later.

Turning to the teaching of bookkeeping and accounts, the curricula of some Elizabethan schools contain references to 'the art of casting accounts [which] was useful to boys who would later be apprenticed' (Curtis, 1967: 91). Examples provided by Curtis (1967: 91–2) include: 'St Olave's Grammar School, Southwark, 1561: The master to teach children to write and read and cast accounts.' There is evidence of bookkeeping and accounts having been taught over the next couple of centuries in private schools, the old grammar schools, and private academies, as well as by private tutors (Hans, 1951). The Soho Academy, for example (Hans, 1951: 88), was founded by Martin Clare, MA, FRS, in 1718, and located at Soho Square. Clare authored the *Youth's Introduction to Trade and Business, for the Use of Schools* (1720), which indicates that the school was intended as a commercial academy, though the curriculum included Latin and French for the training of aspiring merchants, because the 'businessman needs a liberal education as a basis for his vocational training' (quoted in Hans, 1951: 87–8). Clearly, these institutions were meeting a growing demand for accounting knowledge, and we know that merchants and manufacturing firms such as Wedgwood, Boulton and Watt, the Welsh ironmasters, and many others kept elaborate sets of accounts 'in house', sometimes with the help of specialist bookkeepers (Boyns and Edwards, 1996). Only rarely did these early entrepreneurs see the need to employ outsiders to help manage their accounts, but the situation eventually changed.

SOME NUMBERS AND PRACTICES

Through the latter part of the eighteenth century there was a gradual growth in the number of independent firms offering accounting services, often of a basic bookkeeping nature, to those unwilling or unable to provide their own (Jones, 1981: 24–5). Quantifying the numbers of accountants in this period relies on local trade directories which can give only a rough guide to the number of persons offering accounting services, and must almost inevitably understate the true figure. The figures given by Brown (1905), Kedslie (1990a), and Macdonald (1984) are summarized in Table 1. These show a mere handful of accountants in the major cities in the late eighteenth century, and a significant upsurge in numbers really begins to emerge only around 1850. One of the difficulties in constructing these figures is, of course, the fact that 'accountants' usually undertook a range of non-accounting activities, particularly early on. Macdonald, for example, points to the fact that accounting work was often combined with occupations 'such as writing master, teacher, agent or broker' (1984: 179). As late as 1880, the *Post Office London Directory* included accountants under the broader heading 'Accountants & Referees'.

The rise in the number of accountants naturally reflects the growth of accountancy practices. Some of the earliest include: Tribe, Clarke & Co. (1780) of Bristol, which merged with Deloitte, Plender, Griffiths & Co. (1969) (see Appendix, Deloitte Haskins & Sells), now part of Coopers & Lybrand; Edward Thomas Jones (1788), also Bristol, now Chantrey Vellacott; and Joseph Reddish (1796), Liverpool, now Kidsons Impey (see Appendix, Hodgson Impey, Kidsons), although the Liverpool office of Hodgson Impey in fact merged with Pannell Kerr Forster (1990) (Boys, 1994: 17). North of the border, William Cuthbertson set up in business in the eighteenth century, with his son Donald training with the family firm

Table 1. Numbers of accountants in various British cities, 1780 to 1870

Decade	London	Liverpool	Manchester	Bristol	Edinburgh	Glasgow	Aberdeen
1780s					7	6	
1790s	5	5		1			
1800s	25		4		17	10	
1810s	47		14				
1820s	99		24	20			
1830s		37	32	28			6
1840s	107	69	52		111	48	8
1850s	264		66		132	135	13
1860s	310	91	84	74	129	169	25
1870s	467	139	159		160	238	28

Sources: Brown, 1905: 183, 202; Kedslie, 1990a: 183, 199, 208; Macdonald, 1984: 180.

and being admitted to partnership in 1810 (Stewart, 1977: 74). These independent accountancy firms contained the seeds of the profession, and Jones's conviction that the growth in accountancy as a separate profession was part of the specialization process for services which traders had previously performed for themselves may be somewhat misplaced. Most firms had always maintained and, despite the recent rise in outsourcing arrangements (*Accountancy Age*, 18 Jan. 1996: 1), usually still today maintain their records on a day-to-day basis, and this preference probably explains early increases in the number of clerks employed by companies in England and Wales, which rose from 92,012 in 1861 to 236,125 in 1881 and 518,900 in 1901 (Kirkham and Loft, 1993: 556). The growth of the accountancy profession and independent firms of accountants in the nineteenth century, therefore, was primarily based on the supply of services which companies or their management could not, by definition, do for themselves, such as insolvency, auditing, and investigation work.

THE PATHWAY TO 'PUBLIC ACCOUNTANT'

The process through which accountancy firms developed in England mirrors, in some respects, the experience of banking during the same period since 'early private banks generally originated as the ancillary business of traders, manufacturers, and mining concerns' (Sayers, 1957: 1). Lloyds Bank, for example, grew out of the Birmingham iron trade. Likewise, the accountant's business sometimes started as a sideline for merchants or for suppliers of other business services who had developed an accounting expertise for their own purposes and, in due course, found it profitable to market their new-found knowledge. One entrant in the *Liverpool Directory* of 1790, for example, is described as a 'mercantile accomptant' as well as a 'dealer in tin-plates' (Brown, 1905: 234). John Mallard, who was also in business as a merchant around this time, undertook accounting work as a sideline, and his son, having trained in his father's firm, left in the 1820s to establish himself in public practice as an accountant (Hill Vellacott, 1988: 9 and 20). In Scotland, the designation 'merchant and accountant' was quite common in Glaswegian trade directories of the mid-nineteenth century; certainly much more so than in the directories of its historic rival Edinburgh, reflecting the less commercial and greater legal orientation of the profession in the latter city (Macdonald, 1984: 181).

This juxtaposition of accounting with other trades is well illustrated by the history of the Jones family. Edward Thomas Jones, who was also trained by Mallard in the 1780s, in due course founded the accountancy practice that eventually became Hill Vellacott. Jones, who sold bookkeeping systems to major firms in Scotland, Yorkshire, and Lancashire, was also the author of a controversial manual (Yamey, 1956) entitled *Jones's English System of Bookkeeping*, published in Bristol in 1796. Jones guaranteed that his text 'would measure up to the most exacting standards and supply what the commercial world, we may be sure, had long been seeking—an infallible system of book-keeping' (Etor, 1985: 356; Yamey, 1956: 313). Jones was successively proprietor of Waunfawr Colliery in Risca, south Wales, and a coal merchant in Bristol until 1821, when he finally moved to the City of London with his three sons (Orlando, Edwin, and Theodore) to set up an accountancy practice in Poultry and, later, at the top of Coleman Street (Hill Vellacott, 1988: 10–13). Following Edward's death, the firm was continued by Theodore whose two brothers left to develop their own business. Orlando set up as 'a public accountant and patent starch manufacturer' in the City of London and, when he died in 1847, his son Theodore Brooke Jones, aged 16, trained with Theodore, and eventually became a partner in his uncle's firm (Hill Vellacott, 1988: 20). Theodore Brooke Jones went on to become a founder member of the Institute of Accountants and, later, the ICAEW.

It is quite clear, then, that many newcomers to 'public practice' had developed some of the skills required at an earlier stage in their career, sometimes while apprenticed in businesses not closely connected with accountancy. In 1849, Frederick Whinney, a future president of the ICAEW, was employed as a senior clerk by Harding & Pullein, perhaps having acquired knowledge of accounts either at his family's livery stable in London, or in ship and insurance broking (Jones, 1986b: 766). Edwin Guthrie, who was later to play a prominent part in setting up the first British accountancy practice in the United States (Barrow, Wade & Guthrie in New York in 1883; Bywater, 1984: 685; Wise, 1982: 1–2), worked as a bookkeeper to a Liverpudlian general merchant before entering into business as a contractor in the 1860s. At the time of his marriage, in 1869, he was described as an estate agent, but six years later formed the Mancunian accountancy partnership Thomas, Wade & Guthrie, with John Thomas and Charles Henry Wade (Kitchen and Parker, 1980: 8–9; Jones, 1981: 67). Although their partnership was dissolved in 1895, both Wade and Guthrie achieved considerable subsequent success; Wade's firm was eventually to become part of Spicer Oppenheim (see Appendix), while Guthrie's practice became part of Peat, Marwick & Mitchell (see Appendix, Peat Marwick McLintock), now KPMG.

Henry Edge started life as a clerk on the railway near Bury around 1850, and we may infer that he developed his accounting expertise during this period as he then joined with a Mr Cane in an accountancy partnership in Blackburn, later becoming a founder member of the ICAEW (*Accountant*, 23 Feb. 1901: 255). Alfred Allott commenced his business career in the Sheffield and Hallamshire Bank, leaving to set up in business as a public accountant, in the 1850s, serving for many years as professional auditor to the Midland Railway Company. Like many others, he maintained his interest in business, being 'Largely connected with the development of the coal industry in South Yorkshire and was closely identified with some of the most successful undertakings of that character in the district' (*Accountant*, 16 Feb. 1901: 221). William Grisewood moved from Whitehaven to Liverpool at the age of 20, in the mid-1860s, and joined the accounting department of the Mersey Dock & Harbour Board before moving into practice (*Accountant*, 3 Apr. 1915: 458–9). Jarvis William Barber joined the Sheffield Banking Company where his father was a managing director in 1862, and five years later started business as an accountant and share broker (*Accountant*, 17 Dec. 1921: 854). In a similar vein, William Francis Moore began practice in Preston, in 1869, having obtained his early accounting experience as a bookkeeper in the corn warehouse of Joseph Pyke & Sons (Moore and Smalley, 1992). In Scotland, Robert Scobie was a clerk and cashier with a firm of wholesale warehousemen before setting up as an accountant in Glasgow in 1847 (Stewart, 1977: 149), while Robert Fletcher was a clerk in an insurance company until he started his own accountancy practice in Aberdeen in 1866 (Howitt, 1966: 242).

Not all late recruits to public practice moved from trade to their new position. Jonas Dearnley Taylor, about whom, like many others, more will be said later, started out in the offices of a solicitor (*Accountant*, 13 Sept. 1902: 908), while Henry Davies, on leaving Manchester Grammar School in the mid-1850s, entered the office of the Town Clerk of Salford where, as an indentured apprentice, he served the corporation for several years. He moved to the borough treasurer's office during his apprenticeship, and we may assume that it was there that he developed an accounting expertise. He subsequently became Preston's borough accountant, leaving in 1864 to set up in practice (*Accountant*, 23 Mar. 1908: 768).

In Scotland, young men often moved into accountancy after receiving their initial training in a solicitor's office. This reflected, in the main, the Scottish accountant's need for legal knowledge to equip him to carry out his duties efficiently. Many of the early Edinburgh accountants received at least part of their training in legal offices (for example, William Milne, James Meston), also partly reflecting the fact that a number had family connections in the legal profession (Stewart, 1977: 26, 109, 112; Walker, 1988). A similar situation appears to have prevailed in Aberdeen where six of the 22 members admitted to the society up to 1879 either practised as advocates or trained in the offices of advocates.

There is also no shortage of examples of businessmen moving into accountancy having previously tried, and sometimes failed, in another line of business. Brown (1905) tells us that merchants sometimes moved into accountancy as a means of employing their commercial skills following bankruptcy. This may have been the sequence of events in the case of Alexander Morris who 'made a small fortune as a merchant and lost it as a manufacturer' in the drapery business (Morris, Gregory & Co., 1953: 1). It is certainly the case that the firm which he subsequently established, Alexander Morris & Son, was listed in Slater's *Manchester Directory* of 1852 as 'Accountants and Agents to the County Fire and Provident Life Assurance Companies' (Morris, Gregory & Co., 1953: 1). William Holyland appears to have been a partner in 'a soap manufactory which came to grief' (Jones, 1995: 32) before becoming, around 1850, partner in a firm of warehousemen and outfitters. This manufacturing and mercantile environment appears to have enabled Holyland to develop the bookkeeping knowledge required to set up in practice as an accountant, at the age of 49, in 1856. Soon afterwards, he joined the eminent City firm Coleman, Turquand, Youngs, as principal clerk, leaving to help found Price, Holyland & Waterhouse in 1865 (Jones, 1995: 33; see Appendix, Price Waterhouse).

The existence of a critical mass of professional accountants in a large city in Britain was, of course, often the trigger for the establishment of a professional body. It is likely that the creation of such a body in turn encouraged at least some local businessmen to redirect their attention to this area of operation. Alexander Moore, for example, was employed in the counting house of William Easton & Co., commission agents, Glasgow, before becoming a partner in a similar firm, but he left to set up as an accountant in 1855. Perhaps the formation of the Institute of Accountants in Glasgow (renamed the Institute of Accountants and Actuaries in Glasgow (Glasgow Institute) in 1855) two years earlier encouraged a change of direction 'for which I had long had a predilection' (quoted in Stewart, 1977: 115). We find, also, some fairly sharp changes, mid-career, in order to qualify for membership of a newly formed professional body. W. J. Carswell, for example, was in business as a house factor and insurance agent when he applied for membership of the newly formed Glasgow Institute in 1855. The council decided that his previous occupation did not sufficiently qualify him for membership, and his successful re-application in 1857 states that he had by this time been apprentice and clerk to Richard Hall, writer in Glasgow, where he was principally engaged on sequestrations and trust estates (Stewart, 1977: 60).

The movement from various trades into accountancy can also be illustrated by reference to some of the early leaders of the profession. The story is often told of how Robert Palmer Harding, son of an auctioneer and house agent, began by running a West End hatter's which encountered financial difficulties. Harding's books were produced in the court appearance that ensued, whereupon the court official complimented his record keeping and suggested he would be more gainfully employed in accountancy. This advice was heeded; Harding set up in business as a sole practitioner in 1847. One year later he formed a highly successful partnership with Edmund Pullein (see Appendix, Ernst & Whinney), described in the

Post Office London Directory of 1850 as 'accountants and arbitrators' (Jones, 1981: 33). The Glasgow Institute council member James Gourlay, born 1804, was initially apprenticed to a smallwares manufacturer before setting up in business as a wholesaler with his brother in Paisley. His main role was that of commercial traveller covering the whole of Scotland and parts of Ireland by horse and gig. Following retirement from this occupation, he set up in business as a Glasgow accountant in 1841, using his previous experience and connections to develop a good business in the valuation and disposal of bankrupt stocks to wholesalers in Glasgow, London, and Manchester (Stewart, 1977: 83).

NON-ACCOUNTING SERVICES

Once established as reputable public accountants, firms continued to conduct non-accounting business, often a vestige of their origins. '[A]ccountant and auctioneer' was a common designation, while another widespread associated activity that was subsequently frowned upon by the newly established professional bodies was the collection of debts and rents for clients. The Glasgow-based accountant Andrew Harvey charged 5% commission on rents collected in the 1830s (Mann Judd Gordon, 1967: 20). Even one of the most prestigious firms, led by founder members of the ICAEW—Harding & Pullein—was acting as a debt collector for a 5% commission in the 1840s (Jones, 1981: 59). Cooper Brothers were also engaged in this work in the 1860s (Jones, 1984a: 778).

The original members of the Edinburgh Society contained many who were connected with the insurance business and, indeed, designated themselves as actuaries (Stewart, 1977: 11, 18). One outcome of the close connection with actuarial work and law was that Scottish accountants were more likely to possess more than one professional qualification than their English counterparts (see Stewart, 1977: 41–165). The founder member of the Edinburgh Society, Henry Callender, for example, was also an actuary, and for some time manager of the Scottish Life and Mercantile Assurance Company and Edinburgh director of the Scottish Imperial Insurance Company (Stewart, 1977: 58). Unfortunately, his career ended in ignominy, being 'removed from the Society following some publicised unprofessional activities that induced his fleeing to the USA to avoid prosecution' (Walker, 1988: 28).

Some of the Scottish actuarial experts moved south of the border and utilized their skills to great advantage in the firms that they joined. James Hill, who joined Theodore Jones's practice in 1867, was a mathematics graduate from Edinburgh University, whose expertise was used to calculate interest and repayment tables for building societies. This proved to be both an immediate source of income and a vehicle for establishing links with financial institutions in the years that followed (Hill Vellacott, 1988: 21) and, from the date Hill joined, the firm described itself as actuaries as well as accountants (Hill Vellacott, 1988: 21–2). The English accountant, too, often had an actuarial background. Howard Smith took his articles with Edward Carter (see Appendix, Coopers & Lybrand), started his own accounting practice in 1867, and became a fellow of both the Society of Actuaries and the Actuaries Institute of Scotland. Smith undertook actuarial consultancy engagements for Birmingham Corporation and 'several local provident societies', also assisting 'as an actuary in the preparation of tables, etc. for Joseph Chamberlain's old age pension scheme' (Howard Smith, Thompson, 1967: 2; see Appendix, Price Waterhouse). Thomas Young Strachan combined the work of accountant and actuary in Newcastle upon Tyne. He became a fellow of the Institute of Actuaries by examination in 1868, and was on the council of that body for 20 years, but he was also a well-established accountant and a founder member of the ICAEW. He set up the Newcastle-upon-Tyne Building Society, for which he acted as secretary and actuary, and resigned from the council of the ICAEW in 1888 to take up the appointment as manager of the Mortgage Insurance Corporation. Henceforth, he 'practised as a consulting actuary, and was known as an able and sound advisor, more especially in matters relating to Building Societies' (Accountant, 25 Apr. 1903: 568). The Bolton chartered accountant Peter Kevan also held the appointment, from 1884, of actuary to the Bolton Savings Bank (Accountant, 22 Dec. 1900: 1, 183). George A. Touch (later Sir George A. Touche; he added the 'e' in 1906 because of annoyance concerning the incorrect pronunciation of the family name; Richards, 1981: 4), the founder of the firm known today as Deloitte & Touche (see Appendix, Touche Ross & Co.), and David Begg of Mann, Judd, Gordon & Co. provide further examples of leading accountants who possessed advanced actuarial knowledge (Richards, 1981; Mann Judd Gordon, 1967).

Early Glasgow accountants were often more closely connected with stockbroking than actuarial work, and it is therefore a curiosity that the Institute of Accountants and Actuaries in Glasgow should have explicitly linked itself with actuarial work through its title. The Glasgow Stock Exchange was formed in 1844, and most of the Glasgow Institute's initial membership of 28 combined accountancy with stockbroking (Stewart, 1977: 11–12). Those who straddled the two areas of expertise early on include Alexander Black, who was in practice from at least 1841 and became a member of the Glasgow Stock Exchange Association in 1845, and T. G. Buchanan, who was vice-chairman of the Association from 1844 to 1865. Other Scots practising as accountants and stockbrokers include Andrew McEwan (from 1836), James Wilkie (1845), John Miller (c.1845), and Robert Forrester (from 1852) (Stewart, 1977: 49, 57, 81, 111, 123, 163). An insight into the range and relative proportions of work undertaken by a Glasgow accountant is provided by Shackleton and Milner, who have analysed the books of Alexander Sloan, who commenced business as 'a Chartered Accountant, stockbroker and joint resident Secretary of the Standard Life Assurance Company Ltd' in mid-1867 (1996: 106). Between 1867 and 1878 (he took his brother Charles into partnership in 1874) the total income of £16,409 was split: accounting 35%, stockbroking 38%, and insurance and sundries 27% (Shackleton and Milner, 1996: 107).

We can therefore see that work as insurance agents was another source of remuneration. It also provided a steady income for Andrew Harvey as the result of his connections with the Caledonian Insurance Company; in the 1830s, for example, a 15% commission was earned on premiums collected (Mann Judd Gordon, 1967: 19). Such work was also undertaken in the 1860s by the Scotsman Robert Fletcher (see Appendix, Peat Marwick McLintock), not to be confused with the Bristolian of the same name (see Appendix, Coopers & Lybrand), while the 1867/8 *Aberdeen Directory* records the fact that the Glasgow chartered accountant Alexander Brand specialized in advice on insurance and was an agent for four insurance companies (Stewart, 1977: 52). Moving south of the border, 'house and general agency and insurance business' were the 'two main roots' of James Grace & Son, established in 1861 (Grace et al., 1957: ch. 1). Estate agency, an activity also later banned by professional rules of conduct, was often a constituent element of the early accountant's business. A circular sent to clients by Theodore Jones, in the mid-nineteenth century, advertised 'the management and improvement of estates and the negotiation of sales by private contract' (Hill Vellacott, 1988: 22). Indeed, James Hill joined the firm in order to strengthen the estate agency side of the business.

We can therefore see that individuals continued to reach accounting through a variety of routes into the late nineteenth century, and that the services offered ranged well beyond those that were to become the major areas of operation for the accountant. Where these more mainstream accounting services proved more successful and profitable than the more peripheral operations, they became the predominant and even sole focus of activity. We can therefore see the profession coalescing as individuals respond to the promptings of the market with opportunities for increased income. Indeed, a number of specialist accountancy firms, not entirely dissimilar to today's local firms in the broad range of work undertaken, had begun to emerge by the early nineteenth century. A prominent example is the Bristol practice of Robert Fletcher, established in 1816 (eventually part of Coopers & Lybrand, see Appendix). Fletcher drew considerable fees from insolvency in the early years, but this work, which admittedly fluctuates with the business cycle, does seem to have become less important as the practice expanded. By 1828, just 11% of the £1,423 fee income was derived from insolvency, whereas seven years previously the share was 56%. The 1828 client list of the firm provides clear evidence of the evolution of a comprehensive professional accountancy practice, with services supplied comprising: 'in addition to routine accounting and bookkeeping: auditing; arbitration work; management of estates . . . ; consultancy services regarding the installation and operation of bookkeeping systems; and partnership dissolutions' (Cornwell, 1993: 159–60). The firm's historian concludes that, by the late 1820s, the practice

enjoyed close and continuing contact with both old and new industries, and was particularly heavily involved in the financial and administrative affairs of companies active at the dawn of the railway age. These factors serve to show that, no later than 1828, Robert Fletcher's activities had 'come of age' as an established and fully-fledged 'professional' practice. (Cornwell, 1993: 162–3)

TRAINING NEW ENTRANTS

The training of new entrants was an issue of growing importance and, by the late eighteenth century, we find the specialist accountancy firms adopting the time-honoured procedure, developed by the old professions and crafts, for training aspiring accountants. From the Middle Ages, training through apprenticeship, 'characteristic of the gild system', was the method adopted by surgeons, apothecaries, and barristers, whose moots and eating of dinners at the Inns of Court formed an important element of pupillage (Carr-Saunders and Wilson, 1933: 307). The Glasgow firm of accountants, auctioneers, debt collectors, and general dealers headed by John Gibson and Richard Smellie placed the following advertisement in the *Glasgow Mercury* in 1784: 'Wanted an Apprentice: None need apply unless they intend to give an Apprentice-fee' (McDougall, 1954: 12). James Kerr trained in the office of (probably) his father David Kerr, 'a practising accountant and clerk to the Commissioners for the Tax on Income'. Kerr set up his own highly successful firm in 1804, and his name survived until 1974 when the successor firm merged with Deloitte & Co (see Appendix, Deloitte Haskins & Sells; McDougall, 1954: 16). James McClelland was the initial holder of what was to become another of the great names of Scottish accountancy, disappearing only when Arthur Young, McClelland, Moores & Co. shortened its name to Arthur Young in 1985 (see Appendix). He was apprenticed to James Kerr, in Glasgow, in 1815, and remained there until he set up in business on his own account in 1824 (Stewart, 1977: 121).

William Quilter, who believed his practice to be the most extensive in England in the mid-nineteenth century, left the family farm in Suffolk in 1825 to enter articles with the leading public accountant of the day, Peter Harris Abbott (Bywater, 1985*b*: 791). In turn, Quilter, Ball & Co., established in 1833 upon Abbott's appointment to the post of Official

Assignee in Bankruptcy, became the 'nursery of the accounting profession' (Bywater, 1985*b*: 794). Prominent accountants who learned their
trade with Quilter, Ball & Co. include William and Arthur Cooper,
founder partners of today's Coopers & Lybrand, John Reeves Ellerman,
the shipping magnate, and Thomas Abercrombie Welton and John B. Ball
(John Ball's nephew), both future presidents of the ICAEW.

Samuel Lowell Price, the son of a small-scale pottery manufacturer in
Bristol and one of the founders of Price Waterhouse, is believed to have
been articled, from the late 1830s, to the local firm of Bradley & Barnard,
'public accountants, auctioneers and general agents to assignees and
creditors in bankruptcies' (Jones, 1995: 26). In 1842, Price moved to the
firm's London office, later commencing business on his own account,
before briefly partnering William Edwards who himself trained a 'considerable number of chartered accountants later to achieve success in the
City' (Jones, 1986*a*: 582). The indentures of Edward Mounsey to Thomas
Whinneray of Liverpool in 1840 provide a brief insight into the life of the
articled clerk, with Mounsey entitled to 'good wholesome and sufficient
meat, drink and lodging, becoming wearing apparel and the mending
thereof' (Howitt, 1966: 237). The nature of the arrangement between principal and clerk is spelt out colourfully in an indenture between William
Francis Moore and James Blakey dated 1 November 1876:

James Blakey shall and will well and truly serve the said William Francis Moore
as such his apprentice in his trade or business of an Accountant in such way or
manner as the said William Francis Moore or his Copartner Francis Alfred Moore
or either of them shall direct and is usual in the said trade or business. And shall
and will at all times during the said term obey the lawful commands of the said
[partners] and in all things demean and conduct himself as a faithful and honest
apprentice and shall not nor will waste spend damage or injure the goods moneys
and other the Estate and effects of the said [partners] nor disclose secrets nor
absent himself from their service without leave first. (Moore & Smalley, 1992: n.p.)

Each partner agreed, for his part, 'according to the best of his skill and
knowledge during the said term of five years [to] teach and instruct or
cause to be taught and instructed the said James Blakey in the said trade
or business of an Accountant and all things incident thereto' (Moore &
Smalley, 1992: n.p.).

GETTING STARTED

It is clear that by the 1860s, in England, accountancy was already recognized as a suitable career for the sons of the bourgeoisie, such as Edgar
Waterhouse (1841–1917). Price Waterhouse's historian, Edgar Jones,
profiles his early career, and demonstrates the struggle of even well-

connected accountants to establish themselves (Jones, 1995: 33–40; see also Edwards, 1986: 674–9). Waterhouse, the son of a well-to-do partner in a merchanting and broking business in Liverpool, was, unusually for the time, a university graduate who joined the City firm of Coleman, Turquand, Youngs & Co., as apprentice to William Turquand in 1861. Turquand had become acquainted with the Waterhouse family through his three sisters who were their neighbours in Reading. Edwin recounts in his diaries how he contemplated medicine, but 'My father considered a training in an accountant's office, giving me an insight into City and commercial life, just what was wanted for me' (quoted in Jones, 1995: 35). A premium of £210 was paid to Turquand and the young Waterhouse studied bookkeeping and the various methods of insolvency. During his training, he examined the accounts of a workhouse, put the accounts of an army agent in order, and helped one of the partners, Coleman, in his role of assistant to the shareholder auditors of the London, Chatham & Dover Railway.

In general, the occupations followed by parents of the early Scottish accountants, often that of a lawyer, seem to have ranked rather higher on the social scale than those of their English and Welsh counterparts. The familial background of six Scottish accountants helps to illustrate this point: the Borthwick family (Archibald Borthwick, in common with the other five specifically mentioned here, joined the Edinburgh Society on, or within a year, of its formation), which traces its descent from the eleventh century, with its ancestor, a Livonian knight, coming to Scotland in the train of the princess who married Malcolm Canmore; the family of James Brown (first president of the Edinburgh Society), which traces its descent to the Browns of Fordell Castle, Perthshire, and Fairmount, Fife, in 1250; that of John Maitland, who was the eighth son of Alexander Gibson Maitland, Bt., of Cliftonhall in Kirkliston parish; that of William Moncreiff, whose father, an advocate, became Lord Moncreiff; that of Alexander Weir Robinson, who 'came from a family of lawyers and founded a family of chartered accountants', both his father and grandfather being a Writer to the Signet; and that of Kenneth Mackenzie, who was the son of the Deputy Keeper of the Signet of Dolphinton (his elder brother succeeded to the Dolphinton estate of upwards of 3,000 acres) (Stewart, 1977: 50, 54, 106, 114, 124, 143).

The fact that the pioneers of the Scottish profession often came from a few rungs higher on the social ladder than their counterparts south of the border is reflected in their education, with a fair number of the early members of the Scottish professional bodies having attended university, in most cases in Edinburgh. That relatively few graduated, reflecting the fact that they attended only selected classes, mainly law, does not undermine the significance of the distinction (Stewart, 1977: 27). Those who did graduate include the following. Donald Cuthbertson was the son of

William Cuthbertson, described as a merchant in the *Glasgow Directory* of 1757, who is the acknowledged originator of the accountancy profession in that city. Donald was educated at Glasgow High School and Glasgow University, where he graduated in law, before joining his father's office, becoming a partner in 1810 (Stewart, 1977: 74). The legendary George Auldjo Jamieson (Walker, 1996), son of a doctor in the naval service, graduated from Aberdeen University before obtaining his early training in a firm of advocates, moving to Edinburgh, and becoming a partner in Lindsay, Esson & Jamieson in 1855 (Stewart, 1977: 94; Walker, 1996: 13). Its successor firm, like so many others in Scotland, eventually became part of Arthur Young (see Appendix), now Ernst & Young.

With three years' experience under his belt, Waterhouse began to practise independently as a public accountant. He found it hard going, however, despite sending out business cards and letters to friends and acquaintances soliciting work, drawing on his Quaker and nonconformist connections like Fry, the chocolate manufacturers, and Huntley and Palmers, the biscuit makers. An entry in Edwin Waterhouse's diary of 1864 tells us that 'no work came in for some weeks, and I began to think I might have made a mistake . . . my father had given me £2,000 to start on which, with my small savings, made a sum of £2,078 18s 5d and I made calculations and estimates as to how long, with compound interest, I could subsist on this sum at my current rate of expenditure' (quoted in Edwards, 1986: 675). The only business forthcoming in the first few months was putting the accounts of his brother's architect's practice in order. He obtained contracted work from Harmood Banner, possibly by exploiting his father's Liverpool connections, and certainly by employing the time-honoured ploy of entering the market by undercutting the opposition on price: 'I should of course be very unwilling', he wrote in a veiled way, 'to do business on terms which might be thought too low for a first class accountant but under the present circumstances, I beg to leave the question of terms entirely in your hands' (quoted in Jones, 1995: 37). This led to the commission of his first audit, Queen Insurance Co., which he completed with great thoroughness. His diary for February–December 1864 shows that he managed to generate 1,052.5 chargeable hours of which 9% was accounted for by audit work, 80% was devoted to the preparation of accounts (and audit), and 11% to the investigation of accounts (and audit) (Jones, 1995: 38, 395). Over 36% of Waterhouse's 1864 chargeable time was devoted to John Fowler, a steam-powered agricultural machinery maker and a Quaker acquaintance of his father, for whom Edwin organized and started 'a system of accounts specially adapted to the business as well as taking charge of and generally superintending them for some months' (quoted in Jones, 1995: 39).

Not surprisingly, therefore, we find it necessary for accountants, just starting out, to draw on the familiar networks of family, friends, religious groups, and previous business contacts, and also to engage in advertising and touting, both latter actions later banned by the ICAEW. A letter to prospective clients from J. G. Carlill in 1835, for example, stated, 'I take the liberty to offer you my services as an Accountant. . . . I have had a few years experience in Book-keeping and flatter myself I am qualified for the undertaking' (Howitt, 1966: 231). This tactic proved successful, with Carlill establishing a thriving practice in Hull. A similar circular was sent out in 1869 by the Bradford accountant H. W. Blackburn (see Appendix, Ernst & Whinney): 'The great experience we have had in the winding up of Insolvent Estates now for more than twenty-five years, and the staff of assistants at our command, enable us with confidence to say we can efficiently serve the commercial public in this department' (quoted in Howitt, 1966: 228). Deloitte's historian tells us that advertising for business was by no means uncommon in the mid-nineteenth century and that the firm's ledger books contained several approaches to potential clients (Kettle, 1957: 11).

Touting for business naturally created friction between professional firms. The history of the Preston firm Moore & Smalley tells of a letter written to a certain Mr Ward on 23 December 1905. This stated that:

The directors of the Leyland Motor Company Ltd. have reported to us that you have been touting for the audit, and have written offering your services at the handsome remuneration of £22. 2s. 0d per year. I do not wish to take any hasty action, or place a wrong construction on your conduct, and hope you will be able to give a satisfactory explanation of what on the face of it seems a direct stab below the belt. (Moore and Smalley, 1992: 3)

There is no recorded reply from the culprit who might have found solace for this attack on his professional integrity in that he retained the audit of what grew into a very large company.

The importance of family and other connections in the choice of an accounting career, in obtaining an initial position, and in developing a subsequent career has been examined in detail by Walker (1988), specifically in relation to recruits to the Edinburgh Society. In this context, Walker concludes that 'Youths were placed in vocations determined by the range of parental occupational and social connections and by their ability to exploit them' (1988: 81). David McLagan, for example, joined the Scottish Union Insurance Office in about 1840 because his father was the company's medical adviser (1988: 82). David subsequently became manager of the Alliance British and Foreign Assurance Company in Edinburgh through John Hamilton, advocate, who was an acquaintance of his father, both of them worshipping at the same church. The appointment of McLagan provided this England-based insurance company, in turn, with the necessary entrée to business in Edinburgh. Later still, McLagan became manager of the Edinburgh Life Assurance Company on the recommendation of his father-in-law who had previously held the position (1988: 193–4). In common with a number of other members of the Edinburgh Society, there is no evidence that he was ever in practice.

ACCELERATING DEMAND FOR ACCOUNTING SERVICES

By the early nineteenth century, therefore, there already existed specialist accountancy firms whose work went beyond mere bookkeeping and who trained up their own workforce via pupillage. Thus accountancy exhibited many of the hallmarks of a profession long before the foundation of the societies from whose creation many writers date the profession's formation. The principal activity undertaken by a number of the elite accountancy firms located in the City of London was undoubtedly insolvency. Indeed, it was their ability to capture the insolvency market which accorded them high status. Their City location reflected the long-established need for accountants to be close to the country's largest bankruptcy court, located in Basinghall Street until 1883 when it moved to Carey Street and merged into the High Court of Justice (Medlam, 1980: 5). The close connection between City accountancy firms and insolvency work is clearly reflected in the following contemporary gibe: 'if an accountant were required, he would be found at the bar of the nearest tavern to the Bankruptcy Court in Basinghall Street' (Cooper, 1921: 554).

Nineteenth-century legislative changes appear to have exerted a significant influence on the work of accountants. Indeed, Chapter 3 draws attention to the fact that the desire to protect spheres of work threatened by new legislation at least partially explains the formation of professional societies in Scotland in the 1850s. South of the border, the Bankruptcy Act 1831 established the bankruptcy court and provided for 'official assignees' who, if not accountants themselves, such as William Edwards who trained William Welch Deloitte, tended to employ accountants to perform investigation work and prepare a balance sheet (Jones, 1995: 28). The growing tendency for accountants to capture work previously undertaken by members of the legal profession is indicated by the oft-quoted remark of Justice Quain in 1875, namely that 'The whole affairs in bankruptcy have been handed over to an ignorant set of men called accountants, which is one of the greatest abuses introduced into law' (quoted in Worthington, 1895: 73). It is equally clear, however, that accountants were increasingly drawn to such work by the burgeoning number and the complexity of company failures, in turn the product of the upheavals of industrial and commercial development. Further legislation helped to reinforce their position.

The Winding-Up Act 1848 'regulated the control of liquidations, making the appointment of a public accountant, as the official manager, a virtual necessity' (Jones, 1981: 45). The Bankruptcy Act of 1861 permitted debtors to absolve themselves of their liabilities by making themselves voluntarily bankrupt; this caused a significant increase in the number of registered failures, which in the period 1862 to 1869 exceeded 7,000 per annum (Weiss, 1986: 180). The 'accountant's friend', the Companies Act of 1862, established the position of 'official liquidator' and brought further opportunities (Edwards, 1989a: 263), while the Bankruptcy Act 1869, which abolished the position of official assignee and instituted a trustee in his place, also 'brought a large accession of business to accountants' (Cooper, 1921: 559). Under the Act public accountants 'could be appointed directly as trustees to administer the debtor's estate rather than having to work through an intermediary' (Jones, 1995: 45). That this legislation provided a further fillip to the profession is evidenced in the history of Pannell Kerr Forster (see Appendix), founded in 1869 by William Henry Pannell. It appears that the act of that year made it 'a very favourable time to start the business', and, 'Pannell, therefore, had a steady flow of winding-up for the first five years of the practise' (Medlam, 1980: 5).

A number of firms had established significant practices, based on insolvency, as early as the 1830s. Joseph Parrinton, the principal of Parrinton & Sons, for example, was listed in the *City of London Directory* for 1828 as 'mainly concerned with administering bankruptcies, liquidations and receiverships' (quoted in Viney Merretts, 1974: n.p.). Peter Harriss Abbott's status as an accountant was recognized by the government which appointed him, in 1829, to a Commission looking into the keeping of the public accounts (Bywater, 1985b: 791). Following his appointment as an Official Assignee in Bankruptcy in 1833, he remained loyal to his former clerks, being then 'in a position to commission the partnership [Quilter, Ball & Co.] to prepare the balance sheets of debtors prior to their appearance in court' (Bywater, 1985b: 791). The commercial crisis of 1847/8 provided the stimulus for Quilter, Ball & Co.'s growth; the firm handled eight of 43 bankruptcy cases, more than any other firm. Similarly, in the crisis of 1857/8, the firm handled 31 out of 147 cases, although the 'largest insolvencies were dealt with by John Edward Coleman who had an invaluable connection with the Bank of England and whose partnership with Turquand, Youngs provided Quilter Ball with an important rival for many years' (Bywater, 1985b: 792).

The history of George Coryndon Begbie's firm provides an insight into a City bankruptcy practice in this early period. Having established himself as an accountant in 1837, 'by far the greater part of [his] early practice was concerned with the Court of Bankruptcy. During the first year of business, he prepared, for the Court of Bankruptcy, the accounts of 23 debtors' (Begbie et al., 1937: 8). One major problem encountered was that of obtaining payment; a process dependent upon the debtor's successful application to the assignee in bankruptcy for an allowance out of which the professional fees could be paid or, alternatively, upon financial assistance provided by friends (Begbie et al., 1937: 9). As a result, 'Begbie was forced to write off as bad debts many of the fees earned in the first years of his practice, including some for considerable amounts and one for upwards of £100' (Begbie et al., 1937: 9). Begbie's response was, as far as possible, to delay delivery of accounts prepared for the court of bankruptcy until he had received his fees, though this proved not to be the ultimate panacea. In 1842, work was undertaken for an insolvent Saville Row tailor amounting to £68 10s., 'but all that Mr. Begbie got out of it was a coat and waistcoat, which he sold for £5' (Begbie et al., 1937: 10). By the mid-nineteenth century, Begbie had developed a clientele for accountancy and audit work, and was 'in a position to refuse insolvency work with its attendant bad debts' (Begbie et al., 1937: 18; see also p. 12). A more general complaint was that association with the sordid circumstances of bankruptcy proceedings tended to lower a firm's standing in the estimation of the public, and we read of William Welch Deloitte's clerk being obliged to attend Newgate prison in order to collect information from a bankrupt (Kettle, 1957: 3).

The Turquands were another family to make a handsome living from insolvency. William Turquand's father, previously a stockbroker, was another of the early Official Assignees appointed under the Bankruptcy Act 1831—a position filled by William himself in 1846/7 (Jones, 1986a: 582). Thereafter, William moved into public practice and undoubtedly made use of the contacts previously built up. By 1856, Turquand, after an abortive partnership with William Edwards, joined with the Scottish brothers John and Alexander Young. One year later, Turquand, Youngs & Co. merged with John Edward Coleman who had been in practice since about 1840, and who, in 1857, wound up twelve companies with liabilities totalling £6.7 million. The new partnership was to become 'one of the largest firms of its kind in London, indeed the world' (Jones, 1986a: 582; *Accountant*, 15 Dec. 1888; see Appendix, Ernst & Whinney). Coleman, Turquand, Youngs & Co.'s fee income averaged £20,895 in the period 1858–64, and then rose to £37,541 (1865/6), before rocketing to £51,005 in 1867 and £90,287 in 1868, partly as a result of the enormous fees earned in winding up Overend, Gurney (Jones, 1981: 263). The crash of that bank in 1866, with liabilities of £18 million, led to the appointment of Turquand as receiver and Robert Palmer Harding as his assistant; an engagement which was to generate £71,000 in fees and £14,000 in expenses over the succeeding thirty years (Jones, 1981: 43). The importance of insolvency to Robert Palmer Harding and his firm is equally clear. Harding & Pullein derived 73.2% of fee income from insolvency in 1848; ten years later this proportion had increased to 93.2%, while in 1884 it accounted for two-thirds of Harding, Whinney & Co.'s business (Jones, 1985c: 33).

Firms grew very wealthy on this work. The fee income of Harding's firms rose from £221 in 1848, to £14,130 in 1863; it then exceeded £23,500 in each of the next six years, peaking in 1866 (£32,268) as a result of the Overend, Gurney failure. Thereafter, until the end of the nineteenth century, fee incomes fluctuated in the range £10,232 (1882) to £18,975 (1870), with the exception of 1879 when fees spiralled to £25,203 (Jones, 1981: 263). In 1867, the City accountant William Henderson prepared a listing of top liquidators in 1866 for a parliamentary Select Committee on the Limited Liability Acts. This showed that Harding, Whinney & Gibbons (see Appendix, Ernst & Whinney), with 61 of the 259 insolvencies of that year and £20.2 million of the £92.1 million capital in liquidation, had 'cornered the market' (quoted in Jones, 1981: 46). Coleman, Turquand, Youngs & Co. (see Appendix, Ernst & Whinney) with 29 companies were second in the unofficial league table, though in terms of the capitalization of their companies in liquidation (£18.4 million), they were not such a distant second as the raw numbers would suggest. Kemp, Cannan, Ford & Co. (12 companies; £13.7 million capital) (see Appendix, Touche Ross), Price, Holyland, Waterhouse & Co. (8, £5.2 million) (see Appendix, Price Waterhouse), Chatteris & Nichols (5, £4.9 million) (see Appendix, Touche Ross), and Quilter, Ball & Co. (5, £1.1 million) (see Appendix, Deloitte Haskins & Sells) were the other firms listed.

Insolvency also formed the backbone of many eighteenth- and nineteenth-century accountancy practices in Scotland (Kedslie, 1990*a*: 7, 12, 39). In 1778, the Glaswegian John Gibson included among the range of services offered: 'Settling of Copartnery or Other Disputes, Making Out Accounts of the Rankings of Creditors, and the Division of Subjects' (quoted in McDougall, 1954: 11). Six years later, on entering into partnership with Richard Smellie, the firm also acted as 'Factors on Estates and Subjects, under the management of Executors or Creditors' (quoted in Murray, 1930: 107). Henry Paul, a Glasgow practitioner, advertised a bankrupt's 'business assets' for sale in 1819, and, by the 1820s, was regarded as an authority on sequestrated estates (Mann Judd Gordon, 1967: 14). Paul continued to undertake a great deal of bankruptcy work through until his death in 1860 (Mann Judd Gordon, 1967: 11).

The Alphabetical Compendium of Scotch Mercantile Sequestrations 1851 (1852) provides an insight into the amount and occupational distribution of sequestrations (a process in Scotland which involves the realization of assets under the supervision of the court), which was work that accounted for approximately one-half of all insolvency engagements. This directory lists 1,155 sequestrations completed in 1851 or still proceeding at that date and shows that accountants had captured 55% by number and, significantly, 78% of the total fee incomes resulting therefrom. Further analysis shows that accountants who later joined one of the three Scottish chartered bodies had captured 38% of the total cases but, as a result of administering the most remunerative and presumably the most complex estates, they obtained 63% of total fee income. This may be contrasted with the shares of 'other accountants' which were 17% of cases and 15% of income respectively, members of the legal profession (13% of cases, 8% of income), bankers (5%, 3%), and a miscellaneous non-professional grouping which sequestrated 27% of the estates but earned just 11% of total fee income (Kedslie, 1990*a*: 40–2).

Insolvency was by no means the only business undertaken by the early nineteenth-century accounting practice, of course, and this was particularly so in the case of provincial firms. The range of work undertaken by Fletcher in Bristol has already been noted, and the 'types of work evidenced by the Accounts Book [of J. W. Sully of Queen Victoria St., London, and also Bristol, 1873–93] are quite widely varied, though no great volume of insolvency business seems to have been undertaken by the Firm' (Sully, 1951: 9). Similarly, 'The Jones' [Edward and Theodore] practices in Leeds were not deeply involved in this lucrative [liquidation] work', having 'been far more interested in helping successful firms, especially in industry' (Hill Vellacott, 1988: 27). Likewise, there is no mention of insolvency work in the surviving archives of the Manchester firm Ashworth Mosley & Co., which traces its history back to 1825 (see Appendix, Robson Rhodes), until the twentieth century when, in 'the days of the great slump, [of] the late twenties and early thirties [bankruptcy work] poured into the office' (Allured, 1980: 3). Similarly, by the 1890s, if not earlier, Howard Smith's Birmingham firm 'was not keen to undertake bankruptcy and liquidation work, and its practice consisted mainly of auditing the accounts of collieries, manufacturing, engineering and steel companies, and of course those of the corporation of Birmingham' (Howard Smith, Thompson, 1967: 5).

The strong ties that existed between accountants and the legal profession in Edinburgh are reflected in the fact that, from 1847, accountants were listed in the Law section of the *Edinburgh and Leith Post Office Directory*. The initial focus in Scotland was very much on insolvency, insurance, and stockbroking, with James Meston, who set up in business in Aberdeen in 1857, rating special mention from Stewart on the grounds that he 'held many important audit appointments not only in Aberdeen, but in London and in cities throughout Scotland and England' (1977: 109). It therefore seems likely that the development of corporate audit work was a particularly slow process in Scotland, though Walker (1993) has underlined the importance of not overlooking the possible significance of the less publicly visible non-corporate audit work. His examination of the records of the leading Scottish firm, Lindsay, Jamieson & Haldane, shows that it derived a mere 2% of average annual fee income from sequestrations in the period 1859–91, 8% from liquidations, whilst over 26% flowed from trusts and executries (mainly involving accounting and trust management work) and 25% from audit (Walker, 1993: 134–6). Indeed, an analysis of the changing profile of over 600 of the firm's clients reveals that, before 1879, 'a substantial audit clientele of landed proprietors, trustees, life assurance societies and learned institutions existed in the non-corporate sector' (Walker, 1993: 145).

It was auditing, of course, that was to form the basis for the accountancy profession's future growth. The early Private Acts of Parliament establishing transport and utility companies contained little by way of provision for the publication or audit of accounts, but quite extensive requirements for accountability had been developed by the 1820s. The statute creating the Liverpool and Manchester Railway, for example, obliged the directors to keep a 'true, exact, and particular Account', for accounts to be made up annually and presented to the 'proprietors' who, if a majority required it, could 'call for and examine the accounts of the said Company, and of the Directors, and of the Treasurer, Receivers or Collectors of the Rates, and other Officers of the said Company' (7 Geo. IV, c. xlix, ss. xciv, cxxii). Initially, audits were usually the responsibility of two shareholders, though the complexity of the task soon ensured that this work became the preserve of the trained accountant. A particular stimulus for this development was the need for shareholders to call in professionals to help them investigate companies whose affairs became the subject of suspicion, particularly following the railway mania of the mid-1840s. Given that there was no long-term growth in insolvencies, these highly lucrative railway audits were also instrumental in the establishment of accountancy as a profession. Moreover, as with insolvencies, an audit assignment required skill well beyond that of bookkeeping, and was sometimes even judged to be unsuitable for professional accountants unless they already specialized in the area. Jones cites Edwin Waterhouse who, having turned down a request to audit the huge Midland Railway in 1883 due to pressure of work, suggested his distinguished partner, Samuel Price. This proposal proved unacceptable to the company, however, apparently because of Price's 'lack of specialist knowledge', despite his previous experience of auditing smaller railways (Jones, 1995: 55).

The acknowledged leader in the field of railway audits was William Welch Deloitte who established a City practice in 1845. Deloitte's appointment to assist the shareholder auditors of the Great Western Railway in 1849 appears to have ensured the success of his practice, as the audits of other railways, docks, collieries, and ironworks soon followed. His reputation was further enhanced when he was called in to investigate the frauds at the Great Northern Railway (1857) and the Great Eastern Steamship Company (1870) (Jones, 1984b: 58). The appointment of Edwin Waterhouse to assist the London & North Western Railway shareholder auditors was an equally important milestone in the history of Price,

Waterhouse. Waterhouse was already known to the staff at Euston, having worked there as a clerk under Coleman. When the latter resigned, in 1866, Waterhouse was the natural successor as 'public accountant'. He was elected auditor in his own right, in 1882, and held this position until succeeded by his son Nicholas in 1913 (Jones, 1995: 50). As with Deloitte, the appointment of Waterhouse as auditor of the London & North Western Railway was the avenue to further railway audits.

Following the Companies Acts of 1856 and 1862, City firms hitherto reliant on bankruptcy increasingly engaged in the audits of a continually widening spectrum of companies. Quilter, Ball & Co., for example, developed 'a substantial audit practise' during the 1860s (Bywater, 1985*b*: 793). Quilter's role in sorting out the fraud at the Eastern Counties Railway in 1854 brought him to national prominence and would appear to have been a significant contributor both to his success and in raising firm's profile, in that it raised shareholder awareness generally of the utility of employing accountants to assist shareholder auditors. The Hudson's Bay Company (in 1863) and Birmingham Joint Stock Bank (1866) were two of the practice's earliest major audit clients, to be followed by a number of banks and foreign railways. As Table 4 shows, Quilter, Ball were second only to Turquand, Youngs in the league table of quoted company auditors for 1886.

The 1921 reflections of Ernest Cooper on his 'Fifty-seven Years in an Accountant's Office' provide an insight into the changing composition of the accountancy profession over time. An examination of the 300 or so practising accountants listed in the *London Directory* of 1864 enabled him 'to recognise only a few names, and none is still carrying on under the same name with the exception of my firm. . . . Only two firms, which in 1864 were, I believe, in a large way of business, now remain' (Cooper, 1921: 553). This might suggest that those firms reliant upon insolvency down to the mid- to late nineteenth century who were unable to transform their practices to incorporate the growth areas, namely auditing, were destined to drop out of the upper echelons of the accountancy profession.

CONCLUDING COMMENTS

This chapter has focused on a number of important developments during the pre-professionalization period which could be said to run up to 1853 in Scotland and 1870 in England. A small number of individuals began to hold themselves out as offering the services of an accountant, beginning in the late eighteenth century, often having developed their financial expertise working in trade or, particularly in Scotland, in the office of a lawyer. The services offered, sometimes within the partnership framework, initially encompassed non-accounting activities with their particular focus reflecting local economic circumstances, such as the rise of stockbroking in Glasgow. We find firms increasingly able to make a living from, and therefore focusing on, a core range of activities which could be seen to constitute the work of a specialist accounting partnership, with particular emphasis on insolvency, audit, and investigation work. Undoubtedly legislation was significant in enabling accountants to gain prominence in insolvency both north and south of the border (see Chapter 4). More fundamentally, however, during the emergence of accounting as an embryo profession, '[I]t was the industrial revolution and the accompanying increase in the scale of industry and commerce, which necessitated the regular employment of accountants by business firms' (Carr-Saunders and Wilson, 1933: 209). Parker (1986: 10) agrees that the growth and proliferation of the corporate entity, and subsequently of company legislation, provided

opportunities for those who could combine the qualities of knowledge of the relevant law, numeracy, independence and integrity. No existing profession had this combination and accountancy practitioners quickly realized that in order to demonstrate these qualities as well as to possess them it was necessary to form professional associations.

The subsequent rise of the accountancy profession is now examined.

3

The Rise of the Accounting Function

The industrial revolution, the development of the transportation network, and rapid technological innovation in a range of industries had produced a demand for business services, during the nineteenth century, amongst which were those provided by the accountant. Indeed, Chapter 2 has shown that, a long time before the professional accountancy bodies were formed in Britain, there were already a significant number of 'accountants' plying their trade.

The purpose of this chapter is to set the scene for the subsequent chronological analysis of the rise of the professional accountant in business management and to document five trends which were both a cause and a consequence of this process. First, we look at the rise of the accountancy firms in terms of their numbers and size. We also see how their scale of operations has expanded both nationally and internationally, the role of mergers among accountancy firms in this process, and the transition, in some cases, from relatively cosy professional practices where personal service was a key feature, into anonymous international corporations as epitomized by the use of corporate logos such as KPMG. We then review the emergence of the range of accountancy bodies which grant the accountant his (and today also her) professional status, and see the factors causing both the proliferation and, periodically, the partial merger of such organizations. The numbers of professional accountants are then identified for 1881, subsequent census years, and 1995, and some international comparisons are made. Next, we examine the progress of women within the accountancy profession. Finally, we consider how entry restrictions imposed by both the professional bodies and accounting practices have helped to define the type of person entitled to the accolade 'professional accountant'.

ACCOUNTANCY FIRMS

The most important institutions driving the development of the accountancy profession have been the firms within which individual members of the profession plied their trade. This organizational structure, comprising sole practitioners or partnerships, has remained dominant from early times right down to the present day. This, despite the option of incorporation provided by the Companies Act 1989, and KPMG's decision, in 1995, to restructure their auditing business as a limited company (Bassirian, 1996: 23). The extent to which KPMG's move, designed to counter the increasing tendency to sue the auditor or investigating accountant, will be followed by other firms remains to be seen, though many believe the 'ultimate test will come when the company is landed with a law suit' (*Accountancy*, Nov. 1995: 11).

The majority of chartered accountants worked in public practice until well into the twentieth century. Taking the published name of the firm in the membership lists of the societies as a guide, 69% of the ICAEW's members worked in their own firm in 1911, while a further 30% worked as clerks. For the SIAA, 61% of its members were partners and 20% were clerks. Although the lists of the London Association of Accountants (LAA) and the Central Association of Accountants (CAA) are less clear, it appears that most of their membership also worked in their own practices. Additionally, there were firms of unqualified accountants, such as G. A. Derrick, an unqualified clerk who left A. G. Gunn & Co.'s Singaporean firm to set up his own, very successful, Far East practice in 1889. In addition to auditing the huge Straits Trading Company, Derrick also rendered audit and secretarial services to numerous rubber companies (Jones, 1981: 103).

The comparatively low capital requirement for setting up in practice has meant that, in financial terms, the accountancy market has always been relatively easy to enter; a pathway taken frequently by clerks leaving to set up on their own. Such an initiative has come about, on occasions, with the blessing of the parent firm, though perhaps more often with a degree of acrimony. Harold Barton and Basil Mayhew appear to have negotiated a fairly smooth separation from Price, Waterhouse & Co., and they were each allowed to take one client to the new partnership set up in 1907 (Jones, 1981: 95). A major dispute ensued, however, when Arthur Hill left Theodore Brooke Jones in 1889, quite possibly exacerbated by Hill taking with him W. E. Vellacott to found the firm of Hill, Vellacott & Co. (Etor, 1985: 536).

New accounting practices were, and still are, constantly being set up. The earliest reliable figures available for the number of accountancy firms practising in the UK are for 1928, when there were 3,880 firms whose members were either chartered or incorporated accountants, or with the professional bodies that, in due course, made up the Association of Certified and Corporate Accountants (ACCA, today called the Association of Chartered Certified Accountants) (Briston, 1979: 458). We can see (Table 2, column 2) that, with the apparent exception of the 1960s, merger activity was more than matched by the formation of new accountancy firms particularly in the 1950s. By 1958, there were over 8,000 accountancy firms in the UK, almost twice as many as twenty years previously. Rapid growth resumed, post-1968, such that the ICAEW lists 17,136 British (and 1,975

Table 2. Membership and firms in the ICAEW, ICAS, ICAI, and ACCA, 1928–1996

	(1) Members in practice in the UK (estimate)	(2) Number of UK firms	(3) Average members per firm (col. 2/col. 3)	(4) Numbers of firms with listed audit clients	(5) Percentage of all listed audits carried out by top 10 firms
1928	13,454	3,880	3.47	2,014	23
1938	17,162	4,127	4.16	1,433	27
1948	18,020	4,831	3.73	1,422	26
1958	23,132	8,005	2.89	1,238	25
1968	25,893	7,857	3.30	1,109	31
1978	33,599	8,711	3.86	511	51
1996	43,605	22,773	1.91	160	75

Note: 1996, column 4, relates to 1993 and is taken from *Financial Times*, 4 Jan. 1993.

Sources: Column 1, 1928–78: as for Tables 8 and 16; columns 2–5, 1928–78: Briston, 1979: 458; for all 1996 data: ICAEW, 1996c; information from ACCA, ICAS, and ICAI head offices; *The Hambro Company Guide*, 1996.

overseas) firms in 1996 (1996c: 1), at a time when there were 4,098 certified firms in existence (information provided by ACCA, Members Service, Glasgow).

Leading partnerships

A striking feature of accountancy is the longevity of the leading firms. This permanence has arisen largely from the absence of bankruptcies among major accountancy firms. Whilst firms might cease practising, often on the death or retirement of the sole partner, once formed, unless taken over, they have tended to survive the vicissitudes of business life. Roderick Mackay did in fact get into financial difficulties but his partner, William Barclay Peat, assumed responsibility for the outstanding debts when Mackay died in Monte Carlo in 1891 (Wise, 1982: 16; see Appendix, Peat Marwick & McLintock). Josiah Wade, formed in 1780, is probably the oldest accountancy firm to trace a continuous existence down to the present day. Following various mergers, this firm is now part of Coopers & Lybrand (see Appendix). Indeed, at least seven present-day English firms have a lineage extending back to 1820 or earlier (Boys, 1994: 17).

Although there is relatively free entry at the bottom end of the market, it has proved very difficult to break into the ruling elite. As a result, the pre-eminent firms of the early years have by and large held their lead. The City of London-based firms associated with the foundation of the Institute of Accountants, in 1870, included Deloitte, Dever, Hollebone & Griffiths (see Appendix, Deloitte Haskins & Sells), Price, Holyland & Waterhouse (see Appendix, Price Waterhouse), Turquand, Youngs & Co., and Harding, Whinney, Gibbons & Co. (see Appendix, Ernst & Whinney). These have a direct line of descent to Coopers & Lybrand, Price Waterhouse, and Ernst & Young which comprise three of the five largest firms in the UK today. Partners in twelve firms represented on the ICAEW's first council can be traced to seven of the top two dozen firms of recent years (Boys, 1989a: 100). An examination of the list of 45 original ICAEW council members reveals even more familiar names. Table 3 lists thirty of these 'founding fathers', not all of whom were household names, but every one was a partner in a firm which in due course became part of one of today's largest practices (see also Parker, 1980b).

A sampling of the auditors of listed companies at twenty-year intervals from 1891 confirms the continued dominance of the largest firms (Table 5). Particularly striking is the fact that, bearing in mind Deloitte, Haskins & Sells' merger with Coopers & Lybrand in 1990, and that Turquand, Youngs and McAuliffe, Davis & Hope (in seventh position in 1911) are constituent parts of Ernst & Young (see Appendix, Ernst & Whinney), the top five firms in 1911 differ from those of 1995 only by the entry of Arthur

Table 3. First council of the ICAEW—original firms and 1996 equivalents

Name	Firm name	Location	1996 equivalent
Beddow, Josiah	Josiah Beddow & Son	London	Littlejohn Frazer
Blackburn, John	H. W. & J. Blackburn	Bradford and Leeds	Ernst & Young
Bolton, James Charles	J. C. Bolton & Son	London	Pannell Kerr Forster
Cape, George Augustus	Cape & Harris	London	Saffery Champness
Carter, Edward	Carter & Carter	Birmingham	Coopers & Lybrand
Cash, William	Cash & Stone	London	Coopers & Lybrand
Chadwick, David	Chadwick, Collier & Co.	London and Manchester	Coopers & Lybrand
Chalmers, Arthur Wigham	Chalmers & Wade	Liverpool	Kidsons Impey
Cooper, Arthur	Cooper Brothers & Co.	London	Coopers & Lybrand
Davies, Joseph	Davies, Voisey & Davies	Warrington	Kidsons Impey
Deloitte, William Welch	Deloitte, Dever, Griffiths & Co.	London	Coopers & Lybrand
Fisher, Walter Newton	Walter Newton Fisher	Birmingham	Coopers & Lybrand
Griffiths, John George	Deloitte, Dever, Griffiths & Co.	London	Coopers & Lybrand
Guthrie, Edwin	Thomas, Wade, Guthrie & Co.	Manchester	KPMG

Harding, Robert Palmer	Harding, Whinney & Co.	London	Ernst & Young
Kemp, Charles Fitch	C. F. Kemp, Ford & Co.	London	Deloitte & Touche
Ladbury, George Herbert	Ladbury, Collinson & Viney	London	Binder Hamlyn
Mackay, Roderick	R. Mackay & Co.	London and Middlesbrough	KPMG
Peirson, Edward Thomas	Edward Thomas Peirson	Coventry	Kidsons Impey
Price, Samuel Lowell	Price, Waterhouse & Co.	London	Price Waterhouse
Read, Thomas William	Thomas William Read	Liverpool	Deloitte & Touche
Saffery, Joseph John	J. J. Saffery & Co.	London	Saffery Champness
Shuttleworth, Thomas George	Tasker & Shuttleworth	Sheffield	Grant Thornton
Swithinbank, George Edwin	G. E. Swithinbank & Co.; G. E. Swithinbank, Briggs & Co.	London and Bristol	Price Waterhouse
Tilly, John Henry	Tilly & Co.	London	Baker Tilly
Turquand, William	Turquand, Youngs & Co.	London	Ernst & Young
Wade, Charles Henry	Thomas, Wade, Guthrie & Co.	Manchester	KPMG
Welton, Thomas Abercrombie	Quilter, Ball & Co.	London	Coopers & Lybrand
Whinney, Frederick	Harding, Whinney & Co.	London	Ernst & Young
Young, John	Turquand, Youngs & Co.	London	Ernst & Young

Note: The above table lists 30 of the 45 members of the first council of the ICAEW who can be traced through to the leading firms of 1996.

Sources: Parker, 1980*b*; Boys, 1989*a–q*; and *Accountancy*.

Andersen. Of US origin, it opened its first office in England in 1957 (Boys, 1994: 22; see Appendix) but made exceptional progress and achieved second place in the league table of fee income for 1995 (*Accountancy*, July 1995: 19). Indeed, it has been suggested (*Accountancy Age*, 13 June 1996: 7) that the 'big six' boycotted preparation of the 1996 league table, by refusing to supply details of fee income, because 'Andersens would have ascended to the number-one slot'.

The Institute of Accountants and the ICAEW were both, as noted in the first section of this chapter, initiated and dominated by firms with their headquarters in the City of London. Indeed, the profession was 'concentrated in the Gresham Street, Old Jewry, Basinghall and Coleman Street area' (Jones, 1981: 66). By 1911, all but three of the 21 past presidents of the ICAEW were from City practices, 26 of the 45 members of the governing council of the ICAEW in that year were from City partnerships, and the firms of a further seven, although provincial in origin, had branches in the City (Matthews, 1993: 201). At the SIAA, a national body from the outset, eight of its 25 council members in 1911 were City practitioners. The audit appointments identified in Tables 4 and 5, as might be expected, were virtually monopolized by City firms. In 1886 and 1891, the largest four firms were City-based; by 1911 the eight largest auditors were City concerns, by which time 88% of all the auditors in our sample had offices in the Square Mile.

These accountancy firms were, during the second half of the nineteenth century, taking their place amongst the business elite of the City alongside merchant bankers, stockbrokers, and insurance underwriters. They were also woven into the freemasonry of the Square Mile. George Sneath of Price, Waterhouse, for example, was a prominent freemason, having been initiated to the Royal Athelston Lodge, London, in 1878, and he is thought to have been responsible for establishing a tradition of freemasonry in the firm. He was a founder member of the Chartered Accountants Lodge set up in 1906, and this attracted leading lights of the profession such as William Plender, Francis W. Pixley, Arthur Whinney, and Gilbert Garnsey (Jones, 1995: 64). The Lodge had spawned, by the 1960s, no fewer than nine presidents of the ICAEW and three Lord Mayors of London (Howitt, 1966: 55).

A number of the elite chartered accountants came from the City establishment. Pixley, for example, had an uncle who was a stockbroker and another who was a bullion broker. It was said of Pixley, who set up as an accountant in 1878: a 'member of the Conservative and City of London Clubs, he is closely connected, by family and association, with what is most solid and of best standing in the mercantile world' (quoted in Kitchen and Parker, 1980: 26). The location of major accountancy practices in the City reflected, as we have seen, the early need for accountants to be close to the country's largest bankruptcy court. Increasingly too, accountants were attracted to the proximity of the stock market and the head

Table 4. Top 22 auditors, 1886

Rank	Firm	No. of audits
1	Turquand, Youngs	69
2	Quilter, Ball	48
3	Deloitte, Dever, Griffiths	42
4	Price, Waterhouse	36
5	Harmood Banner	24
6	Roderick Mackay	22
7	Cooper Brothers	19
8	C. F. Kemp, Ford	16
9	Edwin Collier, Beardsall	15
10=	Lindsay, Jamieson & Haldane	12
10=	Cash & Stone	12
12=	James Fraser	11
12=	Howden & Molleson	11
12=	Harding, Whinney	11
15	Chatteris, Nichols, Atkins	10
16	Halliday, Pearson	9
17=	Drury & Elliot	8
17=	Chalmers & Wade	8
17=	Aitken & Mackenzie	8
17=	Monkhouse, Goddard	8
17=	Broome, Murray	8
17=	Carter & Carter	8

Note: The table was compiled from the 943 companies (out of a population of 1,100 companies) whose auditors could be identified from the sources listed below.

Sources: *Burdett's Official Intelligence*; corporate reports housed at the Guildhall Library, London.

offices of their major audit clients—59% of the sample of companies in the survey of auditors in 1911 had headquarters in the City.

There were also, of course, some large and successful provincial firms. Referring to Table 4, the fifth largest quoted company auditor in 1886 was the Liverpudlian firm of John Sutherland Harmood-Banner (see Appendix, Deloitte Haskins & Sells), whose business was centred around local banking, insurance, and shipping companies. Liverpool also spawned the firm of Chalmers & Wade (see Appendix, Hodgson Impey), whilst three of the top 22 auditors of 1886—Edwin Collier, Beardsall & Co. (see Appendix, Coopers & Lybrand), Halliday, Pearson & Co., and Broome, Murray & Co. (see Appendix, Robson Rhodes)—were based in nearby Manchester. Monkhouse, Goddard & Co. (see Appendix, Price Waterhouse), centred in Newcastle upon Tyne (by 1886 it also had branches in London,

Table 5. The top auditors 1891–1995

(a)

Rank	1891 Firm	%	1911 Firm	%	1931 Firm	%	1951 Firm	%	1971 Firm	%	1991 Firm	%	1995 Firm	%	£m
1	Deloitte, Dever, Griffiths	5.0	Deloitte, Plender, Griffiths	5.0	Price, Waterhouse	10.3	Deloitte, Plender, Griffiths	6.9	Peat, Marwick, Mitchell	8.0	KPMG Peat Marwick McLintock	9.6	Coopers & Lybrand	19.0	253.0
2	Turquand, Youngs, Bishop & Clarke	5.0	Price, Waterhouse	5.0	Deloitte, Plender, Griffiths	5.5	Price Waterhouse	6.1	Price Waterhouse	7.2	Coopers & Lybrand Deloitte	7.0	KPMG	17.8	223.7
3	Price, Waterhouse	3.7	Turquand, Youngs	3.7	Cooper Brothers	3.9	Peat, Marwick, Mitchell	2.0	Deloitte	5.4	Price Waterhouse	4.7	Price Waterhouse	11.5	163.3
4	Welton, Jones	2.8	W. B. Peat	2.8	McAuliffe Davis & Hope	3.4	Cooper Brothers	1.9	Cooper Brothers	2.4	Ernst & Young	3.7	Ernst & Young	9.5	158.0
5	Monkhouse, Goddard	2.5	Cooper Brothers	2.5	Peat, Marwick, Mitchell	3.2	Turquand, Youngs, McAuliffe	1.9	Thomson, McLintock	2.2	Touche Ross	3.1	Arthur Andersen	8.9	128.0
6	Harmood Banner	2.1	J. H. Duncan	2.1	Turquand, Youngs	1.6	Kemp, Chatteris	1.8	Turquand, Youngs	1.8	BDO Binder Hamlyn	2.8	Touche Ross	5.5	121.8
7	C. F. Kemp, Ford	2.0	McAuliffe, Davis & Hope	2.0	Kemp, Chatteris, Nichols, Sendell	1.4	Harmood Banner, Lewis & Mounsey	1.7	Touche Ross	1.6	Arthur Andersen	2.8	BDO Stoy Hayward	3.6	50.0

	1891	1911	1931	1951	1971	1991	1996
8	1.8 R. Mackay	1.4 Jackson, Pixley	1.6 Whinney, Smith & Whinney	1.6 Whinney, Murray	2.6 Grant Thornton	3.1 Grant Thornton	41.7
9	1.7 Cooper Brothers	1.1 Annan, Dexter	1.6 Ford, Rhodes, Williams	1.5 Arthur Young, McClelland, Moores	2.1 Stoy Hayward	2.2 Clark Whitehill	36.3
10	1.6 Chatteris, Nichols & Atkins	1.1 Ford, Rhodes & Ford	1.4 Sharp, Parsons	1.3 Spicer & Pegler	1.7 Pannell Kerr Forster	2.0 Pannell Kerr Forster	31.0

Note: the rank-8 1891 firm is listed as "R. Mackay" with sub-entry "Monkhouse, Stoneham"; rank-9 as "Cooper Brothers"/"Harmood Banner"; rank-10 as "Chatteris, Nichols & Atkins"/"Armitage & Norton".

(b)	1891	1911	1931	1951	1971	1991	1996
No. of audits in sample	705	435	624	538	571	641	2,300
% by top 5	19.0	26.3	18.8	25.0	28.1	66.7	61.4
% by top 10	28.2	32.9	26.9	32.8	40.1	83.1	75.0
% by top 20	35.8	41.9	37.6	42.5	52.7	89.7	n./a.

Notes: % = percentage of total sample audited.
The 1995 rankings are based on 1995 fee income derived from audit/accountancy work.

Sources: Burdett's Official Intelligence; The Stock Exchange Official Intelligence; The Stock Exchange Official Year-Book; Accountancy, July 1995: 18–20; *The Hambro Company Guide,* 1996.

West Hartlepool, and Middlesbrough), and the Birmingham partnership of Carter & Carter (see Appendix, Coopers & Lybrand), were the other leading English, non-City, firms of auditors. Three Scottish firms had penetrated the quoted audit market by this date; two—Lindsay, Jamieson & Haldane (see Appendix, Arthur Young) and Howden & Molleson (see Appendix, Deloitte Haskins & Sells)—were Edinburgh-based, whilst Aitken & Mackenzie was Glaswegian.

Despite the growth of provincial firms, a sizeable proportion of listed companies based in the provinces came to the City of London to have their accounts audited. This was probably because of the prestige and experience of the City accountants, and the boost to public confidence bestowed by their signature on a company's audit report (Jones, 1981: 60). The banking sector, whose confidence was shattered by the spectacular collapse of the City of Glasgow Bank in 1878, provides a graphic example: 61 of the 65 UK listed banks that registered with limited liability following the débâcle had engaged professional auditors by 1886. Significantly, 32 of the auditors engaged were City firms, 23 of whom were taken onto audit banks located outside London (Anderson et al., 1996: 361).

Whilst there has been a continual diminution in the importance of the City in terms of the geographic locations of members of the leading professional bodies (see Table 6), the headquarters of the major partnerships are still located in or near the City. Of the top ten firms in 1996,

Table 6. Geographical distribution of membership of accountancy societies, 1891–1991

	1891			1911					1931				
	ICAEW (%)	SAA (%)	Total (%)	ICAEW (%)	SIAA (%)	CAA (%)	LAA (%)	Total (%)	ICAEW (%)	SIAA (%)	CAA (%)	LAA (%)	Total (%)
England and Wales	97.1	90.7	95.7	80.5	73.4	83.5	89.2	80.0	88.3	81.1	83.7	76.7	84.2
Including:													
City of London	42.2	27.8	39.1	36.3	17.7	12.1	2.2	24.2	24.3	15.2	15.3	11.5	19.3
Rest of London				6.7	9.6	28.6	18.2	11.1	13.1	13.4	19.0	13.5	13.5
Manchester	11.1	5.7	9.9	9.0	5.1	1.8	3.4	6.5	6.1	5.5	1.8	3.7	5.4
Birmingham	8.9	3.0	7.6	6.6	3.4	2.1	1.6	4.6	4.0	3.4	3.6	2.4	3.6
Abroad	2.9	9.3	4.3	19.5	26.6	16.5	10.8	20.0	11.7	18.9	16.3	23.3	15.8
Total membership	100.0	100.0	100.0	100.0	100.0	100.0	100.0	100.0	100.0	100.0	100.0	100.0	100.0

Notes: Figures are based on a count or, when the numbers became too large, an estimate from the topographical sections of the membership lists in the yearbooks. 'Abroad' includes Scotland and Ireland. The reliability of our figures receives a degree of confirmation from the fact that the estimate for the proportion of ICAEW members abroad for 1991 (14.5%) compares reasonably well with the figure of 13.4% (non-English and Welsh members as a proportion of the total) obtained

Coopers & Lybrand, Clark Whitehill, Deloitte & Touche, KPMG, and Pannell Kerr Forster have their head offices in the City; Ernst & Young and Price Waterhouse are just across the river in SE1, whilst Arthur Andersen, BDO Stoy Hayward, and Grant Thornton are in the West End.

It is a significant feature of the leading accountancy practices that the establishment of branches remained uncommon prior to the First World War. One early exception was Theodore Brooke Jones who, although based in the City of London, had generated clients in Glasgow, Manchester, and south Wales. Jones began to develop a network of local partnerships in the 1860s, though he did not follow the twentieth-century practice of using the same name for each office (Etor, 1985: 536). By 1870, Jones had offices in Leeds, Manchester, and Belfast. Of the twenty-two leading auditors of 1886, all but Roderick Mackay (with offices in Middlesbrough and London) and Monkhouse, Goddard (with four offices) were single-office firms. Mackay's connection with the north-east was as a result of the previous activities of his partner W. B. Peat. Peat, though initially articled to a lawyer in Montrose, never qualified and, in 1870, at the age of 18, joined the London office of Robert Fletcher. Wise tells us that 'In 1877 he was despatched to Middlesbrough on an investigation into the affairs of the corporation of the town. Sensing the potential of iron and steel there, Peat obtained Fletcher's permission to open an office and was made partner' (1982: 16). By 1911, Roderick Mackay's successor firm, W. B. Peat & Co., had five UK offices.

1951					1971				1991			
ICAEW (%)	SIAA (%)	ACCA (%)	ICWA (%)	Total (%)	ICAEW (%)	ACCA (%)	ICWA (%)	Total (%)	ICAEW (%)	ACCA (%)	CIMA (%)	Total (%)
89.7	80.4	80.3	80.7	84.5	86.4	75.0	70.7	81.9	85.5	59.1	72.7	77.1
15.8	11.5	9.3	3.2	12.2	4.6	8.1	3.0	5.0	2.0	2.5	3.0	2.3
13.0	14.4	17.4	13.4	14.3	14.8	15.2	10.5	14.2	14.9	8.2	8.1	12.1
4.5	3.4	2.5	4.7	3.8	1.8	1.7	2.4	1.9	1.6	1.0	1.6	1.5
4.3	1.9	2.5	5.1	3.4	1.9	2.2	2.4	2.0	1.2	0.5	2.0	1.2
10.3	19.6	19.7	19.3	15.5	13.6	25.0	29.3	18.1	14.5	40.9	27.3	22.9
100.0	100.0	100.0	100.0	100.0	100.0	100.0	100.0	100.0	100.0	100.0	100.0	100.0

by the ICAEW in 1992 (*ICAEW Membership Questionnaire*, 1992: 2). The final 'Total' column is an estimate of the geographical distribution of the membership of all societies based on a weighted average of the societies counted.

Sources: As for Table 8.

Most of the relatively big City chartered accountancy practices were remarkably slow to establish branches in the provinces, however, and this partly reflects the relatively small scale of accountancy firms generally down to the Second World War. A further factor seems to have been the desire to supervise personally the work undertaken; a perfectly natural concern, particularly in circumstances where it was common practice for the partner responsible to sign the audit report in his personal capacity. The policy laid down by the founders of Cooper Brothers & Co., for example, was that 'the business should be conducted only from the office in London. They felt that unless they could give personal supervision to the work of the firm they would not be able to maintain the standards which they felt to be important' ([Benson] 1954: 37). Price, Waterhouse & Co. was also initially sceptical of opening branch offices for this reason, but also 'in deference to clients' wishes that staff with homes in the district where the clients' offices were located should not be allowed to examine their private books' (Richards, 1950: 8–9).

The national coverage of the leading London-based firms has increased dramatically, particularly since the 1950s, with the market leaders having a presence in most of Britain's major cities. Of the 'big six' firms in 1995, KPMG had the largest UK branch network with 38, closely followed by Coopers & Lybrand's 36, and Arthur Andersen lagging well behind with just thirteen offices (*Accountancy*, July 1995: 18), possibly reflecting its traditional emphasis on consultancy work and relatively weaker performance in the audit market. Then, as in 1886, the number of offices did not determine a firm's volume of business. Arthur Andersen was the second largest firm by volume of business, while Clark Whitehill (ranked tenth), with 55 more UK offices, generated just over 10% of Andersen's fee income.

Firm size

There is an absence of data concerning the size of late nineteenth- and early twentieth-century firms, but it is nevertheless clear that the largest firms were minute by today's standards. In 1891, Howard Smith, Thompson & Co., the successful Birmingham firm, had partners and staff totalling 32 (Howard Smith, Thompson, 1967: 4). The staff at W. H. Pannell & Co., the forerunner of Pannell Kerr Forster (see Appendix), numbered 30 immediately after the First World War and just 40 by 1939 (Medlam, 1980: 8). In 1900, Price Waterhouse's staff, including partners, numbered 86, all working in the City; fifty years later there were fifteen partners and 544 staff working in eight UK offices and 93 branches overseas (Boys, 1994: 29). Deloitte, Dever, Griffiths & Co., which under various guises has almost continually featured among the top three UK firms (Table 5), had a professional staff of 30 in 1882, which had risen to 80 by 1900, 193 (including four partners) by 1914, and 351 by 1939 (Kettle, 1957: 99).

A number of factors contributed to the relatively small scale of accountancy firms in the early period, and we have already noted the ease with which clerks (the term used by accountancy practices to describe qualified staff who were not partners) could form their own firms rather than work in branches of established partnerships. There was little incentive for the City firms to venture out into the possibly less profitable provinces, particularly given concerns with supervision, while the absence of significant economies of scale meant they had no particular competitive edge over regional firms who themselves had the advantage of local knowledge. The limitation on the number of partners to 20, introduced as part of the Joint Stock Companies Act 1856, undoubtedly placed some restriction on the size of accountancy firms, even though it could be circumvented by the establishment of legally separate partnerships to act in association with one another through cross-partnership agreements (Boys, 1989a: 100). In 1952, for example, Peat, Marwick, Mitchell had 44 partners spread over eighteen offices in the UK (*Financial Times*, 6 Jan. 1994).

The Companies Act of 1967 ended the restrictions on the number of partners in an accountancy firm, thus finally opening the way to almost unrestricted growth (Boys, 1994: 22). Deloitte Haskins & Sells, for example, had 251 partners by 1986 in addition to their professional staff of 3,002 (*Financial Times*, 15 Dec. 1986). Coopers increased their staff from 173 in 1945 to 2,445 in 1979 and, following the merger with Deloitte, Haskins & Sells, the combined firm had 735 partners and 7,807 staff in 1990 (*Accountancy*, June 1991: 17; Boys, 1994: 27). Following a degree of rationalization, the 1995 data for partners and professional staff stood, respectively, at 607 and 6,268, which made Coopers & Lybrand the largest of the 'big six' by staffing levels at that date (*Accountancy*, July 1995: 19). Second largest firm in 1995 was KPMG with 573 partners and 5,998 staff—a position unrecognizable from 1952 when Peat, Marwick, Mitchell had 44 partners and 1,000 staff, and representing giant strides even compared with 1981, at which time the professional staff numbered 3,046, including 170 partners (*Financial Times*, 18 June 1981; *Accountancy*, July 1995: 19). The staff of Price Waterhouse, a firm untouched by major mergers, has increased greatly from fifteen partners and 544 staff in 1950, to 160 partners and 2,022 staff in 1981. Fourteen years on, the number of partners had more than doubled to reach 399, whilst the professional staff numbered 3,836 (Boys, 1994: 29; *Accountancy*, July 1995: 19). Today, the six largest UK firms employ over 30,000 professional staff, in addition to 2,700 partners and an unpublished, though substantial, number of practice support staff.

The merger movement

Accountancy practices have achieved this growth through both internal expansion and a continuing series of mergers, though individual firms naturally differ dramatically in terms of their growth strategies which have also not remained constant over time. The merger movement, graphically illustrated by the painstaking reconstruction of the family trees of leading firms by Boys (1989*a*–*q*), pre-dates the formation of professional bodies. For example, the Appendix (Coopers & Lybrand) shows that Arthur Daniell, having established himself in practice in 1827, merged with W. R. Kettle, formed in 1840, to become Kettle & Daniell in 1857. In 1860, they were joined by Edward Carter, who had established his own practice three years earlier. Carter & Co., the successor firm of the 1860 partnership, merged with Cooper Brothers & Co. 100 years later, and from 1973 has been known as Coopers & Lybrand. The diverse manner in which three of today's top ten firms have been shaped will further illustrate the process of growth by merger.

Thornton, Webb & Co. (see Appendix, Grant Thornton) was established in Oxford in 1904, and the story is told that Reginald Thornton was waiting to see an inspector of taxes when he became engaged in conversation with William Morris, later Lord Nuffield. Thornton's suggestion that Morris needed an accountant produced the following reply: 'Well, in that case, you'd better deal with it for me' (Hubbard, 1991: 3). Thornton & Thornton thereafter grew along with Morris Motors and opened new offices as work increased. In contrast, Baker & Co., of Leicester and Northampton, whose origin dates from 1868, and who merged with Thornton & Thornton in 1959, expanded by a series of amalgamations. Ten years later, Thornton Baker & Co., as the firm became, was led by two incorporated accountants, David Sirkin and Cyril Riddington, with the former 'inspired by the ambition to create a nation-wide firm of accountants' (Hubbard, 1991: 3). Looking back in 1988, Riddington claimed that 'Their philosophy was one of controlled decentralisation with areas of specialism and regular meetings of partners to build up a partnership spirit and avoid bureaucracy' (Hubbard, 1991: 3).

From 1959 onwards, there was impressive but somewhat random growth at Thornton Baker, resulting in 50 successful mergers with small local practices (too small to be recorded in the Appendix) and a number of others which proved abortive (Boys, 1989*h*: 98). The firm became known in the profession as 'the thundering herd'. Many of the merging firms, however, had long histories stretching back into the nineteenth century, and 'almost all were established and had deep roots in their local communities' (Hubbard, 1991: 4). The firm's new 'leading lights' were Arthur Green and Michael Lickiss who took it through an enormous expansion in the 1970s and 1980s, and were respectively president of the ICAEW in

1987 and 1990 (Hubbard, 1991: 7). In 1977, the partners' conference decided to expand out of the traditional areas of auditing and accounting and to give priority to all-round financial services and, in particular, tax, financial planning, and management advisory services. The firm was the first to set up a corporate finance department in 1977, but was somewhat tardy in recognizing the need to invest and develop the management consultancy side (Hubbard, 1991: 11, 13). In 1979 the firm joined with US accountants Alexander Grant & Co. to set up the international firm Grant Thornton International, and in 1986 Thornton Baker cemented the merger with Alexander Grant to become the world-wide firm of Grant Thornton (Hubbard, 1991: 16).

The post-war growth, by merger, of the well-established firm of Touche Ross is also demonstrated in the Appendix. We have seen that this firm was founded by the Scotsman George A. Touch in 1899; it opened its first overseas branch in Canada in 1909, and entered into its first international partnership with J. B. Niven, a fellow Scot, in the United States in 1900 (Richards, 1981: 5–6). The firm grew slowly at home, however, such that its UK staff numbered a mere 67 in 1939. The Canadian branch of the firm joined with the Canadian accountants P. S. Ross & Sons in 1958, two years prior to their fusion with the American branch, by which time the firm had twelve partners and 200 staff (Boys, 1994: 25). Thereafter the partners decided to expand nationally, by merger with major and long-established firms such as Kemp Chatteris (merged 1963) and Mann Judd (1979), so that it had 157 partners and around 2,300 staff by 1981. Following their 1990 merger with Spicer & Oppenheim, themselves the product of the 1988 coming together of the American firm of Oppenheim, Appel, Dixon & Co. and Spicer & Pegler in Britain, Touche Ross moved into the top five UK firms (Table 5, Appendix). By 1995, Touche Ross had 345 partners and 4,303 professional staff in 22 UK offices (*Accountancy*, July 1995: 18). From 1 February 1996, the UK practice changed its name to Deloitte & Touche following an interesting series of events. Deloitte Haskins & Sells entered into a world-wide merger with Touche Ross International in 1989 (*Accountancy*, Feb. 1996: 13), with the exception of the British arm of Deloitte whose partners decided, late on in the negotiations, to remain independent. In the modern era of international business, this was clearly an untenable position and, in 1990, they merged with (many would say they were taken over by) Coopers & Lybrand to form Coopers & Lybrand Deloitte. The firm reverted to the snappier title Coopers & Lybrand in 1992, leaving the way open for Touche's UK operations to add Deloitte to its name, thereby bringing it into line with other members of the world-wide organization Deloitte Touche Tohmatsu International (*Accountancy*, Feb. 1996: 13).

The third illustration of expansion and merger considered here concerns the provenance of Ernst & Young (see Appendix, Ernst & Whinney,

Arthur Young). Turquand, Youngs & Co., founder members of the English profession, merged with Barton, Mayhew & Co. in 1972, and in 1979 took over Whinney, Murray & Co., itself able to trace its history to Harding & Pullein, founded in the 1840s. Also in 1979, Turquand, Barton, Mayhew & Co. and Whinney, Murray & Co. merged with the American firm of Ernst & Ernst (who had acted for Whinney, Smith & Whinney in America since 1918) to form Ernst & Whinney (Jones, 1981: 246; Boys, 1994: 34). Arthur Young, which joined forces with Ernst & Whinney in 1989 to form Ernst & Young, has its origins in the USA in 1894. It had previously achieved substantial growth in the UK through a succession of

Table 7. Top six firms by 1995 fee income

(*a*)

UK ranking	Firm	Fee income (£m.)	UK offices	Partners	Professional staff
1	Coopers & Lybrand	575.0	36	607	6,268
2	Arthur Andersen	539.5	13	389	4,873
3	KPMG	528.4	38	573	5,998
4	Ernst & Young	401.2	27	386	4,389
5	Price Waterhouse	383.2	26	399	3,836
6	Touche Ross	336.8	22	345	4,303

(*b*)

World-wide ranking	Firm	Fee income (US$m.)	Offices	Partners	Professional staff
1	Arthur Andersen	8,100	361	2,563	82,121[b]
2	KPMG[a]	7,500	840	6,003	49,884
3	Ernst & Young International	6,870	685	5,288	46,779[b]
4	Coopers & Lybrand International	6,200	755	5,228	70,500[b]
5	Deloitte Touche Tohmatsu	5,950	680	4,650	42,000
6	Price Waterhouse	4,460	434	3,246	38,985

[a] KPMG data is revenue reported in the form of total billings to clients rather than as net fee income.

[b] Total staff, including partners.

Sources: *Accountancy*, July 1995: 18; Feb. 1996: 17.

mergers with Scottish and English firms, notably Broads, Paterson & Co. (1923) and McClelland, Moores & Co. (1968), themselves tracing histories back to the 1820s.

All three of these studies exhibit the trend, which culminated in the 1980s, towards international, especially transatlantic, merger among accountancy firms. The Appendix also shows that Cooper Brothers and the American firm Lybrand, Ross Bros. & Montgomery, with which it had been in close association from 1957, merged in 1973 to practise world-wide as Coopers & Lybrand. In 1978, Deloitte & Co. merged with the American firm Haskins & Sells to create Deloitte Haskins & Sells, again building on a previous association which dates back at least to 1931. In 1987, Peat Marwick Mitchell merged with KMG Thomson McLintock, itself a merger of the old Thomson McLintock partnership of largely Scottish origin and the international Dutch-, American-, and German-based firm of KMG (see Appendix, Peat Marwick McLintock). By 1991, they had emerged as KPMG Peat Marwick and in 1995 became KPMG (Boys, 1989*l*: 82; Boys, 1994: 22). The Appendix depicts the 1988 creation of BDO Binder Hamlyn following the merger of the UK firm Binder Hamlyn with the European firm BDO. Subsequently, BDO Binder Hamlyn has splintered, with its larger offices joining Arthur Andersen, and the bulk of the provincial and Scottish operations teaming up with Stoy Hayward to form BDO Stoy Hayward (see Appendix, BDO Binder Hamlyn, Stoy Hayward).

The merger movement has, therefore, not only resulted in all the major UK firms having close global ties but also witnessed their transformation into large multinational organizations. Measured by 1995 fee income, the world-wide 'big six' differs from the UK listing only in terms of their relative positions (Table 7). World leader Arthur Andersen was the second largest UK firm. At the other end of the scale, the fifth and sixth largest world-wide firms of Deloitte Touche Tohmatsu and Price Waterhouse were ranked sixth and fifth respectively in the UK.

The quiet revolution

The massive expansion of today's dominant London-based firms therefore dates from the 1970s, but was preceded by essential organizational reforms which had begun to emerge much earlier. The inter-war period had witnessed the establishment of specialist departments—for example, a tax department at Thomson McLintock in the 1920s, an 'organization and methods' department (a forerunner of their management consultancy arm) at Deloitte, Plender, Griffiths in 1933—but it was not until the post-Second World War period that the departmentalization of accountancy firms became much more common (*Accountancy*, Aug. 1988: 97). An early radical overhaul of the organizational framework was undertaken at Cooper Brothers, in 1945/6, as the firm came to the conclusion that the problems upon which the profession were asked to advise were of such a specialised character that they could not be undertaken efficiently unless they were dealt with by partners and staff who devoted the greater part of their time and energy to those subjects. Accordingly, separate departments were established to deal with executorship work, liquidations and receiverships, registration and share transfer work, costing and organisation, secretarial work and investigations. ([Benson] 1954: 16–17)

Organizational changes therefore underpinned growth which was undoubtedly facilitated by a number of technical factors noted earlier in this chapter, such as the removal of legal restrictions on the number of partners in an accountancy practice. Of even greater significance, however, has been the way in which *attitudes* have altered as accountancy firms responded to changing economic conditions and client requirements. This process is vividly illustrated by Jones in his history of Price Waterhouse. A strong theme throughout the book is the fundamental change which took place in the nature of this accounting practice, and possibly others, between about 1965 and 1975. Price Waterhouse in 1965 continued to be run by a small group of partners who met every morning to discuss business. Indeed, although considerable expansion had taken place over the previous 100 years or so, the essential features of the professional practice initially developed by Price and Waterhouse in the second half of the nineteenth century remained in place. The main reason for this similarity was that, up to the 1960s, the traditionalists within the firm had won the battle against the reformists, an outcome which may well have been the product of debates that were paralleled within other leading accounting practices, except possibly Cooper Brothers, where the highly ambitious Henry Benson and S. John Pears mounted a successful coup designed to inject more dynamic leadership into the firm as early as 1946 (Benson, 1989: 43).

An important reason for the slower rate of change at Price Waterhouse was the belief that 'a client would expect a partner to be fully conversant with every aspect of their business' (Jones, 1995: 215). It appears that Sir Albert Wyon, senior partner 1916–37, was highly conservative, and is portrayed as having 'scuppered' the advanced negotiations with Peats for amalgamation in 1921. Although criticized for his insularity, Wyon's arguments against the big business partnership can alternatively be interpreted as commendable foresight in view of the problems increasingly encountered in recent decades: 'What methods', he asked, 'assure to a large accounting organisation, composed for the most part of salaried employees, the same sense of professional responsibility as that attained by an individual practitioner or small group of practitioners working together as partners?' (quoted in Jones, 1995: 126). The answer according to Wyon was that the small partnership, limited both in numbers and territorially, would 'secure uniformity of standards and the preservation of traditions, ideals and a high sense of responsibility' (Jones, 1995: 127). These broad concepts were also dear to Sir Nicholas Waterhouse who was senior partner between 1945–60, while, in the post-war period, influential figures such as Sir Thomas B. Robson, senior partner 1961–6, and G. E. Richards continued to resist innovation.

Both, in their different ways, attempted to maintain standards of conduct, technical excellence and professional integrity. Neither saw themselves as businessmen or as men who were running a commercial enterprise for profit. They were, of course, concerned to generate a healthy surplus but would have seen this as the natural outcome of a well run practice. (Jones, 1995: 211)

Criticisms were voiced from time to time by partners concerning the leadership and the slow rate of expansion, for example, by F. S. Tull in 1946, but no significant changes took place (Jones, 1995: 213). The leadership of W. E. Parker between 1966 and 1971 marked a tentative move in the direction of expansion, but

Parker, like Robson, believed that the professional ethic was more important for a firm such as Price Waterhouse than mere business considerations. While recognising, of course, that the partnership could survive only so long as it earned profits, he believed that its status relied upon technical excellence and high standards of personal conduct rather than in competing with rivals to win new clients and extending the range of services. (Jones, 1995: 251)

It was only under the influence of the post-war hero of Jones's story, Michael Coates, that Price Waterhouse worked hard to change its image. Coates's 'seminal paper' of June 1973, which contained ideas and proposals which were 'to exercise the firm for the next decade', drew attention to the fact that

the financial community still thought of PW as too 'superior', too fussy and not commercial enough. Some partners think we tend to breed introverts . . . there is a general feeling that too few partners are well-known outside the firm. There is also a recurring comment that we have a reputation of being uninterested in medium and small-sized clients. (Jones, 1995: 258)

From the 1970s, therefore, fundamental changes identified by Jones include an increasingly commercial attitude, new strategies for recruitment, training, and career development, a hierarchy of functional committees, and other innovations designed to manage an ever more complex organization. The construction of Southwark Towers, at London Bridge, is seen to symbolize the fundamental change which was occurring within the firm. As a result of this move,

The elegant terraced offices of Frederick's Place, which outwardly symbolised tradition, reserve, discretion and probity, had been replaced by a purpose-built, eye-catching tower block described by Pevsner as having 'screens of reflecting glass' which 'break up the surfaces and give the building a glittering elegance but secretive face'. Southwark Towers was an outward expression of the firm's professionalism, stability and ambitious approach to business. (Jones, 1995: 273)

One further manifestation of this growing commercialization has been a greater mobility amongst senior staff, with individuals for almost the first time both coming in at the top and leaving for alternative attractive engagements.

The 1970s also saw, of course, the rise of what the accountancy press captioned the 'big eight' (now, of course, it is the 'big six') and what Jones describes as 'the quiet revolution'. The appearance of the 'big eight' marked a fundamental change in the nature of the profession, with the large organizations having almost wiped out the medium-sized firm. At the same time, the leading firms adopted many of the essential features of what might be called 'big business'. For example, loose world-wide networks were replaced by a single corporate style and the endeavour to introduce common procedures and technical standards across the board. Moreover, whereas accountancy firms had traditionally looked to their professional bodies for guidance, they now became major business concerns in their own right and 'turned to their own committees and research groups when matters of policy and practice arose' (Jones, 1995: 248). With commercialization gaining pace, the 1980s is identified as the period when Price Waterhouse, for example, having previously been 'essentially reactive', became proactive. The firm recognized the need to protect its audit portfolio as an important source of new work, but the burgeoning management consultancy department was the main engine for growth. Of particular relevance in this context was the reversal of an earlier key strategic decision *not* to offer advice on production problems, marketing and sales policies, or time studies on the grounds that such work, requiring the employment of specialists such as engineers, would 'give rise to fundamental problems for the firm and for the accountancy profession' (quoted in Jones, 1995: 234).

Price Waterhouse was not, of course, alone in making these changes. The other leading firms also operated increasingly like the major companies they had become, with large and impressive head offices (for example, Cooper's glass palace at Charing Cross strategically located across the river from Southwark Towers) and partners who gave up practising accountancy to become full-time executives responsible for managing their firms.

ACCOUNTANCY SOCIETIES

The development of the accountancy firm reflected the burgeoning number of accountants qualifying with a growing array of professional bodies (see Appendix). We have seen that the Scots were the first to establish British accountancy societies—in Edinburgh and Glasgow in 1853 and Aberdeen in 1866. They remained three separate bodies, although they worked closely together (using common examinations from 1892), until they formally merged in 1951 (Boys, 1990*a*: 110). The formation of professional organizations in Scotland earlier than in England perhaps has something to do with the fact that, in Scotland, accountants were a more established part of the commercial system at an earlier date. From the late seventeenth and early eighteenth centuries, for example, Scottish accountants began to emerge as part of the legal establishment, advising the courts on the ranking of creditors and handling the estates of bankrupts and others; work that in England was undertaken, at this time, by court officials and lawyers (McDougall, 1954: 4; Jones, 1981: 81–2). The willingness of the courts to refer a range of work to accountants is reflected in the charter application of the Edinburgh Society:

That in the extrication of these numerous suits before the Court of Session which involve directly and indirectly matters of accounting, an Accountant is almost invariably employed by the Court to aid in eliciting the trust . . . such investigation cannot be prosecuted by the Court itself without professional assistance on which it may rely, and the Accountant . . . performs in substance all the more material functions which the Petitioners understand to be performed in England by the Masters in Chancery. (Quoted in Stewart, 1977: 6; see also p. 15)

Indeed, as mentioned above, this involvement with the courts is thought to have provided the specific spur for the formation of the Edinburgh Society in the 1850s, when changes in Scotland's bankruptcy laws threatened to deprive accountants of some of their work (Kedslie, 1990*b*: 8–9; Boys, 1990*a*: 110; Macdonald, 1995: 191; Walker, 1995).

South of the border, the elite Institute of Accountants, formed in 1870 and based in the City of London, was founded by the leading contemporary figures. We are able to infer that William Quilter was the principal actor in the establishment of this body from the fact that the initial meeting took place in the offices of Quilter, Ball & Co. Quilter became the Institute's first president; the other eight attending the initial meeting were his partner John Ball, Samuel Price, William Turquand, John Young, J. B. Gibbons, G. A. Cape, Robert Fletcher, and Charles Fitch Kemp (Howitt, 1966: 5). This elite corps, through successor firms, can trace a massive influence on the profession down to the present day.

The meeting resolved to form an association of accountants and to obtain a royal charter in order to 'maintain and secure the efficiency of the profession' (Howitt, 1966: 5). At a subsequent meeting, 63 City accountants decided that the object of the Institute was to 'elevate the attainments and status of professional accountants in London, to promote their efficiency and usefulness, and to give expression to their opinions upon all questions incident to their profession' (Howitt, 1966: 6). As in Scotland, therefore, the Institute's founders saw themselves not as the creators of a profession but as enhancing, in a variety of ways, the status of an existing profession. Gibbons, Fletcher, and Ball were instructed to find an office, start a library, and take responsibility for publicity. These three also formed the committee which admitted members by oral examination. The entrance fee was 50 guineas for fellows and 25 guineas for associates. By the first annual meeting, in 1872, membership stood at 134 (Howitt, 1966: 8).

Little is known of the provincial societies that sprang up around this time. The Incorporated Society of Liverpool Accountants pre-dated the London Institute of Accountants, having been formed in January 1870. The Society of Accountants was formed in 1872 and aimed for a nation-wide membership. This prompted the London Institute to condescend to admit 'properly qualified' provincial accountants, but their stipulation that a new member be recommended by three fellows restricted numbers entering from outside London. This helped the Society to achieve a faster rate of growth; it had reached a membership of 286 by 1880, compared to the Institute's 188. The Society attacked the Institute for holding to conditions which excluded competent accountants, also because it had been formed without taking provincial interests into account. Additional provincial bodies were set up based in Manchester in 1871 and Sheffield in 1877 (Howitt, 1966: ch. 1; see Appendix).

It is a reflection of the growing significance of accountancy at this time that the profession's own journal, the *Accountant*, was established in 1874 (Howitt, 1966: 13; Parker, 1986: 56). It was a private venture, edited by Alfred Gee, and immediately began campaigning for the amalgamation of societies and the application for a royal charter. The move towards amalgamation was facilitated when Quilter, who opposed any enlargement of the Institute on elitist grounds, resigned as president in 1877 and gave up his seat on the council and membership of the body in the following year (Bywater, 1985b: 794). Turquand, his successor, was more open to progressive moves and, in 1878, a process began that eventually led to the amalgamation of the five societies and the granting of a royal charter in 1880 (Howitt, 1966: 17).

The petition for a royal charter argued: 'That the Profession of Public Accountant in England and Wales is a numerous one and their functions are of great and increasing importance in respect of their employment in the capacities of Liquidators . . . and of Receivers . . . also in the auditing of the accounts of public companies and of partnerships and otherwise' (royal charter of 11 May 1880, reproduced in ICAEW, 1994b: 5). The stated aim of the ICAEW was the 'elevation of the profession of public accountants as a whole and the promotion of their efficiency and usefulness by compelling the observance of strict rules of conduct as a condition of membership and by setting up a high standard of professional and general education and knowledge and otherwise' (ICAEW, 1994b: 5–6). Future membership was confined to those with five years' articles as a public accountant's clerk (reduced to three years for a university graduate) and a 'strict system of examination' (ICAEW, 1994b: 6).

All members of the merging bodies were entitled to join and, of the 638 members of the five original bodies in 1880, 587 became ICAEW members. A further 606 individuals were admitted by the council on the basis of being continually in practice as public accountants—three years for an associate and five years for a fellow—up to the time of the granting of the charter. Despite having fewer members than the Society, the Institute of Accountants clearly dominated the newly formed ICAEW. It had 20 seats on the council including both the presidency and vice-presidency; the Society had fourteen seats and the provincial societies three each. The figure of 45 council members was made up by Charles Henry Wade and Edwin Guthrie of the leading Manchester practice Thomas, Wade & Guthrie, who had joined the presidents of the five original bodies in signing and presenting the petition for a charter (Howitt, 1966: 24). Table 8 demonstrates the subsequent pre-eminence of the ICAEW, accounting for 81% of UK qualified accountants in 1881. This proportion fell to just over a third in the inter-war period, reflecting the formation of new bodies, but, following the merger of the original chartered bodies with the Society of Incorporated Accountants in 1957, the ICAEW's share was restored to over half the total UK membership and has remained at or around that level down to the present time.

In 1888, the accountants of Ireland from Dublin, Belfast, and Cork obtained a royal charter (Robinson, 1964: 87). There were 31 signatories to the petition but, even by 1910, the Institute of Chartered Accountants in Ireland (ICAI) still had only 106 members (Robinson: 1964: 95 and 369). Since that date, though, numbers have grown at a faster rate than in either the English or Scottish societies.

The chartered societies were therefore formed to protect and regulate the provision of the specialist skills which, by the second half of the nineteenth century, were in growing demand as the result of economic development. Membership of a society, if properly regulated, could offer proof to the outside world of the quality of services on offer. Moreover, once these credentials were established, the economic value to existing members of monopoly control over the supply of their specialist services was obvious. As with any monopoly, equally predictable is the fact that 'outsiders' will seek to establish their own credentials. The pattern became established whereby accountants excluded from membership by the rules of existing societies—the process which, as discussed in Chapter 1, sociologists call 'exclusionary closure'—established their own organizations which in turn became exclusive and created, once again, scope for the

Table 8. Membership of major accountancy bodies in the UK, 1881–1995

	(1) ICAEW	(2) SIAA	(3) ICAS	(4) ICAI	(5) LAA	(6) CAA/ACCA	(7) CA	(8) ICWA/CIMA	(9) IMTA/CIPFA	(10) Total	(11) Estimated members abroad (%)	(12) Accountants working in Britain (i.e. col. 10 adjusted by col. 11)	(13) Col. 12 as % UK employed labour force
1881	1,185		285							1,470	0	1,470	0.01
1891	1,796	492	450	46			7		97	2,888	4	2,764	0.02
1901	2,813	1,639	757	59			283		213	5,764	10	5,188	0.03
1911	4,391	2,440	1,298	100	1,251	800	622		439	11,341	20	9,072	0.05
1921	5,642	3,360	1,788	138	2,234	700	868	372	472	15,574	17	12,926	0.07
1931	9,666	5,664	3,322	280	2,935	673	1,967	830	669	26,006	16	21,897	0.12
1941	13,694	7,882	4,565	485		6,390		1,430	1,242	35,688	15	30,335	0.13
1951	16,079	9,000	5,130	787		7,965		3,293	1,805	44,059	15	37,238	0.16
1961	35,600		6,928	1,713		11,006		7,387	3,140	65,774	16	55,251	0.23
1971	51,660		8,558	2,433		13,680		12,003	5,759	94,093	18	77,109	0.31
1981	73,781		10,586	4,280		24,265		20,328	8,673	141,913	19	114,399	0.47
1991	97,720		12,653	7,584		37,765		31,976	10,792	198,490	23	153,015	0.58
1995	109,233		14,016	9,505		47,230		41,634	12,002	233,620	20	186,826	0.73

Sources: ICAEW, 1996*b*. SIAA—Garrett, 1961: 337; yearbooks. ICAS—McDougall, 1954: 173–5; yearbooks. ICAI—information from ICAS head office. ICAI—information from ICAI head office. LAA, CAA, CA/ACCA—yearbooks; BPP, 1936: 4–5; information from ACCA head office. ICWA/ICMA/CIMA—Banyard, 1985: pp. ii, 11, 19, 20, 51, 79; Loft, 1990: 47; information from CIMA head office. IMTA/CIPFA—Poynton, 1960: 141–2; information from CIPFA head office. Labour force data in column 13 from Mitchell, 1962, *OECD Quarterly Labour Force Statistics*, and CSO, 1996: table 6.2. The source of the estimates in column 11 is the same sampling exercise as detailed in Table 6, and for 1995, information provided by ICAEW, ICAS, ICAI, ACCA, CIMA, and CIPFA head offices.

formation of rival organizations (Edwards, 1989*a*: 278; Willmott, 1986: 555–80; Boys, 1990*a*: 110).

The ICAEW's initial requirement that members should usually serve five years' articles in an accountant's office and pass an examination kept out, for example, people who could not afford articles, accountants working in local government, and 'all "official" accountants employed by railway, dock or other companies, even when, as often happened, such accountants engaged in outside professional work with their employers consent' (Howitt, 1966: 12). Such groups helped form the SAA in 1885 (Garrett, 1961: 4) which comprised 'established accountants who had either not applied to join the ICAEW, or had been refused entry' (Kirkham and Loft, 1992: 12). More specifically, this membership comprised practising accountants and their clerks, municipal and county treasurers, and 'in smaller numbers, accountants occupying responsible positions in business and in the Government' (Garrett, 1961: 5). The SAA/ SIAA always trailed the ICAEW in both membership numbers and prestige, but it grew as rapidly as the profession generally, accounting consistently throughout its life for about a fifth of all professional accountants. The SAA created the *Incorporated Accountants Journal* in 1889, which was later renamed *Accountancy* and is now the journal of the ICAEW (Parker, 1986: 56).

From its genesis, the ICAEW attacked the SAA, 'ridiculing its membership and intentions' (Millerson, 1964: 69). Stacey notes that, 'initially, the Society was an outcast; an air of lofty negativism and displeasure at its existence [was felt] by the Institute' (1954: 28). A leading article in the *Accountant* claimed that the membership of the SAA consisted of 'a formidable array of clerks of all kinds—rent collectors, corn merchants, shopkeepers, valuers, collectors of taxes, bailiffs, secretaries of various concerns, civil engineers, school board clerks, overseers, timber agents, pawnbrokers and manure merchants' (20 Mar. 1886: 160). Having obtained a foothold despite these and other outbursts, the SAA soon also required some of its new members to pass an examination and excluded, by degrees, alternative routes into its ranks, such as long service in an accountant's office (Garrett, 1961).

It was the process of closure, in Scotland, that led to the creation of the Scottish Institute of Accountants founded in Glasgow in 1880 and the Corporation of Accountants Ltd. (CA), formed in 1891 by a group of accountants, mostly in public practice, who did not require members to have taken articles and had no compulsory examinations. Attempts to achieve chartered status were, however, thwarted by the three bodies already established north of the border (Walker, 1991). The Scottish Institute therefore became a branch of the SAA in 1899 (see Appendix), while the CA looked to England for its future (Walker, 1991: 280). It quickly built up a membership south of the border where, for legal reasons noted in

Chapter 1, a further rash of new bodies came into existence at the turn of the century. These organizations—the Institution of Certified Public Accountants formed in 1903, the LAA in 1904, and the CAA in 1905—initially ran no examinations (Boys, 1990*a*: 110). The four newcomers, which were later to become the core of the ACCA, were also confined primarily to practising public accountants.

However, 'The initial willingness of these bodies to embrace all aspiring accountants did not last long. Once the monopoly position of the existing bodies was breached, the "new boys" lined up with the old establishment to form a new order' (Edwards, 1989*a*: 278). The LAA's policy of instituting examinations for all aspiring members by 1919 exemplifies such action. The *Accountant* remained unimpressed, however, referring to the membership of the LAA as 'questionable characters who make up the dregs of the profession' (1908: 514). The LAA nevertheless proved highly successful in recruiting members; indeed, at the outset of the First World War, it accounted for about one-tenth of all 'qualified' accountants. As early as 1905, their journal, the *Certified Accountants' Journal* (later to become the *Certified Accountant*), began publication. The LAA established its first branch, in Manchester, in 1906, followed by Sheffield (1908), Scotland (1912), Belfast (1913), and Eire (1925) (Osbourn and Bell, 1954: 8–9, 17, 18, 35). By 1954, the ACCA had 31 district societies in Britain.

Not all new accountancy bodies, it has been argued, were created solely as a reaction to closure or in response to changes in the law. It is suggested that some were formed to cater for accountants specializing in particular branches of the profession (Boys, 1990*a*: 110). In 1885, the Corporate Treasurers' and Accountants' Institute was established by the treasurers of municipal corporations, primarily in Lancashire and Yorkshire, to look after their particular interests. Even here, however, a reaction against exclusion appears to have played a part. '[I]t was an injustice to Corporate Accountants', said the chairman at the inaugural meeting, 'that unless they had a public practice, they were not eligible for the Association of Chartered Accountants [*sic*]' (quoted in Poynton, 1960: 8). The initial membership of the new body was around 60 and proved as exclusive as its predecessors. Fellowships were restricted to the responsible officer in charge of the accounts of a municipal corporation or similar body, while associates had to be in a post immediately next to him in terms of seniority (Poynton, 1960: 30). As a result, numbers in the Institute of Municipal Treasurers and Accountants (IMTA, renamed the Chartered Institute of Public Finance and Accountancy—CIPFA—in 1973), as the society became known on incorporation in 1901, remained small (Table 8). It had about 3% of total qualified accountants in 1921 and has never accounted for more than 7%. The IMTA was always strong in the northern municipalities; the first branch was set up for Lancashire and Cheshire in 1897, the south-west in the following year, and Scotland in 1906 (Sowerby, 1984: 24–5).

Another of today's major societies, the Chartered Institute of Management Accountants (CIMA), was not formed until 1919, then under the title of the Institute of Cost Accountants. It was renamed the Institute of Cost and Works Accountants (ICWA) later in the same year, the Institute of Cost and Management Accountants (ICMA) in 1972, before assuming its present title in 1986. It has been argued that this body also came into being to cater for a separate branch of the profession, that is, to promote the interests of cost accounting as distinct from the financial accounting interests served, primarily, by the then existing bodies. According to Kirkham and Loft, the new body's aim was 'one of copying the professionalisation strategies of the chartered accountants in order to create a profession of cost and works accountants' (1992: 27).

Certainly the ICWA focused from the outset on the cost and management function in its activities, its examinations, and its journal, the *Cost Accountant* (established in 1921 and subsequently renamed *Management Accounting*). Concern with *exclusion* as a principal motivation for the formation of the ICWA, however, can be inferred from the attitude of the existing bodies who could have, had they so wished, opened their doors to accountants in industry. But their doors remained firmly closed. Stacey laments the fact that the status quo neglected 'for so long an important branch of accountancy . . . [and] made no provision for the acquisition of special skills in costing or took an interest in its exploration' (1954: 99). It was not until the cessation of hostilities in the Great War that a progressive element among chartered accountants, led by Mark Webster Jenkinson and supported by Gilbert Garnsey, attempted to move the ICAEW in the direction of greater openness to accountants working in industry, and encouraged it to show more interest in managerial accounting (Loft, 1990: 38). Other chartered accountants strove to set up a separate branch within the ICAEW to further the interests of cost accountants (Loft, 1990: 39). The failure of both initiatives paved the way for the establishment of the above-mentioned independent organization catering exclusively for accountants working in industry.

The determination of the established elite to stifle competition is reflected in the fact that, in 1922, the ICAEW and the SIAA successfully opposed the ICWA's petition for a charter of incorporation on the grounds that cost and works accountants 'are not engaged in professional work, but are employed in the service of traders' (quoted in Jones, 1981: 130). The accounting press was also highly critical of 'the intentions and status of those involved' (Loft, 1986: 153), with a contributor to the *Accountant* alleging that 'the Memorandum [of Association] is subscribed by men of whom we have never heard, and all manner of works accountants, cost clerks, and the like will no doubt range themselves under its banner with a view to "trading" henceforth as "qualified" Cost Accountants' (quoted in Loft, 1986: 153). Whilst the existing accountancy bodies were suspicious of the ICWA, 'a number of prominent industrialists . . . gave their wholehearted support to the new body' (Loft, 1986: 153–4). Moreover, some chartered and incorporated accountants, who had become closely involved with costing matters as a result of employment in government departments during the First World War, joined the society. Reginald Townsend, for example, a chartered accountant who was Director of Ordnance Factories in the inter-war period and took a special interest in costings, became its president in 1932/3 (Loft, 1990: 17, 73 and 82; Parker, 1980a: n.p.).

The ICWA held examinations from the outset, but admission was also at the discretion of its governing body. As usual, elitism surfaced almost immediately, and only those 'with a good job' in industry were admitted. The clear intention was, again, to exclude mere clerks, while people in senior positions, even those having little or no connection with cost accounting or even accounting in general, were admitted. This latter finding provides further support for the view that the ICWA was also set up to provide accountants working in industry, and thereby excluded from the established bodies, with a society of their own, rather than solely to serve the needs of cost accounting. In 1923, 43% of ICWA members had job descriptions which did not link them with cost accounting (Loft, 1986: 99). Many of these were company secretaries; indeed over 10% of the membership in 1923 were also members of the Chartered Institute of Secretaries (Loft, 1986: 100).

The combined effect of examinations and elitism was that the IWCA's membership grew slowly and had reached only 830 in 1931, a year when the population census revealed 28,364 'costing and estimating clerks' (Banyard, 1985: 20; Loft, 1990: 111). The proportion of members admitted by examination had, however, risen from 14% in 1923 to 50% by 1930, indicating that, at least by the latter date, a much greater proportion of the membership had a reasonable grounding in the theory of cost accounting than was the case seven years earlier. This proportion increased over the years, with a rapidly rising membership (Table 8) reflecting the growing importance of management accounting within business organizations (Loft, 1990: 90). The ICWA quickly established branches in locations which reflected its base in manufacturing—first in Birmingham (1919), soon to be followed by Glasgow, Sheffield, Bristol, and Manchester—and in 1921 a London branch was formed (Banyard, 1985: 8; Parker, 1986: 56).

By 1919, then, the nucleus of today's accountancy societies had been established (see Appendix), but this was far from the end of the formation of new bodies. Part of the reason was the continued process of closure. Paradoxically, the institution of examinations by the IMTA in

1903 had in the first instance widened membership, since junior local government finance officers could now gain admittance. Nonetheless, by 1909 IMTA membership was confined to those passing examinations (except under exceptional circumstances at the discretion of the council) and thus became fully exclusive (Poynton, 1960: 31), and the remaining professional bodies gradually followed suit. For example, the LAA made the passing of examinations a compulsory qualification for membership in 1920, and the CA did so in 1928 (Osbourn and Bell, 1954: 28; Boys, 1990a: 110).

The new wave of societies set up in the 1920s and 1930s was prompted, in common with the creation of the LAA and CAA, by a renewed threat of legislation, this time designed to restrict the practice of accounting to those named on a national register of accountants. New societies formed, together with their date of incorporation, were as follows: Institute of Poor Law Accountants (1923); British Association of Accountants and Auditors (1923); Society of Statisticians and Accountants (1927); Professional Accountants' Alliance (1927); Faculty of Auditors (1928); Institute of Company Accountants (1929); Association of International Accountants (1931); Incorporated Association of Cost and Industrial Accountants (1936); Society of Commercial Accountants (1942) (BPP, 1936: 5; Banyard, 1985: 2–3). Apart from the Institute of Company Accountants, none of these bodies achieved a significant membership and, by the time the last of them had been formed, the tide had turned firmly in the direction of amalgamation and rationalization among accountancy bodies.

The first major merger saw the CA combine with the LAA (by then renamed the London Association of Certified Accountants) in 1939 to form the ACCA. The new body absorbed the Institution of Certified Public Accountants in 1941, which had itself taken over the CAA in 1933 (see Appendix). The espoused reasons for consolidation 'were the relatively small number of members, a common history and aims, and the confusion among the public caused by the multiplicity of associations with similar titles' (Boys, 1990a: 110). The ACCA was successively renamed the Association of Certified Accountants (1971), the Chartered Association of Certified Accountants in 1984 (having received a royal charter in 1974) (see Appendix), and the Association of Chartered Certified Accountants in 1996.

We have seen that the three Scottish societies amalgamated in 1951, formalizing a close relationship that had existed almost from the start, while the last of the big mergers saw the original chartered bodies absorb the membership of the Society of Incorporated Accountants in 1957. The reasons given for merger are familiar: there were administrative economies to be made; the distinction between qualification requirements for membership of each body had long since disappeared; there were unnecessary difficulties in the designation of firms where partners belonged to different societies; and there was an avoidable public confusion due to the existence of two bodies performing similar functions (Boys, 1990*a*: 110).

In 1974, the Society of Company and Commercial Accountants was formed by the amalgamation of the Institute of Company Accountants, the Incorporated Association of Cost and Industrial Accountants, and the Society of Commercial Accountants. In 1981 this body also absorbed the British Association of Accountants and Auditors (Henderson and Henderson, 1992), giving it a combined membership of over 10,000. In 1990, the Society of Company and Commercial Accountants reverted to the title of Institute of Company Accountants, but it remained a relatively small organization with its membership estimated to be 'approximately 6,000' on 13 January 1997 (figure supplied by head office), having tried and failed to achieve recognition for its members as auditors under the Companies Acts.

From the mid-1960s, a scheme for the amalgamation of all six remaining major bodies was actively planned. When the final vote was taken, in 1970, the memberships of the Institute of Chartered Accountants of Scotland (ICAS), ICAI, ACCA, ICMA, and IMTA voted in favour, but 55% of the ICAEW members objected and effectively blocked the scheme (Banyard, 1985: 60). More modest schemes for amalgamation have subsequently been attempted (for example, the ICAEW and the ICAS in 1989, CIPFA and the ICAEW in 1990, *Accountant*, June 1990: 2, and the ICAEW and CIMA in 1996, *Accountancy*, Mar. 1996: 11), but all have failed. What did emerge from the first of these initiatives was the formation, in 1975, of a permanently staffed Co-ordinating Committee of Accountancy Bodies to speak for the profession on public matters and do work that is best undertaken on behalf of the profession generally. The most significant development in this direction was the eventual involvement of all professional bodies in the affairs of the Accounting Standards Committee (initially formed by the ICAEW, in 1970, as the Accounting Standards Steering Committee, and replaced in 1990 by the Accounting Standards Board) to guide the form and content of company accounts.

Perhaps the most important development of recent years, in the context of professional associations, has been the loosening up of the right to use the prized designation 'chartered accountant'. We have seen that a number of bodies succeeded in obtaining royal charters in recent decades, but use of the term chartered to describe its members continued to be vigorously defended by the ICAEW, ICAI, and ICAS. A key event, therefore, was the Privy Council's decision, in late 1995, that any accountancy body that had a royal charter could be granted the right to use the term 'chartered' as part of the members' designation. This move had been opposed by the ICAEW, ICAI, and ICAS on the grounds that use of the chartered title by all would be confusing in the minds of the public (*Accountancy*, Jan. 1996: 11). Subsequently, in October 1996, the Privy Council gave its consent to the ACCA changing its name to the Association of Chartered Certified Accountants. It also ruled that the ACCA's members may from 1 January 1997 be known as chartered certified accountants. The ICAEW's forlorn attempt to block this further development again failed (*Accountancy*, Nov. 1996: 11).

COUNTING THE ACCOUNTANTS

Pursuing our examination of the growth of the accountancy profession, we consider now a matter already touched upon in Chapter 2, namely the ever rising number of accountants. In tackling this exercise, there is the fundamental problem of defining what constitutes an accountant (Kirkham and Loft, 1996). Due to the lack of appropriate classifications in the Census of Population (Matthews, 1993), we conclude, in accord with Carr-Saunders and Wilson (1933), that the only meaningful definition of an accountant is one who is a member of a qualifying body. We acknowledge that this is a sub-optimal measure of the number of practising accountants and, therefore, the amount of accounting work performed, in that it excludes part- or unqualified practitioners.

Whilst bookkeeping is the foundation on which accounting is based, and although there is a degree of interchangeability in the work of accountants and bookkeepers (probably more so in the nineteenth century than today), we argue that a distinction can be drawn between bookkeeping activity and the more difficult and analytical work justifying the term 'accounting'. For this reason, we exclude from our count members of the junior accountancy and bookkeeping bodies. These include: the Association of Accounting Technicians established in 1980 from the amalgamation of the Association of Technicians in Finance and Accounting and the Institute of Accounting Staff; and the International Association of Bookkeepers founded in 1972. The respective memberships of these two bodies in 1996, according to their head offices, were 24,558 (also 62,500 students) and 1,413.

Table 8, columns 1–10, sets out the membership of the major accountancy societies identified in the previous section for the census years from 1881 to 1991, and the most recent figures available, namely those for 1995 (the annual updated figures are graphed in Figure 1). Certain further limitations of these figures as a measure of the number of active, professionally qualified, accountants must be acknowledged. A number of other, smaller, societies for which no or incomplete records remain are excluded from the statistics. The Board of Trade Committee on the Registration of Accountants in 1930 listed seventeen societies (BPP, 1936: 4–5),

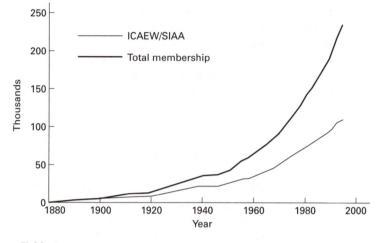

Source: Table 8.

Fig. 1   Membership of UK accountancy bodies, 1881–1995

ten of which (counting the three Scottish bodies separately) are included in Table 8. The remaining seven had 2,175 members in 1930 (of which 600 belonged to the Institute of Company Accountants, formed in 1928), compared to the total of 26,006 for the 'major' bodies one year later. The Irish chartered body is included in Table 8, even though from 1920, of course, Eire was recognized as a separate republic. We are reasonably confident that the numbers omitted, by excluding the smaller bodies, are insufficiently material to alter the broad picture, such that Table 8, column 10, captures well over 90% of total membership of all senior accountancy societies.

Further computational problems need to be resolved in order to measure accurately the number of qualified accountants practising in Britain. Ideally, adjustments are required to eliminate the double counting of those members belonging to more than one society and the fact that, when attempting to identify practising accountants, a certain proportion of the membership will be retired, as Table 9 shows in the case of the ICAEW. There is also an unknown, although probably small, number of qualified accountants whose membership had lapsed by virtue of not having paid their subscriptions.

The figures in Table 8 take no account of the above matters because it is impossible to measure precisely the numbers involved. The *major* inaccuracy of column 10 as a measure of practising accountants in Britain, however, is the proportion of the membership which works abroad. An adjustment to take account of this factor is made in columns 11 and 12, based on the estimates presented in Table 6. Finally, there are an unknown

Table 9. The occupations of ICAEW membership in the UK, 1983–1996

	1983 (%)	1986 (%)	1992 (%)	1995 (%)	1996 (%)
Partner in practice	25	26	20	22	22
Employed in practice	18	17	15	15	14
In business	42	39	35	41	43
Retired	2	10	11	10	10
Unknown	13	8	19	12	11
Total	100	100	100	100	100
or					
In practice	51	53	49	48	45
In business	49	47	51	52	55
Total	100	100	100	100	100

Note: 1983 data relate to all ICAEW members, not UK members.

Sources: *ICAEW Membership Questionnaires*: 1983: 2; 1986: 2; 1992: 2; ICAEW, 1996*b* 2; 1996*c*: 2.

number of foreign accountants practising in Britain for which no adjustment is possible.

Irrespective of the above problems of definition, we can be certain that Britain has large numbers of qualified accountants and that the numbers have been growing rapidly throughout the past 100 years, both absolutely and relative to the occupied population as a whole. Table 10 gives decennial growth rates in total membership of the leading UK accountancy bodies and the combined membership of the ICAEW and SAA/SIAA. The membership nearly doubled in each of the decades up to the First World War. Since then, significant, though lower, rates of growth have been maintained, with a relative slowdown in the decades spanning the two world wars. Since the Second World War, ten-yearly growth rates have fluctuated in the range 40%–50%. As a consequence, the proportion of accountants in the workforce has roughly doubled every twenty years to reach 0.73% in 1995 (Table 8, column 13, and Figure 2).

Accountancy has also been by far the fastest growing of the major professions in Britain in the last 100 years, outdistancing doctors, lawyers, teachers, and engineers/scientists (Halmos, 1970: 32–3). Looking at perhaps the closest comparable profession, law, the 1911 census counted 4,121 barristers and 17,259 solicitors (reproduced in Reader, 1966: 154–5), which compares with the figure of 11,341 accountants in Table 8. In 1991, there were 9,313 barristers and 57,167 solicitors (Hobson's Casebook Series 1993, 1992), together a roughly threefold increase on 1911. The

Table 10.   Growth rates and relative size of leading
UK accountancy bodies, 1881–1995

	Growth rates		Relative size (ICAEW/SIAA as % of total membership)
	Total (%)	ICAEW/ SIAA (%)	
1881–91	96.5	93.1	80.6
1891–1901	99.6	94.6	79.2
1901–11	96.8	53.4	77.2
1911–21	37.3	31.8	60.2
1921–31	67.0	70.3	57.8
1931–41	37.2	40.7	58.9
1941–51	23.5	16.2	60.5
1951–61	49.3	42.0	56.9
1961–71	43.1	45.1	54.1
1971–81	50.8	42.8	54.9
1981–91	39.9	32.4	52.0
1991–5	17.7	11.8	49.2

Notes: Growth rates are ten-yearly except for 1991–5.
The third column of figures is taken at the earlier of the
two dates in each instance; e.g. 80.6% relates to the
1881 fraction.

Sources: Table 8, col. 10 for total membership and cols.
1 and 2 for ICAEW/SIAA.

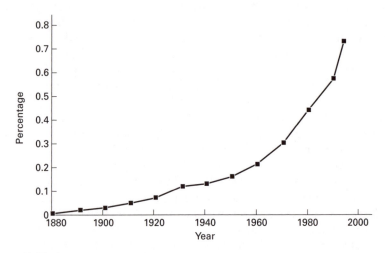

Source: Table 8.

Fig. 2   Accountants as a percentage of the labour force, 1881–1995

engineers did rather better. Buchanan (1989) shows that the size of the engineering profession grew from around 40,000 members (belonging to seventeen British professional institutions) in 1914, to over 375,000 by 1979 (being members of sixteen Engineering Council-nominated bodies and nine affiliated bodies)—a ninefold increase. Turning to accountants, however, by 1991 they numbered 198,490, representing a seventeenfold increase compared with 1911 (Table 8). Put even more dramatically—in 1911 there was approximately one qualified accountant for every 633 jobs in manufacturing in the UK; in 1951 the number was 215, and by 1991 there were only 31 people making things for every one professional accountant adding up the figures.

It is also the case that Britain has a high number of accountants compared with many other leading countries. Table 11 gives the approximate membership of accountancy bodies in the seven leading industrial countries in 1990, and shows the extent to which Britain has by far the highest proportion of accountants relative to the workforce generally and the size of national income. Unfortunately, Nobes and Parker's international figures (used in Table 11) include only accounting societies entitled to undertake audits (Nobes and Parker, 1991), but the indications are that, when all other accountancy societies in these countries (for

Table 11. International comparisons in the G7 countries between numbers of qualified accountants and other economic indicators in 1990

(1) Country	(2) Number of accountants ('000)	(3) Total labour force (millions)	(4) Labour force per accountant	(5) GDP at current prices and exchange rates (US$bn.)	(6) Domestic companies on major stock exchanges 1988
UK	144	28.5	198	974.2	1,804
USA	296	126.4	427	5,464.8	5,783
Germany	6	30.4	5,066	1,496.4	609
France	11	24.9	2,264	1,192.2	459
Japan	11	63.8	5,800	2,940.4	1,571
Italy	46	24.5	533	1,094.8	228
Canada	47	13.8	294	566.7	1,147

Note: Nobes and Parker's figures (column 2) only include accountants qualified to conduct audits.

Sources: Columns 2 and 6: Nobes and Parker, 1991: 4, 9; columns 3 and 4: *OECD Quarterly Labour Force Statistics*, 1993; column 5: *OECD National Accounts*, 1993.

example, those of cost accountants) are added, there is no significant change to the picture presented in Table 11. The pattern is of course distorted to an extent by the fact that some work undertaken by accountants in Britain, for example taxation, is the province of other professionals, such as lawyers, abroad. The heavy provision of professional accountants in Britain compared with these other countries nevertheless remains an indisputable fact.

Within the UK profession, by size of membership, the ICAEW remains dominant. This body, based in Moorgate Place, admitted its one hundred thousandth member in 1993/4. In terms of recent growth rates, however, it has been left trailing by both CIMA and ACCA, who have more than doubled their memberships in the last twenty years. Further, such growth appears set to continue given the vast numbers of students each has in training, particularly abroad. Whereas the ICAEW had 8,599 'active students training' as at 1 October 1996 (ICAEW, 1996c: 1), the ACCA, reflecting its traditional determination to become an international body and its overseas training facilities, has broken the 100,000 barrier, with 100,557 students registered at the end of 1996 (data supplied by head office). CIMA's international pretensions are also reflected in a large student body of 60,206, which includes 10,087 who have passed the examinations and are awaiting admittance to full membership (data supplied by head office). The combined qualified membership of CIMA and ACCA, following recent rapid growth, now totals approximately 85% of that of the ICAEW.

GENDER

A feature of the accountancy profession, in common with professional society in general, has been that of male domination from its inception. Indeed, we referred in Chapter 1 to the fact that the process of closure and the exclusion by the societies of outsiders is seen to have been on the basis of sex (Kirkham and Loft, 1992, 1993). Kirkham and Loft argue that the professionalization of accountancy has been based on the establishment of boundaries between high-status public accountancy and 'a separate occupational sphere for the non-professional accountant, primarily within clerical work', increasingly the domain of the female (Kirkham and Loft, 1993: 552). They therefore categorize 'the professionalisation project as fundamentally gendered', whose success 'was not simply a matter of establishing accountancy as a profession but involved creating and maintaining a masculine identity for the "professional accountant"' (Kirkham and Loft, 1993: 552).

Women were specifically excluded by the constitutions of all the early societies and, whilst a few women did practise accountancy, any applications for membership were rejected. Among that number was Miss Harris Smith, who applied to the SIAA in 1888, but was refused entry despite her obvious competence, having been in practice for ten years (Jones, 1981: 136). This rejection was frequently 'justified' by contrasting women's natural abilities with the qualities demanded of an accountant. '[A]ccountancy was among those professions which required for their proper fulfilment those masculine qualities and experience of the world and intellectual capacity and courage which were rarely to be found in members of the weaker sex', commented one speaker at the SIAA annual meeting in 1891 (Garrett, 1961: 7). Two years earlier, the body held a plebiscite which found only 88 out of 309 members (28.5%) in favour of the admission of women.

The ICAEW had always been steadfastly opposed to the admission of women as chartered accountants. In 1894, the Society for Promoting Employment of Women approached the council to explore the possibility of admitting females, but this initiative was resisted and the *Accountant* added that 'there are few occupations more unsuitable to women' (6 Oct. 1894: 867). The views of the president in 1895, as revealed by the ICAEW's historian, could not have been clearer or more damning: 'it would be so embarrassing to manage a staff composed partly of women that he would rather retire from the profession than contemplate such a position'; a stance greeted with 'loud laughter' by the audience (quoted in Howitt, 1966: 54). Prior to the First World War, the LAA stood alone in admitting women—a step taken in 1909. The *Accountant* at this stage showed some sympathy for this arrangement, provided they had first obtained the degree of Bachelor of Commerce (8 June 1910: 807). Further comment in the journal two years later, however, suggests that this was a temporary aberration: 'We have no desire to say anything that might tend to encourage women to embark upon accountancy, for although many women might make excellent bookkeepers, there is much in accountancy proper that is, we think, altogether unsuitable for them' (*Accountant*, 14 Sept. 1912: 341).

Indeed, it was not until 1914 that Whinney, Smith & Whinney employed its first woman, and then in a secretarial capacity. This policy was soon to change dramatically due to recruitment into the armed forces and the consequent wartime shortage of male labour (Jones, 1981: 135). Many women were employed as audit clerks and in other areas of work, though it appears that the majority lost their jobs at the cessation of hostilities. Price, Waterhouse did continue to employ a number of women during the 1920s but stipulated that they should be single (Jones, 1995: 115).

It was, however, in response to these wartime experiences that the SIAA voted to allow women into the profession in 1918. One year later followed the Sex Discrimination (Removal) Act of 1919 which opened both accountancy and the legal profession to women for the first time (Kirkham and Loft, 1993: 540). It was legislation, therefore, which forced the elitist and chauvinistic ICAEW to admit women, though the floodgates could hardly be said to have opened. Miss Harris Smith was immediately admitted to fellowship of the ICAEW, then able to claim the distinction of being 'the first and only woman chartered accountant in the world' (Howitt, 1966: 65). In the following year, however, just five women entered articles, whilst the first woman to be admitted by examination was Miss Ethel Watts in 1924 (Jones, 1981: 136). There were still only 119 qualified women accountants in 1931, accounting for fewer than 1% of the members of the profession, but this at least represented something of an increase from the position in 1911 when there were just nineteen (BPP, 1913: p. lxxviii; Jones, 1981: 136).

Women entering the profession were confined to the 'exceptionally placed and ambitious', frequently being the offspring of leading accountants who thus enjoyed a privileged position that most women lacked (Kirkham and Loft, 1993: 547). The minority with the necessary education and the funds still had to 'overcome the hurdles the profession had erected over the previous decades', such as attendance at evening classes, a requisite of the ICWA which clearly had social and domestic implications (Kirkham and Loft, 1993: 547). The first woman to be admitted by examination to the SIAA in 1920, Miss H. M. Claridge, was the daughter of that year's president and had been articled to her father (Margerison, 1980: 27). In 1930, four women passed the ICAEW final examinations, twice the number at the SIAA, while the total female membership of ICWA in the following year amounted to just two (Kirkham and Loft, 1993: 547). The LAA, the most advanced in this regard, had 56 women members, but even this number accounted for less than 2% of its overall membership (Kirkham and Loft, 1993: 547).

The Second World War also saw a temporary change of attitude. At Price, Waterhouse, for example, women were taken on in increasing numbers, but a decision was made in March 1944 not to accept female articled clerks. In addition, the firm retained the rule that female employees had to leave on marriage. The partnership therefore remained exclusively male and women could find jobs only as secretaries, comptometer operators, and, more rarely, as audit clerks (Jones, 1995: 200). Based on this kind of attitude, the number of female ICAEW members inevitably remained small for many years. In 1945, the ICAEW boasted just 105 women members (0.8% of the total), and by 1960 this had grown to just 342, or 1% of the total (Kirkham, 1992: 293). The 1970s upsurge in the ICAEW's recruitment of women is evident from the following statistics. As late as 1969, just 2% of articled clerks were female, but this figure had risen to 22% ten years later and 36% by 1994 (Stacey, 1954: 217; Jones, 1981: 242; *ICAEW Member-*

ship Questionnaire, 1992: 3; Boys, 1994: 14). This trend was naturally slower to impact on full membership statistics, such that by 1982 a mere 3% of ICAEW members were female, by 1986 it was 7% and by 1994 it had reached 15% (*ICAEW Membership Questionnaire*, 1986, 1; 1994, 1). Of the ACCA membership in 1993, 19% were women; in CIMA, 9%. Turning to their positioning within the management of accounting societies, the SIAA was the first body to elect a woman to its council, as late as 1949, while the ICAEW followed suit only in 1979. The first woman president was Margaret Downes of the ICAI in 1983 (*Accountancy*, Aug. 1994: 19), while Sheila Masters of KPMG is expected to be the ICAEW's first female president in 1999.

The situation in accountancy, of course, is merely a reflection of trends within British business management generally. Women had been admitted to the lower levels of office work 'associated with the increasing use of shorthand and typing' in large numbers, as the following figures serve to illustrate (Anderson, 1976: 60). At the commencement of the twentieth century, for example, female government employees accounted for '45 per cent of all telephonists and telegraphists, 29 per cent of local government clerks and 25 per cent of civil service clerks' (Anderson, 1976: 109). As early as 1911, there were 124,843 female clerks (18% of the total), whilst seventy years later the 2,342,570 female clerks outnumbered their male counterparts by more than three to one, accounting for 77% of the total (Loft, 1992: 367). However, the upper rungs of the managerial ladder have remained, almost exclusively, a male preserve. Whilst the proportion of 'managers' who were women increased from 1.8% in 1974 to 9.5% twenty years later, by 1994 just 2.8% of company directors were women (*Independent*, 3 May 1994).

Crawford's Directory of City Connections, 1995 edition, showed that just 20 out of a total of 1,376 financial directors were women, at a time when they accounted for 30% of the students of the six main accountancy bodies and 14% of all qualified accountants. The list of women finance directors among FTSE 100 companies now includes, in addition to Rosemary Thorne and Kathleen O'Donovan, referred to above, Pippa Wicks of Courtauld Textiles (*Accountancy Age*, 30 Mar. 1995: 2). Another who has also reached the top is Hilary Wild, managing director of Kleinwort Benson Charities, who initially left Whinney Murray for a client company because she was frustrated by not being able to see the 'whole picture' (Grey, 1994b: 30). She sees 'no glass ceiling at Kleinworts' and, more controversially, 'there are quite a lot of occasions when women think they are being prejudiced against and they are not; it is because they are not as good as the next person'. She does, however, acknowledge the fact that 'I would not have achieved what I have done in my career if I had got married'. A similar picture of bias against women appears to emerge when the positions of financial controller and chief accountant are considered, with women representing just 10.7% of the total in 1994, albeit a significant increase over the comparable figure of 3% in 1992 (*Accountancy Age*, 10 Mar. 1994: 3).

SOCIAL AND FINANCIAL BACKGROUNDS

Accountants have been highly successful in terms of income generation, the achievement of professional status, and in their ability to rise to positions of prominence within business. It may well be the case that the social background of many of the pioneer accountants, and the restrictions placed on entry to the profession in terms of wealth and ability, were initially important contributory factors in this process. Certainly, the leading accountants of the Victorian era appear broadly comparable in terms of social standing with the leaders of the other professions during this period. Perkin found that, among the presidents of seven major professional bodies (including the ICAEW) for the period 1880–99, 64.6% came from the middle class (deemed to account for 18% of the population generally), 32.9% were from the upper class (comprising 3% of society), and 57% were from professional families. Just one president had risen to that position from the manual working class. Seventy-six per cent of society presidents went to private (including grammar) schools, but only a minority had attended university, 'reflecting the apprenticeship training of most professions before the twentieth century' (Perkin, 1989: 87–8). Between 1900 and 1919, the situation had changed a little: 56.3% of presidents of the professional bodies were middle class, 66.3% were from professional families, and 65% had attended private schools. The social spread of the leaders of the professions has increased in more recent times, but not by much. Between 1880 and 1899, 2.1% were from the working class (70% of the population as defined) while, by 1960–70, this had risen to only 12.3%. In the same time-span, those presidents of professions that had been to state schools increased from 17.6% to 20% (Perkin, 1989: 261–2).

An important factor affecting the type of person who could enter the accountancy profession was the cost of articles. The constitution of the ICAEW was modelled on that of the Scottish chartered bodies which, in turn, had copied the lawyers, reflecting the fact that the founders saw themselves as seeking to emulate the law and medicine (Stacey, 1954: 24). We have seen that the ICAEW also set out to create an exclusive body, with the requirements that articled clerks normally serve five years in an accountant's office and pass an examination representing stiff obstacles. In addition, the pupil (or more probably his parents) had to pay a premium which varied widely in amount, presumably depending on the prestige and location of the firm. A. R. Hollebone was probably William Welch Deloitte's first articled clerk in 1861, paying a premium of £499. At Comins & Co., by way of contrast, the premium was £150 in 1885, while Baker Sutton's first articled clerk, indentured in 1903, paid £150 which was shared between the partners (Baker Sutton, 1978: n.p.). The premium might be repaid during training. At Cooper Brothers, 'it was the custom until the outbreak of the second world war to charge a premium of 500 guineas and 300 guineas respectively for five and three year articles with part of the premium being returned over the period of the articles. After the war the firm felt that the practice of charging a premium was out of keeping with modern conditions and the practice was discontinued' ([Benson] 1954: 27). Deloitte, Plender, Griffiths & Co., then also charging a premium of £525, took the same step in 1945 (Kettle, 1957: 35).

The *Pall Mall Gazette* offered the opinion, in 1890, that it was 'inadvisable and altogether imprudent' to become a chartered accountant unless one had a capital of at least £2,000 or £3,000 (equivalent to about £80,000–£120,000 at 1996 prices) or influential friends in business circles. It considered both conditions desirable, but the latter the more important (quoted in Kitchen and Parker, 1980: 26). These kind of factors explain the decision sometimes made to waive the premium of a bright young prospect or for the sons of friends and relatives. Bernhard Binder was 'given' articles by McAuliffe, Davis and Hope and qualified in 1908, while the leading chartered accountant and academic Sewell Bray was similarly treated by Tansley Witt (Parker, 1980a: n.p.). Accountants were not embarrassed to acknowledge the elitism underlying the practice of charging a premium. In 1933, Pixley argued that it was intended to limit membership of the English Institute to the same class of persons as those at Woolwich, Sandhurst, and the Inns of Court, while, as late as 1942, an editorial in the *Accountants' Magazine* argued that 'the premium brings a good type of young man, in the same way as the law of supply and demand brings an economic price for goods of other kinds' (quoted in Parker, 1980a: n.p.).

It was not only financial considerations and the ability to secure articles that served as restrictions on entry. There were also the examinations for those who did not benefit from the usual privilege accorded by founders to themselves, or from the special provisions used more extensively by societies formed later to allow the admission of individuals based on experience. The first professional body established in Britain—the elite Edinburgh Society—did not, however, initially make their examinations all important. According to a senior Scottish chartered accountant writing in the *Accountants' Magazine* in 1909:

The examinations were of secondary importance and were to a great extent oral, which enabled the Examiner to bring his personal observation of the candidate into play. His judgement, therefore, rested on wider grounds than a mere report of the value per cent of a candidate's answers to certain questions put to him. Weight was attached, and rightly, to the character of the instruction he would be likely to receive in the office in which he was trained and to the intelligence shown in oral examinations; and if in certain branches of his profession the candidate revealed deficiency, he was informed of his defects and told how best to remedy them. (Walker, 1988: 138)

The minor role of the examination is reflected in the lack of evidence of anyone having ever failed this test. Indeed, Walker believes that the introduction of a formal three-tier system of examination in 1873 was principally to satisfy demands from aspiring accountants, and perhaps more pertinently their parents, that, in common with other new professions, there would be 'a sophisticated examination system and a recognised qualification of high academic standing' (Walker, 1988: 141). Examinations, when instituted by the various bodies, were usually a stiff test of ability. In the first ICAEW examination held in 1882, for example, only five of the thirteen candidates passed the preliminary examination and fifteen out of 25 passed the finals. Roughly this level of passes has continued ever since. In 1913 only 62% of those ICAEW clerks registering for articles were finally admitted (Howitt, 1966: 198), while the *Education, Training and Student Salary Statistics—1994/95* shows the comparable figure for 1995 to be 63.5% (ICAEW, 1996a: 31).

As we have seen, the organizations set up subsequent to the original chartered bodies were equally keen to impose restrictions. The fact that conditions for entry were rather less restrictive than those of the ICAEW probably signifies nothing more than that their junior position in the market required a lower price to be paid for membership. In the case of the SAA/SIAA, for example, articles were never a fixed requirement and, although usual, could be replaced by ten years' pupillage. The pupils were usually paid during articles and were not required to pay a premium. In the SIAA, working as an assistant in an accountant's office or in central or local government was an alternative route to membership. Examinations were introduced in 1887, although membership continued to be mainly through election by council. In 1893 there were altogether 124 examination candidates (of whom 30 failed), but 155 new members were admitted (including those of the 124 who had passed the *final* examination in that year) (Garrett, 1961: 6). An extensive revision of the SAA's constitution took place in 1902 and, from that date, the power to admit members based on experience and professional standing was used sparingly, being dropped in 1912 except for the admission of members of 'other bodies of standing' (Garrett, 1961: 22). The examinations seem, again, to have represented a stiff test; 378 out of 552 (68.5%) candidates passed the 1913 examinations, while only 61% did so in 1924 (Garrett, 1961: 121).

The cost of articles, the premium combined with the need to support the trainee over a five-year period, meant that chartered accountants could, in most cases, come only from comfortably off, middle- or upper middle-class backgrounds. This situation received some reinforcement from the fact that indentures could often be arranged only through personal contacts within the various social and business networks. The financial and social barriers to membership of the SAA/SIAA, and even more so for the remaining bodies, was less onerous, but generally involved the need to obtain a suitable situation and pass testing examinations. An indication of the backgrounds of leading accountants is chronicled in Table 12, which contains data drawn primarily from Jeremy's *Dictionary of Business Biography* (1984–6) and the obituaries of 65 leading accountants included in Parker's *British Accountants: A Biographical Sourcebook* (1980). Four Scottish farmers' sons—John Young, Richard Brown, T. P. Laird, and W. B. Peat—carved out successful careers, as did the founder of the Edinburgh Society, James Brown, the 'son of the manse' (Parker, 1980a: n.p.). Harold Judd was also born of religious stock, his father having been a missionary. Of the two famous Scots who set up an American partnership, Alexander Mitchell, Jr., born in 1860, was from a wealthy background, whilst James Marwick was the son of Sir James David Marwick LLD, town clerk of both Edinburgh and Glasgow (Wise, 1982: 5). The third of the ancient professions, medicine, also spawned eminent accountants: Alexander Moore's father was a surgeon and Woodburn Kirby's a doctor. The fathers of both Arthur Lowes Dickinson and Lawrence R. Dicksee were artists, while Francis W. Pixley descended from a long line of ships' captains. Arthur Cutforth was the son of a prosperous linen and woollen draper (Kitchen and Parker, 1980: 25, 66). There is, of course, bias in these profiles, in that the aforementioned all reached the top of their profession. Moreover, where those who reached the top came from humble origins, this fact may not have been mentioned in their obituaries.

The comprehensive analysis of the occupations of fathers of Scottish chartered accountants, undertaken by Kedslie (1990a), provides a reliable insight into the social status of early members of the Scottish profession. From their date of formation to 1904, 50.3% of those admitted to the three Scottish societies came from a professional or privileged family;

with a further seventeen per cent coming from a mercantile background, this would suggest that two-thirds of such accountants came from upper- or middle-class families [whilst] fewer than twenty per cent of chartered accountants admitted to membership are known to have come from the lower social classes. (Kedslie, 1990a: 79–81; see also Walker, 1988: 174–6)

Such statistics conceal social variations in the backgrounds of early members. Undoubtedly, the Edinburgh Society's early membership could claim the greatest social distinction, with a significantly higher proportion

Table 12. Prominent accountants—their estate and family background

Accountant	Father's occupation	Education	Year of death	Estate (£)	At 1996 prices (£m)[a]
William Quilter	Farmer	[b]	1888	580,934	30.4
Arthur Cooper	Banker	[b]	1892	32,223	1.7
Sir Robert Palmer Harding	Auctioneer	[b]	1893	54,530	2.9
William Turquand	Official assignee	[b]	1894	45,319	2.7
David Chadwick	Accountant	[b]	1895	2,726	0.2
William Welch Deloitte	Company secretary	[b]	1898	74,707	4.2
George Jamieson	Doctor	Aberdeen University	1900	188,023	9.1
Edwin Guthrie	Engineer	[b]	1904	14,199	0.7
Frederick Whinney	Inn and stable keeper	[b]	1916	98,434	2.6
Edwin Waterhouse	Merchant and broker	University College, London	1917	257,136	5.1
John Manger Fells	Tailor and draper	Deal College	1925	5,378	0.1
Ernest Cooper	Banker	Abroad at a Roman Catholic school	1926	194,403	5.5
Sir John Harmood-Banner	Accountant	Radley	1927	449,279	13.1
Emile Oscar Garcke	[b]	[b]	1930	167,150	6.1
Andrew Wilson Tait	Grocer and spirit dealer	Daniel Stewart's College and Edinburgh University	1930	529,266	19.5
Sir Gilbert F. Garnsey	Butcher	Wellington School, Somerset	1932	151,466	6.7
Sir John Reeves Ellerman	Corn merchant and shipbroker	King Edward VI School, Birmingham	1933	36,685,000	1,650.8

George Alexander Touche	Banker	Edinburgh University and Bonnington Academy	1935	201,564	7.5
Sir Mark W. Jenkinson	Accountant	Wesley College, Sheffield, and privately	1935	10,918	0.4
Sir Arthur L. Dickinson	Painter	Charterhouse and King's College, Cambridge	1935	27,168	1.0
Sir William Barclay Peat	Farmer	Montrose Academy	1936	604,644	21.8
James Ivory	Advocate	Harrow	1939	103,466	3.5
Charles Ker	Merchant	Glasgow Academy and Glasgow University	1940	100,187	2.5
Sir Francis d'Arcy Cooper	Accountant	Private school and Wellington College	1941	648,012	12.1
Lord Plender	Grocer and draper	Royal Grammar School, Newcastle upon Tyne	1946	325,788	6.5
Sir William McLintock	Accountant	Dumfries Academy, Glasgow High School	1947	430,005	8.0
Frederic R. M. de Paula	Solicitor	b	1954	48,499	0.7
Sir Harold M. Barton	Seed-crushing mill owner	Oundle School	1962	50,895	0.6
Sir Basil E. Mayhew	Accountant	b	1966	136,398	1.3
Sir Ronald Edwards	Foreman	Southgate County School, University of London	1976	208,563	0.8

[a] The 1996 equivalents are obtained using indices contained in 'Back to an Age of Falling Prices', 1974, for the period up to 1974, and those published monthly in *Accountancy* after that date.
[b] Unknown.

Sources: Jeremy, 1984–6; Slaven and Checkland, 1990.

being born of legal, financial, and governmental parentage (see also Chapter 2), whereas in Glasgow and Aberdeen the commercial orientation of the economy was reflected in the backgrounds of early members. Among the 180 members of the Edinburgh Society, 1853–79, the backgrounds of their fathers (these were established for 81% of the group) showed 11% to be of the gentry or military, 45% to be professional (45% of whom were lawyers, 23% ministers, and 18% accountants), 6% to be from the lower professional class, with just 5% merchants, 10% tradesmen, and 4% farmers. The contrast with Glasgow and Aberdeen is marked. In Glasgow, nearly one-half of fathers were either merchants (25%), tradesmen (11%), or farmers (10%), with just 2% from the gentry or military, 27% professional (42% of whom were accountants), 9% lower professional, and 16% unknown. In Aberdeen (where 9% were unknown), nearly two-thirds of accountants were sons of merchants (32%), tradesmen (18%), or farmers (13%), whilst 23% were of professional descent, and just 5% derived from the gentry or military (Briston and Kedslie, 1986: 126).

In terms of education, Table 12 reinforces Perkin's findings for the leaders of all the major professions in the period 1880–1919, in that the corresponding group of professional accountants contained the sons of the middle class who had attended public or grammar school but not university. Accountancy, in the nineteenth and first half of the twentieth centuries, was apparently considered an alternative to university, the cost of articles being comparable to that of reading for a degree at Oxford or Cambridge (Napier, 1994: 5–6). Table 12 gives some indication of the education of the leaders of the profession, to which can be added the places of learning of the textbook writers, Pixley and Dicksee. The former was educated at St Peter's School, York, Keir House, Wimbledon, and by his private tutor, the Reverend Dr Frost; the latter at the City of London School before he became indentured, aged 17, in 1881 (Kitchen and Parker, 1980: 25, 54).

Recruits to the Scottish accountancy profession were, on average, even better educated, particularly in Edinburgh. William Home Cook, who attended Edinburgh Academy before going on to St Andrews University, and James Haldane, who attended Edinburgh High School and Edinburgh University, are just two of a number of early graduates. Indeed, even for non-graduates wishing to qualify for the Edinburgh Society, there was a requirement, from 1866, to attend law classes at the University—a move made as part of the general determination to 'upgrade its system of theoretical training' (Walker, 1988: 151). From 1889, Scottish law and conveyancing were courses specified for attendance, and from 1908/9 attendance at classes in political economy and commercial law were also recommended (Walker, 1988: 151). Having analysed the education of Scottish chartered accountants for the period 1853–79, Macdonald (1984) and Briston and Kedslie (1986) broadly concur that, in Edinburgh, 18% had attended university, 3% public school, and 35% an 'other named school'. Walker's detailed analysis of all Edinburgh Society apprentices extends over the longer period 1837–1921, and this shows that 72% attended 'High Class Private' schools, 10% 'High Class Public', and 4% 'The Great Public' schools (1988: 179). In Glasgow and Aberdeen, no cases of public school attendance were found, with 6% of the former's members having attended university and between 9% and 17% (cf. Macdonald, 1984: 183; Briston and Kedslie, 1986) an 'other named school'. In Aberdeen, the latter proportion was between 5% and 14% (cf. Macdonald, 1984: 183; Briston and Kedslie, 1986), with 9% having attended university. Briston and Kedslie acknowledge that such research is hindered by the lack of published registers for Glaswegian schools' former pupils, which necessarily and unsurprisingly indicate a lower proportion of Glasgow accountants as having an educational background as prestigious as their counterparts in Edinburgh (1986: 127).

Moving forward in time, the chartered accountants whose careers are analysed in Chapter 6 strongly suggest that a grammar school background became far more common after the Second World War, and that an increasing number also attended university. Fifty-eight per cent from a sample of company directors for 1955 had attended public school but only a third of these had gone on to university (Aldcroft, 1992: 101). The incidence of a university education was growing although, between 1950/1 and 1960/1, the numbers of the population graduating increased by only 6,000 to 25,699; a rise from 1.4% of the labour force to 1.9%. Following the stimulus provided by the Robbins Report (1963), which recommended an expansion in higher education, however, the number of first degrees trebled to 75,000 in 1975 and 127,000 in 1987. By 1980, 6% of the labour force were graduates (Aldcroft, 1992: 76–8). In view of this trend, therefore, the accountancy profession increasingly had little option but to recruit graduates. In 1963, only 10% of chartered articled clerks were graduates (40% from Oxbridge and 13% from London); by 1969 the proportion had reached 19%; and by 1979, 72% (Howitt, 1966: 140–1; Jones, 1981: 242). The transformation is now almost complete, with 94% of today's trainee chartered accountants being graduates according to the ICAEW *Statistical Circular on Members, Students and Offices* (ICAEW, 1996c: 1). Indeed, the large firms confine recruitment to graduates, actively recruit from only a relatively small number of the old universities, and, in the main, insist on *at least* an upper-second-class honours degree.

As will have become clear, within the accountancy profession, in terms of social class and education, the chartered branch was always the elite, with the later societies, generally speaking, recruiting from a lower rung of the social ladder. Incorporated accountants such as James Martin and John Manger Fells, a tailor's son, and certified accountants such as Ronald Edwards, Julian Hodge, and Charles Latham, 'rose by ability and hard work from comparatively humble beginnings' (Parker, 1980*a*: n.p.). Of the early ICWA membership, Loft says that: 'Few of their members had been to public schools . . . they came from lower middle class and upper working class backgrounds' (1986: 157). In terms of education, one-third of current CIMA students are graduates (data from CIMA head office).

Finally, it can be asserted with confidence that, as was also the case in other walks of British society in the nineteenth century and beyond, many sons followed in their father's footsteps; the Harmood Banners, Joneses, Coopers, McClellands, McLintocks, Peats, Waterhouses, Whinneys, Mayhews, and many others established dynasties. The Whinneys, for example, had an unbroken succession from when Frederick Whinney became a partner in Harding & Pullein in 1859, down to the 1980s (Jones, 1981: 37).

CONCLUDING COMMENTS

The enormous growth of the accountancy profession over the last one and a half centuries has been based until relatively recently on the development of the public practice. Many accountancy practices, today, continue to operate on a small scale, but the largest firms increased steadily in size until the 1960s when a number of factors, including removal of restrictions on the number of partners, conspired to produce a dramatic increase in their scale of operations. Accountancy firms have proved extremely resilient to changing economic circumstances, and many of today's leading firms can trace their ancestry back to the nineteenth and even eighteenth centuries. Their growth has been the product of both internal expansion and merger as graphically illustrated by the contents of the Appendix. Merger activity in the 1970s resulted in the emergence of the 'big eight', while further growth and amalgamation has produced today's 'big six'. Merger activity has naturally caused some famous names from the nineteenth century to disappear, such as Whinney, but many others survive, such as Cooper, Deloitte, Price, and Waterhouse.

The emergence of accountancy as a recognized profession in Britain therefore pre-dates significantly the creation of the professional bodies, first in Scotland and then in England, during the third quarter of the nineteenth century. The existence of a critical mass of accountants in public practice was of course a necessary precondition. A further requirement was the emergence of some environmental circumstance—the changes in bankruptcy legislation have been identified as a causal factor in Edinburgh—to trigger a determination on the part of a group of individuals to make their affairs the subject of joint regulation, in turn based on a degree of public recognition of their right to function as associations operating in the interests of both their members and society in general. The professional organizations set up in Scotland and England, respectively, in the 1850s and 1870s have flourished and, in response to exclusionary closure, have been joined by numerous other organizations designed to cater for groups either excluded from or inadequately served by the existing elite. The first half of the twentieth century, in particular, witnessed a number of mergers resulting in the creation of, for example, today's Association of Chartered Certified Accountants. The last major merger saw the coming together of two of the early elite—the ICAEW and the Society of Incorporated Accountants—with all subsequent major moves towards amalgamation thwarted for one reason or another. These professional bodies have naturally done much to enhance the position of their members but not through obtaining a statutory monopoly of work undertaken. Indeed, many of the Acts of Parliament which seem to have been important in encouraging the appointment of public accountants relate to bankruptcy and insolvency and were enacted prior to the creation of professional bodies. The thesis which we continue to pursue throughout the remainder of the book, therefore, is that accountants in public practice and in industry flourish primarily because they succeeded in supplying services and skills required by business.

We have seen that the numbers of accountants have grown dramatically from a few here and there in the late eighteenth century, to a few thousand in the late nineteenth century and over a quarter of a million today (Tables 1, 8). The ICAEW has been numerically the dominant professional body for much of this period, though its grip is weakening in this respect due to the rapid recent growth of the ACCA and CIMA, to a great extent fuelled by their drive for overseas membership. Women are of necessity not a major part of the story told in this book. This is because they were excluded from membership of the leading bodies until such action was rendered illegal by the Sex Discrimination (Removal) Act of 1919, but their numbers remained modest for at least the next sixty years. It is therefore only in the last decade or so that a significant number have trained and in due course qualified, and the numbers appointed to what might be regarded as top jobs remain small. From the outset, the members of the chartered bodies appear to have come principally from middle- or upper-class backgrounds, reflecting both the connections necessary in order to 'get started' and the financial backing required for those subsequently wishing to train in an established office. In general, the standing of those joining the professional bodies formed later on came from rather lower down on the social scale. Indeed, entry requirements in terms of both funding and education imposed by such bodies were usually less demanding, reflecting the potential of their intended clientele. In the chapters that follow, we shall see how these armies of financial experts have achieved a dominant position in the conduct of British business, with the chartered accountant to the fore almost throughout.

4

Accountants and Business Management in Victorian and Edwardian Britain

In the next three chapters we undertake a chronological examination of the rise of the professional accountant to a position of prominence in the management of the British business enterprise. We start with the period stretching from the mid-nineteenth century to the outbreak of the First World War. We will see that, during this period, professional accountants were only just beginning to move from public practice into industry on a full-time basis. Many more, of course, served at board level on a part-time basis whilst continuing as partners in their professional practice. This chapter focuses on the range of services supplied to industry by public practices in order to demonstrate the relevance of such training and experience for those accountants who subsequently move into industry, which is a matter that is the subject of detailed analysis in Chapter 7.

THE ECONOMIC BACKGROUND: ECONOMIC DECLINE AND THE RISE OF THE CORPORATE ECONOMY

In the middle of the nineteenth century Britain was at the peak of its economic power. It had been the first country in the world to industrialize, starting in the eighteenth century, and by 1870 it had the world's largest industrial output and the highest per capita income of any nation (Matthews et al., 1982: 32). Britain dominated world trade in both goods and services, based on its policy of free trade and supported by the world's greatest empire. Yet, even around that time, relative economic decline became apparent, and has continued down to the present day (Matthews et al., 1982: 31). There was, of course, no absolute decline. Output and living standards continued to grow but, relative to other industrialized countries (the UK was overtaken, in terms of industrial production, by the USA in 1882 and by Germany in 1912), Britain's economic performance was poor and its leadership slipped away. In 1880 Britain had 41.4% of the world trade in manufactured goods; in 1995 it had 5.4% (Pollard, 1989: 15; World Trade Organization, 1996: 18). The growth of the accountancy profession and its involvement in industry and commerce in the last hundred years has, therefore, been in the context of an economic system which has under-performed relative to its competitors.

Within this setting, a number of other changes occurred which are of direct relevance to the history of accountants, the fortunes of whom are inextricably tied to that of the company as an institution.

The British industrial revolution was carried through mainly by businesses organized as sole traders or partnerships, and these were usually family firms spanning several generations. As the scale of the business organization grew, the need for outside capital increased and, in 1855, Parliament took the major step of granting limited liability to joint-stock companies through the simple expedient of registering under the Joint Stock Companies Act. This opened the way for companies to raise 'blind' capital from investors through the stock exchange. In his review of the histories of the major companies of the time, Gourvish identifies the following additional reasons for companies registering with limited liability: the fear of bankruptcy; the desire to release funds for personal use; and the death or advancing age of the founder of the firm (1987: 24–5). The old family-based firms, none the less, were initially relatively slow to adopt limited liability status, and even less keen to raise capital on the

Table 13. Limited companies registered and liquidated in Great Britain, 1880–1996

	Registered in the year	Total registered		Total	Liquidations
		Public	Private		
1880	1,302			8,692[a]	
1890	2,789			13,323	1,091[b]
1900	4,966			29,730	1,804
1910	7,184			51,787	1,960
1920	10,783	16,941	62,600	79,541	3,158
1930	8,866	16,263	95,598	111,861	3,113
1940	6,422	12,423	141,089	153,512	2,584
1950	13,746	17,202[c]	241,063[c]	258,265[c]	3,109[c]
1960	34,312	16,705	376,789	393,494	4,252
1970	30,262	15,425	503,232	518,657	8,782
1980	69,374	9,163	751,642	760,805	11,481
1989/90	126,300	11,100	998,700	1,009,800	15,851
1995/6	146,700	11,500	1,024,700	1,036,200	18,463

[a] Figure is for 1884.
[b] Figure is for 1892.
[c] Figures are for 1949.

Sources: *Returns of Joint Stock Companies*: BPP, 1886: 550–2; 1902: 70–1; *General Annual Report by the Board of Trade*, 1920, 1930, 1940, 1949, 1960, 1970, 1980; Department of Trade and Industry, 1993, 1996.

stock exchange. As Table 13 and Figure 3 show, however, the number of company registrations eventually increased at a rapid rate. New company formations rose from 1,302 in 1880 to 7,184 in 1910, while the number of registered companies extant around these two dates was, respectively, 8,692 and 51,787.

Most limited companies were comparatively small, of course, and the private company (legally defined for the first time in 1907) was the most rapidly growing corporate form. Moreover, of the public companies incorporated during the first half of the period covered in this chapter, relatively few were quoted on the London Stock Exchange where trading was dominated by government stock, foreign issues, and the huge capital of the railway companies. The early industrial companies often arranged first for a quotation on a provincial stock exchange, reflecting their reliance on local finance, though the number of companies engaged in domestic manufacturing and distribution, listed on the London exchange, rose from 60 in 1885 to almost 600 by 1907 (Hannah, 1983: 20).

The average size of companies continued to increase in the nineteenth century, to some extent fuelled by the advent of mergers and takeovers. Probably the largest manufacturing venture in the 1840s was the Dowlais Iron Company, which had a workforce of 5,192 in 1842 (BPP, 1842: appendix, part 2, 594; Hyde, 1977: 178). By a process of merger, this company became Guest Keen and Nettlefolds with a nominal capital of £4.5 million in 1905 and a workforce of 12,451 by 1907 (Payne, 1967: 539; Shaw, 1983: 52). GKN was ranked, at that time, thirteenth in terms of employment and fifteenth in terms of capital. At the turn of the century, the largest manufacturing company by the employment measure was the Fine Cotton

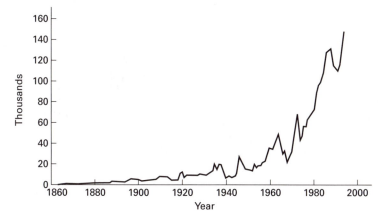

Source: See Table 13.

Fig. 3 Companies registered in UK annually, 1860–1996

Spinners' and Doublers' Association with 30,000 workers, and by size of capital Imperial Tobacco at £17.5 million. Moreover, Imperial Tobacco was itself dwarfed by the mighty railways, the largest of which was the Midland, in 1904/5, with a market value of £136.7 million (Wardley, 1991: 278).

As Figure 4 shows, merger activity has occurred in cycles since 1880 and, during at least the pre-First World War period, booms and mergers corresponded strongly with an upsurge in share prices and to a lesser extent with economic conditions generally (Hannah, 1983: 21). The first major burst of activity occurred at the end of the nineteenth century and was characterized by multi-firm combinations in the textile-finishing industry, typified by the formation of the Calico Printers' Association in 1899 (Hannah, 1983: 21). Concentration remained at a low level, however, with the largest 100 manufacturing firms (excluding railways; Wardley, 1991: 278–81) accounting for 10% of the market in 1880 and still only 15% in 1907 (Hannah, 1983: 180). Moreover, despite public issues of shares, the old families (for example, the owners of the three largest industrial companies in 1905, Coats in cotton yarn, Wills the cigarette makers, and Watney the brewers; Hannah, 1983: 24) proved to be remarkably adept at retaining control. The divorce between the ownership and the control of companies that was to become a major feature of the so-called 'managerial revolution', in the twentieth century, gained ground only slowly in the period prior to the First World War: 'before 1914 British firms made very few significant organisational changes to match their growth, technological change, and a competitive world increasingly shaped by the corporativism of the United States and Germany' (Gourvish, 1987: 21).

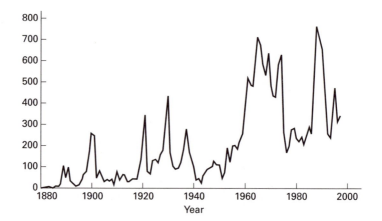

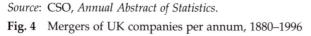

Source: CSO, *Annual Abstract of Statistics*.

Fig. 4   Mergers of UK companies per annum, 1880–1996

Yet, significant corporate developments did occur, and accountants benefited from a rapidly rising demand for their services. Limited companies needed their books kept properly, their external affairs (for example, dealings with the Registrar of Joint Stock Companies) handled by company secretaries, and their accounts audited. There was also a need for improved costing procedures to help with price fixing, planning, monitoring, and controlling business enterprises during a period which saw increased levels of competition in many industries. Public companies needed evidence for the outside world, including the capital market, that proposed ventures had a promising future and that existing businesses were healthy; such companies also required technical support in connection with the issue and registration of shares. Some required tax advice, and others required guidance on a wide range of issues, particularly when in financial difficulty or embarking on acquisitions or mergers. Finally, of course, insolvent individuals and companies required their affairs to be wound up—30% of the public companies formed between 1856 and 1883, for example, ended in liquidation (Hannah, 1983: 19).

We now turn to a detailed consideration of the types of work undertaken by the accountant in the Victorian and Edwardian eras.

INSOLVENCY

We saw, in Chapter 2, that insolvency work was the bedrock of a number of the great City firms that founded the accountancy profession in England and Wales and, to a great extent, still dominate it today. The work of the Victorian public accountancy practice has been the subject of an active, but inconclusive, debate. Parker has pointed to the absence of any reference to auditing in the original charters of each of the two Scottish societies formed in the 1850s (1986: 17), and to its inclusion as 'an afterthought' in the constitution of the ICAEW (1986: 20; see also Napier and Noke, 1992: 36), as evidence of the relative lack of importance of this aspect of the professional accountant's work up to the 1880s. The conventional wisdom (Jones, 1981: ch. 2; Parker, 1986; Stacey, 1954: 97; and Stewart, 1977) therefore argues that insolvency was the most important fee-earning activity for professional accountants down to the late nineteenth century, when auditing began to assume centre-stage. Such a conclusion is borne out elsewhere in the literature including the histories of professional bodies, the 'house' histories of accountancy firms, the biographies of leading accountants, and in specialist articles. The oft-quoted remark that the accountancy profession 'was born through bankruptcies, fed on failures and fraud, grew on liquidations and graduated through audits' is consistent with this school of thought (Robinson, 1964: 30).

The move of professional accountants into auditing in the late nine-teenth century is largely attributed to the growth, outlined above, in the number and scale of limited liability companies, the consequent divorce between ownership and control, and the demand from 'blind' investors for information on the state and progress of companies (Howitt, 1966: 40–2; Edwards, 1989a: 201–2; Jones, 1981: 50–2). This change of emphasis in the work of the accountant is usually illustrated by reference to the information available in respect of the fee income for Whinney, Smith & Whinney and its predecessor firms (the firm-name Whinney, Smith & Whinney dates from 1894. Previous names include Harding, Whinney & Co., 1859–66, and 1872–86, Harding, Whinney, Gibbons & Co., 1866–72, Whinney, Hurlbatt & Smith, 1886–94). Jones's (1981) analysis of the fee income of these firms is reproduced, in summary form, in Table 14, and shows insolvency as accounting for over 70% of total income up to 1880. Indeed, in 1858, 1865, and 1870, 93% of fee income came from that source (Jones, 1981: 47). Whilst insolvency fees as a proportion of total fee income declined in the second half of the century, and the audit proportion of total fees rose, it was not until the 1890s that audit became the most lucrative source of work for the firm (measured in terms of total fee income). These numbers have been widely quoted as evidence of the nature of a Victorian accounting practice (for example, Parker, 1986: 22), with Napier and Noke (1992: 35) drawing particular attention to the fact

Table 14. Breakdown of fee income for Whinney, Smith & Whinney and pred-ecessor firms, 1849–1960, Ernst & Whinney, 1988, and Ernst & Young, 1995

Year	Insolvency (%)	Accounting and audit (%)	Taxation (%)	Trustee and executorship (%)	Special work, consultancy, and government (%)	Total (£)
1849	74.6	8.2	—	11.9	5.2	804
1860	85.8	10.0	—	3.6	0.6	8,873
1870	93.6	4.6	—	1.7	0.1	18,958
1880	72.3	22.1	—	3.5	2.2	13,790
1890	45.6	46.8	—	4.3	3.3	14,237
1900	19.9	69.8	—	5.6	4.7	14,274
1910	53.0	39.3	0.6	3.5	3.8	28,317
1920	45.1	47.8	2.0	1.4	3.2	64,960
1930	6.2	78.4	5.9	3.2	6.2	60,410
1939	2.7	83.5	6.3	1.5	6.0	58,341
1950	4.3	71.2	11.2	1.4	12.0	152,600
1960	0.2	68.1	11.0	2.4	18.2	344,944
1988	6.1	56.3	21.6	—	16.0	148.4 m.
1995	8.4	39.4	30.1	—	22.1	401.2 m.

Sources: Jones, 1981: 47, 99; *Accountancy*, July 1989: 10; July 1995: 18–19.

that, as late as 1880, insolvency work generated 72% of fee income while audit generated only 11% at Harding, Whinney & Co.

Despite the above findings, there is evidence to suggest that the importance of insolvency to mid-Victorian accountants has been somewhat overstated and, consequently, the variety of their work underestimated. Assertions in earlier house histories (for example, Kettle, 1957: 3) have probably been accepted too readily at face value by subsequent writers (for example, Edwards, 1989a: 202; Parker, 1986: 20–2). Indeed, the bankruptcy-auditing thesis has been the subject of criticism by Walker (1993: 128–9) on the grounds that it is not based on the records of accountancy practices and that there has been a tendency to adopt a teleological approach to history by focusing excessively on changes in accounting work explicable in terms of identifiable economic and legislative developments.

There is of course a danger, particularly in a young discipline such as accounting history, for a conventional wisdom to develop on the basis of a single, well-regarded, piece of research. The validity of such generalization relies on the firm in question being representative of the population. We suggest that Whinney, Smith & Whinney (and its predecessor firms) were atypical in two important respects. First, Robert Palmer Harding, the senior partner in Harding, Whinney & Co. until 1883 and the ICAEW's second president, was clearly a leading expert if not *the* leading expert in insolvency matters. He informed the 1877 Select Committee on the Companies Acts that he had been personally involved with the liquidation of 62 companies and that his firm had administered a further 142 (BPP, 1877: minute 1387). Such was Harding's reputation in insolvency that, when on the point of retirement in 1883, he was persuaded by Joseph Chamberlain to take the post of Chief Official Receiver (Jones, 1988: 224). His seven years' service in that capacity ultimately brought Palmer the distinction, in 1890, of being the first member of the ICAEW to receive a knighthood. Secondly, the Report from the 1867 Select Committee on the Limited Liability Acts, as noted in Chapter 2, showed that Harding, Whinney & Gibbons was responsible for administering as many as 61 out of 259 liquidations proceeding in 1866 (Jones, 1981: 46–7). Other major firms of the day, such as Price, Holyland & Waterhouse and Quilter, Ball & Co., were responsible for just eight and five liquidations respectively (see also Chapter 2). Table 4 shows that Harding, Whinney & Gibbons's successor firm was backward in developing its audit business, being ranked equal twelfth in the league table that we have constructed for 1886 (see also next section). The statistics for Ernst & Young's predecessor firms, therefore, are almost certainly unrepresentative of the importance of insolvency even to City firms.

The focus on auditing came earlier for firms such as Quilter, Ball & Co. and Turquand, Youngs & Co., while, for others, such as Price, Waterhouse

& Co., insolvency remained a low priority right through to the 1970s (Jones, 1995: 135, 270). The last-named firm did not gain their first railway audit until late 1866 (Jones, 1995: 50), but Samuel Lowell Price was able to inform the Select Committee on the Companies Acts 1862 and 1867 that he conducted a 'considerable amount of auditing of public companies' (BPP, 1877: minute 1185). We are able to obtain further insight into the nature of this firm's work from the following assessment made by Jones: 'Although not one of the oldest nor one of the first-rank practices of the 1860s, a consistent and determined commitment to auditing propelled Price Waterhouse ahead of many of its better-established rivals' (1995: 44). The nature of Edwin Waterhouse's early work is made clear in an analysis which shows that, between February and December 1864, 80% of his time was spent on the preparation of accounts and audit, 11% on investigation of accounts and audit, and 9% exclusively on audit (Jones, 1995: 395). This trend was also evident at Cooper Brothers & Co. (Boys, 1994: 38). In general, the firms established later appear less likely to have been heavily reliant on insolvency work. As Wise notes of the firm founded in 1891: 'In the earlier days bankruptcy work was important to the growth of accountancy, but this was never a factor in the success of W. B. Peat' (1982: 17).

One plausible explanation for the relative decline in insolvency work throughout the profession is the reduced number of bankruptcies. In Scotland, Kedslie's figures for sequestrations, which admittedly account for only a proportion of total insolvencies, show a fall from an average of 512 per year, in the six years after 1856, to 324 per year for the three years 1892, 1897, and 1902. There was, however, an increase in the value of average gross receipts from sequestrated estates from £6,933 in the early period to £18,737 in the latter three years (Kedslie, 1990a: 121, 130, 134). Kedslie does not give figures for the breakdown of fee income for any Scottish accountancy firms, though the above figures nevertheless suggest that insolvency may have remained more important to practices north of the border than to their English counterparts.

An important causal factor in the relative decline of insolvency south of the border is seen, by some, to be the impact of legislation. According to the president of the ICAEW, in 1915:

the profession experienced a serious setback on two occasions. In 1883 when the Bankruptcy Act of that year transferred much profitable business formerly undertaken by accountants to officials, and in 1890, when by the Companies Act of that year, the Government performed the like service to the profession with regard to compulsory liquidations. (Quoted in Stacey, 1954: 56)

The Bankruptcy Act of 1883, which applied to England and Wales, apparently hit the accountancy profession in two ways (Cooper, 1921: 559; Edwards, 1989a: 263). First, it abolished the position of Trustee in Bankruptcy and created instead that of the Official Receiver. We have seen that a small number of accountants, including Robert Palmer Harding, benefited from appointments to this post, but the bulk of the profession may have lost out because they were no longer directly appointed by the courts. Second, Foreman-Peck has suggested that the 1883 Act had a fundamental effect because it made 'becoming bankrupt more unpleasant' (Foreman-Peck, 1990: 39). The bankrupt was unable to hold civil office, property could be requisitioned until he was discharged, and, until then, the bankrupt was obliged to inform any substantial creditor or seller of his status. Consequently, according to Foreman-Peck, 'The higher the penalties of bankruptcy, the greater the attraction of limited liability, and the lower the level of bankruptcy, both because of the shift to limited liability and because of any deterrent effect encouraging better management' (1990: 39). Further, the 'liquidation risk' fell as the first flush of ill-judged incorporations subsided. Nearly 26% of all public companies set up between 1856 and 1865 ended in insolvency, 30.3% of those from 1866–74 and 33.4% of those founded between 1875 and 1883 (Shannon, 1933; reprinted in Carus-Wilson, 1954: 387). As matters improved the numbers of bankruptcies and liquidations in the economy generally declined from previously high levels; indeed, the excess of liabilities over assets fell from £19 million in 1879 to £6 million in 1885.

The crucial factor in the relative decline in insolvency work, of course, was the growth of audit work buoyed up by the increased number of limited liability companies registered under the Companies Act in each decade covered by this chapter: in the 1860s, 628 per annum; 1870s, 872 per annum; 1880s, 1,643 per annum; 1890s, 3,412 per annum; and in the first decade of the twentieth century, 4,206 per annum (*The Stock Exchange Official Intelligence*, 1933: 1,995; see also Table 13 and Figure 3).

AUDITING

According to Brown, 'The origin of auditing goes back to times scarcely less remote than that of accounting' (1905: 74; see also Chatfield, 1977: 111; Mills, 1990; Woolf, 1912: ch. 13), and he rehearses some of the audit practices engaged in by the ancient Egyptians and, later on, by the Greeks and Romans. Moving rapidly forward in time and to Britain, there is ample evidence of audit practices in use in medieval times, when the accounts were read out and the auditor checked on the lord's behalf that the steward had been neither negligent nor fraudulent (Edwards, 1989a: 37; Noke, 1981). In the government sector, also, the need for a periodic audit to keep track of public funds was quite naturally keenly felt (*Accountant*, 27 Jan. 1912: 124–6; Coombs and Edwards, 1990). Watts and Zimmerman (1983) have traced audit reports back to the merchant guilds and, by the eighteenth century, public accountants were engaged to produce this document. An audit certificate worded 'Examined and found right, Bristol, December 20, 1797' forms part of the records of the firm of Josiah Wade which we have seen was founded in 1780 (Howitt, 1966: 245).

An audit is required to attest to the accountability and stewardship of company management. Its purposes are to detect losses due to error and fraud, and to reduce the possibility that management's stewardship statements contain inaccuracies resulting from innocent mistakes and deliberate misstatements. The latter may take the form of either falsification of accounting records (a device used typically but not exclusively by employees to conceal defalcations) or the manipulation of information contained in the financial statements themselves (most often the device used by management intending to deceive shareholders, lenders, or other outside parties). The term 'fraud detection' is sometimes used to refer to audits aimed only at detecting employee fraud (and the commission of errors), and the phrase 'verification of financial statements' to refer to audits where the objectives would include detection of misstatements due to management manipulation.

Several writers (for example, Brown, 1962; Flint, 1971; Lee, 1979) have commented on the change in audit objectives over the last 150 years. According to these writers, the primary objective of the audit was initially the detection of fraud and error but, by the middle of the twentieth century, it had developed into the verification of financial statements. More recent research suggests that, at least in certain sectors of the economy, the need to provide shareholders with information suitable for investment decisions was appreciated as early as the second quarter of the nineteenth century (Chandler et al., 1993). It therefore seems likely that each of the audit objectives identified above has received a degree of recognition ever since the emergence of the corporate audit, though the attention devoted to each of them has varied between auditors, the types of institutions audited, and over time (Chandler et al., 1993).

In the first half of the nineteenth century, however, the accounts of many, perhaps most, firms were not the subject of an external audit. Those of the Dowlais Iron Company (a partnership), for example, described as the 'the first [ironworks] in the world' (quoted in Edwards and Baber, 1979: 139) in 1842, remained unaudited until the firm registered as a limited company in 1899. The level of accountability even among incorporated companies was highly variable. Companies incorporated by private statute or by royal charter, mainly the public utilities (canals, railways, gas and water companies), but also the old trading companies, the banks, and insurance companies, seem usually to have made audit arrangements, though this task was normally devolved on two shareholders. Ernest Cooper stated that 'In the [eighteen] sixties professional auditors were the exception. Comparatively few large concerns, railways or banks, were audited by accountants' (1921: 554). The practice of appointing an amateur/shareholder auditor was the subject of determined attack as the accountancy profession sought a monopoly of this work in the second half of the nineteenth century (Pixley, 1897: 15; Coombs and Edwards, 1996: ch. 7; Parker, 1986: 23–39) and some of the criticism was no doubt justified. The technical ability, not to mention the time at the disposal of these amateur auditors—they were often appointed by the shareholders on the day of the general meeting with the remit to inspect the books—was severely limited. When Robb, in his catalogue of Victorian frauds, concludes, rather too boldly: 'Throughout much of the nineteenth century, the audit of company accounts was farcical', he has in mind mainly these amateur audits, the superficiality of which led them to be known as 'biscuit and sherry audits' (1992: 129).

It was the pervasive nature of fraud in Victorian business which, together with the level of failure among early limited liability companies, helped to produce an environment conducive to the emergence of the professional auditor. The increasing scale and complexity of companies during the second quarter of the nineteenth century, particularly associated with the development of banking, insurance, and the railways, placed greater responsibilities on the audit function and, as we have said, the shareholder auditor typically appointed by early companies was often ill-equipped for the task. The appointment of Gladstone's Select Committee on Joint Stock Companies, 1841–4, was partly a consequence of concern with the lack of regulation highlighted by recurrent failures and fraud. As noted in Chapter 2, allegations of 'cooked' accounts (Edwards, 1989a: 104, 144) at the time of the railway mania provided a major fillip for the rise of the professional auditor.

The most famous revelations, in this early period, concern the affairs of the Eastern Counties Railway whose chairman was the notorious George Hudson, the 'Railway King'. The report prepared by Quilter, Ball & Co. (called in to assist the shareholders' committee; the report was reproduced by the 1849 Parliamentary Committee on the Audit of Railway Accounts, BPP, 1849: 409–14) revealed the full extent of the ingenuity displayed by Hudson and his staff. Costs amounting to £318,144 were wrongly omitted from the revenue account, comprising expenditure incorrectly debited to the capital account, £233,925, accrued expenses of £61,013, and bad debts of £23,206. In addition, £35,315 was incorrectly credited to the revenue account, and interest capitalized instead of being written off against profit totalled £84,591 (figures quoted in Edwards, 1989a: 167). In aggregate, profits were overstated by £438,050 (roughly equivalent to £18 million at 1997 prices). According to Parker, therefore: 'the railways provided the first example of the need not only for an audit, but also for an expert and independent audit'; a need which was expressed forcibly at rebellious shareholders' meetings around 1850 (Parker, 1986: 7–8; see also

Broadbridge, 1970: 41; Edwards, 1989a: 265). An important stage in the professionalization of the audit function occurred, therefore, when incumbent shareholder auditors brought in public accountants to help them do their job or to sort out problems which had arisen, sometimes because of their own shortcomings.

Increasingly companies changed their articles to allow public accountants to be employed directly as auditors and, to facilitate this process, the initial requirement of a share qualification was gradually phased out. In 1849, J. E. Coleman was drafted in by the London and North Western Railway to assist the shareholder auditors in restoring investor confidence after the malpractices exposed in the previous years (Jones, 1981: 53). William Welch Deloitte was similarly called in by the shareholder auditors at the Great Western Railway, in this case without the knowledge of the board, four of whose members were forced to resign as a result of his 1849 investigation. Deloitte thereafter assisted the shareholder auditors until his appointment as one of the shareholder auditors in 1887; a position held until his retirement in 1897 (Kettle, 1957: 7; Jones, 1984b: 57).

The amateur auditor tradition, although breached, nevertheless persisted in some companies though its frailties were starkly exposed in the Redpath scandal. Leopold Redpath, registrar at the Great Northern Railway, maintained his Regent's Park lifestyle 'of great elegance' in the 1850s by defrauding the company (Kettle, 1957: 22–4). The amateur auditors, blissfully unaware of what was going on, reported as follows to the shareholders:

Gentlemen. The accounts and books in every department continue to be so satisfactorily kept, that we have simply to express our entire approval of them, and to present them to you for the information of the shareholders, with our usual certificate of correctness. (Robb, 1992: 53)

The Redpath frauds involved sums totalling £150,000; even in 1854, when they knew that the dividend payments were not in accord with the authorized capital, the shareholder auditors continued to declare the accounts correct. They never examined the registration books nor thought it their duty to do so. It was not until 1857, when Deloitte was called in to investigate, that the fraud was unravelled (Kettle, 1957: 22–4). This led a shareholder to question the role of the amateur auditor:

Of what earthly use are auditors at all to us? . . . I have, year by year, attempted to show what a miserable farce it is to have these gentlemen as auditors. When there is real work to be done, they employ a professional auditor, and these gentlemen come down and sign their names, declaring that they have nothing to do with the registration department. I say these gentlemen have manifestly neglected their duty. (Robb, 1992: 54)

Clearly, then, the professional audit found favour among companies following the dictates of the financial and capital markets long before it was a legal requirement for most concerns. Sometimes, however, corporate failure did result in the introduction of 'crisis-driven' legislation which, although not necessarily specifying an obligation to employ accountants or arrange for an audit, reflected the need for improved provision in each of these areas. The government passed the Companies Act of 1879, for example, in order to help restore confidence among the investing public following the collapse of the City of Glasgow Bank in 1878. This Act also allowed unlimited companies to re-register as limited, with the proviso that they must have an independent annual audit. Forty-three years earlier, in 1836, only nine out of 107 banks had auditors; indeed fourteen companies who had an explicit power to appoint auditors chose not to do so (Sikka et al., 1992: 13). As noted in Chapter 3, however, of the 65 banks formed prior to 1855 which registered with limited liability after 1878, 61 had arranged for a professional accountant to undertake the audit by 1886 (Anderson et al., 1996: 381).

There were other statutory provisions which, although by no means the explanation for the development of the professional audit in the second half of the nineteenth century, nevertheless provided some encouragement for that process in certain quarters. The Companies Clauses Consolidation Act 1845 (s. 108) and the Companies Act 1862 (table A, clause 93) anticipated the possible engagement of an accountant to assist the auditor, and statutory audit requirements were introduced for specialist categories of company: railways (1867), metropolitan water companies (1871), building societies (1874), banks (1879), insurance companies (1909), and industrial and provident societies (1913). The Railway Companies Act 1867 made it clear that the auditor need not be a shareholder; a move which simplified the appointment of public accountants to this position. This process was repeated by the 1894 legislation pertaining to building societies which followed the frauds at the Liberator Building Society (Robb, 1992: 141).

We have seen, in Chapter 1, that a number of Acts relating to friendly societies, industrial and provident societies, and building societies encouraged or made compulsory the engagement of public accountants as auditors in the pre-First World War period. The Building Societies Act 1894 stated that 'one at least of the auditors of the Society shall be a person who publicly carries on the business of an accountant' (s. 3), and the Industrial and Provident Societies Act 1913 required registered societies to 'once in every year submit [their] accounts for audit to one or more of the public auditors appointed under the provisions of the principal [1893] Act' (s. 2). The Companies Act 1900 introduced an external audit requirement for limited companies in general, but failed to include even the requirement that the work should be performed by a public accountant, despite the fact that contemporary events were suggestive of the fact that such personnel were best qualified to do the job.

There was therefore a growing tendency for the legislature to insist on an external audit, but there was no mention of the need to appoint a professional in the period covered by this chapter, and the overall impact of legislation on the development of the professional audit seems unlikely to have been great. In the absence of explicit statutory support, the chartered accountant had, nevertheless, substantially wrested the role of quoted company auditor, at least, from the unqualified accountant and amateur shareholder auditor as early as the 1880s. A comprehensive study was undertaken, by Anderson et al. (1996), of the audit arrangements of the 1,100 UK quoted companies of 1886. It proved possible to establish the audit profile of 960 companies from this total population and, of these, 98.2% were found to be audited. The study also revealed the fact that over three-quarters (75.5%) were the subject of a professional audit, and that chartered accountants had a virtual monopoly of this work. Of the 725 companies subject to a professional audit, 605 had selected members of the ICAEW, 110 companies had engaged members of one of the Scottish societies, three companies were audited by a combination of English and Scottish chartered accountants, whilst one utilized the services of a Scottish chartered accountant in tandem with a member of the SAA. The six remaining professional audits were undertaken by members of the SAA. By the early 1880s, then, it had become an established practice for most quoted companies to have their accounts drawn up annually and audited, generally by a qualified accountant. With the huge increase in the formation of joint-stock companies in the latter decades of the nineteenth century, the success of the new profession was thereby assured.

The amount of work involved in the audit of a quoted company appears, as today, to have varied a great deal. At Price, Waterhouse in 1897, fees ranged from 25 guineas in the case of the Santa Rita Nitrate Company, through £210 in the case of the City of Baltimore United Breweries audit conducted in Baltimore and London, to £850 for the London and North Western Railway (Anderson et al., 1997). Using known figures for charge-out rates, it is possible to make some estimate of the amount of time devoted to the audit. Available evidence suggests a charge-out rate around this time of 15 guineas per week for a partner, 10 guineas per week for a senior clerk, and 5 guineas per week for an articled clerk (Sully, 1951; see also Kettle, 1957 and Letts, 1980). Assuming each category of staff spent an equal amount of time on the audit of the London and North Western, and that the fee was designed to cover charge-out rates exactly, the number of man days worked would have amounted to approximately 386.

The professional auditor thus drove out the shareholder auditor, and was voluntarily employed by companies, sometimes at significant cost, to undertake the job. It would be utterly misleading, however, to present this narrative as one of unmitigated success. Indeed, there were plenty of examples of audit failure involving the professional accountant, and it possibly reflects widespread recognition of the difficult task undertaken, or at least the absence of a superior alternative, that the professional audit remained the cornerstone for assessing financial probity.

The deficiencies of the professional audit were the subject of both broad-based press comment and litigation. Indeed, throughout the latter part of the nineteenth century, the accountancy profession had to deal with a level of public concern about the value of audits that is familiar to us today. Chandler and Edwards (1996) have drawn attention to the fact that then, as now, the criticism was provoked by the financial failure of well-known companies that had previously been held in high regard. Articles containing attacks on accountants and auditors frequently appeared in contemporary journals such as *Vanity Fair*, *The Economist*, *Money*, the *Bullionist*; in specialist journals such as the *Warehouseman*, the *Journal of Gas Lighting*; and in the wider press including the *Financial Times*, the *Pall Mall Gazette*, the *Daily Chronicle*, the *Westminster Gazette*, the *Scotsman*, and the *Western Press*. The importance attached to these criticisms is reflected in the fact that the *Accountant* reproduced, verbatim, the text of some of the articles, indicating that its editors felt no embarrassment in publishing articles which roundly condemned the profession. The language used by the profession's critics was highly provocative, with the audit certificate described as 'a delusion and a snare' (*Vanity Fair* reprinted in *Accountant*, 3 Nov. 1883: 10) and 'a simple farce' (a letter to *Pall Mall Gazette*, reprinted in *Accountant*, 17 Mar. 1894: 242).

The 1890s also saw the start of negligence suits against professional (as opposed to amateur) auditors which caused accountants and their methods to be the subject of scrutiny by the courts. The defendants in these cases included some famous auditors of the time, including the following: F. W. Pixley (an ICAEW council member, and author of the first textbook on auditing, published in 1881, which was widely used as preparation for the examinations of the ICAEW) in *Woodhouse Rawson United, Lim.* (*Accountant Law Reports*, 30 June 1894: 121–4); W. B. Peat (founder of the firm today known as KPMG, an ICAEW council member at the time of the case, president 1906–7, and knighted in recognition of public services 1912) in *The Millwall Dock Case* (*Accountant*, 21 Oct. 1899: 1,037–8); and J. Sutherland Harmood-Banner (senior partner in Harmood Banner & Son and president of the ICAEW 1904/5) in *Astrachan Steam Ship Company and others* v. *Harmood-Banner and others* (*Accountant Law Reports*, 17 Mar. 1900: 49–50).

In the Millwall Dock Company case, for example, it was shown that the auditor, Peat, had accepted from G. R. Birt—the manager of the company—a certification for debts outstanding which had been artificially inflated, 'to maintain the appearance of prosperity', from £34,000 in 1884 to £208,000 in 1898. The case also revealed that over the fourteen years the auditor had never visited the docks to examine the cargo ledgers (Newton, 1899: 486–9). Public accountants who had based their case for appointment as auditor on their ability to supply a much more effective service than the amateur were, not surprisingly, the subject of derision: 'If auditing by chartered accountants is usually conducted on the lines followed by those employed by the Millwall Company, what is the good of paying auditors at all?' (Newton, 1899: 486–7). Birt was tried in the Central Criminal Court on 12–13 May 1899 and sentenced to nine months' imprisonment with hard labour (*Accountant*, 20 May 1899: 568–70).

Negligence suits against professional accountants sometimes resulted in compensation being paid, with the defendants in *Astrachan Steam Ship Company and others* v. *Harmood-Banner and others* agreeing 'to pay a considerable sum'. The *Accountant* (17 Mar. 1900: 263) was naturally keen to point out that the court's sympathies lay very much with the defendants,

his Honour stating that—in view of the eminent position occupied by Messrs. HARMOOD-BANNER & Son, and the fact that they frequently gave evidence to his Court—he thought it right to state that there was no imputation on their honour or capacity as auditors or accountants, 'it being perfectly obvious that TAPSCOTT [manager of the plaintiff companies who had defrauded them of approximately £45,000] had been manipulating the assets, and that they—like other people— were taken in.'

Finally, in this section, brief mention may be made of an important related development of the late nineteenth century, namely the 'continuous audit'. This was a monthly, quarterly, or six-monthly audit undertaken for the directors, and it was thought to possess the following advantages: it revealed irregularities more quickly; it reduced the likelihood of fraud due to constant supervision; and it avoided delay in the publication of the accounts (*Accountant*, 18 Oct. 1884: 4; see also *Accountant*, 9 Apr. 1892: 298). One firm involved in the provision of this business service was Wenham, Angus & Co., who were called in by Pilkington, the glass makers, in 1884 (Barker, 1960: 170).

CONSULTANCY

The professional work of accountants in this period was not confined to insolvency and auditing. Nineteenth-century accountants were often drafted in, on an *ad hoc* basis, also to help management solve a wide variety of problems. Whilst the nomenclature 'management consultancy' is of recent origin, the work itself is of a long-standing nature. Victorian accountancy firms certainly undertook a great deal of general advisory work for management, which they called special work, and provided services indistinguishable from latter-day management consultancy, some examples of which we cite as illustration in this section.

With fraud 'endemic in the Victorian economy', professional accountants were 'the physicians employed to drive it out' (Jones, 1981: 56). We have seen that William Welch Deloitte was called in to investigate fraud in the Great Northern Railway's registration department, in 1856; he was also recruited to sort out the affairs of the Great Eastern Steamship Company in 1870 (Kettle, 1957: 7) and the London and River Plate Bank fraud in the 1880s (Kettle, 1957: 46). In this context, Pixley informs us that professional accountants were frequently called in as expert witnesses at trials in the late nineteenth century where books had been manipulated (1897: 15–16; see also Howard Smith, Thompson, 1967: 3). The memoirs of Edwin Waterhouse also contain numerous examples of fraud investigations including a particularly clever scheme perpetrated at the offices of the Metropolitan Railway in 1880 (Jones, 1988: 109). This often led to more work. According to Sir John Mann, writing about his early experience in his father's office in the 1870s, the investigation of defalcations 'almost invariably developed into routine audits' (Mann Judd Gordon, 1967: 27).

Another early source of consultancy work was the installation of bookkeeping systems, and this kind of work continued throughout the nineteenth century. In 1854, John Mann, Sr., 'was called in to report upon and make recommendations in regard to the [Western Friendly] Society's books and accounts' (Mann Judd Gordon, 1967: 23), while Howard Smith & Slocombe were, in the 1870s, 'actively engaged in the preparation of the accounts of many leading public and private companies and business firms in Birmingham and the Midlands' (Howard Smith, Thompson, 1967: 3). When, in 1872, Pilkington embarked upon a heavy capital expenditure programme, it was decided to call in outside accountants, Wenham, Angus & Co., 'to put the accounts upon the best commercial footing', and they were also instructed to produce a twice-yearly balance sheet from 1874 (Barker, 1960: 170). The accounts book of the Victorian accountants Sully & Girdlestone includes reference to the introduction of a new bookkeeping system at Offord & Sons, coach-builders, in 1882 (Sully, 1951: 11). Around the same time Theodore Jones 'installed a book-keeping system for Budgetts, wholesale grocers in Bristol' (Hill Vellacott, 1988: 28).

More generally, de Paula tells us that, in the 1890s, it was 'by no means uncommon to find primitive records upon a single entry basis or alternatively most complicated double entry systems' (de Paula, 1948: 22). The need to introduce new systems of bookkeeping sometimes emerged as the result of a firm's appointment as auditor. Again, according to de Paula, 'It commonly fell to the auditor [in the 1890s] to balance the books and prepare the annual accounts' (de Paula, 1948: 22). Frederick Whinney tells us, in 1891, that his firm were also 'frequently asked to finish the balance sheet and take out the balance, and write up the books' (Jones, 1981: 54). The continuing scope for this kind of work is shown by the fact that large organizations such as the Sun Fire Office did not introduce the double-entry system until 1890, while the Capital and Counties Bank was still using various single-entry methods at the time of its amalgamation with Lloyds in 1918 (Jones, 1981: 23). It also appears that professional accountants made creative contributions to accounting's development. Deloitte is credited with being the originator of a system of hotel accounting, having been the auditor of the Langham from 1883 and the Savoy from 1890 (Jones, 1984b: 58). In the late nineteenth century, John George Griffiths, who had acted for many years as joint honorary secretary of the King Edward Hospital Fund for London, designed a standard system of hospital accounting (Howitt, 1966: 44).

Consultancy services often covered a range of matters quite distant from accounting and bookkeeping. The Bristol accountant Robert Fletcher (whose successor firm became the Bristol office of Cooper Brothers in 1966) was engaged to investigate a client's affairs in order to calculate the price of shares in 1834 while, two years later, he prepared calculations for damages and compensation claims (Cornwell, 1991: 75). In 1838, Fletcher was invited to prepare a report for the Queen Elizabeth Hospital which was in dispute with the City Corporation concerning loan interest and, in that year, spent 60% of his time on that engagement (Cornwell, 1991: 84). The important role sometimes played by accountancy firms as external advisers is reflected in the fact that, in 1864, the board of the Telegraph Construction and Maintenance Company Ltd. 'Resolved that Messrs. Deloitte, Greenwood & Dever be appointed Consulting Accountants to the Company' (Kettle, 1957: 15). Other examples of more or less permanent advisory roles undertaken during the third quarter of the nineteenth century were between Theodore Brooke Jones and the Fosters, owners of Black Dyke Mills near Bradford, 'as well as . . . other famous textile firms' (Hill Vellacott, 1988: 28). He (and later Arthur Hill) also acted professionally for co-operative and building societies, and many missionary and charitable organizations (Hill Vellacott, 1988: 28). Gilbert Courtenay Clarke, who became a partner in W. H. Pannell & Co. in 1896, after gaining early experience working in the United States, became heavily involved in advisory work for Harris, Lebus Furniture partnership, a chain of tobacconists which later merged with the Imperial Tobacco Company, and a network of tea shops which became J. Lyons and Company (Medlam, 1980: 6). At the Midland Bank, from as early as the 1870s, accountants were drafted in as consultants to check on the viability of companies which owed them money (Holmes and Green, 1986: 63).

As is the case today, it was often the nineteenth-century accountants' position as auditor that led to client contact in a wider managerial capacity. At Boot & Co. Ltd., forerunners of Boots the Chemist, for example, the auditor's services were by no means confined to certification of the accounts. The Birmingham firm Sharp, Parsons & Co. became auditors when Boot & Co. Ltd was incorporated in 1883, and its partners were present at every subsequent shareholders' meeting 'to assure the small gathering of the continuing strength of the Company' (Chapman, 1974: 121). Sharp, Parsons & Co. were also a vehicle for channelling funds into Boots; its senior partner had family connections with Birmingham stockbrokers, and it is thought to have been more than a coincidence that 'some of the largest subscriptions to Boot's early issues of preference shares came from the Birmingham area' (Chapman, 1974: 121). Further managerial involvement occurred in 1891 when, with the company suffering acute liquidity problems, 'Parsons strongly recommended the restriction of dividends and diversion of part of the profits to a newly-created reserve fund' (Chapman, 1974: 122).

Edwin Waterhouse was engaged in 1870 to determine the profits of the Fox Head Company for the purpose of a profit-sharing scheme. Seven years later, he was employed to devise a sliding scale which related wages to the selling price of iron for the Consett Iron Co. (Jones, 1988: 29). As the reputation of Price, Waterhouse & Co. grew in the last quarter of the nineteenth century, the firm was called upon to make a wide variety of investigations (Edwards, 1986: 675). One such client was Huntley & Palmer which regularly consulted the firm on decisions of strategic importance. In 1894, Price, Waterhouse was requested to investigate the possibility of converting the Huntley & Palmer partnership into a joint-stock company. The firm's report 'set out objectively the pros and cons of such a step' (Corley, 1972: 151). The firm was again called in, in 1918 and 1919, to consider respectively the purchase of Huntley, Boorne & Stevens and possible conversion into a listed company. Incorporation was under consideration as a means of enabling the immediate family to maintain control at a time when the number of family directors and shareholders was continually falling (Corley, 1972: 200). This course was adopted, whilst the further option 'of selling out to an American syndicate which had asked the accountants Price Waterhouse to approach likely firms' was rejected (Corley, 1972: 204).

In 1886, the Birmingham firm of Howard Smith & Slocombe undertook an investigation for the committee of shareholders of the Birmingham Cab Company Ltd. In a report described by the *Accountant* as 'one of the ablest and best drawn up of its kind we have seen' (Howard Smith, Thompson, 1967: 5), Smith reported as follows:

I have inspected the Birmingham Cab Company's books of account, valuation and other documents relating to the Balance Sheet of 30th June last and I am of the opinion that the accounts issued to the shareholders on August 13th of that year and the Chairman's explanations of the item 'Cost of acquiring business and goodwill of same' given at the meeting of shareholders on the 3rd September, were not full and true statements of the Company's affairs. Further, I am of the opinion that the amended Balance Sheet contained in the report of the Committee of Investigation is a fair and proper account, and that it gives the most favourable view that can reasonably be adopted of the Company's position on the 30th of June 1886.

Company formation was also a common area of engagement, Deloitte undertook prospectus work as early as 1855 (Kettle, 1957: 15), and some late nineteenth-century examples of the reports made are those prepared by Ernest Cooper for inclusion in the first prospectus issued by Lever Brothers in 1894 (Hodgkins, 1979: 40–1), and by Harding, Whinney & Co. for the Channel Islands Bank in 1897 (Jones, 1981: 57). The same period saw Theodore Jones advise Guest Keen & Nettlefold on the formation of a new partnership (Hill Vellacott, 1988: 28). The prospectus of Joseph Lucas Ltd., in 1897, provides a typical accountant's endorsement from around this time. It states 'that the average profit for the past three years had been £23,664. 3s per annum, without charging interest on the capital employed, income tax or for partners services, but after ample provision had been made for depreciation and bad debts' (Nockolds, 1976: 3). The nineteenth-century predecessors of J. & A. W. Sully & Co. also undertook a 'good deal' of this type of work (Sully, 1951: 11). We should also record the fact, however, that some commentators considered it appropriate to take a jaundiced view of the value these reports. In 1887, the *Statist* was of the opinion that 'an honest accountant's certificate, honestly applied is one of the rarest features in an industrial prospectus' (quoted in Kennedy, 1987: 127).

Sometimes accountants were even more closely involved in company formations. There are a number of examples of public accountants who were primarily company promoters, amongst whom David Chadwick is by far the best known. Chadwick started his career in local government and became Salford's borough treasurer in 1844, aged 23, and went on to form his own accountancy practice in 1859 (Parker, 1980*a*: n.p.). He specialized in the arrangement of finance for companies going public and 'between 1862 and 1874 he was involved in the formation of at least 47 limited companies, most of which were the conversion of family-owned industrial concerns', and many of whom were important mid-Victorian iron, steel, and coal companies of which he became auditor (Cottrell, 1984: 626). In 1889, the Mancunian accountants Broome, Murray & Co. established a separate company to facilitate corporate flotations called 'The North of England Trustee Debenture and Assets Corporation Limited'. Adam Murray was a director, and its creation 'led to a considerable extension of the firm's business, as many of the companies floated by the

North of England appointed Broome, Murray & Co. as their auditors' (Allured, 1980: 2). It was naturally also quite common for the reporting accountant to be appointed auditor of the new company, as happened following Deloitte, Dever, Griffiths & Co.'s report on the Shelton Iron, Steel & Coal Co. Ltd., in 1889 (Edwards, 1980: 257; see also Jones, 1981: 56). The ongoing provision of capital for existing business also became an important source of fees for some accountancy firms. Price, Waterhouse & Co., for example, was just one firm where 'the work done in connection with the provision of finance for business undoubtedly led to a big increase in the practice both at home and abroad', in the last quarter of the nineteenth century (de Mond, 1951: 5).

We have seen that the amalgamation of companies was a natural consequence of the establishment of the limited liability company and the increased incorporation of businesses as joint-stock concerns. Figure 4 shows that mergers, although cyclical, have seen a secular, upward trend, and the need to value companies that were parties to a merger and to report on past performance produced a commensurate increase in the demand for the accountant's financial expertise. Examples abound of accountants engaged in this area of work although, in contrast to some of the activities outlined above, it was undertaken by the leading account-ants of the day rather than the average practitioner. Peat, for example, advised on many amalgamations in the steel industry (Parker, 1985: 603). Francis d'Arcy Cooper briefed William Lever on possible takeover targets before the First World War and, in this context, investigated a German company in 1910 (Edwards, 1984a: 781). The decision of private banks to publish a balance sheet, in a move designed to restore confidence follow-ing the collapse of the City of Glasgow Bank, was followed by a series of amalgamations with the larger joint-stock banks in the early 1880s, and this provided Edwin Waterhouse's firm with 'scope for services in arrang-ing the terms of amalgamation' (quoted in Jones, 1988: 131). This kind of work sometimes proved highly sensitive. In the 1890s, Waterhouse relates how he was involved in

arranging the terms of amalgamation of Prescott, Cave & Co. of Threadneedle Street, my cousin's firm of Dimsdale, Fowler, Barnard & Co. of Cornhill, Messrs Miles, Cave, Baillie & Co. of Bristol and Messrs Tugwell, Brimmer & Co. of Bath. I had to report upon the profit earning power of each business, and this without creating any suspicion as to what my visits to the banks were for. At Bristol, where it was thought I might be recognized by old friends . . . I was put for my work in a 'first floor back', and the blind drawn down at midday. (Jones, 1988: 131–2)

Frederick Jenkins of Curtis, Jenkins & Co., the accountants of W. D. & H. O. Wills, was called in to advise on the formation of the Imperial Tobacco Company as a defensive merger to counter the influence of the American

Tobacco Company in 1901. There followed the problem of devising a scheme of amalgamation acceptable to companies previously in competition and sometimes antagonistic towards one another. The details of the above case illustrate how complex the arrangements could become. When called in to advise on an earlier (aborted) scheme for amalgamation, Jenkins had identified the crucial problem as the valuation of goodwill (Alford, 1973: 254). At Wills, the tactic to deal with this was to avoid detailed financial disclosure until agreement was reached concerning sensible terms for the amalgamation. Wills' plan, which they realized would be advantageous to them in view of their high, but undisclosed, levels of profitability, was to value goodwill at eight years' purchase of net profits. When the amalgamating parties accepted this proposal and the profits of Wills were revealed, the result—Wills were credited with £700,000 of the £1 million goodwill attributed to all the amalgamating companies— produced astonishment amongst the new partners. The outcome was that Wills received £7 million out of a total consideration of approximately £12 million. William Plender, who had been responsible for valuing goodwill, seems to have ameliorated dissatisfaction, however, by pointing out that the adoption of any of the alternatives put forward for arriving at the figure for goodwill would increase Wills' share even further (Alford, 1973: 263).

With the Imperial Tobacco Company led by W. D. & H. O. Wills as a model, the first decade of the twentieth century also saw attempts to establish a nation-wide biscuit combine under Huntley & Palmer's leadership. Concern with confidentiality and a certain amount of natural suspicion between companies, who were currently in competition with one another, inhibited progress. Some of the firms targeted for the combine 'did allow Sir William Plender, senior partner of the top-ranking accountants Deloitte Plender and Griffiths [who audited Peek Frean], to report to one another their aggregate turnover, profits and fixed asset figures, but one by one they had second thoughts, so that no more was heard of the proposals' (Corley, 1972: 174).

A nineteenth-century insolvency engagement could, in common with audit work, result in accountants providing more general managerial assistance. The engagement might require the accountant to manage a company in receivership for a considerable time-period, and it sometimes involved an attempt to reconstruct and rehabilitate the financially embarrassed concern. In 1850, George Begbie was appointed official manager of the bankrupt Shrewsbury and Leicester Direct Railway Company. Three years' work was devoted to winding up their affairs, but the job did not prove remunerative, with £565 having to be written off as a bad debt, including the costs of solicitors advising him 'during his period of official management' (Begbie et al., 1937: 12).

According to Ernest Cooper, his most interesting experiences as a chartered accountant were when carrying on businesses as liquidator, receiver, or manager. Indeed, he considered himself to have been a 'jack of over thirty trades' during his professional career. For three years in the 1880s he carried on, in liquidation, a company producing 1,000 tons of salt per week from brine. In the same decade, he wound up a company which had established a factory in Vienna for manufacturing electric machinery and lamps, carrying on the business for a year 'I think fairly successfully' (Cooper, 1921: 558). Other assignments included receiver and manager of one of the principal London marine engine building companies, 'a Texas cattle ranch of great dimensions for several years' which was eventually sold to an American, a large Canadian lumber property extending along many miles of the St Lawrence river, which he had to hold on to for years before selling to an American company, a steel merchant and bridge-building business, a large brewery, two paper-making companies, a 'pugilistic establishment in the east end of London, a brewery in York-shire, a large gas lamp factory, a stud farm, and asbestos mines in Sicily' (Cooper, 1921: 559).

It is, however, the career of George Touche which probably provides the greatest insight into the potential provided by this type of work. Touche, having 'distinguished himself in actuarial science in his profes-sional examinations', was 'fortunate enough to uncover a fraud on his first auditing engagement' (Richards, 1986: 540; Parker, 1980a: n.p.). He was then drawn into management as a liquidator with, it was said, a prefer-ence for reconstruction rather than winding up. He first became involved in rescuing investment trusts in the 1890s, and afterwards also developed a general reputation in salvaging derelict businesses. It was to handle this work that he formed his own accountancy firm, George A. Touch & Co., in 1899 and took on Andrew Wilson Tait, a fellow Scot, as partner (Dav-enport-Hines, 1986b: 429–33). Indeed Tait and Touche at first earned most of their income from directors' fees, receiverships, and reconstructions (Richards, 1981: 16).

One of Tait's major achievements was the reconstruction of Ferranti and, according to Wilson, the company's historian, when the electronics firm neared bankruptcy in 1903, its bankers called in two accountants as receiver-managers, being the only people 'capable of relieving the financial chaos in Ferranti Limited's balance sheet' (1988: 81). One of these accountants, Arthur Whittaker, was from a local Manchester firm; the other was Tait, who became chairman. Following reconstruction, Sebastian Ziani de Ferranti, the firm's founder, was 'reduced to a rela-tively insignificant position within the company. Tait in fact ensured that Ferranti was virtually excluded from the Crown Works, after 1905, be-cause of his alleged obstructive influence on profitability' (Wilson, 1988: 83). In that year, another leading City accountant, J. M. Henderson, MP, who held five other directorships, was appointed to the board to represent the interests of Ferranti's shareholders. Wilson concludes: 'Ferranti stands out as an excellent example of the growing importance of professionally-trained businessmen, and especially accountants, in the management of manufacturing companies in the two decades preceding the First World War', and 'only when chartered accountants were brought onto the Board in 1905 did his [Sebastian Ziani de Ferranti's] company begin to exploit the profit potential in the products he designed' (Wilson, 1988: 148).

Accountancy firms were also often engaged to undertake a wide range of investigations overseas. The investment of increasing amounts of British capital in American enterprises in the latter decades of the nineteenth century 'resulted in a growing demand for the services of City accountants whose expertise was required to assess the viability of projected companies and to audit those in existence' (Jones, 1988: 223). George Sneath of Price, Waterhouse made several trips to the United States for this purpose, and in 1889 was accompanied by Joseph Gurney Fowler to investigate the Bartholomay breweries prior to their amalgamation and subsequent flotation on the London Stock Exchange (Jones, 1988: 223). Ten years later, George's brother H. G. J. Sneath, also of Price, Waterhouse, was asked by Fowler to undertake another brewery investigation (Jones, 1988: 222) which lasted for about a year and also required him to take on 'a quasi-managerial role' (Wilkins, 1988: 279).

Lewis Davies Jones and William James Caesar, who were responsible for opening Price, Waterhouse's offices in New York and Chicago in the early 1890s, investigated the following British-financed concerns: 'breweries, packing houses and stockyards (all funded by the City of London Contract Corporation), insurance companies and other ventures including International Okonite, Liptons, and J. & P. Coats (Pawtucket)' (Jones, 1988: 223). Before joining William Henry Pannell's firm in 1893, Gilbert Courtenay Clarke, when a manager with Hart Brothers, Tibbetts & Co., spent some time in Denver, Colorado, where he drew up figures for the merger of the Rocky Mountain and Denver Breweries, preparatory to a public issue of capital in London (Medlam, 1980: 6). The turn of the century also saw members of J. & A. W. Sully & Co. travelling to Angola to institute a 'watertight set of books' and arrange monthly returns for the London office of the clients (Sully, 1951: 14).

COST ACCOUNTING

Cost accounting and management accounting today combine to provide managers with the accounting information required to help them conduct business operations in an efficient manner. Parker has pointed out that, in its modern meaning, cost accounting is difficult to distinguish from management accounting (1984: 47). However, the latter term is of recent origin, achieving widespread use in Britain only after the Second World War.

Cost accounting may usefully be described, for the purpose of the period covered in this section, as 'the accumulation of relevant costs to be used by managers for the purposes of planning, decision making and control' (Edwards, 1989b: 305).

Given Chandler's (1977, 1990) assessment of the impact of the large-scale business enterprise on cost accounting developments, it is not surprising to find that progress in this direction had been made early on by companies at the forefront of Britain's industrial revolution (Boyns and Edwards, 1996, 1997a, 1997b; Edwards et al., 1995; Edwards and Boyns, 1992; Edwards and Newell, 1991; Fleischman and Parker, 1990, 1991, 1992; Fleischman et al., 1991; H. Jones, 1985; McKendrick, 1970; Stone, 1973). The growing interest in costing matters during the period covered in this chapter witnessed an upsurge also in the costing literature which Solomons has referred to as the 'costing renaissance' (1952: 17; see also Edwards et al., 1996).

Whereas professional accountants successfully developed many services in the nineteenth century, there have been some suggestions that they were slow to become involved in the provision of cost accounting information. One contemporary was severely critical of the accountant for failing to meet the needs of 'the manufacturer who may feel that he does not possess the information he desires, but may be unaware of the source from which it can be obtained' (Strachan, 1903: 7). This alleged absence of a close connection between chartered accountants and business in its technological and operational aspects has been put down to snobbery (Parker, 1986: 42). A driving feature of Solomons' 'costing renaissance' was the publication, in 1887, of Garcke and Fells's *Factory Accounts*; a publication today widely acknowledged as a breakthrough, being the earliest standard text on cost accounting. A rather sniffy review in the *Accountant*, however, dismissed this major work on the grounds that

It does not purport to deal with the ordinary financial books. It is rather concerned with the wages and time books, stock books, and matters of a similar nature, which, as a rule, do not come within the scope of an accountant's duties. (5 May 1888: 278)

It is also certainly true that the ICAEW did little to encourage an interest in cost accounting, with the topic not rating a mention in the ICAEW's original charter (1880). In the 32 years up to 1916, only 41 costing questions were included in that body's 128 examinations, and nineteen of these were practically identical. Parker explains this indifference on the grounds that: 'Most practising accountants at this time had little contact with manufacturing companies, even in audit work, their clients being mainly engaged in banking, insurance, railways, water, docks and mines' (1986: 42). However, while it is true that most large companies fell into these business categories, a good number of manufacturing companies

(as noted above) were quoted on the London or provincial stock exchanges in 1880, by which time we know that most were the subject of a
professional audit and were also developing contacts with accountants for
other reasons. There is no evidence of snobbery or an anti-industrial
culture among accountants of this period—what Wiener (1981) has
termed 'The decline of the Industrial Spirit'. Indeed, given the scope for
profitable engagements, it would be surprising if there was.

The explanation for the slow development of costing work among
public accountants, if this indeed was the case, might be the result of quite
different circumstances. There is the possibility that such work, being
ongoing, was more efficiently conducted by company employees. Linked
with this scenario might be an antipathy towards the external auditor on
the part of management. According to Jones, the story of the auditor being
told by the chairman of a large textile company to keep his opinions to
himself, as 'Thow's nowt but scorer', 'represented a commonly held view
among management' (Jones, 1981: 117). In a similar vein, one contemporary writer tells us that 'the average man of business does not look upon
his accountant as of any direct assistance to him in the shaping of his
plans. He rather regards him as the scrutineer and compiler of aggregate
results' (Strachan, 1903: 6). The chartered accountant Thomas Plumpton
(1892: 268) provided further support for these ideas:

This department [the cost office] has hitherto been a secret closed chamber to the
professional accountant, for it has been presumed by the public that an accountant's duty is simply to furnish a financial statement; and manufacturers have
considered that such work could best be accomplished by the election of men who
had been trained as specialists, even so much so that whenever a vacancy has
occurred in the cost office they have seldom sought assistance from the ranks of
Chartered Accountants.

Dicksee also believed there to be a lack of attention to costing, and that this
neglect was reflected in the poor staffing and low status of internal accounting departments at the beginning of the First World War (Dicksee,
1915: 18–19). By this, he almost certainly meant that few chartered accountants were employed there.

We have also found ample evidence to suggest that public accountants—many of them with leading firms—were perfectly prepared, indeed
keen, to earn fees from offering advice on costing systems on a consultancy basis. We have found no evidence to suggest that British accountants turned away requests from industry for assistance in this direction.
Indeed, recent archival research by Boyns and Edwards (1997*a*) into the
coal, iron, and steel industries reveals that the opposite was often the case.
Bolckow, Vaughan & Co. Ltd. was incorporated in 1864 and the directors'
minutes of 3 December 1864 tell us that the firm's auditors, Chadwick,
Adamson & Co., had been engaged to advise on which books needed to be

kept by the company, and also on the duties of the general manager, secretary, and chief cashier. Two years later it was 'Resolved that Mr Chadwick be instructed to send a clerk to examine into the system of account keeping at the outlying works and collieries and report thereon to this company at the next meeting with a recommendation to adopt what improvements may be thought necessary' (NERRC, location no 04603, directors' minutes 17 Oct. 1866, fo. 287). Their 'report on the system of account keeping at the outlying works, mines and collieries was submitted to the meeting' of 20 November 1866 (fo. 294), when it was 'Resolved that the suggestion contained in the report of Messrs Chadwick & Co. be adopted and carried out as far as practicable and that instructions be given at the various places for this purpose forthwith.'

The Shelton Iron, Steel and Coal Co. Ltd. was incorporated in 1889 and, at a directors' meeting held on the following 18 February 'It was resolved that Messrs Deloitte, Dever, Griffiths & Co. and Messrs John Adamson & Co. be requested to arrange the best method for keeping the company's books, such books to commence from the dates when the old companies were taken over. It was decided that the monthly cost sheets relative to the various departments should be made out' (NWRRC, location no. 6720). On 26 March it was decided 'to adopt the forms of new books, cost sheets, and system of book-keeping recommended by Messrs Deloitte'. The continuing involvement of the auditors with the internal accounting system is evidenced in the minutes of the directors' meeting held on 8 September 1891, when we are told that the accounts and cost sheets for the half-year ended June 1891 were submitted together with a report thereon by Deloitte and the secretary. Again, at the South Durham Iron & Steel Co. Ltd., the auditors, W. B. Peat & Co., also provided additional services. On 20 December 1898 they submitted a draft scheme of uniform cost accounts for each works to the board. Peat's firm were also responsible for presenting what was called the 'auditors report' to the board every six months (NERRC, location no. 04879). The report was very much more than the type of audit report prepared for external consumption, however, setting out, in great detail, the costs of each department on a total and per ton basis, quantities consumed both in total and per ton of output, the profits earned, comparisons with previous periods, and a detailed analysis of changes which had taken place.

There are numerous other examples of solid practical contributions made by accountants in the area of cost accounting in the nineteenth century. We noted in Chapter 2 how, in 1864, Edwin Waterhouse was engaged to undertake 'a heavy piece of work in planning a system of cost accounts' for John Fowler, the Leeds machinery manufacturer (Jones, 1988: 79). As auditor of the London and North Western Railway, from 1866, Waterhouse worked with the accountancy department of Captain Mark Huish's railway at Euston and 'facilitated the compilation of operating statistics which were used, in turn, to assess performance and the allocation of resources' (Jones, 1995: 53). Waterhouse's diaries also record the fact that

It was also in the Spring of 1873 that I received from David Dale, who had just been taken into the business of Joseph Pease & Partners, a request to put the accounts of their large colliery and ironstone departments on a good footing, and to audit them in future half yearly. The matter was a difficult one, for the methods of book-keeping were antiquated, and the staff, to a large extent Quakers of mature years, averse to change. (Jones, 1988: 96)

We cannot be entirely sure that the system installed included cost calculations, but this seems likely in view of the fact that costing systems, as we have seen, were introduced for similar types of company by firms of public accountants around this time. Wenham, Angus & Co., who were first called in by Pilkington in the early 1870s (see above), were again engaged in the 1890s to calculate the company's unit costs per foot of glass down to two decimal places of a penny (Barker, 1960: 166). We are told that later 'A careful system of costing was gradually evolved and at the beginning of 1913 a central cost department (one man, T. B. Steane, in charge of two clerks) was set up, equipped with a Hollerith machine' (Barker, 1977: 234), an important innovation that could 'process accounting data with great speed, and which facilitated significant improvements in the collection and diffusion of information in large companies' (Hannah, 1983: 78). We can infer from the fact that Pilkington is recorded as being Hollerith's second oldest customer that this represented an early move into office machinery.

Gilbert Courtenay Clarke possessed considerable experience of factory accounting. On joining W. H. Pannell & Co., he arranged for clients'

factory accounts [to be] drawn up to show turnover, direct costs and gross profits for each main product or division of the business. Accounts presented in this way could be linked with the cost methods used by the client and cash flow statements were provided perhaps 60 or 70 years before it became customary or obligatory to do so. (Medlam, 1980: 7)

As indicated earlier, the accountant Frederick Jenkins was regularly called in to advise W. D. & H. O. Wills, the tobacco firm, on major matters. In the late 1880s, he made recommendations for 'each branch of the business to keep separate trading accounts to be consolidated at the end of each year [and this] enabled a much closer watch to be kept on costs and profitability' (Alford, 1973: 166). A little later Jenkins in conjunction with Hopkinson, a consulting engineer, recommended that the annual accounts of each branch of the business should be analysed on 'dissection sheets'. The analysis

broke down trading accounts into minute detail showing how individual items of cost and revenue had changed. The advantage of such a method was plain because, on very small margins and a large turnover, variations of a fraction of a penny added up to big changes in profits. (Alford, 1973: 167)

When Wills was converted to a limited company in 1893, Jenkins, and James Inskip, the company's solicitor, were instructed to prepare a scheme of incorporation and, following this organizational change, 'decisions concerning production and marketing' continued to be firmly based on the 'dissection sheets and questionnaires to travellers' (Alford, 1973: 241). The former were prepared for each branch on a monthly basis, with sales and production the subject of detailed analysis in terms of value, volume, brand, area, costs, and prices. When Jenkins was called in on the formation of the Imperial Tobacco Company, the Wills' method of analysing performance was extended to all the amalgamating companies. Whereas accounting and costing methods had previously varied considerably, the dissection sheets provided a comparative measure of efficiency and competitiveness in each of the company's branches. The company's executive committee set each branch's total budget and prices and sanctioned new cigarette and tobacco brands based on annual reports received from each of them. These also provided data for forecasts for the coming year which, in turn, formed the basis of claims for capital and marketing expenditure. Costs, including depreciation of capital, were expressed as totals and per pound of sales to three decimal places of a penny (Alford, 1973: 331–2).

In no sense, therefore, did public accountants, generally, consider cost accounting inappropriate work for a professional practice; indeed they were keen to publish work on the subject. In 1874, the Scottish accountant F. Hayne Carter detailed the methods of costing the different workings in a mine (Edwards, 1937: 313). Another book, of 1878, by the Manchester public accountant Thomas Battersby, was entitled *The Perfect Double Entry Bookkeeper and the Perfect Prime Cost and Profit Demonstrator (on the Departmental System) for Iron and Brass Founders, Machinists, Engineers, Shipbuilders, Manufacturers. &c.* This detailed, in particular, a range of methods which could be used to enable the recovery of overhead costs. Neither of the authors of the highly acclaimed *Factory Accounts* (1887) (Parker, 1986: 41; Solomons, 1952: 35), however, were in practice. Garcke was an electrical engineer while Fells was, in 1887, the assistant secretary of the Anglo-American Brush Electric Light Corporation. He became a member of the SAA in 1902 and, in due course, a fellow of the ICWA. Their book was followed two years later by George Pepler Norton's *Textile Manufacturers' Book-keeping*. Norton was a chartered accountant and partner in the firm of Armitage, Clough and Norton, having previously been a 'prize man' in the final examinations of the ICAEW, June 1883. His firm was heavily involved in the installation of costing systems.

By the 1890s, cost accounts were receiving attention in general accounting textbooks. Dicksee's *Bookkeeping for Accountant Students* (1893) contained an example of a builder's cost ledger, while Lisle's *Accounting in Theory and Practice* (1899) included a chapter on cost accounts. One of George Touche's partners, Leslie Hawkins, wrote *Cost Accounting: An Explanation of Principles and a Guide to Practice* in 1905. This book—in its ninth edition by 1934—became standard reading for students and was also of considerable practical value, as it 'set out simply and clearly the relatively new concept [cf. Boyns and Edwards, 1997*a*] of an integrated system of cost and financial accounts' (Richards, 1981: 16). John Mann made a number of major contributions to the costing literature in the late nineteenth and early twentieth centuries; work which was continued by his partner from 1906, the Scottish chartered accountant Harold Godfrey Judd (Mann Judd Gordon, 1967: 55–6).

Costing material also appeared in contemporary journals, and Solomons's pioneering essay (1952) gave particular attention to the content of engineering journals such as *Engineering*, the *Engineer*, and the *Engineering Magazine*. These are important sources of illumination concerning early costing developments that are augmented by other contemporary trade journals such as the *Mechanical Engineer*, the *Railway Times*, the *Journal of Gas Lighting, Water Supply and Sanitary Improvement*, and the *Electrician*. Costing also featured prominently in the accounting journals, with the chartered accountant Arthur H. Gibson writing (1887) the first article published in the *Accountant* to give significant attention to this topic. A small sample of the costing material published in the *Accountant* is reproduced in Edwards et al. (1996), which also contains a summary of the issues covered. The growing interest in costing matters is also reflected in the fact that the *Accountant* devoted a series of leading articles to 'Cost Accounts' in 1894 (28 July: 655–7; 4 Aug.: 673–5; 11 Aug.: 687–9; 18 Aug.: 702–4). In 1908, Pixley still described cost accounting as 'a new branch of the science' of accounting (1908: 131), and set out what he considered to be its principal objectives (1908: 134; see also Strachan, 1903: 2–3; Dicksee, 1928: 6). The rapid development of the costing literature, thereafter, is indicated by Nicholson and Rohrbach's estimate, made eleven years later, that 'more than 90% of this literature has been published in the last decade, and fully 75% in the last five years' (1919: 1).

The precise extent to which cost accounting was being used by management in their decision-making by the end of this period, let alone its effectiveness, is not easy to judge. This must await more detailed analyses of individual company records than are at present available. The use of and quality of costings certainly varied from industry to industry, and from company to company. According to Dicksee, 'good costing' procedures could already be found in the basic industries, such as coal and iron, by the turn of the century (1928: 4). It is probably true to say, however, that the use of unsophisticated and piecemeal cost calculations remained widespread, and was mainly the work of engineers and unqualified accountants. At the same time, we have seen that it is possible to produce numerous examples of professional accountants in public practice providing a wide range of costing services for management.

TAXATION

Taxation does not appear to have figured prominently in the activities of most accounting practices up to the First World War, though it was then to change dramatically spurred on by the introduction of Excess Profits Duty and the increased rates of income tax imposed to help finance the war effort. Up to this time, however, the tax system had been based principally on indirect taxation (Mitchell, 1988: 582), with the structure and implementation of stamp, customs, and excise duties rarely giving rise to the need for an accountant's services. Income tax had been imposed, temporarily, to help finance the Napoleonic Wars, but had been discontinued following the cessation of hostilities in 1815. The tax had proved its worth as a revenue raiser, however, and was reintroduced by Sir Robert Peel, in 1842, to finance a reduction in tariffs; it has been with us ever since.

Up to the First World War, however, rates of income tax were relatively modest. Throughout the period, the top rate was the 1s. 4d. in the pound (6.7%) imposed on incomes above £150 per annum, in the 1850s, to help finance the Crimean War. With lower rates varying between 5d. and $11\frac{1}{2}d$. in the pound on incomes of between £100 and £150 (Mitchell, 1962: 427–9), it was a levy confined to the middle and upper classes. It therefore seems quite likely that, with the rates imposed on individuals and of course business (income tax was only replaced by corporation tax on companies in 1965) at relatively modest levels, the average nineteenth-century accountancy practice was rarely consulted for advice, to prepare computations and negotiate with the Inland Revenue. Certainly, we are told that 'There is not a word in the accounts book to show that J. & A. W. Sully ever touched tax work, nor knew the first thing about taxation.' The firm's history continues: 'This absence of tax work strikes a cold chill in the spines of the mid-twentieth-century partners and senior staff, whose livelihood springs so largely from computations and returns of tax and duties of various kinds. It is, however, only the natural reflection of the insignificant level of taxation in the Victorian era' (Sully, 1951: 12). Deloitte's historian strikes a similar note: 'There is hardly a mention of taxation work [between 1845–1900], perhaps not surprising with a rate of income tax in 1874 of 2d in the £' (Kettle, 1957: 65).

There is of course the possibility that taxation work was undertaken but tends not to show up in the above archives because it was regarded as a (minor) part of the overall service in the area of audit and accountancy. Certainly, it surfaced elsewhere in a variety of guises. The Bristol firm of James and Henry Grace secured appointments, in the 1860s, as 'Government Collectors of Income Tax' for the parishes of St Stephens and St Nicholas (Grace et al., 1957: ch. 2, n.p.). Some years later, James Grace wrote: 'This was a capital appointment. We had uncommon looking notices, printed green or pink for the different parishes, with our advertisement as being Accountants, General Agents, etc.' It seems that the new arrangement was much favoured by businessmen who preferred it to the previous situation, where the collectors changed every year or so. Further, 'being able to pay at any time at our office pleased all and we had calls from large numbers some with cheques and cash for part [of the amount due]. . . . The collection paid us well when the tax was high and to get into touch with everyone worth £160 a year in Queens Square, Welsh Back, St. Stephen Street, St. Nicholas Street, Bridge Street, Prince Street, etc. did us good in more ways than one' (Grace et al., 1957: ch. 2, n.p.).

There was also early income tax work for John Mann, Sr., 'being one of those who filled up the first assessment forms after Peel's reimposition of the tax in 1842' (Mann Judd Gordon, 1967: 27). Similarly, at Theodore, Jones, Hill & Co., the agreement of the tax liabilities of Charles Hope & Son, for 1880/1, is cited as 'proof that accountants were engaged in this work much earlier than historians had hitherto supposed' (Hill Vellacott, 1988: 44). Adam Murray, of the Manchester firm Broome, Murray & Co., a founder of the Manchester Institute of Accountants and vice-president of the ICAEW in 1889/90, was joint author, with Roger Carter, of the first textbook on income tax (Murray and Carter, 1895). Thomson McLintock's first 'big tax job', in about 1914, involved negotiations with the Inland Revenue on behalf of the Lanarkshire coal owners to establish 'uniform rates of depreciation on colliery wagons'; such specialization in taxation is seen as the most important factor in the expansion of the firm for fifty years following the establishment of the London office in 1914 (Winsbury, 1977: 34–5). The history of Begbie, Robinson, Cox and Knight confirms the fact that, as a result of the introduction of Excess Profits Duty, during the First World War, 'the subject of income tax began to assume an importance such as it had never enjoyed before' (1937: 36).

PUBLIC SECTOR WORK

The involvement of professional accountants in government work, at local and central level, has undoubtedly been important in raising the status of both the profession and the accountants personally involved.

Their accountancy practices have benefited from greater exposure while the accountants, themselves, have increasingly received recognition in the honours lists.

Public accountants were heavily involved in local authority work in the second half of the nineteenth century, though it appears to have been mainly confined to audit and advice on the improvement of bookkeeping and financial reporting practices (Coombs and Edwards, 1996: chs. 5–8). At Bradford in 1872, for example, Blackburn & Co. (see Appendix, Ernst & Whinney, Robson Rhodes) were appointed, following the discovery of a cash deficiency, to examine the accounts and 'prepare a fresh set of books for simplifying the accounts in the borough accountant's office' (quoted in Coombs and Edwards, 1996: 45). The finance committee then decided to engage a public accountant to undertake a three-monthly audit, and the voluntary appointment of a firm of accountants to undertake a 'professional audit' in addition to the statute-required ratepayers' audit became common practice amongst municipal corporations in the late nineteenth and early twentieth centuries (Coombs and Edwards, 1996: 135–6).

The successful involvement of professional accountants in central government work also explains the growing willingness of the political establishment to seek the advice of accountants when taking major strategic decisions. Whilst this trend becomes more evident in the inter-war years, it is clear that the process began much earlier. Indeed, the accountant Charles Snell was drafted in by Parliament to investigate the affairs of a firm belonging to one of the directors of the South Sea Company in the early eighteenth century (Edwards, 1989a: 143). Moving on to the nineteenth century, Quilter, Ball & Co. were called in by the government, in 1859, to examine the accounts of the Army Clothing Store at Weedon after the storekeeper had absconded (Bywater, 1985b: 793). They were also engaged to make confidential reports to the Board of Trade on the financial position of private firms wishing to convert into limited liability companies. In 1887, Edwin Waterhouse and Frederick Whinney were engaged to investigate the accounts of the Woolwich Arsenal for a parliamentary committee under the chairmanship of Lord Randolph Churchill (Edwards, 1986: 677). He described their report as 'lucid and valuable'. All their recommendations were adopted (Howitt, 1966: 44), and there followed invitations to advise on developments within the War Office and the Admiralty. Waterhouse and Whinney were also asked to report on the accounts of the Ordnance Department, while William Plender acted for the Metropolitan Water Board in acquiring the London Water Companies in 1903. Five years later he assisted in the setting up of the Port of London Authority and, in 1911, sat on the National Health Insurance Commission. Finally, the story of the most prestigious public appointment of all is told by Wise (1982). The banker Sir Ernst Cassel, when asked by King Edward

VII if he could recommend a reliable accountant to handle the accounts of the privy purse, replied: 'well, I know an honest man I can recommend: William Peat' (1982: 16), whose firm has been the monarch's accountants ever since.

Accountants were called in, from an early stage, to give evidence and advice to parliamentary and government committees. We have seen, for example, that 'the leading public accountant of the day', Peter Harriss Abbott, was a member of the commission inquiring into the method of keeping the public accounts, in 1829, and was appointed to the post of Official Assignee in Bankruptcy in 1833 (Bywater, 1985*b*: 791). Quilter gave evidence to the Select Committee on the Audit of Railway Accounts, 1849, while J. E. Coleman and John Ball both appeared before the Select Committee on the Bank Acts in 1858 (Bywater, 1985*b*: 792). Quilter and Turquand were the permanent inspectors appointed by the Board of Trade to investigate and report on businesses whose shareholders called management into question under the Companies Act 1856 (Bywater, 1985*b*: 793).

Professional accountants were also, quite naturally, called in to present evidence to successive government committees appointed to consider possible amendments to company law. Prior to Britain's entry into the European Community in 1973, the company law amendment committee was the traditional means used by governments to generate new ideas and make recommendations on company law reform. Nine company law amendment committees were appointed and reported between 1841 and 1962, with accountants involved in all but the Gladstone Committee of 1844. The first accountant to give evidence was David Chadwick, in 1867, to the Watkin Select Committee on Limited Liability Acts. Chadwick, by then a Member of Parliament, sat as a member of the Lowe Committee on the Companies Acts 1862 and 1867 in 1877, with leading accountants of the day, Harding, Price, and Turquand, all giving evidence. Edwin Waterhouse was a member of the Davey Departmental Committee on Joint Stock Companies (1895); an appointment indicating 'further government recognition of the contribution accountants could make to the conduct of business life' (Edwards, 1989*a*: 201). Frederick Whinney, another past president of the ICAEW, gave evidence to the Committee, and a number of his proposals were included in the report. In 1906, the Loreburn Company Law Amendment Committee reported on its deliberations over the filing and dissemination of company information. It witnessed the first contribution from a professional accountancy body, with the SAA submitting a memorandum. In 1906, the Board of Trade appointed Peat to a committee looking into the laws on insolvent estates and Edwin Waterhouse, who helped draft the Companies Act 1900, to the next company law amendment committee in 1917 (Howitt, 1966: 44).

The above discussion has sought to demonstrate the growing involvement of accountants in the legislative process. The actual debates and concerns of these committees are not discussed here (see Edwards, 1989*a*: ch. 16 for a useful discussion; also Aranya, 1974), but the presence of members of the profession is significant in two respects. First, the appointment of accountants to committees can be seen as a reflection of the utility and esteem in which the profession was held by the government. Second, the influence can have worked in the opposite direction, in that accountants were provided with a platform to demonstrate their competence, and this served to increase further their utility and profile, not only in the eyes of the government, but also to those in the business community to be affected by the changes in legislation.

The growing involvement of accountants at both local and central levels of government did not pass unnoticed. We have seen that the first chartered accountant to receive a knighthood was Sir Robert Palmer Harding, in 1890, for his work as Official Receiver. A small number followed in his footsteps in the pre-war period. Sir John Sutherland Harmood-Banner—an active politician at both local and national level (he first joined Liverpool City Council in 1894, was Lord Mayor in 1912/13, and 1905–24 was Member of Parliament for the Everton division) and a member of numerous government committees—was knighted in 1913 and created a baronet in 1924 (Davenport-Hines, 1985*a*: 44). Sir Frank Brown, who was first elected a member of Durham County Council in 1892, and was chairman of that authority for many years, was awarded a knighthood 'in acknowledgement of his life of public service' in 1913 (*Accountant*, 18 Apr. 1931: 499). The entrepreneurial John Reeves Ellerman, who left public practice for industry in the mid-1890s to make a fortune, was awarded a baronetcy in 1905, for making 'his rapidly expanding empire' available to the government during the Boer War, and for his 'growing presence behind the scenes in the Conservative party' (Rubinstein, 1984: 251). In general, however, progress in this direction was slow, with the expectation that some members of the profession might receive titles at the time of Queen Victoria's Jubilee of 1887, for example, remaining unfulfilled (Cooper, 1921: 555). It was not until the First World War, when accountants proved their worth as administrators, that the titles began to flow.

COMPANY SECRETARIES AND DIRECTORS

The accountant involved in the formation of a company would sometimes become responsible, not only for the audit of the new concern, but also for handling at least some of the administrative duties of the company secretary. The holder of this office, 'the true civil servant of business', handled the company's dealings with its shareholders and the registrar of joint-stock companies, serviced the requirements of the board of directors, as well as fulfilling a number of other roles (Carr-Saunders and Wilson, 1933: 238).

We know that Robert Fletcher supplied secretarial services to the Bristol and Gloucestershire Railway Company, in 1836, and attended the meetings of the executive committee of that railway (Cornwell, 1991: 74). Secretarial services were provided by Harding & Pullein for the Caledonian Railway in the 1850s (Jones, 1981: 56). The first explicit appointment as company secretary of which the authors are aware, however, is Quilter's engagement by the Edinburgh Silk Yarn Company in 1842 (Bywater, 1985b: 792). Later examples include: John Curtis, appointed secretary to the Aberdare Railway Company sometime before 1882 (Cornwell, 1991: 117); George Touche, to the Threlfal Brewery Company in 1889 (Richards, 1986: 540); and Frederick Augustus Jenkins, to the Bristol Channel Malting and Milling Company in 1890 (Cornwell, 1991: 123). Turning to Scotland, A. T. Niven promoted the Edinburgh Railway Access & Property Co. in 1853, and served the company as manager and secretary until his death in 1918 (Stewart, 1977: 129).

A distinction must be made, however, between these cases (which involved the provision of secretarial services by accountancy firms) and the qualified accountant leaving practice to become company secretary as a full-time employee. The latter arrangement, at least among chartered accountants, appears to have remained rare until after the First World War.

The pinnacle of achievement of the public accountant in British management in this period may be seen as appointment at board level. Here, it is possible to quantify the accountant's role, and the results of a statistical exercise are shown in Table 15. Samples of companies were taken from *The Stock Exchange Official Year-Book* at twenty-year intervals from 1891 to 1991, and the names of their directors were checked against the lists of members contained in the yearbooks of the accountancy societies (for a fuller statement of the methodology, see Matthews, 1993). This revealed the proportions of directors, chairmen, managing directors, and secretaries that were qualified accountants in each bi-decennial year, and the percentage of companies that had at least one accountant on the board.

The results chart the remarkable rise of qualified accountants in the hierarchy of British management, and describing and explaining this rise forms a major part of this history. Before the First World War, a small proportion of directors, managing directors, and chairmen were professional accountants. Since then the proportion has increased significantly and, at the present time, about one in five of all three posts are held by a qualified accountant. In both 1891 and 1911, the proportion of company chairmen, directors, and managing directors who were accountants was

Table 15. Analysis by sampling of the involvement of qualified accountants in company management, 1891–1991

	1891	1911	1931	1951	1971	1991
1. Companies in sample	541	437	340	340	322	324
2. Directors in sample	2,651	2,011	1,653	1,592	1,870	2,084
3. % of companies with an accountant-director	4.0	7.6	19.1	39.1	65.8	81.2
4. % of managing directors who were accountants	0.0	2.2	2.6	4.8	13.8	19.3
5. % of company secretaries who were accountants	7.1	7.3	14.3	29.0	41.7	47.4
6. % of chairmen who were accountants	0.8	0.6	4.6	7.6	13.6	20.7
7. % of company directors who were accountants	0.8	1.7	3.8	9.4	15.2	22.0
8. % of accountant directors who were in ICAEW (+SIAA)	92.7	75.8	74.6	75.1	77.1	80.1
9. % of directors in ICAEW who were in practice	100.0	100.0	66.0	53.0	22.0	13.1
10. % of accountants who were directors	4.5	5.2	9.3	8.6	8.7	10.3

Sources: *The Stock Exchange Official Year-Book*; *Directory of Directors*; yearbooks and lists of members for accountancy bodies given in Table 8.

not significant—2.2% or less in each case. We can therefore conclude that, prior to the First World War, accountants were minor players in top management. At the same time, however, one in 20 qualified accountants of this period was a company director, and the number of companies that had at least one accountant on the board was increasing, with 7.6% of listed companies having an accountant around the board table by 1911. Chartered accountants again predominated; ICAEW members accounted almost entirely for the handful of accountant-directors in 1891, and three-quarters of them in 1911.

There were differences of opinion within the accountancy profession concerning whether it was appropriate for partners to accept company directorships. Many did, but at Deloitte it was the policy of the firm, 'from the first', not to accept positions on the board (Kettle, 1957: 56). The Companies Act 1900, section 21 (3), outlawed the appointment of a director as auditor (previously only the Companies Act 1862, table A, article 86, when adopted, ruled out this linkage) and so, henceforth, it was possible for an accountant in practice to be appointed only to the board of a non-audit client. The effect of statutory and other regulations, however, could easily be circumvented, even by the profession's leaders. The best example of how this could be done may be the Cash family's association with the Abbey National Building Society where, on appointment to the board, the auditor's job was passed on to the next generation. F. G. Cash was appointed director to the Abbey National in 1855 and his nephew William, a founder council member of the ICAEW, was appointed auditor in the same year. William served as auditor until 1874 when he joined the board (until his death in 1891), and his son, also William (president of the ICAEW, 1921–3), became auditor in his place. The second William was in turn succeeded as auditor by William Cash, Jr. (knighted 1959), who resigned in 1938 in order, again, to occupy a seat on the board, becoming chairman of Abbey's finance committee (Bellman, 1949: 122).

In later years, Thomson, McLintock was another firm where the partners seldom took on outside directorships; the policy being 'not to take such positions as a routine part of business' (Winsbury, 1977: 5). We find, as a result, William McLintock 'steadfastly refusing all offers of directorships, though he received many' (Winsbury, 1977: 42). Most accountants had no such qualms. While only 5.2% of qualified accountants were company directors in 1911 (Table 15), the leaders of the profession were habitués of the City boardrooms. The *Directory of Directors* reveals that, of the 45-man ruling council of the ICAEW in 1911, 22 (all but four of whom were with City firms) held 60 company directorships between them. Among these were Sir John Sutherland Harmood-Banner, MP, director of thirteen companies, Sir John Craggs, chairman of Fortnum & Mason, and Edwin Waterhouse, chairman of the Riverside Trust and the London board of the Life Association of Scotland. John George Griffiths held four directorships including the GWR, whilst William Peat had seats on the boards of Ind Coope, a large brewery, and British Ropes, of which he was the first chairman. Three of Sir William's sons were partners in the firm, and another, J. B. Peat, was a director of the firm's audit client, the huge steel firm of Dorman Long & Co. Ltd. Of the 25-strong council of the SIAA, seven members together held directorships in sixteen companies. Significantly, the councils of the less prestigious LAA and CAA had no company directors. For 1995/6, by way of comparison, the ICAEW's 88 council members included fifteen who held, between them, directorships in 90 companies; of the ACCA's ruling body of 36 in 1994/5, six held directorships in eighteen companies (*Directory of Directors*, 1995).

Board membership was not, however, confined to the major City-based accountants. James Wood Sully, having established a firm in Sheffield in 1865, had, by the late 1880s, become chairman of Offord & Sons, local coach-builders and later motor engineers, and his 'directorships and other interests were already taking him away from the business of the practice' (Sully, 1951: 6, 10). Sully was considered, within his firm, to have been better equipped for the 'cut and thrust' of industry than the, then perhaps, more prosaic work of a provincial professional practice.

The above evidence casts doubt on the views expressed by early accounting historians (for example, Stacey, 1954: 176), and more recent commentators that, prior to the inter-war period, accountants had 'only rarely taken important positions in the directorates of large companies' (Hannah, 1983: 80; see also Armstrong, 1985: 135). Our findings instead support Jones's conclusion that: 'it was common at this time for leading accountants to be appointed to the boards of major companies' (1986*b*: 767). However, Jones's assertion, quoted earlier, that such accountants were usually valued for their 'expert knowledge of book-keeping' implies a rather too narrow assessment of their contribution (Jones, 1981: 156). Locke is equally mistaken in stating that a public accountant 'rarely entered a business or factory, except perhaps to do an audit. Management concerns were none of his own' (1984: 128). When the accountants assumed prominence at Ferranti in the early years of the twentieth century, for example, we have seen that they took all the managerial decisions including the detail of the company's product range (Wilson, 1988: 82). In 1906, the Scot James Ivory, with his successful background in the investment trust business, became a director in the Standard Life Insurance Company and was closely involved in formulating its investment policy (Munn, 1990*a*: 408).

Indeed, accountants became company directors for a remarkable variety of reasons which, together, give some clues to the cause of the upward trend in their board membership in the twentieth century. In this early period, some accountants were on the board because they were wealthy shareholders in their own right, which corresponded with the contemporary practice of drawing directors from the companies' major shareholders. Table 12 suggests that a fair number of the leading accountants of the period came from comfortable and sometimes wealthy backgrounds, and many went on to amass fortunes, enhanced by profitable investment in corporate securities. When Quilter died in 1888, for example, the pre-eminent Victorian accountant left £332,000 of his estate in shares, including £276,000 in railway shares alone. It was therefore quite natural that he should have held appointments as director or chairman of a number of railway companies (Bywater, 1985*b*: 793). In a similar vein, Harmood-Banner inherited wealth and succeeded to a place on the board of a coal and iron company on the death of his father-in-law (Davenport-Hines, 1985*a*: 43). Indeed Harmood-Banner's own father, an accountant who left approximately £160,000 when he died in 1878, was also a company director, serving as chairman of both the Liverpool & Harrington Water Co. and Liverpool & Harrington Gas Co. (Davenport-Hines, 1985*a*: 43).

Many accountant-directors were on the boards of companies that they had been instrumental in setting up. Almost two-thirds of capital that flowed through the London Stock Exchange from 1865 to 1914 went abroad (Davis and Huttenback, 1988: 56), and a common feature of this period was the appointment of accountants to the boards of companies established in London to raise the finance required to conduct business overseas—what have been called 'free standing companies' (Wilkins, 1988: 259–82), but which we will style 'foreign'. It is likely that most of these 'foreign' companies were speculative in nature, and the name of a reputable accountant on the board might have been expected to increase the marketability of their shares.

All the accountants involved with 'foreign' companies in 1911, identified in the sample which forms the basis for Table 15, were from City firms (compared with 48% of all the accountant-directors identified), and their role seems to have been different from that of accountant-directors in most 'domestic' companies. The *Directory of Directors* reveals that they appear to have specialized in 'foreign' companies to the exclusion of others, and they were also more likely to have multiple directorships, giving rise to what has been described as 'clusters' of interests (Wilkins, 1988: 266). For example, F. G. Clarke of the SIAA was a director in seven companies, all operating in the nitrate mining sector, six of which were formed at the height of the 1904–6 boom in nitrate shares. Patrick Gow of the ICAEW held seven directorships in Far Eastern rubber and tea plantations, while George Thomas Rait, a founder member of the ICAEW, was on the board of no fewer than fourteen companies (chairman of five), with interests in property and mines in Canada, Uruguay, and Australia. An incorporated accountant, G. Parker, was also on the board of two of Rait's gold-mining concerns, both wound up in 1911. J. M. Fells, of the SIAA, was director of three mining companies operating in Burma and Australia formed between 1906 and 1908, two of which were also being wound up in 1911. Indeed, the companies in which accountants became involved were typical of foreign mining ventures generally in this period in terms of their lack of success and their short-lived nature.

Accountants, active in the foreign sector, also seem to have been involved as promoters of these speculative enterprises. Recent research into international mining investment of this period refers to accountants as company promoters (Harvey and Press, 1990: 98), and our survey identified a number of apparent examples. C. I. Beavis of the LAA was on the boards of seven Australian and Malayan mining companies formed between 1897 and 1904, and at least one of his roles as the instigator of companies may be inferred from the fact that they all shared Beavis's address in Leadenhall Street (Matthews, 1993: 210–11). Charles Samuel Beale of the CAA was a director in three mining companies, formed in

1909/10 at the height of the speculative boom in foreign mineral mining, and all operated from the address of Beale's accountancy firm (Matthews, 1993: 211). Speculative company promotion was not confined to foreign issues, though it was an untypical feature of the domestic companies with which accountants were closely associated. The chartered accountant William Lacon Threlford, however, was a founding member of the boards of four cinema companies (chairman of two), all formed in the boom period in 'electric theatres' around 1909.

The majority of accountant-directors in the period up to the First World War, however, were unlikely to have held this position due to factors such as wealth, inheritance, or speculative company promotion. Our research suggests that a high proportion had been consciously appointed to the board in recognition of their personal qualities or their professional expertise. This, despite the fact that, during this period (Table 15, row 9), almost all accountant-directors remained in practice and were therefore not full-time salaried employees. As was to be expected, a number of biographies show that accountants were drafted into the boardroom after having impressed companies in their professional role as auditor. This is a process with a long history. In 1825 the Scot James Brown was elected auditor of the Edinburgh Life Assurance Company and, within fifteen years, had become a director (Anderson, 1994: 151). Frederick Whinney was a director of the London, Tilbury and Southend Railway in the 1890s, his firm having been the company's auditors since 1892. Likewise, Deloitte, Plender, Griffiths & Co. had audited the books of the Great Western Railway for many years before Griffiths gave up his partnership to join their client's board (Kettle, 1957: 25). John Dent became the Co-operative Permanent Society's first auditor in 1884 and was elected to the board in 1920 (Cassell, 1984: 15). Again, when margarine makers Van den Berghs took over Meadow Dairy in 1909, they installed their auditor Basil Mayhew on the board; while in 1935 Mayhew accepted a directorship in J. & J. Coleman Ltd., having been the auditor of some of its subsidiaries (Jones, 1985a: 208, 209).

Other accountants clearly made an impression serving as company secretary. Henry Portlock of the firm of incorporated accountants Portlock & Smith, having previously acted as secretary to Mappin & Webb, the Oxford Street silversmiths, was appointed liquidator in 1908 and became a director of the re-formed company. Touche, whom we discussed above, made his mark at the newly formed Industrial and General Trust, in 1889, as its company secretary. After the financial crisis of the early 1890s, he served as manager with the job of reconstructing the company and restoring it to profitability. Four years later, in 1898, he was appointed a director and, in 1908, chairman (Richards, 1986: 540). In similar circumstances, Touche also became director and chairman of the Trustees & Securities Corporation in 1901. According to his biographer, Richards,

He quickly became prominent in the investment world and his personal reputation as a man with great financial flair and a personal integrity which was above suspicion was well known in the City and far beyond and his services as a director were much sought after. (1986: 540)

When Touche died in 1935, 'he was a director of twelve major trust companies and chairman of nine of them' (Richards, 1981: 4). His obituary notice acclaimed him 'as essentially a creator and restorer of the trust company movement' (Richards, 1986: 540), and as responsible for establishing many of the principles of administration on which such companies continue to be managed. Touche also served as chairman of the Anglo-Argentine Tramways Company, the Midland Railway Company of Western Australia, and the Mexican Southern Railway (*Accountant*, 13 July 1935: 39). James Ivory, too, was in the vanguard of the investment trust movement that had started in 1873, becoming one of the most successful fund managers in Edinburgh. In 1898, he set up the British Assets Trust with a capital of £15,000. By 1928 he had attained board level, which position he held until his death in 1939, by which time the fund held over £7 million in investments (Munn, 1990a: 408).

We have noted, above, that accountants sometimes became involved with companies in financial difficulty, and their success in helping to reconstruct these ailing enterprises also sometimes led to board membership. Tait, the saviour of Ferranti, in common with Touche, made his reputation in company reconstruction and, again following in his senior partner's footsteps, the *Directory of Directors* 1911 lists him as chairman of five companies and a director of a further six. Tait was 'acknowledged in the City as a force in industrial finance' (Davenport-Hines, 1986b: 429); 'in his comparatively short career'—he died, in 1930, at the age of 54—'he had become one of the best-known entrepreneurs of the business world and had been able to amass a fortune of about half a million pounds' (Richards, 1981: 20).

Another accountant who had outstanding success in rehabilitating companies was the Scot George Jamieson, admitted to the Edinburgh Society in 1854 and, in the following year, a partner in the firm Lindsay, Jamieson & Haldane, which eventually became part of Arthur Young (see Appendix). Jamieson, one of the leaders of Edinburgh's late Victorian business community, was director of seven companies, including the Royal Bank of Scotland and the North British & Mercantile Insurance Co., 'both at the heart of Scotland's close-knit financial community' (Schmitz, 1990: 410). Already a small shareholder in the Arizona Copper Co. Ltd., set up in 1882 to mine and smelt copper in America, Jamieson was elected chairman to salvage the company as it hit trouble when copper prices tumbled. He reconstructed the firm, modernized the mines, and set it on the road to recovery. It became comfortably the most profitable British mining investment in North America before 1920, and one of the best

British overseas investments of the period. Significantly, Jamieson steered the company to a position of technological leadership, 'pioneering both copper leaching and low grade ore extraction techniques' (Schmitz, 1990: 410).

Accountants joined the boards of distressed companies in other ways with which we are today familiar. Again, it is possible to trace the linkages by reference to the contents of the *Directory of Directors* and *The Stock Exchange Official Year-Book*. Frank Woodley Mason, for example, had for some time been the auditor of Charrington's brewery when financial difficulties caused it to pass its dividend in 1906. He was immediately drafted onto the board. At National Explosives, based in Cornwall, Charles Jermyn Ford, who had been auditor of the troubled company, was appointed receiver in 1908, and joined the board after the company's reconstruction. He did the same after acting as liquidator at the Saccharin Corporation in 1909. At Singer, the bicycle and motor manufacturers, the accountant, receiver, and manager appointed by the debenture holders re-formed the company and installed the leading City accountant Arthur Charles Bourner on the board in 1909. When the Quebec Central Railway defaulted on its debentures, in 1887, an accountant was appointed as secretary to the bondholders' committee and subsequently became company secretary; in 1906, he was promoted to a position on the board. Others were drafted straight in, at board level, such as J. M. Fells as chairman of Kent Collieries, re-formed in 1905.

The accountant's role in amalgamations, discussed above, was another common conduit to board membership. This sequence of events is well illustrated by the burst of mergers in the late nineteenth century. Following formation of the Bradford Dyers' Association, created by the combination of 22 firms in 1898, two (possibly three) accountants joined the executive committee of the board. A chartered accountant was an executive director of the Calico Printers' Association, which resulted from a merger of 46 companies in 1899, and another was on the board of the Bleachers' Association, created by a merger of 53 firms in 1900 (Hannah, 1983: 23). The formation, in 1910, of the British Aluminium Company from the federation of a number of small firms comprising most of the aluminium industry was largely attributed to the work of Tait who became the company's first chairman (Richards, 1981: 16). A reasonable inference might be that, in the above cases, top management had reached the conclusion that it was useful to have accountants in the boardroom to wrestle with the problems of co-ordination, control, and consolidation of these unwieldy new combines.

It does not appear that companies with accountants on their boards conform to any obvious size pattern. For example, there were accountants on the boards of the largest companies in the land—like the GWR, with a market value of £92.3 million the third largest company in the country in 1904/5 (Wardley, 1991: 278). There were also accountant-directors at the Calico Printers' Association, with capital of £8.2 million, and Charrington's the brewers with £4 million, respectively the fifth and 22nd largest industrial concerns in 1905 (Payne, 1967: 539). At the other end of the scale, as we have seen, Bourner was on the board of Singer, the cycle, and later motor, manufacturer, while the Birmingham accountant John Arter was chairman of the James Cycle company. Both of these companies had an authorized capital of only £50,000.

Moreover, as the above indicates, there seems to be no pattern as to the type of companies with accountant-directors. These included: railways and other utility companies, such as gas, electric, and water; financial services, such as banks and insurance; and a wide range of manufacturing concerns. Among our 1911 sample (used for Table 15), there was a good spread of textile, steel, and engineering firms, while the so-called 'new industries' also had their share of accountants. For example, in 1911 Arthur Henry Gibson, a Birmingham accountant and ICAEW council member, was on the board of the local Lancaster Motor Company and also W. & T. Avery, the weighing-scales maker. Another provincial ICAEW council member, John Gordon from Leeds, was a director of Henry Berry, hydraulic machinery makers, and chairman of T. H. Bracken, paper makers.

The inclusion of directors on the board was not, of course, a guarantee against corporate collapse. Again, tracing company histories through *The Stock Exchange Official Year-Book* from the earliest years reveals that the Lancashire Watch Company first registered in 1888, for example, fell on hard times and was reconstructed in 1897 with two accountants on a six-member board. By 1911, it had failed to pay a dividend and had accumulated losses of £361,496. The West India and Panama Telegraph Company had an accountant on the board from 1883, but still struggled to pay a dividend in 1911. Likewise, the New Peterborough Brick Company, where the accountant C. H. Wells had been a director since 1899, was still not paying a dividend in 1911. Finally, the accountant E. R. Painter seems to have been instrumental in the formation by merger of the Petersfield and Selsey Gas Company in 1901 which, unusually for a gas concern, remained unprofitable until Painter's departure in 1911.

ENTREPRENEURS AND EMPLOYEES

Companies, as they grew in size and increasingly went public during the late nineteenth and early twentieth centuries, established and expanded their accounts departments. The responsibilities of these departments included drawing up, for publication, the financial statements that were the subject of the annual audit, namely the balance sheet and profit and loss account. There is little detailed information available concerning the historical development of the accounts department, but we do know that, even before the industrial revolution, firms of any size already had their own counting house. In the nineteenth century, inevitably led by the railway companies, these offices developed into sizeable bureaucracies. Some of the bookkeepers and unqualified accountants made their way up the management ladder. For example, in 1868, having been the accountant at the Lancashire & Yorkshire and then the Midland Railway, Samuel Swarbrick was appointed general manager of the Great Eastern Railway (Jones, 1981: 116–17). Such elevation, however, was probably rare.

We have drawn attention to the fact that Dicksee considered accounts offices to be 'indifferently staffed', that is, staffed by unqualified accountants, at least down to the First World War (quoted in Jones, 1981: 116). Even before the war, however, the larger or more efficient companies began to recruit chief accountants and secretaries from accountancy firms, and often from their auditors. This represented the culmination of an interesting sequence of events. In the eighteenth and nineteenth centuries, individuals, who had often gained their bookkeeping knowledge in business, left to establish independent accounting practices. This led, in due course, to the establishment of a new profession, chartered accountancy, whose members, by the end of the nineteenth century, were reversing the earlier trend and leaving public practice in increasing numbers for industry.

This movement, accelerating through the twentieth century, created a significant division among qualified accountants, between those who worked in a practice, either as partners or clerks, and those who worked as employees in industry and commerce. Until recently, an accountant who worked outside public practice was said to have 'left the profession', and tended to be regarded as a second-class citizen. Indeed, some of the accountants who have moved to industry continue to complain that they are still perceived that way by their professional body (see, for example, the views expressed by John Corrin, Peter Davies, and Richard Close profiled, respectively, by Irvine, 1993*a*, 1993*b*, 1994). Some Victorian accountants probably shared the prevailing snobbery, still perhaps with us, whereby high status was accorded to the 'learned professions', such as the Church and the law, to which accountancy aspired, whereas to be 'in trade was scorned' (Mumford, 1991: 124). The ICAEW's initial constitution barred chartered accountants from following 'any business or occupation other than that of Public Accountant or some business which in the opinion of council is incident thereto or consistent therewith' (section 19 (3)). There is no evidence, however, that the ICAEW ever disciplined members who, once qualified, went to work in industry, and in the revised charter of 1948 this restriction on non-accounting work was explicitly applied only to members in practice (Howitt, 1966: 183).

The distinction between practitioners and employees was, in this period, as it still is today, sometimes blurred. Some accountants, though remaining in practice, clearly devoted much of their time to a single client. For example, Jonas Dearnley Taylor was in practice as J. D. Taylor & Co., Halifax, when, as secretary, he took the minutes of the first meeting of the Halifax Building Society in 1852 (Hobson, 1953: 16). At the annual meeting of the Society, held fifty years later, the president described Taylor as 'really the founder of the Society' (Hobson, 1953: 53). He was its chief executive between 1853 and 1902, and 'it was chiefly owing to his organising ability, his persevering efforts, his power of concentration and his strict integrity that it now stood in a higher position than ever before' (Hobson, 1953: 53). A director of the Halifax described Taylor 'as having a genius for organisation. In particular he had a talent for book-keeping and patented several labour-saving devices in that connection' (Hobson, 1953: 56). But Taylor remained in practice, 'which in the early days of the Society must have provided him with the greater part of his means of subsistence' (Hobson, 1953: 56). Unsurprisingly, his work at the Halifax meant that he took little part in his accountancy firm's activities in later years, leaving this to his son.

Although exceptional, there are early examples of accountants transferring from public practice to industry. For example, Alfred Richard Hollebone, who was probably William Welch Deloitte's first articled clerk in 1861, was promoted to partner in 1867 but resigned six years later to join the stockbroking firm of Hollebone Brothers & Trench; he later became senior partner. In 1877, James Halliday left Deloitte's Manchester branch partnership, styled Deloitte & Halliday, and later became managing director and subsequently chairman of the Manchester and Liverpool District Bank (Kettle, 1957: 20). Hollebone may conceivably have been a member of one or other of the five bodies (formed 1870–7) which merged to form the ICAEW in 1880 (most likely the Institute of Accountants in London), but we have not been able to confirm this possibility due to the absence of comprehensive surviving lists of members for those bodies. *The Accountants' Directory for 1877*, however, shows that Halliday was a member of the Manchester Institute of Accountants (Harper, 1877: 8), and we do know, of course (see Chapter 2), that Thomas Young Strachan was not only a member of the ICAEW but also on its council when he resigned his seat, in 1888, to join the Mortgage Insurance Corporation.

Evidence of early transfers from public practice into industry is more readily available in the case of Scottish accountants, partly reflecting an oversupply of professional accountants following the establishment of three professional bodies, although this could not have been the explanation in the case of the first known transfer. Robert Aitken, a partner in Henry Paul's Glasgow accountancy practice, left to join a stockbroking partnership in 1831, and later became a founder member and subsequently chairman of the Glasgow Stock Exchange (Mann Judd Gordon, 1967: 12). In 1856, G. A. Esson left his partnership with Donald Lindsay to become Accountant in Bankruptcy at Register House. He took with him as an assistant James Watson, who later became head clerk to the Bankruptcy Office. In 1871, Watson was appointed manager of the Standard Property Investment Co., holding the office for 37 years (Stewart, 1977: 161). David F. Park was admitted to the Edinburgh Society in 1873, but spent virtually all of his professional career with Crédit Foncier of Mauritius in London, which he joined two years later (Stewart, 1977: 130). James Pringle of the Edinburgh Society (1870) also chose to make his career outside account-ing, becoming a partner in John Robertson & Co., stockbrokers. He also acted as director of a number of companies, including the Scottish New Zealand Investment Co., and was chairman of the Scottish Lands and Buildings Co. Ltd. for 34 years (Stewart, 1977: 141). William Ross qualified in Edinburgh in 1869 and, after spending about eight years in practice in the City, went to the Far East and ended up in business as a merchant in Yokohama (Stewart, 1977: 149). T. P. Gillespie was apprenticed to Dr J. Turnbull Smith, LL D, CA, and was admitted to the Edinburgh Society in 1878. He never seems to have been in practice and spent most of his career as manager of a paper mill at Longcroft, Linlithgow (Stewart, 1977: 82).

The list continues. William W. Naismith served a five-year apprentice-ship with McClelland, MacKinnon & Blyth before leaving, it seems, imme-diately on qualification in 1879, to spend the whole of his career with the County Fire Office (Stewart, 1977: 128). John Lamb qualified with the Edinburgh Society in 1874 and practised for a few years before leaving public practice, in 1880, to join the Scottish Provident Institution as chief assistant. To underpin this change of career, he became a fellow of the Faculty of Actuaries in 1885, having taken first place in the final examina-tions, and became secretary of Scottish Provident in 1890 (Stewart, 1977: 96). Nathaniel Spens was in practice for a number of years and served on the Glasgow Institute's Council, 1885–7, before moving to London, in 1890, to serve for 38 years as the chairman and managing director of Stock Conversion Trust Ltd., as well as being actively involved in the direction and management of numerous finance and investment companies, and with railway finance (Stewart, 1977: 155). J. H. W. Rowland, having served his apprenticeship with Lindsay, Jamieson & Haldane, and spent some time in partnership with G. T. Chiene, and also having qualified as an actuary, was appointed secretary to the Standard Life Assurance Co. In 1892 the company moved him to London as their general secretary and he was in due course promoted to manager (Stewart, 1977: 147).

A few professional accountants left public practice to become entrepre-neurs, with the extraordinary business career of John Reeves Ellerman a shining example of this type of move. Ellerman left Quilter, Ball & Co. to set up his own accountancy business, J. R. Ellerman & Co., in 1887. Five years later, when the great shipowner Frederick Leyland collapsed and died, Ellerman formed a syndicate which acquired and reorganized Leyland & Co.. Ellerman became chairman and managing director, ceasing to practise as an accountant from around 1895. There followed a period of rapid expansion with Ellerman's method being

to purchase control of old-established shipping firms which, though still possessing a perfectly sound fleet and trading network, and much business goodwill, had entered into a period of entrepreneurial decline, often because of the incompetence of the heirs of the firm's founder. (Rubinstein, 1984: 249)

Ellerman is seen as the 'forerunner of the modern professionally-trained business manager . . . [and] far more than a shipowner, he was a profit maximising financier by training and inclination' (Rubinstein, 1984: 250–1). He was a 'loner', who had not the benefit of a major public school or a university, and 'owed nothing to family friends or business associates' (Rubinstein, 1984: 257). His success is attributed to a huge 'business intellect', and the fact he was 'a professionally trained and highly competent accountant . . . strikingly able to use his professional knowledge to his independent advantage' (Rubinstein, 1984: 257–8). Ellerman was hugely successful and, when he died in 1933, he left the massive sum of £36,685,000, by far the largest British fortune left by any industrialist up to that time (Rubinstein, 1984: 255) and perhaps, in real terms, since.

Bernhard Heymann Binder is another example of a chartered accountant leaving public practice for industry. His career commenced as a junior clerk in Yorkshire and later Nottingham. Thereafter, having taught himself shorthand, he moved to London as a correspondence clerk, and then joined the office of McAuliffe, Davis & Hope, with whom he qualified in 1908 (Parker, 1980*a*: n.p.). He left shortly afterwards to help run various public utility companies in South America, including the Brazil Railway Company and the Brazilian Traction, Light and Power Company, first as accountant and financial manager, then as director (*The Times*, 12 July 1966).

Ellerman and Binder were entrepreneurs rather than employees, but there are many more clear-cut examples of leading accountants moving from practice into employment in top management as we move forward in time. Allan Macdiarmid qualified as a Scottish chartered accountant in 1905 and, by 1910, had joined the steel makers Stewarts & Lloyds Ltd., holding the post of secretary and, from 1918, executive director (Boswell, 1983: 64). James Hornby Jolly, the son of a bookkeeper, qualified as a chartered accountant in 1909, having served his articles with Bowman & Grimshaw in Blackpool (Jones, 1985*b*: 524). Following a move to Cardiff to work as clerk to W. B. Peat & Co., Jolly left practice to work for the Blaenavon Co. in 1911 to implement his own proposals for improving the management of the concern. This move represents an early example of a chartered accountant joining a client, previously investigated, to give practical effect to recommendations made. In 1918, he became company secretary to Guest Keen & Nettlefolds at their head office in Smethwick, and we follow his career more fully in the next Chapter. The first example we have found of a professional accountant joining the staff of an audit client, however, is Charles Weatherley who left Cooper Brothers & Co. to join the British South Africa company in 1889, but returned, following the death of two of the Cooper brothers, as partner in 1893, remaining there until his death in 1917 ([Benson] 1954: 7, 30).

These then are examples of some of the major figures in the accountancy profession who had moved over to industry before the First World War. With regard to the generality of the profession, there is a diversity of views concerning the extent of their employment in industry and commerce at the beginning of the twentieth century. According to a contemporary, Richard A. Witty, author of *How to Become a Qualified Accountant*, published in 1906: 'Many accountant's clerks are successful in obtaining appointments as accountants and secretaries to companies and other commercial concerns' (quoted in Jones, 1981: 116). Also, 'there has during the past few years grown up a big demand for qualified accountants to fill every kind of important position in the mercantile world'. It is quite possible, however, that Witty was overstating the case in order to improve the marketability of his book. Other writers date the transfer of manpower, on any significant scale, rather later. According to one view, 'from early in the twentieth-century members of the professional auditing bodies left public practice in increasing numbers . . . [and] by 1930 the majority of British accountants' worked in industry and commerce (Mumford, 1991: 124). Further, 'the move of chartered accountants into industry accelerated from the 1930s' (Mumford, 1991: 125).

Table 16 offers estimates of numbers in industry based on sampling the lists of members of the accountants' societies. It reveals that just 7% of professional accountants worked outside public practice in 1911, and that the move into industry in significant numbers does indeed date from the inter-war period. Whilst the ICAEW membership list for 1911 does show one member employed by a savings bank and another in a textile mill, overwhelmingly, members of the ICAEW remained in practice; fewer than 1% worked elsewhere at that date. This low figure probably owes little to the implied proscription, noted earlier, on outside employment by the ICAEW. It was not against the rules of the other accountancy bodies and was undoubtedly more common among their members, though still relatively insignificant before the outbreak of the First World War.

The sample from the membership lists revealed that 6% of SIAA members and 5% of the predecessor bodies of the ACCA (CA, CAA, and LAA) worked 'outside' the profession in 1911. Among these, the most common occupation was as borough or county treasurer, or a lesser role in the

Table 16. Estimates of the proportion and implied number of accountants 'in business', 1891–1991

	1891 (%)	1911 (%)	1931 (%)	1951 (%)	1971 (%)	1991 (%)
ICAEW	1	1	12	28	36	50
SIAA	3	6	38	52		
ICAS	1	3	15	35	49	40
ACCA		5	38	58	60	70
All (see *Notes*)	5	7	29	48	53	64
Implied numbers	128	642	6,253	17,491	39,960	94,917
% of employed population			0.03	0.07	0.16	0.36

Notes: The data are based on a count in 1891 and 1911 and a random sampling from every tenth page of the membership lists of each society's yearbooks for the later years. For 1891 and 1911 there was a clear indication of the nature of employment for almost all names. By 1931, however, the number of 'unknowns' rose to a third or more of the sample and it is possible that these were skewed toward those working in business. However, Fea (1957: 6, 7) did the same exercise and reached comparable figures for the ICAEW members in business of 16% in 1932 and 32% in 1957. The ICAEW's own 1992 figure was 51% (*ICAEW Membership Questionnaire*, 1992: 2). Our % total for 'All' accountants assumes ICWA/CIMA and IMTA/CIPFA at 100% 'in business' and weights the figures according to the relative importance of each body in the total number of accountants, as in Table 8. This % is then used to imply the numbers 'in business' in Britain using Table 8, column 12, and these numbers are given as a % of total UK employment using OECD, *Quarterly Labour Force Statistics*.

Sources: As for Table 8.

treasury departments of local councils. Around two-thirds of SIAA members working outside an accountancy firm were in local government in 1911—a connection which, as we noted in Chapter 3, dated from the Society's foundation. About a third of the non-practising members of the CAA and a fifth of those in the LAA also worked in local government. Significantly, none of the membership lists make reference to jobs in central government which, traditionally, trained its own accounting staff. Other positions held by SIAA members included company secretaries of gas works, collieries and manufacturing companies, and 'accountants' working for water boards, banks and insurance firms, and, *inter alia*, a theatre company. The CAA and LAA had members employed by home and foreign railways and gas and electricity companies; one was the chief accountant of Harrods, another was the secretary and superintendent of a hospital.

CONCLUDING COMMENTS

The period reviewed in this chapter, principally the mid-nineteenth century to the outbreak of the First World War, saw the emergence of accounting as an organized profession, a rapid growth in the work undertaken, and changes in the relative importance of different areas of specialization. Insolvency work was an important factor in the rise to prominence of a number of City practices, and for some of them remained the major source of revenue for much of the period. Naturally, however, the scope for this work was very much a function of the general economic climate, with improvements in systems of internal organization and changes in statute law also seen to be important independent variables in this relationship.

It was the growing importance of the audit function which brought the most significant growth in work to the public accountant in the period covered by this Chapter, and the driving force here was the rise of the limited liability company. The stimulus which this provided for increasing the average size of the business unit led to the need for checks by management on employees and by shareholders on both of these groups. The areas of risk were the loss of money through embezzlement and inefficiency, and the concealment of financial problems and inefficiency through the manipulation of financial reports prepared for management and published for consumption by external user groups. The professional accountant, who had based much of his initial reputation on the ability to administer efficiently the financial affairs of individuals and companies following business failure, sometimes also requiring him to unravel the machinations of ingenious fraudsters, was well qualified to undertake such work. Over a relatively short time-period the professional replaced the incumbent amateur shareholder as auditor of at least Britain's largest companies.

It was therefore the decision to register a company with limited liability, and, perhaps to an extent, the arrangement of a stock exchange listing, that imposed a greater level of discipline on companies' accounting and auditing practices. During the second half of the nineteenth century, irrespective of the law, companies' articles frequently included requirements, not only for the appointment of an auditor, but sometimes for the appointment of a professional or, more specifically, a chartered accountant (Edwards and Webb, 1985: 188–9). Equally, these companies published accounts comprising balance sheets and, in many cases, a certain amount of profit and loss account data either in a separate statement, or in the directors' report, or on the face of the balance sheet. Thus we see evidence, within a *laissez-faire* environment, of market forces producing a voluntary improvement in levels of accountability and therefore the efficiency of the market by improving the credibility of published data (see also Watts, 1977; Watts and Zimmerman, 1979, 1983).

The changing management/ownership structure of joint-stock companies required modifications to be made to the nature of the audit process reflecting, in turn, the need to revise the principal audit objectives (Chandler et al., 1993). Transitions in the late nineteenth century, as today, did not proceed smoothly, and there occurred litigation, sometimes against leading accountants, and much public debate. It is a significant feature of this period that leading accountants became fully involved in the debate, reflecting a healthy willingness to face public criticism and play a full part in attempting to obtain the consensus necessary to help close any 'expectations gap' (Chandler and Edwards, 1996), that is the gap between what the users of published accounts expect from auditors and what they think they are currently receiving (Parker, 1992: 26).

We have seen that certain legislative regulations required companies to arrange for an external audit, and there were one or two provisions that pointed to the need to appoint an accountant to this position, but there was no mention of an obligation to enlist the services of a professional. It is therefore clear that the development of the professional audit was market driven, in the main, and, although work undertaken was sometimes the subject of strong criticism, the increasing engagement of the professional reflects a broad-based recognition of the value of this business service.

Firms of accountants also secured a wide range of business appointments which we have explored in the section entitled 'Consultancy'. We have used this term as it is usually applied today, namely as a 'catch-all' category to cover activities not captured by the headings auditing, taxation, and insolvency. The involvement of professionals in the installation of cost accounting systems and in advising management on the significance of this information is of sufficient importance in the context of this study to justify separate consideration. The driving force here, again, was the growth in size of business organizations, giving rise to the need for financial information, in place of direct supervision, to fill the gap which had emerged between management and the shop floor. The interest shown by professionals in this source of work is reflected by their willingness to devote time to contributing to the emerging literature on the subject.

The period also saw professional accountants becoming directly involved in the management of companies, in two different ways. First, there were those professional accountants, small in number but significant as a proportion of their population, who sat on the boards of quoted companies. This was the start of a trend which today sees accountants as comfortably the dominant professional grouping in the corporate boardroom. Second, we find a few professionally qualified accountants leaving public practice for full-time employment in business. Once again, this was the start of a trend which, in this case, accelerated rapidly during the inter-war period. The pervasive importance of the audit for the growth of the accountancy profession is reflected in the fact that it was the source of many of these engagements, that is, the accountant transferred his talents to the company which he had previously audited.

The 1995 survey of the fee income of the 50 largest UK professional accountancy firms showed that they earned 9% of total income from insolvency work, 40% from audit and accountancy, 23% from consul-tancy, 24% from tax, and 4% from 'Other' sources (*Accountancy*, July 1995: 19). We can therefore see that, although the proportions of income derived from different areas of specialization may have changed significantly since 1914, the broad range of work undertaken by today's leading prac-tices was firmly established by that date.

5

Accountants in the Economic Maelstrom: The First World War and the Inter-war Years

ECONOMIC BACKGROUND

The inter-war years were turbulent times for the British economy and it was certainly a period when great structural change was under way, although economic historians now doubt whether the period was unusual in this respect. Once-mighty industries, such as coal mining and cotton textiles, began what we now know to be all but terminal decline, while so-called 'new industries', like motor manufacture, rose in their place. The main problem with the old industries was that competitive weaknesses, already visible before the war, now became more apparent. These failings were particularly evident in the great staple industries that had once made Britain the 'workshop of the world'. The old industries were the source of the high level of structural unemployment in the inter-war period, while the lack of demand for their output left them with chronic over-capacity. Unemployment rarely fell below one million or 10% of the insured workforce, reaching 18% in 1921 and 22% in 1932 (Howson, 1981: 265). Companies grew in size, family firms continued to decline, and management gradually became more 'professional'.

While there was an irreversible decline in the old staple industries, structural change in the inter-war period produced some positive results, in particular the growth in the so-called 'new' industries. Although previously slow to take root in Britain, the beneficial impact of wartime conditions on industries such as electric power and electrical goods, motor vehicles and road transport, synthetic fibres, processed foods, and new chemicals and drugs, together with the growing service sector and the booming building industry, ensured that overall growth rates in the economy, particularly in the 1930s, were at or above the UK's long-run average. These new industries, together with the service sector, largely account for the high level of company formation during the inter-war period. New company registrations reached hitherto unequalled levels in the post-First World War boom of 1919/20, remained high during the Great Slump, and scaled new peaks in the late 1930s (Hudson, 1989: 119; Figure 3). Between 1920 and 1940, the number of limited companies increased by 93% (derived from Table 13).

During the inter-war period, the stock exchange became more important as a primary market in corporate securities, this despite the fact that four-fifths of all investment continued to be financed from retained earnings (28% of earnings on average in manufacturing were ploughed back) (Hannah, 1983: 62). The stock market's growing importance may be attributed to the buoyant demand for capital, particularly from the new industries, and family firms selling out and/or going public. There were, for example, 569 firms in manufacturing and distribution quoted on the London Stock Exchange in 1907, with a capitalized value of £500 million. By 1924 and 1939 there were 719 and 1,712 companies respectively, worth £2,500 million at the latter date (Hannah, 1983: 61). Table 13 shows that private companies vastly outnumbered public companies, but the latter accounted for 57% of all profits in the early 1920s and 71% in 1951 (Hannah, 1983: 61). The growth in the number and size of firms quoted on the stock exchange, therefore, provided scope for professional accountants to increase both their number and prosperity during this period. They proved equal to the challenge.

As we have argued in previous chapters, these churning developments in the fundamentals of the economy had a determining influence on the changes in the accountant's work, which, in this period, were indeed profound. It is probably fair to say that, during the inter-war period, the accountancy profession first reached national importance. Their rapid growth in numbers, wartime service, brief notoriety during the Royal Mail case (Edwards, 1976), their role in rescuing crippled companies, and their evident rise as business managers generally brought accountants a certain public prominence not previously enjoyed. Chapter 2 illustrates how accountancy firms and the profession itself to an extent sprang out of business, with people who had developed their bookkeeping skills in industry and commerce leaving to set up as specialist accountants. In the inter-war period, the reverse process, which began in the pre-war period, gathered pace, with accountants trained by accountancy firms moving to industry for employment. This sequence of events was undoubtedly related to the growing bureaucratization of capitalism during this period, itself a function of increasing scale. For example, after allowing for inflation, the largest manufacturing company in 1934/5, Imperial Tobacco, had a market valuation four times the size of the largest in 1904/5, J. & P. Coates (Wardley, 1991: 278–9). Moreover, mass production in the new industries led to an overall increase in plant size. Factories employing over 1,500 workers in manufacturing rose from 15% of total employment in 1935 to 24% in 1951 (Hannah, 1983: 138). The increase in the size of firms led inevitably to changes in management structures.

Business historians talk of the 'corporate lag' in Britain, by this time, compared to the mature 'managerial capitalism' of the USA. In his survey of the major British companies of this period, Gourvish found 'a

continuation of the unitary or departmental form, a preference for inter-
nally-recruited directors, and the retention of owners in entrepreneurial
positions' (1987: 33). Only two companies (ICI and Unilever) seem to have
'achieved "managerial status" by 1939, with salaried managers dominating key decision-making at the top, supported by a structured hierarchy
below' (Gourvish, 1987: 34). According to Hannah, only ICI (between 1928
and 1931) adopted a truly divisionalized form of structure, most fully
analysed in the literature by Alfred Chandler (1990). In its purest form,
this involved major capital and other strategic decisions being made at
head office, and manufacturing carried on by semi-autonomous divisions.
Spillers, Turner & Newall, and Dunlop were said to have progressed some
way down this road, while even at ICI there was still a centralized pricing
policy.

The growth of the large-scale company through takeover, merger, and
rationalization during the inter-war period in Britain was commonly
structured as an investment holding company (distinguishable from the
industrial holding company where an operating company also holds
shares in other companies), as parent, owning a range of, largely independent, operating subsidiaries. According to Kitchen, the holding company did not play a significant part in the early amalgamation waves at
the turn of the century, but it became important in the half-dozen years
before 1922, with notable examples being Imperial Tobacco, GKN, and
EMI (Kitchen, 1979: 87, 90).

Even if Britain lagged behind America, growth in corporate scale, whatever the corporate form, usually meant an increasing role for a head office
staffed with managers and clerks. The growth in this industrial bureaucracy was undeniable. Clerical workers grew from 887,000 or 4.8% of the
workforce in 1911 to 2,404,000 or 10.7% in 1951 (Perkin, 1989: 272). Administrative staff in manufacturing increased from 567,000, 11.8% of production operatives in 1924, to 1,201,000 or 19.7% of operatives in 1948
(Hannah, 1983: 72). Alongside this came the 'increased functional differ-
entiation of managerial tasks', amongst which flourished the accounts
department (Hannah, 1983: 78). Firms often had difficulty finding trained
managers and no more than a dozen major manufacturing companies
had graduate management training schemes in place during the 1930s
(Hannah, 1983: 88). Managers were recruited (or poached) from railway
companies, the Civil Service, the army, and of course accountancy firms.
According to Hannah, 'it was particularly through developments in accounting that the introduction of new methods for the oversight and
assessment of subsidiaries was encouraged and facilitated' (1983: 80). The
accountants 'were quickly familiarised with the problems of imposing
uniform accounting on a merger and of controlling capital expenditure
by forward budgeting' (Hannah, 1983: 86). Once again, therefore, we see
basic changes in the economic structure creating new opportunities for

trained accountants, towards which they were drawn by tempting salaries and career prospects.

This chapter examines the rise of the professional accountant in business management, in the inter-war period, in light of these economic and social upheavals. In the first three sections, we consider broad developments in the workload of professional firms during the period 1914–39, the contribution of accountants as accountants to the war effort, and the part which they played in the reorganization and rationalization of industries in the 1920s and 1930s. These studies are designed to demonstrate both how it was that work undertaken within a professional practice helped accountants develop the skills valued by industry and commerce, and the events and engagements that provided accountants with the opportunity to advertise the possession of a wide range of advisory skills on high-profile public platforms. We then proceed to an examination of the accelerating exodus to industry of professional accountants who qualified in public practice, and we measure the extent to which they reached board level and chief executive status.

PROFESSIONAL PRACTICE

Chapter 4 showed that professional firms had developed, in the period up to the First World War, to supply services which could be classified into the same four categories that are used today to analyse fee income, namely auditing, taxation, consultancy, and insolvency. The quarter of a century up to 1939 saw an expansion of the size of professional practices, with Table 17 giving some figures for five medium-sized and large firms.

We can therefore see that the fee income of each of these firms grew dramatically during the inter-war period. The number of employees required to service this rising level of operations no doubt also showed significant increase. Price, Waterhouse had 86 staff in 1900, 107 in 1913 (Jones, 1995: 99), and 409 by 1939, including eleven partners and 23 managers (Jones, 1995: 99, 404; Richards, 1950: 11). Turning to the breakdown of fee income, the historian is even less well served than for the pre-world war period, with the only figures available being those for Whinney, Smith & Whinney. There are really no grounds for believing that these figures (Table 14; see also Jones, 1981: 99 for the detailed amounts) are any more representative of the profession as a whole than was the case in earlier times but, with this caveat, the figures are rehearsed here since they are all that we have.

Insolvency income had been the mainstay of Whinney, Smith & Whinney, and its predecessor firms, during much of the nineteenth century, but this source of revenue collapsed dramatically in the inter-war

Table 17.   Fee income of professional firms, 1914–1939

Year	Whinney, Smith & Whinney (£)	C. Herbert Smith & Russell (Birmingham) (£)	Baker, Sutton & Co. (£)	Barton, Mayhew & Co. (£)	Price, Waterhouse & Co. (£)
1914	24,953	3,535	6,330	5,000	69,927
1923	83,464	12,161	27,680	19,482	211,306
1931	58,598	20,864	32,264	54,399[a]	319,327
1939	71,657	34,546	40,806	68,434[b]	381,334

[a] 1932 figure.
[b] 1940 figure.

Note: There were considerable fluctuations in the price level during the period 1914–39, but the overall rise between those two dates was 34.2% ('Back to an Age of Falling Prices', 1974: 62).

Sources: Jones, 1981: 264–5; 1995: 399.

period. In 1920, Whinney, Smith & Whinney earned £29,321 from insolvencies (45.1% of total fees); by 1930 this work earned just £3,733 (6.2% of the total), and by 1939 £1,580 (2.7%). These figures are not easy to explain and Jones, the firm's historian, makes no attempt at doing so. Table 13 shows that the number of liquidations did not fall in this period and, as might be expected, compulsory company liquidations rose dramatically during each of the depressions, probably reaching a greater total than ever before in 1933, and remained at a high level throughout the 1930s (Hudson, 1989: 104). Paradoxically, Whinney, Smith & Whinney earned most from insolvency in 1920, the peak year of the post-war boom, and their insolvency earnings seem to have dwindled into insignificance during the depths of the 1930s depression. The high earnings in some years in the 1920s are probably a reflection of the erratic impact of one or two large insolvencies. Nevertheless, the long-run downward trend in insolvency earnings seems clear.

So far as can be judged on the basis of information currently available, it seems likely that, for many firms, there was an increase in the relative importance of taxation and consultancy work between 1914 and 1939 but, in absolute terms, auditing was the main engine for growth. These trends are discussed in the remainder of this section.

As noted in Chapter 4, the increase in taxation work for accountants arose directly from the impact of the First World War. Between 1910 and 1914, income tax had been levied at the modest standard rate of 1s. 2d. in the pound (5.8%), and even this rate was paid only by the comfortably off;

supertax was also levied on the rich following Lloyd George's 1909 budget. During the war, income tax was raised to 5s. in the pound (25%) and 6s. (30%) in the pound in the immediate post-war period. Although it subsequently fell, income tax never reverted to the pre-war level, and rose again to a maximum of 10s. in the pound (50%) in 1942–6 (Mitchell, 1962: 427–9). An income of £10,000 in 1914 attracted tax at 8%; in 1919 this was 42.5% and it was still 39.1% in 1939 (Perkin, 1989: 246). Although estate duty had been introduced in 1894, at 8% on estates of £1 million and over, and extended by the 1909 budget to 15%, it was then, as now, relatively easy to evade its full rigours (Perkin, 1989: 245). During the inter-war period, estate duty rose to 40%, and the financial incentive to seek a means of avoidance, usually based on advice from an accountant, increased accordingly. Professional accountants, therefore, obtained the major slice of taxation work for individuals, but also for companies, with the latter, as a result of the First World War, facing the complexities of two new taxes: the Munitions Levy and Excess Profits Duty (in place until 1926) designed to curb profiteering (Margerison, 1980: 25; Jones, 1981: 133).

Fees from taxation work appear to have been virtually non-existent at Whinney, Smith & Whinney before the war, but rose to 6.3% of income by 1939 (Table 14). For Thomson McLintock, taxation is seen as the most important factor in the expansion of the firm for fifty years following the establishment of the London office in 1914. F. J. Cooksey joined the firm from the Inland Revenue early in 1920, and 'it has been said that William McLintock was very aware of the increasing importance of taxation work at this time and that with this usual astuteness "he brought or even some say bought" Cooksey as a specialist to run this department' (Winsbury, 1977: 34). Their tax department apparently grew at a phenomenal rate and, in addition, was 'always a big breeder of audit work' (Winsbury, 1977: 5). Cooper Brothers set up its tax department in 1925 (Coopers & Lybrand Deloitte, 1990), while Brown, Fleming & Murray (Jones, 1981: 210), Merrett, Son & Street (Viney Merretts, 1974: n.p.), and George A. Touche (Richards, 1981: 28) did so in the 1930s. At Price Waterhouse, the negotiation and agreement of Excess Profits Duty liabilities with the Inland Revenue fuelled the development of its tax department. A shipping line (probably the Royal Mail group) was making little headway in its negotiations with the Inland Revenue; Price Waterhouse were called in, recovered £250,000, and were paid 20,000 guineas for their services (Jones, 1995: 138). By 1930, the tax department headed by H. E. Seed numbered ten, and had swelled to 22 by 1939. Seed had started his career in the Post Office, but then qualified with a firm of incorporated accountants before joining Price Waterhouse. He qualified as a chartered accountant in 1933, but was barred from achieving partnership status by the firm's rule that only general practitioners could be admitted (Jones, 1995: 138–9).

Turning to consultancy work, a major source of new business for accountancy practices arose from the need to restructure industry to meet changes in world demand and the growth of foreign competition. In view of its implications, and its significance in raising the profile of professional accountants, this involvement is examined in a separate section entitled 'Special work in rationalization, rescues, and mergers'. Consultancy appointments in the kinds of areas discussed in Chapter 4—such as installing accounting systems, reporting on prospectuses, advising on company purchases and amalgamations, and managing companies in receivership and liquidation—naturally continued. We saw in the previous chapter that it was common for a company's auditors to become their ongoing management advisers, as the case of Sir Basil Mayhew serves to illustrate. From 1926, when he became Bowater's auditor, Mayhew virtually took over the financial affairs, reconstructed the company and continued to be its close adviser (Jones, 1981: 159–60). Although Chandler, in his attack on British family-run firms, argues that Bowater lacked a managerial team during this period (1990: 315), this highly professional advice from accounting consultants should not be ignored.

A growing aspect of consultancy work, at this time, was cost accounting. According to Loft, the First World War was a time when cost accounting, previously functioning in 'obscure corners of great industrial concerns . . . came into the light' (1986: 141, 147). Chapter 4 demonstrates the fact that cost accounting was rather more developed in the nineteenth century than was thought to be the case even ten years ago, however, and we have shown that accountancy firms were actively involved in installing, monitoring, and interpreting the information generated by cost accounting systems. At the same time, it is clear that the First World War provided an important stimulus for the development of cost accounting, and helped to raise its profile significantly in many industrial enterprises.

A key factor is seen to have been events at the Ministry of Munitions, set up in 1915 to co-ordinate production, to bring to an end a serious shortage of ammunition, to achieve a more rapid and efficient production of war materials, and to improve the quality of goods produced. The huge increase in government contracts during the war necessitated the accurate estimation of costs of production. It is thought that the Ministry's accountants, assisted by advice from engineers, had, by July 1917, undertaken some 700 investigations into production costs (Marriner, 1980: 136–7). These exposed the backward nature of British cost accounting and, according to John Mann, reporting in 1917, 'the Ministry's investigation has often been beneficial in showing the contractor his real costs and in stimulating better methods of costing' (Marriner, 1980: 136). The deputy Minister of Munitions informed the House of Commons, in 1919, that: 'The [engineering] contractors at first were very suspicious of this [costing] system for although it had been a common industrial practice in America for some years, it was foreign to the practice of this country. I believe today we can say it has become an integral part of the method of most up-to-date industrial firms' (quoted in Loft, 1986: 146).

The post-war period witnessed further efforts to introduce costing systems into government departments and business generally (Garrett, 1961: 123; Marriner, 1980: 139). For Workman, this 'led to the development and installation in many cases of efficient costing methods' and brought to the attention of manufacturers 'the value of accurate cost accounting' (1929: p. iii). Loft agrees that 'the institution of cost accounting systems in manufacturing industries seems to have proceeded quickly' (1986: 141). In 1919, the *Accountant* acknowledged that 'Many manufacturers are today keeping Cost Accounts who hardly knew there were such things five years ago' (quoted in Loft, 1986: 146). The 1921 census of population provides evidence of a mountain of costing work undertaken, in revealing that, out of nearly one million 'clerks and draughtsmen and typists', there were almost 20,000 costing and estimation clerks (Loft, 1986: 143). We have seen that a further significant event, in this process, was the creation of the ICWA, in 1919, to serve the interests of cost accountants.

Loft believes that it was the war which also forced cost accounting to the attention of the chartered accountancy 'elite', and 'gave the work greater status'. In her view, a 'profound metamorphosis' overtook accountants in the five years of the war when younger accountants had become involved in costing, 'a subject many had previously thought beneath their dignity' (Loft, 1986: 157). Cost accounting was first recognized as a final examination subject for the ICAEW's students in 1928 (Dicksee, 1928: 5; and Loft, 1986: 147) and, although there was growth in the number and sophistication of costing questions from that date (they were previously merely descriptive), it was still not until 1957 that the final examination syllabus of the Institute included a separate paper on cost and management accounting (Howitt, 1966: 124). The lower esteem attached to members working in industry meant that they were not allowed to become fellows (Howitt, 1966: 108–9) and, until 1942, were ineligible to serve on the ICAEW's committees (Mumford, 1991: 125). The official history of the Society of Incorporated Accountants claims a more enlightened attitude, with steps taken immediately after the war to ensure costing was adequately covered in its examinations so that its members were properly equipped to meet future challenges (Garrett, 1961: 108–9).

Doubt has been cast on whether the Ministry of Munitions' work did have the dramatic effect on cost accounting practice suggested above (Marriner, 1980: 140), and whether indeed much progress at all was made in this area at least during the 1920s (Dicksee, 1928: 4; de Paula, 1926: 141;

Stacey, 1954: 123–4). The likelihood is that some progress was made, but that it was slow and patchy (Solomons, 1952: 36). Perhaps Cornwell's first-hand assessment that 'costing and standard costing were introduced at a languid rate when they were recognised at all' (1991, 137–8), during the inter-war period, is as fair a depiction of the overall position as we are able to get at this point in time. It is certain that there was an increased interest in costing matters, however, and that firms of accountants benefited from work in this area. Deloitte, Plender, Griffiths & Co., for example, began a long-term connection with the Bank of England in 1919, when they prepared a cost accounting system tailored to the Bank's requirements. The firm subsequently acted in a consultation capacity to 'the governor on many occasions on matters outside the domestic economy of the bank' (Kettle, 1957: 11). Some firms were undoubtedly more interested in costing work than others. At Price Waterhouse, for example, costing engagements grew during the inter-war period, but nevertheless remained of minor significance until 1945, principally because the firm regarded itself primarily as auditors. It was Garnsey, however, reflecting a forward-looking attitude which was not typical of the firm at this time, who recruited Albert Cathles, an Edinburgh accountant who had been employed by the Ministry of Munitions as Deputy Controller of Factory Audit Costs, in 1919. Cathles undertook a variety of business investigations specializing in 'works and cost accounting' (Jones, 1995: 118). Indeed, a systems department was set up following Cathles's appointment, but it remained fairly small, 'undertaking specific tasks probably for existing audit clients' (Jones, 1995: 139). We will see, in the next section, that war work enabled professional accountants to develop costing expertise that they were subsequently able to take back to their firms and companies.

We now turn our attention to the major growth area for accounting practices during the inter-war period, namely auditing. The phenomenon of chartered accountants taking a significant proportion of the audits of quoted companies, clearly in evidence as early as 1886 (see Chapter 4), continued to gain momentum during the inter-war period. Members of the ICAEW were solely responsible for auditing 90% of the 5,518 companies listed in 1928, and 95% when those audited in conjunction with members of other bodies are included (BPP, 1936: 22). Whinney, Smith & Whinney's auditing income rose from 38.3% of total fee income in 1920 to 73.3% in 1939 (Jones, 1981: 99). The firm had 218 clients in 1910 and 436 by 1933, including firms in the new industries such as Dunlop Rubber, Imperial Airways, Chrysler Motors, and Thorn Electrical Industries (Jones, 1981: 144). Most of the absolute increase in audit fee income occurred in the 1920s, rising from £13,078 in 1918 to £37,093 in 1925. Over the next fourteen years, it exhibited a relatively modest further rise to £42,765 (Jones, 1981: 99).

We also find a continuing trend in favour of the concentration of quoted company audits among a relatively small number of firms, though by no means reaching today's proportions. As can be seen from Table 5, between one-quarter and one-third of listed audits were undertaken by the ten largest firms during the inter-war period, leaving two-thirds or more of the listed market spread amongst approximately 1,400–2,000 accountancy firms (Table 2). We can assume that most of the 1,866 accountancy firms (49% of the total) with no audits of listed companies in 1928 and the 2,694 (65%) in 1938 (see Table 2) were the smaller firms who prospered on the numerically greater and more rapidly growing pool of unlisted public companies, private companies (see Table 13), sole traders, and partnerships, where auditing merged imperceptibly into accounting—that is 'doing the books'. In view of the volume of audit work undertaken, it is probably not surprising to discover that then, as today, there were cases of audit failure. The potential inadequacies of this business service, even when performed in accordance with best practice, were vividly portrayed during the prosecution of the chairman (Lord Kylsant) and auditor (Harold Morland of Price, Waterhouse) of the Royal Mail Company in 1931. The defendants were accused of circulating a balance sheet considered to be false and fraudulent. The published accounts for 1926 contained a profit figure described as follows:

Balance for the year, including dividends on shares in allied and other companies, adjustment of taxation reserves, less depreciation of fleet, etc.   £439,212. 12. 1.

Investigations showed that the company had in fact suffered an operating loss of about £300,000, which was concealed by making an undisclosed transfer of approximately £750,000 from tax provisions surplus to requirements built up during the First World War. The prosecution failed on the grounds that the caption used, although misleading, was technically correct at a time when there was no statutory requirement to disclose transfers to and from reserves; the key words being 'adjustment of taxation reserves'. Mr Justice Wright's charge to the jury, however, contained severe explicit criticism of the company's reporting practices and, indeed, implied criticism of the external audit function generally (Davies and Bourn, 1972; Edwards, 1976; Hastings, 1962).

ACCOUNTANTS IN PUBLIC SERVICE IN THE FIRST WORLD WAR

Important developments in the British and the world economy during the inter-war period were bound up with the impact of the First World War. By depriving British industrialists of markets which were never regained, by disrupting world trade and the operation of the Gold Standard, which never again worked as smoothly as before, by slashing the value of Britain's overseas assets, and in marking the rise of the American economy and New York as a financial centre to rival London, the Great War saw, if it did not cause, the further decline of Britain as a world economic power. At home, a major long-term effect of war was the increased involvement in industry of the government which, under the exigencies of total war, had taken 'virtually all-pervasive' control over industry and agriculture (Pollard, 1983: 22).

As we saw in the previous chapter, public accountants had been called in to advise government and Parliament since the early nineteenth century, but closer links were undoubtedly forged between professional accountants and central government as a result of the 1914–18 war. Their valuable wartime role in reorganizing and managing departments led Garrett to claim that the war raised accountants and accountancy to the status of 'national importance' (1961: 103), while Ernest Cooper judged that 'the War brought our profession prominently forward' (quoted in Loft, 1990: 17). It might also be the period which saw the transition of accountancy from what Frederick Whinney, speaking as the president of the ICAEW in 1887, modestly judged to be one of the 'semi-professions' in terms of public recognition (Whinney, 1887: 388) to full professional status. The list of leading accountants, from public practice, who undertook heavy government engagements during the war is formidable and includes the following: Frederick Rudolph Mackley de Paula, who served as Assistant Director-General of Transportation at General Headquarters in France (Kitchen, 1984: 72); William Plender, who was controller of the large London branches of sequestrated German, Austrian, and Turkish banks (Edwards, 1985: 738; French, 1996); Ernest Cooper, who also helped to administer a number of enemy banks (Jones, 1984a: 779); W. B. Peat who, as financial secretary to the Ministry of Food, 1917–20, was responsible for introducing a costing system (Parker, 1985: 603); and William McLintock, who was engaged to 'investigate, supervise and, sometimes, wind-up German-owned businesses' (Winsbury, 1977: 31).

The influence of accountants was particularly marked at the Ministry of Munitions where, according to Marriner, the greatest need 'was for cost accountants equipped with the necessary combination of accounting knowledge and a detailed understanding of all the technical, engineering and manufacturing problems involved in costing explosives, iron ore and coal mining, shell, gun and aircraft-production' (1980: 132). In the endeavour to improve the administration of these services, ministers responsible 'appointed as heads of, or advisers to, accounts, finance, and costing divisions, partners in practising firms of accountants; and staff was found from among qualified accountants and senior clerks over a certain age whose military service had been postponed' (Garrett, 1961: 102). Despite a shortage of accountants who could undertake such work, by 1918 there were reported to be 340 chartered and incorporated accountants on the staff of the Ministry of Munitions alone (Loft, 1986: 146).

As noted above, one consequence of the accountants' involvement at the Ministry was the much higher profile subsequently accorded to cost accounting. Heavily involved in arranging major contracts, priced either on an estimate of costs or, less commonly, retrospectively on a 'cost plus' basis, the Ministry necessarily placed great emphasis on accurate costings. Government teams led by accountants and engineers toured factories gathering data on costs. In 1917 alone, 2,500 technical estimates and 1,000 accountancy investigations were made (Loft, 1986: 145). A 'key appointment' at the Ministry was Samuel Hardman Lever as financial secretary (he moved on to become financial secretary at the Treasury in 1917), who had acquired his extensive costing experience and skills in the United States as a partner in Barrow, Wade, Guthrie & Co. (Marriner, 1980: 132; Jones, 1981: 129). Another leading figure was the incorporated accountant James (later Sir James) Martin, who served as Director of Contract Costing (Garrett, 1961: 103).

Lever was succeeded, at the Ministry of Munitions, by the Scottish chartered accountant John Mann, who had first established contact with the government, in 1911, as spokesman for the Friendly Society Movement concerning the implementation of the National Insurance Act of that year. It seems that the favourable impression made by Mann within government circles, at this time, was the reason why he and his partner, Harold Judd, were brought into the Ministry of Munitions (Mann Judd Gordon, 1967: 32). Initially appointed Controller of Munitions Contracts, Mann 'worked hard to estimate the real cost of munitions manufacture, something which neither the War Office nor the manufacturers themselves knew, although some of them maintained a "ring" to keep their prices up' (Mann Judd Gordon, 1967: 33). Mann estimated that the Ministry saved £330 million, and his work brought him a knighthood and Judd a CBE. In a similar vein, Mark Webster Jenkinson, who later boasted that he had cut the cost of one of the first contracts submitted to him by £1 million, was made Director of Factory Accounting at the Ministry (Davenport-Hines, 1985b: 484), where he was assisted by William McLintock (Winsbury, 1977: 31). Given the nature of their work, it is unsurprising to hear that the Ministry's accountants were not popular with industrialists. One disgruntled manufacturer warned: 'I have heard that you [Mann] are the best hated man in the Midlands. It is true. I will see that you pay sweetly for this some day, my man' (quoted in Mann Judd Gordon, 1967: 33).

The contribution of accountants at the Ministry of Munitions was assessed in the following terms by Raymond W. Needham, KC, speaking at the Jubilee dinner of the leading accounting tutors Foulks Lynch, in 1934: 'The accountants certainly brought order out of chaos. There was chaos everywhere, even in the Ministry of Munitions, and I put it to you, Mr Chairman, where would the Ministry of Munitions have been but for the accountants?' Needham recognized that this was, of course, a mutually beneficial arrangement, and he continued: 'I also put it to you, Mr Chairman, where would certain accountants have been but for the Ministry of Munitions?' (Foulks Lynch, 1955: 42).

Marriner is more critical of the contribution of accountants, at least up to the appointment of Garnsey as Director of Internal Audits (1917) and, later, Controller of Munitions Accounts (Edwards, 1984b: 487). Teaming up with J. H. Guy, Garnsey did much to sort matters out (Edwards, 1984b: 487), though their reforms seem not to have had a long-lasting influence (Marriner, 1980: 139). In the earlier war years, there had been severe problems. The Ministry of Munitions had burgeoned into a massive undertaking such that, whereas in 1913 total government expenditure was £184 million, by the year ended 31 March 1918, the Ministry alone had a turnover of £2,000 million and a net cost to the taxpayer of £620 million (prices just about doubled 1913–18) (Marriner, 1980: 130). It is clear from Marriner's research into the public records that the Ministry's accounting systems failed to cope with this administrative monster; the existing government accounting system—on the single-entry and cash rather than accruals basis—was cruelly exposed (Marriner, 1980: 131). Although the influx of accountants—pre-Garnsey—attempted to change the system, 'they did not do so systematically. The inevitable result was confusion' (Marriner, 1980: 133). For Marriner, 'The Ministry's accountants had a dismal history of failure until 1918: many millions of taxpayers' money could never be accounted for and had to be written off' (1980: 130).

Whatever the reason for these shortcomings, the leading accountants involved seem to have attracted no opprobrium—in fact, the reverse. Lever, who presided over the early chaos, was awarded a peerage. Moreover, the perceived achievements of professional accountants led to appointments on numerous government committees and commissions after the war (see Howitt, 1966: 216). The personal lists of memberships and chairmanships of government committees, royal commissions, tribunals, etc., amazing in their length and variety, may be found for the likes of Binder, Plender, McLintock, Garnsey, and Mayhew (Bywater, 1985a: 69; Edwards, 1984b: 488, 1985: 739; Jones, 1985a: 209; *The Times*, 12 July 1966).

SPECIAL WORK IN RATIONALIZATION, RESCUES, AND MERGERS

Accountants were intimately associated with the problems faced by British industry in the inter-war period. The 1921 depression witnessed the abandonment of governmental control and support for the old industries such as coal mining and the railways. Although no sustained attempt was made to manage the economy in this period, the government could not totally ignore the devastation caused by fundamental structural change, however, and it was here that the skills of the accountant were called into use. The fashionable cure for oversupply, the perceived surfeit of small companies, and resulting cut-throat competition and low prices, was rationalization—the merger of ailing companies and the scrapping of surplus capacity. The government provided informal encouragement for this process, often through the Bank of England via its consortium of bankers, the Bankers' Industrial Development Company, formed in 1929. One of the Development Company's creations, the Lancashire Cotton Corporation, took over almost 100 firms between 1929 and 1932 (Hannah, 1983: 64). Another method of inducing mergers was through legislation, the Coal Mines Act of 1930 being a prime example. Whatever the adopted policy, however, successes, measured against the scale of the problem, were modest. Figure 4 demonstrates the fact that merger activity also reached new levels at this time. The three waves of major activity show, more strongly than at any other time, a correlation between mergers and periods of prosperity, coming as they did at or near the peaks of the trade cycle in 1920, 1929, and 1936.

Rationalization, whether brought about with government encouragement or as a result of private initiatives, called forth the skills of leading accountants to act as intermediaries in arranging a compromise between interested parties. The work of firms, such as Deloittes, Price Waterhouse, and others, as the honest brokers in devising rationalization schemes within declining industries, did much to enhance the profession's reputation as business advisers. The Scottish chartered accountant Norman Duthie noted the developing nature of the accountant's work:

The professional accountant is being forced to regard himself less and less as a mere scrutineer and arithmetician, and to appreciate that the business world wants him to be actively helpful in the solution of its problems. . . . [I]t is the general experience that the definitely consulting work of our profession is noticeably increasing. . . . In practically every case the trouble goes much deeper than capital and finance. The wider and more complex issues of the general policy of the business, the scope of its operations, the soundness of its equipment and organisation, the efficient and harmonious working of its management and staff . . . Bearing in mind the diversity of problems which may have to be solved—financial, technical, psychological, and economic—it is a significant fact that there is a clear tendency to offer to the accountant the task of welding together the complete scheme of reorganisation, of which the purely financial adjustments may form only a small, and far from the most important, section. (Duthie, 1927: 984, 985)

Duthie further refers to 'our function as business consultants and advisers' (Duthie, 1927: 986) and, as far as can be judged, accountants did succeed, during this period, in distinguishing themselves above the other professions in fulfilling a managerial role in conducting the diverse aspects of business activity. Midland Bank, for example, regularly called in Whinney, Smith & Whinney to perform special tasks for its clients. One example involved an attempt to rehabilitate the struggling staple industries, with Whinney, Smith & Whinney's scheme, of 1933, favouring the amalgamation of a range of cotton companies under the control of a holding company (Jones, 1981: 161).

The extent to which business turned to accountants for advice on major strategic decisions can be illustrated by reference to their involvement in a series of attempts to rationalize Scottish steel-making in its endeavour to maintain international competitiveness. In 1923, Sir William Plender was 'asked to formulate a scheme of amalgamation or some lesser arrangement conducive to the "better working and administration of the steel trade in Scotland"' (Payne, 1979: 156). Plender, engaged for his financial expertise rather than his knowledge of steel-making, confessed to be 'not at present intimately acquainted with any unusual conditions attached to the industry, or with any peculiar circumstances which may affect the various companies' (Payne, 1979: 157). Indeed, according to Payne, Plender's report focused on important general issues, but was 'lacking in depth and unconvincing in its recommendations' (Payne, 1979: 157). Nevertheless, the parties involved were sufficiently impressed by Plender's contribution to call him in again, later in the year, to produce a second scheme. This is thought to have envisaged a mammoth holding company, though the proposals were not implemented. Another scheme for Scottish steel was put forward in 1926, allegedly the brainchild of Sir William Barclay Peat, then secretary of the National Federation of Iron & Steel Manufacturers. The plan was for the establishment of a separate operating company, at national level, with responsibility for controlling production and commercial policies, but leaving individual firms otherwise free to manage their own affairs. This initiative, promoted by F. A. Szarvasy of the British Foreign and Colonial Corporation, with Peat prominent throughout discussions, was given careful consideration but again came to nothing (Payne, 1979: 163–70).

Three years later, H. A. Brassert & Co., a Chicago firm of consulting engineers, were engaged to prepare a scheme which, among other things, contained detailed costings for the production of various products (Payne, 1979: 170–80). Although the Brassert scheme for full amalgamation of the Scottish steel industry failed, one company, Colvilles, looked instead to possible merger with James Dunlop & Co. It was necessary to obtain Treasury approval for this scheme because Colvilles had not yet completed repayment of the wartime loans granted by the Ministry of Munitions and, with the company indirectly under the control of the Royal Mail group through Harland & Wolff, it was not surprising that the Treasury placed the matter into the hands of Sir William McLintock, one of the trustees for the group after its collapse. McLintock had 'grave misgivings' that the amalgamation would result in an excessive capitalization of the new organization and 'make a more comprehensive amalgamation scheme even more difficult to achieve' (Payne, 1979: 192). Although sympathetic to this criticism, J. Craig of Colvilles informed McLintock that James Dunlop 'would not budge on the question of the capital structure' and feared that, if they were pushed further, there was a very real 'risk of [them] going off altogether' (letter from Craig to McLintock, Payne, 1979: 188). McLintock therefore agreed to the proposed scheme provided Craig was made chairman or managing director, but again the scheme failed to reach fruition.

McLintock was again called in, later in 1930, to advise on a possible merger involving William Baird & Co., the Steel Company of Scotland, Stewarts & Lloyds, Colvilles, and Dunlops (Payne, 1979: 193). It appears that this step was taken as the result of pressure from Montagu Norman, the Governor of the Bank of England, and there were a number of new factors which conspired to ensure a more 'sympathetic reception' for any plan McLintock might now produce. One was that, as many ailing steel companies had fallen unwanted into the hands of the banks, including the Bank of England, during the 1920s, there was an increased willingness on the part of banks to intervene and encourage the adoption of schemes that would be likely to avoid bankruptcy. This represented a reaction against what *The Times* described as a 'policy of benevolent but inert orthodoxy' which had continued to the 1920s (Payne, 1979: 196).

McLintock's new plan was to establish an operating company comprising the assets of certain selected companies. Objections to the scheme by Craig, on the grounds that the valuation of the Steel Company of Scotland, which had a history of losses, was too high, could not be overcome despite a downward revaluation by McLintock. The revised scheme remained unacceptable to Colvilles, while the Steel Company of Scotland naturally clung to McLintock's original calculations (Payne, 1979: 210). All initiatives failed, leaving Craig to move step by step towards rationalization of Scottish steel-making through acquisition and complete domination by Colvilles (Payne, 1979: 213–16). According to Payne, McLintock continued to play a crucial role in cajoling and encouraging Craig to push on with his plans while, at the same time, making no effort to influence the internal workings of the new company and thereby avoided eroding Craig's dominant position (Payne, 1979: 243).

The highly regarded McLintock was also called in to investigate target companies on behalf of clients on numerous occasions during the inter-war period (Bywater, 1985*a*: 69). Amongst his most notable achievements were the creation of the Explosive Trades Ltd. in 1918 and the British Dyestuffs Corporation in 1919. McLintock is also, perhaps, the only leading accountant who deserves to emerge from the Royal Mail affair with an enhanced reputation. It was on the basis of his report on the company, made for the government, that the Royal Mail was reconstructed and, according to Bywater, the reconstruction, 'probably the most important, certainly the most prominent, work that he engaged in', meant that he (and his fellow trustees) reduced investors' and unsecured creditors' losses to one-half of the likely level had the group gone into receivership (Bywater, 1985*a*: 71 and 73; Green and Moss, 1982: 202). McLintock also worked jointly with William Henry ('Harry') Peat (W. B. Peat's eldest son), when advising on the merger of the explosives companies, and the 'Nobel scheme' of 1920 has been described as 'the forerunner of the big business in company mergers which was such a feature of Thomson McLintock's activities in the period following the First World War' (Winsbury, 1977: 32).

By no means all of the companies in distress were from the old, declining, industries, of course, and the new industries faced problems and were involved in mergers which inevitably drew accountants in. The involvement of accountants also underpinned the creation of Cable & Wireless Ltd., from the merger of the Eastern Telegraph Company Ltd. and Marconi. Eastern's predecessor and associated companies, having developed a world-wide communication network based on cables starting in 1851, were threatened by Marconi's ability to transfer messages at a fraction of the cost of cable through its 'beam Wireless' in the 1920s. A solution, with British government support, was the merger of these two rivals through the creation of the Imperial and International Communication Ltd., renamed Cable & Wireless Ltd. in 1934. The respective auditors of the merging companies, Plender (for Eastern Telegraph) and Garnsey (for Marconi), were left to 'hammer out the delicate matter of the financial basis of fusion' (Barty-King, 1979: 205).

The merger of these communications concerns was not a panacea; enormous difficulties arose from the general depression and increased competition, particularly from airmail (Barty-King, 1979: 224–5). An investigating committee was appointed under the chairmanship of the future Master of the Rolls, Wilfred Greene, which referred economic matters, including the question of whether capital should be reduced, to McLintock, Garnsey, and Allan Rae Smith of Deloittes. This group of financial experts opposed any writing down of capital 'on the grounds that it was impossible to estimate "normal revenue"' (Barty-King, 1979: 233). Various options were considered for reorganizing the new company's activities, including one conjured up by McLintock and government officials that involved a *coup d'état* designed to install Sir Alexander Roger of British Insulated Cables as chairman. A note of the meeting records that 'Sir William McLintock said they were all agreed that the present direction and management of C & W Ltd was hopelessly ineffective. The right way was to get rid of the whole gang and even if they had to be compensated on a five years' basis it would be a profitable investment to the company since none of them need be replaced' (quoted in Barty-King, 1979: 242). Although the plan was shelved, for reasons which are not recorded, it is further evidence of the involvement of accountants at the heart of schemes, favoured by government and the Bank of England, designed to restructure British industry during the inter-war period.

Austin Motor Company Ltd., in the early 1920s, provides further evidence of the accountants' role in rescuing and reorganizing firms among the new industries. Declining turnover in the post-war depression, at a time when a major capital expenditure programme was being undertaken to enable large-scale production, had precipitated a cash crisis at Austin. This led the company to request, in February 1921, its 'friendly' creditors (Eagle Star and the Midland Bank) to file a petition for the appointment of a receiver. Sir Arthur Whinney (Frederick Whinney's son, knighted in 1919 for his work on naval accounts) was appointed manager and chairman of a creditors' committee which reformed the structure of the company. In particular, it was decided that, whilst 'the ultimate control of the work should be in the hands of the Board of Directors, a Board of Management should act for them' at operational level (Church, 1979: 64). The financial problems of the company were resolved by 'the issue of a £1.5 million debenture of three different kinds to be repaid over five years' (Church, 1979: 63). In April 1922, the directors were able to resume full control. Sir Arthur Whinney performed a similar investigation on behalf of the shareholders of Dunlop Rubber Company in 1922 which also began the rehabilitation of that company (Jones, 1981: 148).

Attempts to rescue ailing companies did not, of course, always meet with success. In the early 1930s, an advisory committee was set up, in the face of opposition from top management, to investigate the affairs of the Francis Willey group of wool merchants and textile manufacturers. Francis Willey (created Baron Barnby in 1922) succeeded to the position of governing director of the group on the death of his father in 1929, but found that the company had been slackly managed in the last years of his father's reign. The National Provincial Bank—the group's largest creditor—insisted on the appointment of a committee chaired by Sir William Barclay Peat to investigate the company's affairs. But Peat's work was in vain; the bank could not be satisfied and terminated its overdraft facilities, thereby 'pushing the group into insolvency and forcing its reconstruction in 1935' (Davenport-Hines, 1986a: 813).

Further, advice from accountants was not always acted on. Kendricks, the medium-sized Midlands hardware firm, commissioned a report from their management consultants Peat, Marwick, Mitchell & Co. which recommended that they should seek a merger with rivals. The advice was rejected on the grounds that the family feared a loss of control (quoted in

Hannah, 1983: 128). Hannah notes, with approval, Sir Arthur Cutforth's exasperation with the reluctance of owners to lose control of their firms. Cutforth, a partner in Deloittes, was sufficiently immersed in mergers to write a book on the subject (Cutforth, 1926).

ACCOUNTANTS ON THE BOARD

Throughout the inter-war period, it was still the case that 'public company boards retained strong controlling family elements, and the peculiar British tradition of (in cricketing terms) excluding professional "players" from the board positions in favour of "gentlemen" amateurs died slowly' (Hannah, 1983: 88). The majority of company directors either were connected to the family, were major shareholders, and/or were 'the great and the good' whose titles were judged to give favourable signals to the outside world. In Florence's sample of fifteen companies in 1936, 158 of the 300 biggest shareholders (the top 20 in each company) were individuals as opposed to companies. Moreover, 48 (26%) of these companies' 183 directors were among the 300 biggest shareholders (Florence, 1947: 6–10). Turning to titles, Table 18 presents the results of a survey (used also for Table 15) of directors' titles and qualifications. Although not all directors may have chosen to declare their personal details, we have a reasonable amount of confidence in these figures because, when the percentage of accountants who declared their qualifications given in Table 18, column 10, is compared with the comprehensive figures given in Table 15 (repeated in Table 18, column 11), there is the predicted under-recording, but it shows a consistent pattern over time.

Down to 1931, the most popular qualification for board membership in Britain was a titled noble—representing over one in ten directors—followed by military officers—whose numbers were undoubtedly boosted by the Great War—and a relatively small and declining number of MPs. Professional qualifications were few, and less than 1% of directors of quoted companies had degrees or legal qualifications. Beginning to become significant, however, are the accountants. Across the war and inter-war years, the number of accountant-directors increased from below 2% in 1911 to almost 10% in 1951 (see Table 15, row 7, Figure 5). Even more significantly, the proportion of companies having at least one accountant on the board increased from less than 8% in 1911 to almost one company in five in 1931, and doubled in the subsequent twenty years (Table 15, row 3). These estimates are consistent with those of Florence whose random sample of 463 British companies for the year 1936 revealed 127 accountants, implying that a maximum of 27% of companies then had an accountant on the board (1947: 15).

Table 18. Qualifications and titles of company directors, 1891–1991

(1) Year	(2) Total directors in sample	(3) Directors with some qualification/title (%)	(4) Graduates (%)	(5) Engineering qualification (%)	(6) Noble title (%)	(7) Military title (%)	(8) MPs (%)	(9) Lawyers (%)	(10) Accountants (%)	(11) Accountants revealed in Table 15, row 7 (%)
1891	2,651	16.8	0.3	0.0	7.6	5.6	4.7	0.1	0.0	0.8
1911	2,011	11.6	0.3	0.0	7.6	2.4	1.9	0.0	0.0	1.7
1931	1,653	28.9	0.8	1.8	11.4	7.9	1.3	0.7	1.7	3.8
1951	1,592	24.9	2.7	4.9	7.3	6.5	0.3	0.6	7.4	9.4
1971	1,870	37.8	9.1	6.9	5.6	1.7	0.3	1.8	12.1	15.2
1991	2,084	41.3	16.6	5.7	5.9	1.1	0.4	1.5	16.2	22.0

Notes: Directors with multiple qualifications cannot be allocated to a single category and so all qualifications were counted. Columns 4–10, therefore, do not sum to column 3. Qualifications which were numerically insignificant are included in column 3 and are not reported separately. In absolute terms, these statistics are unreliable since qualifications are not given for all directors in the source material.

Sources: As for Table 15.

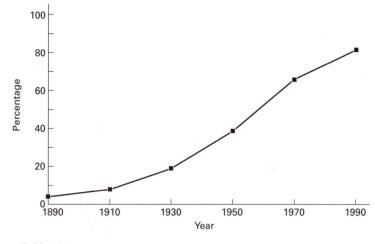

Source: Table 15.
Fig. 5   Percentage of companies with an accountant-director, 1891–1991

Accountants who combined directorships with public practice were still the most common. Whereas prior to the First World War *all* of the accountant-directors in our sample remained in practice, this situation changed rapidly during the inter-war period, so that by 1931 only two-thirds of accountant-directors were in practice (Table 15, row 9). These proportions are helpful indicators of the extent of the accountants' commitment to a particular business, but they are not an accurate measure of the rise of what we would call today the executive director. For example, some of the accountant-directors in the 'not in practice' category held directorships in companies other than their main employer, whilst others were retired practitioners. One notable example was Sir Arthur Dickinson, Price Waterhouse's senior partner in their American operation, 1901–13, and then a partner in London until his retirement in 1923 (Jones, 1995: 130). In 1931, aged 72, as well as being on the board of governors of the London School of Economics, he was a director of twelve companies including Goodyear Tyre and Ebbw Vale Steel, and was chairman of Alvis Cars (*Directory of Directors*; *WWW*, 1929–40: 364).

Another accountant notably active in a non-executive capacity in British boardrooms in this period was Bernhard Binder, who we saw, in Chapter 4, had been involved full-time in the management of certain South American companies in the period up to the First World War. In 1918 he returned to Britain and joined in partnership with R. Ashton Hamlyn. Binder kept, or took on, a wide range of directorships, totalling seventeen by 1939. Again, there is a strong 'rescue' element in Binder's role on these boards, and his obituary in *The Times* refers to a description of him as a 'doctor of industry' (12 July 1966). A less prominent example of an accountant who served on company boards while remaining in practice is Henry Charles Merrett, of Merrett Son & Street (see Appendix, BDO Binder Hamlyn). Although, apparently, never attracted to everyday accountancy, he was one of the first examples of finance directors we have found and was extremely 'successful as financial director of various companies', the fees from which went to a large extent into the firm (Viney Merretts, 1974: n.p.). In the early 1920s, Merrett joined the board of the National Omnibus Company, and 'as this company proceeded to buy up the smaller omnibus companies throughout England each acquisition was preceded by an investigation by the firm [Merrett's]' (Viney Merretts, 1974: n.p.). Merrett also served on the boards of other omnibus groups in London, the Midlands, and abroad.

The circumstances in which accountants were brought in, and the roles they performed, have been the subject of a broad-based study of the hosiery industry by Erickson which spans the pre- and post-war period.

Often an accountant is invited to join the firm as a kind of emergency measure just after the firm has registered as a limited company, shortly before liquidation, or upon the death of the leading investor. Of 126 limited companies in our 1930 and 1952 groups, twenty-eight, or about one in five, have at some time had an accountant as a director. In the case of twelve of these firms the accountant was called upon only briefly, in a time of crisis. Fourteen firms have apparently adopted the policy of having an accountant's advice readily available at least from a part-time director. In the other two cases accountants were leading investors in the firm. (1959: 130)

A significant feature of this period is that the 'non-executive' accountant-directors, although not in numerical decline, became relatively less important compared with professional accountants who devoted the whole of their career to an executive role at board level (Table 15, row 9). One of the first of these must have been Alexander Young, who started his business life while still articled to Fairbairn, Wingfield & Wykes and obtained special dispensation from the ICAEW to become a director of Redhill Tile Company in 1925. Five years later, he moved full-time to the company as managing director (Murch, 1986: 926–9). The decline in the proportion of practising accountants serving as directors may have been driven, to an extent, by bans placed by firms themselves on partners or clerks taking directorships. This sensitivity to a possible conflict of interest might have been a particular concern for large practices, where there was greater risk of a client having business dealings with another company where a member of staff was director. At Peats, we are told that the 'independence question must have spread into full bloom in the 1920s, because in 1925 he [W. B. Peat] decided to remain Director of National Provincial Bank and to allow his son Harry to take over the reins of the partnership' (Wise, 1982: 16).

COMING IN AT THE TOP

The inter-war period witnessed a substantial increase in the numbers of accountants employed full-time in business at all levels. This was particularly significant at the upper rungs of the managerial ladder (Table 15, rows 4, 6), and of course represented an important part of the growing professionalization of management generally during this period. Whereas, in 1911, only one in 50 managing directors was an accountant, 40 years later this had increased to one in 20. Over the same period, accountant-chairmen increased from less than 1 per cent to one in every 13. It is more difficult to get behind these figures to the personalities involved in order to assess their effectiveness as managers, and we stress the fact that this is not the principal purpose of this study. Inevitably, given the nature of our secondary source material (failures tend not to be written about), most of our examples are the major success stories, and cautionary reference to this fact is therefore required. None the less, the successes among accountant-managers are numerous and impressive, and do tell us something of what professional accountants were contributing to business at this time.

The route through which the top accountants were recruited is not without its significance. Personal contact was the rule with, as we have seen, companies frequently recruiting accountants from their auditors. Moreover, there is no strong evidence to support Chandler's suggestion that selection to senior management or the board by personal ties was to the detriment of managerial competence (1990: 242). For example, in the best-known instance of a professional accountant taking on a full-time engagement, during the inter-war period, he proved to be well equipped for the job. Francis d'Arcy Cooper resigned his senior partnership at Cooper Brothers & Co., in 1923, to join his audit client Lever Brothers. Having previously served as a member of the company's policy-making 'inner cabinet', Cooper already possessed the authority of a director and, two years after joining, became chairman on the death of Lord Leverhulme.

Cooper's mission was to convert an 'ill-organised collection of companies into an efficient, modern industrial organisation', through a 'complete metamorphosis of Lever Brothers from a private empire owned and controlled by one man into a public company administered by a professional management' (Edwards, 1984a: 782; Wilson, 1977: 132). Eager to recruit graduates and on the principle of merit not connections, Cooper engendered a sense of personal responsibility among his managers, 'to set their sights clearly on efficiency in production and sales' (Edwards, 1984*a*: 782). By 1929, the year in which Cooper was instrumental in bringing about the merger with the Dutch Margarine Union, making Unilever the largest company in Britain by the market value of its assets, record profits of £5.5 million were reported (Chandler, 1990: 676). Cooper had a clear policy of preserving parity between the two sides of the Unilever business, such that when the power of the British branch waxed in the 1930s, he sold assets to the Dutch to preserve a balance. To pull together the disparate elements of the soap business, he was assisted at Unilever by Geoffrey Heyworth, 'another accountant turned successful manager', who carried through the rationalization of the company's 49 soap-making units which previously had their own sales organizations (Gourvish, 1987: 29). The effect of Cooper's success, at Unilever, in both increasing the demand from industry for their services and demonstrating the willingness of accountants to transfer their skills, appears to have been an important milestone. On the other hand, the relatively slow progress made by Cooper Brothers & Co. during the inter-war period is largely attributed to Cooper's resignation ([Benson] 1954: 10; Benson, 1989: 42).

The career of Arthur Edgar Sylvester provides another example of how personal contact introduced a professional accountant to a future employer. Sylvester had been a partner with Barton, Mayhew & Co. since 1920 but, following completion of a report on the reorganization of the Gas Light & Coke Company, he joined the utility as financial controller in 1934, 'to form a budget and audit department and overhaul the cost accounting systems' (Jones, 1985*a*: 209). Promoted to general manager in 1941, managing director (1942), and then governor (1945), such was Sylvester's success that he became chairman of the South Eastern Gas Corporation in 1945 and, on nationalization, chairman of the Gas Council, 1949–52 (Jones, 1981: 160).

John Greenwood of Boots is another success story, being described as an accountant possessing 'outstanding ability' (Chapman, 1974: 192). Greenwood, the son of a City stockbroker, with a law degree from Cambridge, qualified as a chartered accountant with Gane, Jackson, Jeffreys & Freeman at the age of 29 in 1920. He immediately joined the board of Boots Pure Drug Co. Ltd. (*WWW*, 1971–80: 317) via family connections, possessing, it was said, 'all the qualifications and connections [Jesse] Boot could hope for' (Chapman, 1974: 143). On his arrival, the costing system, such as it was, gave no indication of the contribution to profits made by individual sectors of the firm—manufacturing, retailing, or ancillary services—much less of individual shops and products. The proprietor's drive to increase the number of branches regardless of profitability was challenged by Greenwood, whose analysis of costs showed that small branches were much less profitable than large ones. His influence was such that, on being promoted to joint vice-chairman, Greenwood had helped Boots to grow from the 39th largest company in Britain in 1919, with a market value of £5 million, to the 29th largest firm in 1948 worth £23.7 million (Chandler, 1990: 669 and 683).

Even more noteworthy is the career of Mark Webster Jenkinson, whose work at the Ministry of Munitions was referred to earlier in this chapter. Following the cessation of hostilities, Jenkinson was recruited by Dudley Docker as secretary to the Electric & Railway Finance Corporation and, in view of his special knowledge of armaments production, Docker later engaged him to make an independent report on Vickers, where Docker was also a director. The inter-war history of Vickers provides a useful illustration of the work of accountants as managers, as well as advisers, in the ailing sectors of the economy. Dominated by engineers, who were also the company's salesmen, Vickers was in poor shape in 1921/2, having expanded too quickly in the post-war boom through takeovers and diversification into a wide range of activities (Scott, 1962: 367). In his report, Jenkinson's 'proposed remedies involved a rough awakening. They provided for a decentralization of control and a splitting up of the company into four or more groups' (Scott, 1962: 157). At that time, however, Vickers' management was not ready for fundamental change, and the report was pigeonholed. By June 1925 matters had not improved, and Jenkinson's second detailed investigation, instigated by the board again through Docker, recommended a massive reduction of capital, including a write-down of ordinary shares to one-third of their former nominal value (Scott, 1962: 158). These proposals were accepted, with the 'carrot' for shareholders being the promise of an early resumption of dividend payments. The report earned Jenkinson a knighthood and the reputation as 'one of the ablest financiers in the country' (Davenport-Hines, 1985*b*: 485). In 1926, he went onto the Vickers board and effectively implemented his own report. Subsidiaries were sold off, leaving a compact business in steel and ships (Scott, 1962: 159).

Jenkinson held strong views on corporate governance. He believed that no more than one-third of a board should be aged over 60, and that, 'So long as boards of directors are constituted without regard to the qualifications of those selected, so long as shareholders prefer a man "with a name" to a man "with a future" . . . other nations continue to beat us' (quoted in Scott, 1962: 159). Jenkinson completely restructured the board, creating three 'executive' management boards on functional lines (armaments and shipbuilding, finance management, and industrial management) separated from the overall controlling board. He also ruthlessly manœuvred himself into the job of finance comptroller, in 1926, with the remit to redesign Vickers' procedures (Davenport-Hines, 1985*b*: 486). Jenkinson, who now had 'unrestricted scope to implement his principles of scientific management', introduced formal procedures, systematic planning, and a shake-up of the internal financial system, reflecting his belief in 'full and accurate flows of internal information' (Davenport-Hines, 1985b: 486). In short, we have an example of an innovative and thoroughly modern manager making full use of the skills provided by his accountancy training.

In the early 1920s, Vickers' competitor Armstrong Whitworth were also struggling; indeed they owed the Bank of England £2.6 million. This enabled the Bank to obtain a great deal more information than the public, 'which had perforce to accept Armstrongs' profit and loss accounts, in which the profit was conjured out of optimistic depreciation figures' (Scott, 1962: 162). The Bank arranged for Armstrong's affairs to be investigated by the Scotsman James Frater Taylor, '[b]eing both an accountant and an industrialist' who specialized in reorganizing failing companies (Scott, 1962: 161). Taylor's preliminary investigation revealed an almost disastrous financial state and resulted in his appointment by the Bank as, in effect, controller of the company. The company's accounts for 1925 made public the full extent of its known problems, though a further report by Taylor, jointly with Garnsey, estimated that Armstrong's had about £10 million invested in peripheral business activities on which no return was being made nor likely to be made for some time to come (Scott, 1962: 163).

With Vickers restored to a position of strength, Jenkinson, witnessing Armstrong's share price continuing to fall, put forward a proposal which, in essence, amounted to Vickers taking over Armstrong Whitworth's affairs and the government guaranteeing a certain level of orders for a fixed period of time (Scott, 1962: 163–4). Negotiations, in which Sir William Plender was heavily involved, continued into 1927, with Frater Taylor eventually coming 'round to something like an acceptance of the inevitable' (Scott, 1962: 165). Vickers-Armstrongs Ltd. was created by an agreement signed on 31 October 1927. Jenkinson, together with the first chairman of the new Vickers holding company, Gen. Lawrence, brought about 'one of the most vaunted examples of industrial rationalisation in the period' (Davenport-Hines, 1985b: 486). In 1929, Vickers reached agreement with Cammell Laird whereby their rolling-stock interests were merged to form Metropolitan-Cammell, and their steel-making interests were combined to form the English Steel Corporation. In 1937, control of Vickers passed to another chartered accountant—the Scot Archibald Jamieson—who had been a member of the board since 1928. The deputy chairman since 1930 had been Lt.-Col. J. B. Neilson, a man with a background similar to Jamieson, being also a Scottish chartered accountant, and the influence of Scottish chartered accountancy was further reinforced in 1937 when James Reid Young, 'the man who had cleaned the Augean stables of the Accounts Department', joined the Vickers board (Scott, 1962: 260–1).

Finally, no examination of the movement of the leading professional accountants into top management posts during the inter-war period would be complete without reference to the varied career of Frederick Rudolph Mackley de Paula, though he restricted his involvement to the financial sphere. Having qualified in 1905, de Paula returned to public practice after the First World War, and became also part-time professor of accounting at the London School of Economics during the 1920s (Kitchen, 1984: 72). In 1930, he was recruited as chief accountant of the Dunlop Rubber Company by its chairman Sir Eric Geddes, under whom de Paula had worked in the Ministry of Munitions. De Paula soon became controller of finance and made momentous improvements to Dunlop's accounts for 1931 and 1933. These 'trail-blazing' accounts served as the models which helped to raise the general standard of financial reporting amongst British companies in the aftermath of the Royal Mail case. However, it was 'his work on financial management and control, and the development of budgetary control, [which] represented his greatest contribution from the point of view of the Dunlop board' (Kitchen, 1984: 73). De Paula's career is also significant in that he worked tirelessly to raise the status of the accountant and the accounts department in industry, viewing the chief accountant as 'the chief financial officer of the whole company, who would be responsible to the general manager for the finances of the business and its financial control' (Kitchen, 1984: 73).

ACCOUNTANTS WORKING THEIR WAY UP

Having considered the recruitment of accountants into management at the highest levels, this section highlights the equally significant influx of qualified accountants into the administration of companies further down the managerial hierarchy. Table 16 gives our estimates of the proportion of accountants 'in business', and makes it clear that the period traversing the two world wars saw the most significant increase in numbers. This was the product of chartered and incorporated accountants leaving practice for industry, and the rise in the number of accountants who qualified while working in business, never having been in practice. Certified accountants (from 1939) could qualify in practice or industry, while we have seen that the ICWA (formed 1919) and a number of smaller societies, such as the Institute of Company Accountants (formed 1929), were specifically founded to cater for accountants employed in industry and commerce.

Whereas the proportion of accountants employed outside public practice was insignificant before the First World War, by 1951 it represented one-half of all professionally qualified accountants, though the proportions for the ICAEW (28%) and ICAS (35%) were considerably lower. Stacey estimated, for the profession as a whole, that 50% of accountants were working in business in 1939, but this overstated the true number because he erroneously classified as working in business all professionally qualified accountants employed by public practitioners (1954: 215). Based on our new estimates, the proportion in 1939 is in the region of 40%. This is still, of course, a very significant jump from 7% in 1911 and, in absolute terms, represents an increase from a few hundred accountants in business before the First World War to about 15,000 by 1939.

Our sampling of the accountancy bodies revealed that professional accountants worked for a wide range of employers in 1931. It appears that, at this time, the employment of accountants mirrored employment in the economy generally, except that a higher proportion seemed to work in manufacturing. The spread of manufacturing companies captured by our sample included the Lancashire Dynamo & Motor Co., Wolsey the stocking makers, Lever Brothers, Capper Pass Smelting Works, a newspaper company, and a number of oil companies. Smaller numbers of accountants worked in government departments, such as the Inland Revenue, and for quasi-government bodies, including the Mersey Docks and Harbour Board. Financial services were represented by the major banks, for example the Midland and Lloyds, merchant banks including Rothschilds, and a marine insurance company.

Company secretary was the most common source of employment for professional accountants during the inter-war period. The proportion of quoted companies that had accountants as secretaries increased from under 10% in 1911 to almost 30% by 1951 (Table 15, row 5). The next most important position was probably that of chief accountant, with the title 'Secretary and Chief Accountant' commonplace. It appears that it was not until after the First World War that companies drafted in more than a handful of qualified chartered accountants to act as company secretary and/or to head their accounts departments. In some cases, this reflected the undeveloped state of the accounting function. For example, Arthur Bertram Waring joined Lucas (just two years after qualifying) as its first professional accountant in 1922 (Nockolds, 1986: 666). The Crosville Motor Company Ltd. did not employ an accountant until the 1930s, despite the fact that it was formed in 1906 and quoted on the stock exchange from 1929 (Anderson, 1981: 161). The accounting function also remained undeveloped at Metal Box as late as 1940, being still located in the secretary's department. According to the company's historian, this state of affairs had arisen because the company had been growing so fast that no one had paused to consider setting up the accountant in a separate department (Reader, 1976: 144). Peat, Marwick, Mitchell & Co., brought in as consultants by Metal Box, reported that it was the first time they had encountered so large a company where the secretarial and accountancy functions were combined in that way. They recommended the appointment of a financial comptroller answerable directly to the board.

As was often the case, Peats had a candidate in mind for the appointment, James Maberley Sandford Smith, 'a youngish chartered accountant who for some years had been with the Milk Marketing Board, latterly as Chief Accountant at £2,500 a year', itself a measure of the high salaries earned by accountants who moved over into industry (Reader, 1976: 144). This case-study also shows that the accountant's passage into industry was sometimes far from smooth. Sandford Smith, as financial comptroller, soon clashed with Robert Barlow, the autocratic chairman and managing director of Metal Box and one of Chandler's entrepreneurial heroes, 'who transformed Metal Box' from a loose federation 'into a modern industrial enterprise' (Chandler, 1990: 319). Barlow resented Sandford Smith for not only reorganizing the accounting system but also making suggestions for improvement outside his own department (Reader, 1976: 144–5). The outcome was that Sandford Smith left to join the board of the consultancy firm Harold Whitehead Partners Ltd. His successor, the chartered accountant Henry Chisolm (who qualified with Barton, Mayhew & Co. and initially left public practice for industry in 1933), was appointed in 1945. 'He had barely been in office a year before the pattern of Sandford Smith's experience began to repeat itself', and when he disagreed with Barlow about the rate of dividend to be paid, Chisolm 'joined the lengthening roll of accountants who had passed rapidly through the head office of Metal Box since its foundation' (Reader, 1976: 149). Chisolm moved on to become joint managing director at A. C. Cossar Ltd., electrical and scientific instrument makers.

The route from special work into the employment of a client is evident in the career of Richard Luff who left Deloitte, Plender, Griffiths & Co. in 1928, at the time they acted for the British cable companies in the merger with Marconi. Luff was promoted to chief accountant of Cable & Wireless in 1930, treasurer in 1941, and joint managing director in 1946 (Barty-King, 1979: 318). As with many of our other examples, it would be interesting to know whether Luff's rise through the organization was a reflection of the financial problems and complexities of a vast establishment which required the expertise of a professionally trained accountant, or whether Luff simply proved himself to be an able general manager.

The route into business was, therefore, sometimes from a firm of investigating accountants, but it was more often from auditor to client company. This linkage, familiar even before the First World War, became increasingly common during the inter-war period. In 1920, for example, Stephenson Grace left James & Henry Grace, Bristol, for J. S. Fry & Sons Ltd. (Grace et al., 1957: ch. 4). In the same year, Robert Fowler moved from the Birmingham practice of Gibson & Ashford to the chocolate manufacturers Cadburys at Bournville (Williams, 1931: 242). In 1933, N. Richard R.

Brooke left the Birmingham-based firm Carter & Co. to join one of its major clients, Guest Keen & Nettlefold, to take charge of the accounting department of GKN's East Moors steel works (Jones, 1990: 141). He rose to become a main board director and chairman of various GKN subsidiaries in the 1960s (*WW*, 1981: 324).

A major factor in the growing recruitment of professional accountants by business is that accountancy became established, during the inter-war period, as a management training, and the present-day practice of young people joining an accountancy firm with every intention of leaving, on qualification, to start a career in industry became not uncommon. During the inter-war period, for just about the first time, therefore, there was a clearly defined career progression for the accountant who moved into industry. The following sequences of progression, common today, were firmly established by the 1930s: recruitment as a junior accountant, promotion to chief accountant, then perhaps to financial controller and financial director. Then, increasingly, the accountant made the significant switch into general management, rising to the position of general manager, managing director, and, perhaps, receiving the ultimate accolade as chairman.

We have many instances of accountants leaving their practice within a year of qualifying and then going on to prominence. These include William Ewing Eadie who qualified in 1921, Robert Paterson Smith in 1925, and John Francis Strain in 1928, all Scottish chartered accountants and future chairmen of Burmah Oil (Corley, 1988). Herbert John Inston, formerly a clerk with Blackburn, Barton, Mayhew, joined their audit clients Bowater as chief accountant and secretary in 1928, and rose to board level by 1952 (Reader, 1981: 71–2, 92). George John Regis Leo d'Erlanger (Higham, 1984: 77–9) qualified with George A. Touche & Co. in 1930, and left public practice in the same year to join Imperial Airways, becoming chairman of BEA in 1947 and BOAC in the 1950s. Sir Arthur Eric Courtney Drake (Ferrier, 1984: 169–72) qualified in 1933 and left Jackson, Pixley & Co. a year later to join the Anglo-Iranian Oil Company, becoming general manager by the early 1950s and chairman of the renamed British Petroleum in 1969. George James Harris (Kaner, 1985: 70–4), previously with Deloitte, Plender, Griffiths & Co., joined Rowntree as an accountant on qualifying in 1923, and had risen to company chairman by 1941. Other cases include John Eric Rowe, who joined the accounting department of the US division of the Sun Life Assurance Company on qualification in 1929, and eventually became a board member at BSA. On qualification in 1930, Sir Basil Smallpeice moved from Bullimore & Co. to become accountant and assistant secretary at Hoover Ltd., the vacuum cleaner manufacturers. He joined Doulton & Co. Ltd. in 1937, where he became secretary and chief accountant responsible for costing and accountancy at the factories, and for financial administration and company secretary's work at headquarters (*Accountant*, 7 Jan. 1950: 10–11). Smallpeice later became a director at BOAC and Cunard (see Chapter 6).

Accountancy's potential as a business education was also recognized early on by family firms. Ernest Palmer, founder partner of Huntley & Palmer, arranged for his elder son Cecil, who had initially entered the factory as an apprentice after leaving university, to join Price, Waterhouse & Co., the company's auditors, with whom close links had developed over many years. On qualification in 1911, Cecil Palmer immediately rejoined the firm as a director and had a successful career (Corley, 1972: 184). When Huntley & Palmer went public, in 1919, the junior directors recognized a need to improve the company's administration, and established a finance committee and a committee of management. The former, under Cecil's chairmanship, was charged with the responsibility 'to determine the company's exact financial circumstances and prospects, which even the directors did not know precisely, as events in the next year or two were to reveal' (Corley, 1972: 204). Cecil's brother Eric became chairman in 1926 and, in the endeavour to improve the company's financial performance, he set up an economy committee once again headed by Cecil, now deputy chairman. It carried out a thorough investigation and suggested economies in various parts of the business (Corley, 1972: 216). Cecil Palmer ascended to the family peerage in 1950 and, in Corley's view, 'As a chartered accountant, he had played a key role in the financial affairs of the Company and Group alike' (Corley, 1972: 254). Robert Sainsbury, son of John Benjamin Sainsbury, founder of the grocery chain, is a further example of an aspiring businessman who saw the advantage of obtaining a chartered accountancy qualification before joining the family firm. He qualified with Gane, Jackson, Jeffreys & Freeman in 1930 and immediately joined Sainsbury's head office, becoming director and company secretary in 1934 and four years later joint general manager (Shaw, 1986: 1–11).

There was clearly then a well-established market in managerial talent by the inter-war period, albeit one based very much on personal contact. In accountancy, movement was not all in one direction; some accountants left public practice on what proved to be a temporary basis. Leonard Coates, for example, who joined the Canadian Pacific Ocean Services in 1911, returned as a partner in Blackburn, Barton, Mayhew & Co. in 1922. At the time of his death, twenty-two years later, he was senior partner of Blackburns Coates & Co. of Leeds (Grace et al., 1957: ch. 4). Stanley Hillyer, of Hillyer & Hillyer, went into the forces during the First World War, subsequently joined the Ministry of Food (where he was awarded an OBE for his work), and served as chief accountant of the Bank of London and South America before returning to professional practice (Hill Vellacott, 1988: 41). William McLintock's brother Charles left the firm of Thomson McLintock in 1918 and spent many years in industry, becoming a managing director of British Ropes, but responded to the firm's need for another senior partner in London in 1934 (Winsbury, 1977: 30, 35). A similar vacuum arose at George A. Touche & Co. in 1931, following the death of Touche's partner John Hunter, and this led the firm to 'head hunt' Robert Adams who had left the firm for commerce two years earlier (Richards, 1981: 21). Finally, Norman Gerald Lancaster returned to Howard Smith, Thompson & Co. in 1945, having switched to industry in the mid-1930s, becoming joint managing director of the motor components firm Fisher and Ludlow (Howard Smith, Thompson, 1967: 8). His return was short-lived, as he left again to become a director of Tube Investments in 1949.

ACCOUNTANTS IN CHARGE

How good were the accountants that made their way to the top in industry during this period? Quality of management cannot be measured in any precise way, but a number of case-studies will give some indication of the nature and quality of the work of leading accountants in British management at this time. The existing literature certainly suggests some success stories.

In 1921, Bennet Palmer, a practising accountant (no relation to the founder of the firm which he was soon to join), was appointed secretary of the biscuit makers Huntley, Boorme and Stevens 'with the task of introducing a costing system there. . . . [since] no proper check had been kept on costs and prices' (Corley, 1972: 209). Some form of crude standard costing was attempted by Palmer who, in the endeavour to ensure that costs did not get out of hand, had the responsibility for establishing a comparison of estimated with actual costs of each order or job going through the factory. The company's historian observes that, 'since accurate costing and estimation are the lifeblood of any company, what was good for a tin works was good for a biscuit factory, even though the latter made for stock while the former made to order' (Corley, 1972: 209). In 1921, Palmer also became secretary of Huntley & Palmer, where 'he soon introduced a system of monthly profit estimates, which were to be of considerable value during the next difficult decade' (Corley, 1972: 209). Bennet Palmer retired as financial director of Huntley & Palmer in 1962 (Corley, 1972: 271).

George Morris Wright, a chartered accountant who left public practice in about 1915 to join Debenhams, is attributed with having 'secured Debenhams against what might have been spectacular disaster' (Corina, 1978: 103). Having bought the Drapery Trust at an inflated price from the notorious Clarence Hatry and with public confidence shaken by declining profits and the unfavourable publicity arising from the Hatry connection, Debenhams plunged towards a crisis. However:

The man of the moment proved to be G. M. Wright whose financial recommendations were severe—a comprehensive rewriting of capital and a complete merger of Debenhams, the Drapery Trust and the controlling interests of Debenhams Securities. Put starkly, the plan was to reduce the reorganized group's capital. By a series of share revaluations, cancellations and other changes, the combined issued capital was to be spectacularly slashed from £15,100,000 to £6,000,000. (Corina, 1978: 105)

The removal of 'a large unremunerative slab of capital' brought 'a sense of realism' to the consolidated balance sheet which presented 'a more conservative and considered view of the group's position' (Corina, 1978: 105). The reconstruction scheme, when taken before the High Court for approval, was described by Mr Justice Eve as 'absolutely fair' in distributing the impact between shareholders of all classes (Corina, 1978: 105).

The 1930s were 'vital, lusty years for Debenhams' (Corina, 1978: 113), led by the energetic F. J. Pope. Wright was the perfect foil, 'insular by instinct . . . his influence on financial policy was beyond challenge. The sheer complexities of Debenhams at this time were apparently understood only by Wright' (Corina, 1978: 113). His role was 'to reform accounting systems, often staging large secretariat conferences to impress on everyone the need for more unity among stores in keeping their books. While Pope was driving salesmen, Wright poured [sic] over bought ledgers and reformed counting houses' (Corina, 1978: 113). Wright was subsequently promoted to managing director and, in 1948, at which time Debenhams was the largest departmental store group in Britain, he became chairman.

We have seen that accountants were heavily involved in a rapidly growing industry of the inter-war period, namely oil. Burmah Oil was managed extensively by accountants, many of whom were Scottish, and accountants also enjoyed a degree of prominence at British Petroleum. In 1929, John Francis Strain joined Burmah Oil and, according to Corley, the company's historian, was successful in focusing attention on the company's cash-flow problems, taking action to avoid a financial crisis (Corley, 1988: 369). He became chief accountant in 1950 and deputy chairman in 1967. William Ewing Eadie joined Burmah in Rangoon in 1921, moved to London in 1928, became chief accountant in 1948, and rose through the ranks to board level, ascending to the position of managing director and, finally, chairman in 1957 (Corley, 1988: 60, 164, 217). The third Scottish chartered accountant following Eadie's path, first as managing director and subsequently as chairman of Burmah Oil, was Robert Paterson Smith, who had initially joined Asiatic Petroleum in 1926. The close links between Burmah Oil and BP are reflected in the fact that Eadie and Smith were, respectively, on the board of the latter between 1955–64 and 1957–71. By way of contrast, the Scottish chartered accountant Alistair Frederick Down, who joined Anglo-Iranian Oil Co. in 1938, in due course rose to become managing director of BP. Down was subsequently installed as chairman of Burmah Oil, at the behest of the Bank of England, after it neared bankruptcy in 1975, and remained there until 1983, having brought the company back to profitability (Corley, 1984: 159).

Alfred Chandler's severe criticisms of British corporate governance in this period serve as a helpful framework for pursuing further this analysis of the contribution of accountants to business. Chandler made three substantial points: first, that British companies were dominated by family ownership and control for too long and therefore did not derive economies of scale and scope; second, these firms did not invest in production, marketing, and professional management; and third, the holding company allowed the maintenance of family control through its subsidiaries (1990: 240, 287). Below, we focus on family firms (Courtaulds in synthetic fibres; Joseph Lucas, the motor components makers; and Pilkington, the glass makers) and holding companies (GKN, the steel makers and engineers; Beechams, the drug manufacturers; and English China Clays) all of which (with the exception of English China Clays) come in for criticism from Chandler.

Courtaulds, a company where, according to Chandler (1990: 310), the 'owners' continuing commitment to the ways of personal management retarded the development of managerial and technical skills', was none the less a company well served by professional accountants. Arthur Hugoe 'Loxley' Kilner, recruited as chief accountant in 1913, was at the centre of various financial machinations, including the formation of the American Viscose Corporation, in 1922, both to help conceal the level of profits earned in that country and to enable those profits to be remitted to the UK in a tax-efficient manner (Coleman, 1969: 149)—a reminder that creative accounting is not an innovation of recent origin. One scheme comprised an early example of the 'special purpose vehicle', much in the news since the mid-1980s as a means of arranging 'off balance sheet finance', that is a legal technique designed to enable companies to raise finance in such a way that the liability does not appear in the balance sheet (Pimm, 1991). In the 1920s, under Kilner's tax avoidance scheme, two companies were established in Liechtenstein in such a way that they were controlled by Courtaulds and the profits accrued to Courtaulds, but Courtaulds was not technically the legal owner (Coleman, 1969: 280–1). As a result of his work in this and other directions, Kilner was promoted to the position of director in 1935, and was succeeded by another chartered accountant, Roy Anderson Kinnes, previously of Price Waterhouse. Kinnes, who according to Jones was 'yet another instance of an accountant playing a major part in long-term planning', in turn joined the board in 1939 (Jones, 1981: 158; Coleman, 1969: 222, 224). Kinnes pushed forward the policy of creating a holding company to control the company's subsidiaries and asked his old firm, Price Waterhouse, to prepare a report on the scheme in 1943, although it was not implemented until 1947.

Joseph Lucas was another family firm keen to benefit from the professional skills of talented accountants, somewhat at odds with the picture of amateurism painted by Chandler. The leading accountant in the Lucas success story is Bertram Waring who started his career in practice but later commented, 'though I had every prospect of becoming a partner . . . I decided I would like to get into business or industry and find out what it was all about' (Nockolds, 1976: 194). His was a long and distinguished career. Following a private education and war-interrupted training, he qualified as a chartered accountant in 1920, moving almost immediately into industry where he worked as assistant secretary of a foundry company in Derby. Meanwhile, a visit made by Oliver Lucas to the United States, around this time, demonstrated the importance of the economies of scale. On his return, Lucas immediately introduced organizational changes at his engineering firm designed to obtain these benefits, and Waring was recruited in 1922 to achieve related improvements in the company's information systems. He became company secretary in 1924 and 'proved adept at applying the policies of Lucas and [Peter] Bennett who left day to day management to him' (Jeremy and Tweedale, 1994: 220). Eight years later, Lucas acquired M. L. Magneto Syndicate, which proved highly beneficial, in that 'a bright young cost accountant named Frederick Coleman' was recruited, whom Waring 'decided to train as a sort of administrative consultant or trouble shooter' (Nockolds, 1976: 252). Coleman went through the whole system of costing procedures at the main works and found them 'antiquated, long-handed and individually carried out instead of being co-ordinated. . . . his recommendations helped to set the pattern for the decentralised reorganisation of autonomous companies within the Lucas group' (Nockolds, 1976: 252).

Trips to the United States by Lucas management, undertaken to keep in touch with new developments, were regularly arranged. In 1935, Fred Coleman, attached at this time to the Lucas subsidiary Rotax Ltd., was part of one team and, when in the United States,

used his experience of estimating at Lucas to assess the cost of American products as they visited various factories. It appears that Lucas benefited enormously from the trip, as the Americans allowed Coleman to look at their costing, accounting and financial systems. Waring was doing for his side of the business, through Coleman and others, what Oliver Lucas was doing in terms of technology. (Nockolds, 1976: 299)

Waring was appointed to the Lucas board, in 1935, and took on major managerial responsibilities, with his 'strength as an accountant invaluable in assessing and shaping the company's financial policy and procedures' (Nockolds, 1976: 298). During the Second World War he operationally managed 40,000 employees in 33 factories, and was appointed joint managing director in 1948. He became chairman in 1951 and remained in the top position until his retirement in 1969, when he was invited to become the company's first honorary president (Nockolds, 1976: 195). Waring is judged to have transformed Lucas from a 'Birmingham business producing accessories for the motor industry into an international group with interests spreading into aviation components and industrial engineering. In 1951, sales of £42.5 million produced a net profit of £928,297; in 1969 sales of £251 million, world-wide, made £16.7 million pre-tax profit. Employment numbers rose from [20,000 when he joined the board to] 45,000 in 1955 to 65,000 in 1966' (Jeremy and Tweedale, 1994: 220). Nockolds' assessment of Waring is that: 'Although an accountant by trade, he became, in time, a great all rounder, a wise and far sighted administrator, as shrewd in commercial dealings as he was in finance, and with an exceptional regard for the human basis on which all businesses ultimately depend' (Nockolds, 1976: 224).

At the family firm of Pilkington, there was also evidence of a well-trained professional management team at work. Lord Cozens-Hardy took over the chairmanship in 1931, reorganized the division of responsibility between departmental committees, and introduced a system of budgetary controls (Barker, 1977: 329). In practice, this responsibility devolved upon the company's chief accountant, L. Robson, who, having studied the budgetary controls devised by de Paula at Dunlops, brought the proposals to fruition at Pilkington in 1933. Three chartered accountants assisted him and, in total, fifteen accountants were in posts at Pilkington in 1933 (Barker, 1977: 337).

The widespread practice of arranging British business activity through the holding company structure, during the inter-war period, has been severely criticized, not only as we have noted by Chandler (1990: 12), but also by Armstrong (1987: 429–30, 433). Guest Keen and Nettlefold, the engineering firm, has borne the brunt of Chandler's ire, given that it was said to be a loose confederation run by the original families with virtually no central control (Chandler, 1990: 317). Here, although Chandler makes no mention of him, the career of James Hornby Jolly provides a good example of the functions performed by accountants working inside holding companies at this time (Jones, 1985b: 523). As noted in Chapter 4, Jolly had left the profession in 1911, joining GKN as secretary seven years later, where he was 'surprised by the company's antiquated methods of keeping financial records' (Jones, 1985b: 524). Jolly insisted that he become the chief accountant and, by his own assessment, 'created a certain order out of chaos'. This led to his elevation to the GKN board in 1930, becoming managing director in 1934 and chairman for 1947–53 (Jones, 1990: 288). His contribution is assessed as follows by Jones: 'A finance and administration man but very clear headed in the way in which things should go', and a 'conservative businessman who believed in the value of economy', a 'cautious, conservative chairman, Jolly did not make any strategic changes of direction. His contribution was to hold the group on a steady course during a period of growth' (Jones, 1990: 525–6).

Jolly clearly believed in the holding company form of business organization. The GKN group operated as a set of largely independent concerns, enabling individual subsidiaries to make their own decisions and run their own affairs. A limited range of centralized functions were carried out by the small accountancy staff, so that the head office at Smethwick functioned as little more than 'a central accounting department' (Jones, 1990: 297). Professionally qualified accountants were increasingly recruited at GKN to work at head office and in the major manufacturing units as a result of Jolly's influence (Jones, 1985b: 525). The chartered accountant Eric Charles Drake left the profession in 1911 and ten years later joined GKN as chief accountant, allowing Jolly to concentrate on wider duties. When Jolly became managing director in 1934, Drake also took on the responsibility of company secretary. Other appointments included, in 1948, W. A. Nickle, previously one of Jolly's assistants, as company secretary and W. W. Fea as chief accountant (Jones, 1990: 288).

The financial reports prepared for head office helped top management to monitor individual performance, but the extent to which they were used as a basis for intervening and influencing policy-making at subsidiary company level remains unclear. Jolly analysed the subsidiaries' balance sheets and their performance and his influence was reinforced by appointment to the boards of a number of these concerns. Apparently, however, control was hindered by the absence from subsidiaries' financial reports of any standardized accounting procedures (Jones, 1990: 287, 369). Jolly was not against the consolidation of the accounts but did not give it priority, preferring instead to improve the company's management and reporting policies. As managing director in the 1930s, Jolly masterminded a modernization programme of the company's works and expanded into areas linked to the main business through acquisition. As chairman in the 1940s, he set up holding companies which separated the steel-making business, which was nationalized, from the other activities which remained in the company's hands. Within this framework and under Jolly's management, GKN was a profitable company which grew, on Chandler's own evidence, from nineteenth largest company in 1919 to thirteenth in 1948, benefiting greatly from the growth in the demand for sheet steel from the motor industry (Jones, 1985b: 526; Chandler, 1990: 326). There is, therefore, no prima-facie evidence to show that the holding company was an inefficient mechanism for organizing and running a company.

A similar story may be told for the pharmaceutical company Beechams Pills Ltd., representing an example of the influence of accountants among the new industries. Facing financial difficulties in 1927, the family firm was rescued by Phillip Hill working in association with Louis Nicholas (of Louis Nicholas & Co.), a Liverpool chartered accountant and financier (Lazell, 1975: 77, 90). After the reconstruction, Nicholas became managing director, but strong rivalry between him and another accountant, Stanley Holmes (later Lord Dovercourt, senior partner at Holmes & Sons), who became joint managing director following the acquisition of Yeast-Vite in 1931, resulted in Nicholas being made vice-chairman and concentrating his attention on aspects of the business which did not bring the two into direct conflict with one another. A further important appointment at Beechams around this time was the 'fine [chartered] accountant, particularly in the sphere of investigations', Bernard Hobrow, who joined them as secretary in 1930, one year after qualifying (Lazell, 1975: 27). Soon afterwards, Hobrow was appointed assistant managing director of Beechams. Indeed, Beechams was run by professional accountants in the 1930s since it appears that, once ensconced, they did their best to ensure that new appointees also possessed that qualification.

The structure of Beechams, under the leadership of accountants, is of interest. The firm operated through a large number of subsidiaries and made no attempt to rationalize or consolidate new businesses acquired. They remained the responsibility of local managers who, it is said, were in the main underpaid and under-controlled. On the other hand, as might be expected, 'the whole accounting system of Beechams was first-class' and, as at GKN, the firm's headquarters was essentially an accounting office. At local level, the procedure was for the board of each subsidiary to hold a meeting each month which was 'almost wholly financial in content'. 'The Beechams subsidiary accounts were designed to disclose all indirect and capital expenditure in a whole series of schedules attached to the year-end accounts. No manager could indulge himself without seeing his extravagance in black and white at the end of the year!' (Lazell, 1975: 27). Again, as with GKN, the weaknesses of the holding company structure are by no means apparent in view of Beechams' results in this period, when the company went from being 138th largest British company with a market value of £2.3 million in 1930, to 34th largest with a market value of £22.4 million in 1948 (Chandler, 1990: 676, 683).

In 1929, John Keay joined the English China Clays (ECC) board as secretary; the company having earlier that year taken over William Varcoe, the china clay merchants, an audit client of Bourner, Bullock & Co., the firm with whom Keay qualified in 1921. Keay became managing director in 1931, at a time when the china clay industry 'was doing worse than ever' (Hudson, 1985: 568). The industry's response to crisis was rationalization. In 1932, ECC merged with its two main competitors, Lovering China Clays and H. D. Pochin & Co., to become 'a holding company, its assets being transferred to a new trading company, English Clays Lovering Pochin & Co.' (Hudson, 1985: 568). The survival of English Clays Lovering Pochin & Co. (ECLP) in the 1930s and 1940s 'was largely due to Keay's energy and foresight', an achievement which brought him a knighthood in 1950 (Hudson, 1985: 568). His reconstruction of the company involved the replacement of small-scale methods by mass production, and his 'rare combination of financial expertise and strong technical interests made him an exceptionally suitable person to guide the fortunes of ECC and ECLP' (Hudson, 1985: 568). Keay became chairman of ECC in 1947 and, six years later, chairman and managing director of ECLP. Between 1947 and 1963 (when he retired), the issued capital of ECC was increased from £1,895,661 to £10,549,716.

CONCLUDING COMMENTS

The First World War did much to raise the profile of professional accountants in the administration of public life. They were called into various government departments to help manage the war effort, and their contribution at the Ministry of Munitions was particularly marked. These achievements were no doubt a factor in the increasing willingness of business as well as the government to call in the Plenders, McLintocks, and Garnseys to help, advise, and resolve difficult problems during the inter-war period. The rationalization of the old industries and the reorganization of newer industries to help them compete more efficiently both in British and on world markets earned accountants sobriquets such as 'business doctors' and 'surgeons of commerce' (*Accountant*, 19 July 1919: 58).

The recognition of the broadening role in business played by professional accountants is evident from the following item headed 'In the Highest Spheres', which appeared in the *Accountant* in 1929. The content of the extract also reflects the desire of the still-young profession to advertise growing recognition of the contributions which its members were making to public life.

Hardly a week now passes without some tribute to the profession in spheres outside the usual audit routine. The official announcement was recently made of the provisional agreement for the merger of Dorman, Long & Co., Ltd., and Bolckow, Vaughan & Co., Ltd., two great iron and steel manufacturers. Once again leaders of the profession were called in and the terms under which the fusion will be made are the result of their deliberations. The actual agreement itself is the work of Sir William McLintock, G.B.E., C.V.O., F.C.A., while Sir William Plender,

Bart., G.B.E., F.C.A., and Sir William B. Peat, C.V.O., F.C.A., gave their endorsement on behalf of the two companies. The intricacy of the calculations can be seen from the fact that the interests of ordinary and preference shareholders and four classes of debenture holders were involved, with a total capital of nearly twenty millions. The appointment of Sir Basil Mayhew, K.B.E., F.C.A., and Mr. C. J. G. Palmour, F.C.A., as trustees for the debenture stockholders of the new British Amalgamated Theatres, Ltd., is a reminder of another sphere which accountants are eminently capable of filling. Those responsible for the administration of the two great accountancy bodies rightly insist that general audit practice is merely the foundation of an accountant's work. It is on the wide practical experience which he derives therefrom joined to his theoretical knowledge that he attains to the capacity to fill such posts in the industrial and financial world. (19 Oct. 1929: 485)

The inter-war period also saw professional accountants moving from public practice into industry in increasingly large numbers. Some were appointed directly to top positions, such as d'Arcy Cooper at Lever Brothers, whereas others, such as Richard Luff at Cable & Wireless, worked their way up from relatively junior appointments. Both of these individuals moved from accountancy firm to client company, and this was becoming an increasingly common occurrence with industry able to recruit personnel with whom they were familiar and whose expertise they admired. A further developing trend was the tendency for professional accountants to leave public practice soon after qualifying, reflecting recognition of the period of articles as an entirely suitable training for performing the finance function within industrial companies and as a preparation for business management generally.

We also see growing signs of accountants rising to prominent positions. Between 1931 and 1951, there was a more than doubling in the proportion of companies with a trained accountant on their board (Table 15, row 3), and it is likely that the very largest companies used accountants more than the above figures (from a random sample of quoted companies) suggest. Our survey of the largest companies, which we have culled from mainly secondary sources, indicates the prevalence of their involvement at senior management level. These ranged from the largest companies in the land—such as Unilever (1st in terms of market value in 1930 according to Chandler), Dunlop (11th), GKN (14th), and Vickers (15th)—to even larger public utilities such as Cable & Wireless and the Gas Light & Coke Company, and included the family firms of Courtaulds (6th), Lucas (97th), Pilkington (117th), Huntley & Palmer, and Sainsbury. It is difficult to say whether this demonstration of the involvement of accountants in management amounts to evidence that the British did not suffer from a lack of professional management in this period as Chandler and others have argued. We will return to the question of the quality of accountancy as a management training in the final chapter and, whatever the truth of the matter, Table 15 indicates that only a small fraction of managing directors or company chairmen were accountants at this time. None the less, the overall impact of accountants was undoubtedly formidable, and they were a resource, a fund of business knowledge and experience extending beyond the financial sphere, which probably no other country had in such abundance.

6

Rise of the 'Priesthood' in the Post-Second World War Era

This chapter focuses principally on the continued rise to primacy of the accountant in industry in the post-Second World War period. As in the First World War, the contribution made by accountants to the successful administration of the finance and organization of industry was again important in the Second World War, and we start this chapter with a brief review of the way in which their value was recognized and their profile raised during this latter conflict. We then move on to a discussion of the main economic developments of the post-war period, given that these shaped the environment within which the accountant subsequently flourished. The public accountancy practice continued to be the main reservoir from which were drawn accountants involved in top management, and the continued growth in the size and range of work undertaken by these organizations, for business, is next examined. We see accountants as having found their way into business through a variety of 'routes', and it is useful to summarize these at this stage of the story, and refer to how their relative importance has altered over time. Examples are then provided of individuals entering through each of these routes during the post-war period, and their background and the contribution made to the administration of the firms that they served is discussed. Finally, we close this chapter with a numerical analysis of the involvement of accountants generally in industry, of the rise of the finance director, and the extent to which they occupy positions in top management.

ACCOUNTANTS AT WAR

With war imminent, the ICAEW invited members to enter their names on a Central Register. By the beginning of 1939, 6,000 members (out of a total membership of 13,000) had indicated their readiness 'in time of war or other emergency to offer themselves for appropriate work in their professional capacity, while 3,000 others had indicated that they were prepared to undertake whole-time national service' (Howitt, 1966: 93). Accountancy was in due course placed on the Schedule of Reserved Occupations, with the age of reservation fixed at 30. The 1942 proclamation that all men up to 45 years old were liable for military service produced some consternation, but the special position of accountancy was recognized through a favourable response to applications for individual deferment, often based on 'the continued pressure upon them from the Ministries and the Inland Revenue, and the continued inadequacy in the numbers of trained personnel' (Garrett, 1961: 213).

We saw that, at the start of the First World War, the government possessed little by way of suitably skilled economic and accounting staffs and, with regard to costing for example, outside help was enlisted from the outset in large numbers. Stacey sees a rather different situation arising in the second war: 'the civil service possessed a competent cadre of economists and accountants, therefore securing expert assistance in the initial stages of the war was less vital. But as hostilities progressed an increasing number of specialists were recruited' (Stacey, 1954: 192). The Board of Trade discovered its staff of 2,000 to be totally inadequate; it 'therefore expanded its complement to 6,500 and found the accountancy profession to be a particularly fruitful source of additional administrative personnel' (Walker and Shackleton, 1995: 478) Three new ministries were set up (Economic Welfare, Food, and Shipping) which 'required accountants in large numbers to cost manufacturing processes, discover frauds or profiteering, and to cope with the vast bureaucracies that these ministries created and use their managerial skills to smooth their operation' (Jones, 1981: 189). The Central Register was used to help allocate professional accountants to departments requiring additional expertise (Garrett, 1961: 211), while the services of firms of accountants were also enlisted in certain circumstances. When the Ministry of Supply was concerned to ensure proper control over the supply of raw materials, for example, the Accountants Advisory Selection Panel was set up under the chairmanship of Nicholas Waterhouse to recommend the appointment of firms to undertake certain tasks (Garrett, 1961: 211).

The range of responsibilities undertaken by professional accountants during the Second World War has been summarized as follows:

On price regulation committees, over the problems of clothes, food and raw materials rationing, purchase tax, rent control, custodianship of enemy property and the defence finance regulations, the accountant was brought in to act as an impartial arbiter between the licensing authority, the State, and the trader, or the manufacturer . . . The accountants' task was to prepare returns so that authorities could compute the extent of available supplies. On the fiscal plane the services of the accountant were indispensable to the smooth running of the financial machine. The impartial computation of liability under the excess profit tax, income tax and the national defence contribution ensured that, as much as possible, the burden of war should be covered from current earnings. Profiteering from the miseries of war, if not totally eliminated, was cut down to the minutest proportions, and much of it can be attributed to the untiring efforts of the accountancy profession. (Stacey, 1954: 191)

Overall, it has been argued, the professional accountants' 'services were invoked to a greater degree than in World War I' (Kettle, 1957: 132; see also Jones, 1981: 185). The following examples serve to illustrate the importance of the accountancy profession in providing administrative back-up to servicemen: Horace Owen Harrison Coulson of Barton, Mayhew became Director of Internal Audit to the Ministry of Food; Charles J. G. Palmour of Whinney, Smith and Whinney—a major in the Royal Army Service Corps during the First World War and ICAEW president 1938–44—was knighted in 1946 for sustained public service; John Pears of Cooper Brothers became the Principal Controller of Costs at the Ministry of Supply, responsible for costing contracts (Jones, 1981: 189); Harold Barton of Barton, Mayhew served as financial director of the National Dock Labour Corporation (1941–7), and later became controller of General Aircraft Ltd., building on his First World War experience at the Department of Aircraft Production; and Ivan Spens of Brown, Fleming & Murray served as Accountant-General to the Ministry of Supply (1939–41), Deputy Director-General of Finance and Accountant-General (1941/2), and head of the Industrial Division of the Ministry of Production (1943–5) (Jones, 1981). As in the First World War, accountants were called in to handle the assets of friends and foe alike that fell into British hands. Cooper Brothers, for example, ran the Belgian shipping fleet while McAuliffe, Turquand, Youngs took over Japanese assets in the Far East (Jones, 1981: 195).

The Second World War therefore 're-emphasised the importance of the accountants' skills and in doing so raised them further in public esteem' (Jones, 1981: 196). The continued engagement of professional accountants by government after the war—such appointments were listed in the annual report from 1954—may be found in the official history of the ICAEW (Howitt, 1966: 217–23). Bernhard Binder, whom we have seen undertook a great deal of government work during the inter-war period, was made coal supplies officer of the south Wales district during the Second World War (*The Times*, 12 July 1966). After the war, Binder visited Argentina (1946) as part of the government mission to negotiate the disposal of British-owned railways. As with a number of the leading contemporary accountants from this period, Binder was probably knighted (in 1952) in recognition of public work undertaken over an extended period of time (*The Times*, 12 July 1966). During the Second World War, Henry Benson was seconded from the army into the Ministry of Supply to advise on the reorganization of the accounts of the Royal Ordnance Factories, and was then appointed director to implement the proposed changes. This type of public sector work was undertaken by accountants on an unparalleled scale in the post-war era. Benson's early peacetime appointments, for example, included Controller of Building Materials at the Ministry of Works and adviser to the Ministry of Health on housing production (see also *WW*, 1993: 144; Jones, 1984*c*: 287–9).

ECONOMIC BACKGROUND

Economically, the post-Second World War era falls neatly in two parts. The period to the early 1970s saw low inflation and unemployment, which in the latter case never rose above 3% (Crafts, 1991: 261). Economic growth and the increase in living standards were also historically high (though poor in comparison with Britain's competitors)—real output per worker rose by about 2.5% per annum between 1951 and 1973, faster than at any time since 1873 (Crafts, 1991: 261). In this 'golden age', as economic historians now call it, the accountancy profession prospered in line with the growth in company formation (shown in Figure 3). The high level of personal taxation, a legacy from the Second World War, stimulated the accountants' role as tax advisers, while the re-emergence of the merger movement and growing scale of companies, generally, produced problems of organization and control that provided scope for the rapid development of management consultancy services.

Perhaps the most significant development, for the leading accountancy firms at least, was the growing importance of the stock exchange: 'as a result of the metamorphosis from personal to managerial capitalism City interests were much more influential by the 1970s' (Wilson, 1995: 181). Whereas domestic securities accounted for only 8% of those quoted on the stock exchange in 1913, they averaged over 90% from the late 1940s. The volume of domestic capital issues averaged around £70 million (at current prices) in the late 1940s, but had risen to over £650 million by the early 1970s (Wilson, 1995: 188). This period saw what has been called the 'rise of the cult of the equity' and, whereas retained earnings accounted for about 80% of total industrial investment during the inter-war period, external sources of capital contributed over one-half of all new finance by the late 1960s (Wilson, 1995: 183, 188).

Seemingly encouraged by the sustained economic growth of the 1950s and 1960s, there was an explosion in the number of company mergers. Figure 4 shows that, from a low point in 1950, mergers gathered momentum to reach a peak in the mid-1960s, and remained high until collapsing in the depression of the mid-1970s. In the ten years 1957–67, no less than 38% of quoted companies were acquired by other quoted companies (Hannah, 1983: 150). Important factors encouraging this process were the decline of family control over the larger firms and the disclosure requirements of the Companies Act 1948, with the latter providing potential bidders with more information on asset values and profits. Hostile take-overs became a new feature on the stock market (Hannah, 1983: 130, 149), with the technique pioneered by Charles Clore when acquiring J. Sears & Co. in 1953, 'having discovered that this company, following standard contemporary accounting procedures, had underestimated by £10 million the real estate value of its 900 shoe shops' (Wilson, 1995: 203). Takeovers, therefore, further increased the demand for accounting skills in accurately valuing target companies. Merger activity subsided in the late 1970s and early 1980s due, according to Hannah, to the conviction that recent amal-gamations had improved neither profits nor efficiency (Hannah, 1983: 149).

The 1960s exceeded both the preceding and subsequent decade in terms of the number and value of mergers, though merger activity did remain high in the early 1970s. The consequent growth in size of the leading companies, which Hannah attributes entirely to merger activity (1983: 144), meant that, whereas the 100 largest companies in manufacturing accounted for 23% of net output in 1950, by 1978 this had risen to 41% and Britain had the most concentrated industrial economy in the world (Wilson, 1995: 194–5). The degree of concentration had declined a little by the late 1980s, probably indicating a resurgence of small companies and, perhaps, an increase in competition in business generally. Figure 3 shows that company formations rose throughout the slump of the early 1980s and reached unprecedented levels in the subsequent boom but, as can be seen from Table 13, the growth occurred in the smaller, private companies sector. The numbers of employers and self-employed grew from 1,675,000 or 6.8 % of total working population in 1960, to 3,143,000 or 11.1% by 1990 (CSO, *Annual Abstract of Statistics*).

In the 1970s, the British and world economy, and with them the ac-countancy profession, entered a far more turbulent era. As had been the case for 100 years, manufacturing remained the problem sector, and its lack of international competitiveness seemed to threaten complete deindustrialization. In 1950, manufacturing accounted for 36.6% of GDP, and this held up at 34.4% in 1970; it then collapsed to 26.6% by 1980 and 22.4% in 1990 (CSO, *Annual Abstract of Statistics*). Imports as a percentage of total sales in manufactures increased from 17% to 36% between 1968 and 1989 (Griffiths and Wall, 1993: 593). In the 1970s, even the new industries of the inter-war period, such as motor manufacturing, went into absolute decline. By the early 1980s, the average rate of profit in British manufacturing, also deteriorating for over a century, approached zero (Matthews et al., 1982: 188, 346). The 1970s, the era of 'stagflation', saw both inflation and long-term unemployment begin to rise in Britain, as part of the trend elsewhere in the world. Between 1974 and 1981, inflation in Britain never fell below 11% per annum (Dimsdale, 1991: 121), while the continued rise in unemployment did not peak until it reached over three million or 11.1% of the workforce in 1986.

The post-world war period has also seen a reduction in general tariffs, under GATT agreements, and regional moves towards freeing up international trade, including Britain joining the European common market in 1973. The result has been a startling increase in international trade which, between the early 1950s and late 1980s, grew at double the rate of world industrial production (Mackintosh et al., 1996: 396). Trade in goods and services has become more important as a proportion of national income in most advanced economies. Between 1960 and 1980, for example, the share of trade in GDP increased from 20.1% to 26% in the UK, 4.7% to 10.5% in the USA, 12.6% to 23.0% in France, and from 18.7% to 33% in Germany (Mackintosh et al., 1996: 630). Capital is also now exported in much greater quantities, foreign direct investment as a proportion of GNP having more than doubled for the economies of the USA, UK, Japan, Germany, and France (Mackintosh et al., 1996: 397). Moreover, Britain exported a greater proportion of its capital abroad than almost any of its competitors, particularly after controls on foreign exchange movements were abolished by the Thatcher government in 1979. Between 1985 and 1990 the UK accounted for 17.4% of total world capital exports, second only to Japan (19.5%) (Dunning, 1993: 18; Mackintosh et al., 1996: 631). Britain has also benefited from huge amounts of inward investment, mainly from America but latterly most significantly from Japan (Foreman-Peck, 1991: 151). In 1967, UK inward investment amounted to 7.2% of its GDP, already more than other developed countries; by 1988 the figure was 17%, twice the western European average (Dunning, 1993: 20).

The Thatcher government was committed to liberalization of the markets: exchange controls were abolished, control of bank and building society lending was all but abolished, and banking and other financial services were freed of regulation. The so-called 'Big Bang' of 1986 saw outsiders let in to the London Stock Exchange, minimum commissions ended, and the closed cartels of the jobbers and brokers abolished and replaced by integrated securities houses. These last-named institutions were to play a notorious role in the spectacular company bankruptcies that characterized the end of the long boom of the 1980s. Thus Barclays de Zoete Wedd advised British and Commonwealth and Samuel Montagu advised Robert Maxwell (Smith, 1992: 15). The City of London maintained its competitive edge in world financial markets by, for example, leading the world with 18% of the international bank lending (in excess of $1,300bn.), closely followed by Japan. From 1964 to 1991, at constant factor cost, the service sector grew by 261.3%, in contrast to an overall growth in GDP of 65.3%, and of 32.4% in the manufacturing sector (almost all of which came prior to 1973) (Griffiths and Wall, 1993: 5). The financial sector doubled in importance as part of GDP, rising from 8.3% in 1964 to 16.8%

in 1991, and was ranked a close second in importance to manufacturing by the latter date. This trend in Britain is, however, only slightly more dramatic than in all advanced economies. The leading growth sector in the economy of the Thatcher era was therefore services, but even manufacturing saw a degree of improvement from the mid-1980s (Crafts, 1991: 261). Profits and the real wages of those still in work rose rapidly. It was a period of freewheeling optimism in the City and in the country.

In addition to, or concomitant with, these developments has been, since the 1970s, a transport and communications revolution (Mackintosh et al., 1996: 396). Air travel has mushroomed and satellite and computer-based telecommunications have effectively shrunk the world, furnishing the ability to buy and sell and move funds and information on a global scale instantaneously. All of these changes have led to 'the rapid growth of international economic interdependence' or the 'globalisation' of the world economy (Wilson, 1995: 230). Companies in all countries are now far more likely to operate on an international basis. Britain was at the forefront in developing the multinational enterprise in the nineteenth century, and this process accelerated after 1945. Between 1950 and 1962, 364 foreign subsidiaries (300 American) were established in Britain (Wilson, 1995: 230). In the other direction, of the largest 100 British-owned manufacturing companies in 1950, 29% had six or more overseas production operations; by 1970 the figure was 58% (Channon, 1973: 78). Major companies without overseas operations are now the exception rather than the rule.

The major economic changes outlined above have naturally had the most profound effect on the accountancy profession and, consequently, on the role and public conception of the accountant.

PROFESSIONAL FIRMS

Down to the 1970s accountancy partnerships flourished; recruitment of new accountants was accelerating, but was never quick enough to meet the increased demand. As discussed in Chapter 3, however, the broad manner in which partnership operations were conducted had changed little since Victorian times. Even the largest partnerships had only a relatively small number of partners. Price Waterhouse, for example, had only 37 partners in the whole of the UK in 1964 (Jones, 1995: 405). Growth was steady if unspectacular. The fee income at Price Waterhouse grew, in 1995 prices, from £9.4 million in 1945 to £14.5 million in 1960; while Whinney, Smith & Whinney's income rose from £2 million to £4.2 million over the same period (Jones, 1995: 403; Jones, 1981: 99). Just as important—despite a certain amount of adverse publicity for auditors in connection with the collapse of Rolls Razor, the takeover of Associated Electrical Industries by

GEC, and the Leasco bid for Pergamon (Edwards, 1996: 58–61)—the profession just about maintained its public reputation of reliability and probity, though unable to shake off its dull image. At the level of the individual, the American humourist H. L. Mencken probably still held sway:

'Suppose you had your free choice between going to a convention of Rotarians and going to a convention of accountants, which would you choose? Obviously you would choose the convention of Rotarians, just as you would go to the Folies Bergere rather than to a meeting of the Ladies' Aid Society. Accountants, in their way, are the wisest of men. Once, working as a newspaper reporter, I covered one of their assemblages, and in four days I didn't hear a single foolish word. What they said was sober, sound and indubitable. But it was also as flat as dishwater.'

The increased scale of British companies, together with the growth of multinational activity and the need for international competitiveness in order to survive, has been closely mirrored by British accountancy firms. In the 1960s, the largest firms could still quite clearly be identified as rather gentlemanly, accountancy practices in the nineteenth-century sense; by the mid-1980s, they were more accurately categorized as multi-activity multinational organizations operating in the financial services industry. Whinney, Smith & Whinney's fee income (at 1995 prices) grew from £4.2 million in 1960 to £155.8 million (as Ernst & Whinney) in 1986/7 and £401.2 million (as Ernst & Young) in 1995 (*Accountancy Age*, 18 June 1987; *Accountancy*, July 1995: 18; Jones, 1981: 99). The Appendix (Ernst & Whinney, Arthur Young) shows that much of this growth arose from merger, but this was less so at Price Waterhouse where, as the Appendix also shows, there was little by way of merger activity in the 1970s and 1980s, but where fee income (at 1995 prices) grew from £14.5 million in 1960, to £46.6 million in 1970, to £216.0 million by 1986/7, and £383.2 million by 1995 (*Accountancy Age*, 18 June 1987; *Accountancy*, July 1995: 18; Jones, 1995: 410). And, whereas Price Waterhouse had 37 UK partners in 1964, there were 463 by 1990, though this had been reduced to 399 by 1995 (*Accountancy*, July 1995: 18; Jones, 1995: 405 and 408). The absence of mergers at Price Waterhouse has clearly affected its ranking in terms of fee income; over three times the size of Ernst & Whinney in 1960, Price Waterhouse had been overtaken by that firm 35 years later.

These professional practices, dominated by members of the ICAEW and ICAS, have been the major training ground for accountants as business managers during the post-war period. More accountants were now qualifying in industry with the ACCA and CIMA, but the bulwark of the professional accountant's domination of business management remains attributable to those who obtain their training in public practice. We therefore examine the development of professional firms, both to demonstrate the services which they provided directly for industry, and to indicate the kinds of skill that their staff could take with them when transferring their allegiance to the corporate sector. We also note that the changing nature of the leading professional firms helped equip migrant accountants for their new challenges.

As before, we do not intend to provide a comprehensive history of the functioning of the professional practice, but instead attempt to supply an important contextual ingredient for our understanding of the rise of the professional accountant in business management. A key contribution of the inter-war period—rationalization, rescues, and mergers—does not therefore warrant separate consideration here, and we also leave aside, as no longer central to our story, the insolvency work which initially did so much to establish the reputation of the accountant as a master of figures and financial affairs. We focus instead on taxation work, which grew significantly in importance in the post-war period, auditing, which remains the key link between the accountancy profession and industry, and management consultancy, which was increasingly responsible for driving the growth of accountancy firms and demonstrating the range of valuable skills possessed by their employees.

Table 16 shows that the number of accountants employed directly by business has continued to grow throughout the post-war period, but employment in practice still accounts for a third of all qualified accountants and a half of all chartered accountants. Table 14 gives the unique and much-used income figures for Whinney, Smith & Whinney down to 1995. This shows that earnings from insolvency remained relatively insignificant in their business. This picture receives some confirmation from the staffing ratios at Price Waterhouse's London office. In 1955, apart from the partners and managers (whose work is not apportioned), Price Waterhouse had two personnel each in liquidations and management consultancy, but 22 in tax and 206 in auditing. By 1968 they had 412 in audit (insolvency was subsumed in this figure), 40 in tax, and 45 in management consultancy (Jones, 1995: 404). In 1986, for the first time, we have a helpful breakdown of fee income for six of the top ten firms, Coopers & Lybrand (ranked first), Peat Marwick Mitchell (second), Price Waterhouse (third), Touche Ross (sixth), Arthur Andersen (eighth), and KMG Thomson McLintock (tenth). On average, these firms took 58% of their fees from auditing, 19% from tax, 17% from management consultancy, and 6% from insolvency (*Accountant*, 19 June 1986: 14–15). The relative growth areas in the post-war period had clearly been management consultancy and tax, and this trend continued through to 1995 when the corresponding percentages for the top six firms were as follows: auditing 38%, tax 24%, management consultancy 28%, and insolvency 8% (*Accountancy*, July 1995: 19).

Auditing

It can be inferred from Table 14 that auditing and general accounting work, when expressed as a proportion of the total services supplied by the big firms, has seen a comparative decline in the years since the Second World War. From being regularly well over three-quarters of Whinney, Smith & Whinney's earnings in the 1930s, audits accounted for just over two-thirds of fee income in the 1950s and 1960s. Such proportions can, however, conceal more than they reveal. The phenomenal growth in the business of the big accountancy firms in this period was still due largely to the rising earnings from audit work. Whinney, Smith & Whinney's audit business grew from £64,904 in 1945 (£1.5 million at 1995 prices) to £66.5 million (as Ernst & Whinney) in 1986/7 (£102.8 million at 1995 prices) at which time auditing and accounting still accounted for 66% of their income (Jones, 1981: 99; *Accountancy Age*, 18 June 1987). Even in recent years, with KPMG's audit income falling from 70% of total income business in 1985 to 42.3% in 1995, for example, the bald figures (in 1995 prices) are £126.2 million and £223.7 million. At Coopers, where the proportion has changed little from 48.7% of all business to 44%, the cash equivalents are £91.5 million and £253 million (*Accountancy*, Aug. 1986: 7; *Accountancy*, July 1995: 19).

It is difficult to assess, for any individual firm, the extent to which these rises represent one or more of the following: the effect of takeovers and mergers; a firm's success in obtaining a larger slice of the audit market; and real growth in the audit market. There can be no doubt, however, that the market in company audits was growing rapidly in this period. Table 13 shows that, although the number of public companies was about the same in 1990 as in 1950, and less than it was in 1920, business was boosted by the continued rapid growth in the number of private companies. As Figure 3 shows, company formations reached record levels by the late 1950s, and even greater heights in the boom of the early 1970s. Of perhaps greater importance to the large accountancy firms, however, was the fact that the rising average size of companies justified charging higher fees. The audit fee for ICI, in 1960/1, for example, was £50,000 (£595,000 at 1995 prices); after the company was split in two, for ICI and Zeneca combined it was £5.7 million (plus £2.8 million for additional services) by 1995 (data from company reports for 1960/1 and *Accountancy Age*, 1 June 1995: 7).

There are of course many factors which contribute to the rise in the level of audit fees, and these include the increased scope and coverage of the annual accounts. In 1949, the president of the SIAA suggested that 'Accountants stepping back to admire the products of their skill might well think on reflection that most of the people for whom the elaborate accounting service was being rendered did not understand what they were getting' (quoted in Garrett, 1961: 259). Writing twelve years later, the Society of Incorporated Accountants' historian noted that: 'The form and contents of many companies' reports, which sometimes include coloured illustrations, would be startling to earlier generations of directors, secretaries and auditors' (Garrett, 1961: 259). The increased size of company reports was not driven solely by the desire of company directors to keep the outside world better informed. Indeed, of possibly much greater importance has been the growing weight of regulation which dates from the 1940s. The ICAEW started to issue its series of Recommendations on Accounting Principles, concerning the appropriate form and content of published accounts, in 1942, while a seemingly never-ending stream of statements detailing standard accounting practice have emanated from the Accounting Standards Committee, 1970–90, and Accounting Standards Board since 1990. Added to these, the contents of numerous Companies Acts, most notably in 1967, 1976, 1980, 1981, and 1989, and the additional obligations placed on auditors by the Auditing Practices Board since 1991 explain to some extent the growing length of the published accounts and the increasing cost of the audit.

The major growth of management consultancy since the 1980s and, to a lesser extent, tax (see below) reflected an increased recognition of the fact that scope for developing the audit side of the practice was nevertheless diminishing, at least in relation to quoted companies. The larger firms had achieved an almost total monopoly of the quoted companies audit market, and further growth was almost entirely restricted to a client acquiring another quoted company or through success in the market of audit switching. When, in 1996, Panell Kerr Forster lost the audit of Williams Holdings, an FTSE 100 company, to Coopers & Lybrand, only Clark Whitehill and Kidson Impey, outside the 'big six', were 'left with a toe-hold in the big time' (*Accountancy*, July 1996: 9). Clark Whitehill held the only remaining full-time audit contract, with Smiths Industries, while Kidson's jointly audited the RMC group in conjunction with Coopers & Lybrand (*Accountancy*, July 1996: 9). More broadly, the August 1996 list of stock market clients—fully listed together with the unlisted securities market—showed the top ten auditors accounting for 1,724 UK stock market client companies, representing 75% of the total (*The Hambro Company Guide*, 1996).

The period since the Second World War has undoubtedly seen the role of the accountant becoming even more prominent. Their involvement in the freebooting moneymaking of the Thatcher era embroiled them in many financial scandals and, indeed, their apparent enthusiasm for the entrepreneurial spirit of enterprise has led some to question the accountant's status as a professional. Individual accountants and the leading accountancy firms have been implicated in major frauds, and the 1990s have frequently seen accountants in their insolvency role suing other accountants, in their role as auditors, for sums running into billions of pounds. The increased willingness to pursue the 'deep pockets' of auditors caused the number of outstanding claims against accountancy firms in the UK, which stood at just three as recently as 1983, to spiral to over 600 ten years later (*Accountancy Age*, 3 Mar. 1994: 11).

Many of these cases have made banner headlines including the audit of Barlow Clowes by Spicer & Pegler, Edencorp by Ernst & Young, Astra Holdings and Polly Peck by Stoy Hayward, Bestwood by BDO Binder Hamlyn, the Ferranti subsidiary International Signal & Control by KPMG Peat Marwick, BCCI by Price Waterhouse and Ernst & Whinney, and Maxwell's empire by Coopers & Lybrand. Such events have often led to investigations by the Department of Trade and Industry and the profession's own Joint Disciplinary Scheme, and findings have been highly critical of audit practice in a number of cases. These concerns have been added to by John Knox, deputy director of the Serious Fraud Office, who has gone on record as saying that 'in 95% of cases handled by the SFO, auditors had failed to detect mis-statements by companies' (*Accountancy Age*, 6 Jan. 1994: 9). Actions against accountants have resulted in substantial settlements being made both in and out of court, including the award against the former BDO Binder Hamlyn partnership of £105 million in favour of the electronics security group ADT (see *Accountancy*, Jan. 1996: 11) and KPMG's £40 million out of court settlement in connection with their audit of International Signal & Control, a figure which is believed to have been surpassed in the legal settlement reached by Coopers & Lybrand in connection with their audit of the Maxwell pension funds (*Accountancy*, Mar. 1995: 22). The rising level of litigation at one time looked as if it would bankrupt accountancy firms themselves and indeed it may still do so. In view of these and other events, there has been renewed questioning of the still unresolved issues of the nature and purpose of the accountant's bread and butter activity—the audit.

Taxation

We have seen (Chapter 5) that a small number of accountancy firms set up specialist tax departments in the inter-war period, and this process now developed apace. The practice of poaching expertise from the Inland Revenue also continued. At Baker Sutton & Co., for example, taxation services to clients were significantly improved in 1969 with the recruitment of Paul W. De Voil, previously an inspector of taxes who became tax manager (Baker Sutton, 1978: n.p.). The appointment of taxation specialists as partners was, however, often a slow process. Recruits from the public sector would have to take the chartered exams before qualifying for promotion, and other obstacles continued in place even amongst the leading firms. At Price Waterhouse, for example, the creation of specialist partners for tax occurred only in the early 1960s, with D. O. Bailey and A. M. Inglis achieving partnership status in April 1961. The firm had at last put aside the tradition that all members of the partnership should be 'generalist' or able to offer expertise in auditing (Jones, 1995: 210–11).

The growing importance of taxation work fundamentally reflects the general increase in the level and complexity of taxation in the post-war period, although it also attests to the nimble way in which accountants in Britain capture work which is undertaken in other countries by, for example, lawyers. The high levels of taxation levied during the Second World War—there was a fourfold increase in government receipts from personal taxation between 1938 and 1949 (Jones, 1981: 211)—continued, to a substantial extent, into peacetime. Private individuals increasingly turned to accountants for tax advice, since 'The demand for tax avoidance schemes is naturally most pressing when income tax rates are high, such as in the fiscal year 1952/3 when the top marginal rate was 97.5% on all income, and between 1974–78 when it was 98 per cent on investment income' (Edwards, 1989a: 274).

Perhaps of most significance in driving up accountants' earnings from this source of work were the major changes in corporate and personal taxation that occurred in the 1960s and early 1970s. The Finance Act 1965, which introduced two major new taxes, corporation tax and capital gains tax, comprised the largest package of tax changes up to that date. According to the head of KPMG Peat Marwick's tax department, speaking in 1993: 'This was the moment when multinational companies moved away from allowing in-house departments to handle the Inland Revenue in particular and tax planning in general. They started to consult experts', which meant the accountants (Reynolds, 1993: 47). The year 1973 saw the imposition also of Value Added Tax and, at Price Waterhouse, the combined effect of these new levies 'resulted in professional advisers suddenly finding themselves unable to predict with any certainty the outcome of any dispute with the Revenue' (Jones, 1995: 266). Consequently, negotiations and compromise with the authorities began to displace 'the settlement of disputed points by reference to the law' (Jones, 1995: 266). A further factor underpinning the growth in tax work was rising competition which caused companies to look more closely at this major item of expenditure. Also, the increasingly international character of business produced a need to understand the regulations applying in a range of different countries, particularly with governments themselves competing for revenue and seeking to attract foreign investment (Jones, 1995: 314). At the more mundane level, the introduction of self-assessment in 1997 is likely to result in many more people turning to the accountant for advice, and one might guess that it is the small local accountancy practice that will gain most from the decision to impose on taxpayers this huge increase in compliance work.

The greater emphasis on taxation work has proved extremely lucrative. In 1995, the top ten firms reported that they had earned 23.8% of total revenue from taxation work, with Coopers & Lybrand's fee breakdown showing them to be top of the tree in this area, as well as overall, with £133 million earned from this source. Amongst this group, Ernst & Young was marginally most reliant on tax work, at 30.1% of total income, while the consulting specialists Arthur Andersen trailed at just 18.1%. Lower down the fee income league, Smith & Williamson (ranked seventeenth) earned 66% more from tax than from audit and, for Chantrey Vellacott (ranked twenty-second), 36% of total income came from tax work (*Accountancy*, July 1995: 18–19).

Management consultancy

The most significant development in the work of accountancy firms in the post-war period has been the growth in management consultancy, where a particular stimulus was provided by the achievements of organizations specializing in this area. One of the first independent consultancy firms was set up by James McKinsey (a qualified accountant and lawyer) in the USA in 1926 (McKenna, 1995: 53). As in Britain, engineers, accountants, and lawyers had acted as consultants to business in America since the turn of the century, often working for merchant bankers such as J. P. Morgan (McKenna, 1995: 51–8). When McKinsey came to Britain, in 1959, their early success was bemoaned by the *Accountant* and attributed to the following factors: that the USA led in management theory and 'know-how'; that they were more likely to bring new ideas to a problem; and that the ICAEW's members were at a competitive disadvantage due to the ban on advertising their services (*Accountant*, 9 Nov. 1968: 618). The first 'home-grown' firm of specialist consultants was PA Consulting, established in 1943 (*Directory of Management Consultants in the UK*, 1991). In 1956, the Management Consultancies Association was formed by the leading practitioners, with its objectives including 'to enhance the standing of management consultancy professions by ensuring work is carried out to a high standard' and 'to increase the knowledge, understanding and market for management consultancy'. It sponsored the formation of the Management Consultants' Association in 1962 which has similar aims (Millerson, 1964: 287; *The European Directory of Management Consultants 1995*, 1994: 498). The Association's members had 751 clients in 1960 and 85% of all management consultancy work two years later (Millerson, 1964: 287), but this proportion was down to 65% of fee-earning consultancy work by 1987 (*Accountancy*, Aug. 1988: 94). They shared in a much bigger market at the latter date, however, with business growing at roughly 30% per annum in the late 1980s. The number of their clients rose to 4,524 by 1970 and 12,515 by 1987 (*Accountancy*, Aug. 1988: 94).

We find accountancy firms, as usual, competing for new work and sharing in its growth. The natural outcome was, again, the establishment of specialist departments, and even separate organizations, to give particular focus to this activity. Cooper Brothers were quickly off the mark, establishing a separate consultancy department in 1946, and they launched Management Accountancy Services as a separate company in 1962 (Coopers & Lybrand Deloitte, 1990). Progress was rather slower at Price Waterhouse despite the fact, noted in Chapter 5, that they had set up a small-scale systems department in the inter-war period (but see Jones, 1995: 225). There were just two specialist staff in 1955, and the first systems partner was appointed only in 1961 (Jones, 1995: 216, 225). In recognition of the wider range of operations then undertaken by Price Waterhouse, the systems department was renamed Management Consultancy Services (MCS) in 1963. By 1966, we find Price Waterhouse employing engineers and economists and, since these were ineligible for partnership, the establishment of an unlimited liability MCS company to enable their appointment as directors. MCS staff totalled 53 in 1969, rising rapidly to about 60 in 1975, 218 in 1982, and 1,140 by 1990 (Jones, 1995: 268, 409). During this period, expansion arose increasingly from diversification into non-accounting areas (Jones, 1995: 295). The recruitment of non-accountants blossomed with just nine qualified accountants amongst the 32 consultancy partners in London in 1992 (Jones, 1995: 315). Elsewhere, the establishment of a specialization in consultancy was often through a joint venture. Thomson McLintock formed a consultancy with Brown Fleming & Murray and Mann Judd under the title McLintock Mann Murray in 1959 (Jones, 1981: 211). Fifty smaller accounting practices established the consultancy Annan, Impey, Morrish in 1969, to help make their presence felt in this area (Baker Sutton, 1978: n.p.).

An insight into the difficulties faced by accountancy firms when *initially* striving to make an impact in this new area is provided by Paul Girolami who joined Cooper's management consultancy arm in 1956. The next nine years were 'struggling days for these [accountancy] firms because you were competing with the great names in management consultancy. We were the poor relations, if you like, but it was exciting' (Irvine, 1992a: 26). According to Girolami, the work was varied and 'it broadened my outlook. I learnt that you cannot run a company without management techniques and that accounting techniques are not management techniques' (Irvine, 1992a: 26). The growing pains associated with the development of consultancy work are also addressed in the history of Peat, Marwick, Mitchell & Co. for whom investigations had become a speciality (Wise, 1982: 19). Sir Harry Peat was succeeded as senior partner by his brother Roderick in 1956 and, according to the firm's chronicler, it was under his administration in 1957 that the UK firm jumped into the field of management consulting. It had been an area of practice about which there was quite a lot of dispute; as many times as it came up, it was pushed aside as an activity not suitable for the firm's standards. Some of the partners felt that the firm had been doing consultancy work for years and saw no reason to set up a special department. The debate went on for some time until Ronald Leach found that one of his best clients had been referred to Price Waterhouse for a management consulting job. That came as such a shock to the Peat Marwick organisation that the management consulting operation was set up almost immediately. Responsibility for the new unit was given to Sir Harold's son Tony Howitt, an engineer, a chartered accountant and a member of the Institute of Cost and Works Accountants. (Wise, 1982: 19)

The new department encountered early problems when one of Peat's leading partners John Corbett produced a report on BOAC that was so critical of the company's operation that it was never published (Wise, 1982: 20). The range of management consultancy services provided by accountancy firms such as Peats has been summarized by Burt in the following terms:

Although they owe their origins to the world of accountancy, it is by no means true that such firms have confined their activities to the financial aspects of management. Their spread of activities is just as wide as that of the other general practice consultancies, covering the full gamut from human resources to production management and information technology. It is also not true that the majority of accountancy-based firms' consultancy clients are necessarily drawn from the ranks of their auditing clients. In some cases the overlap may be as much as 50%, but in others the number of audit clients may make up as little as 25% of the total. (1988: 96)

The diverse range of services offered by Peat Marwick Mitchell, at that date, underlines the above point: 'business strategy and planning, financial management, information technology, marketing, operations management, transport, management sciences, training, human resources, executive recruitment and career counselling' (Burt, 1988: 97).

In the immediate post-war period, consultants were brought in to address what many people have seen as a perennial problem within British management, namely the poor quality of cost and management accounting techniques. We saw that cost accounting was the subject of critical comment during the First World War, and this process was repeated after the Second World War. Between 1945 and 1947, the Chancellor of the Exchequer, Sir Stafford Cripps, set up seventeen working parties to investigate the efficiency and boost the export potential of a variety of industries, and every report singled out cost accounting as capable of improvement. These reports demonstrated, not only the lack of advanced techniques, but ignorance of basic matters such as the accurate identification of production costs and the nature and use of standard costing (Stacey, 1954: 201–2). Britain looked across the Atlantic for illumination on such matters, with a management accounting team led by the chartered accountant Ian Morrow visiting the United States under the auspices of the Anglo-American Council on Productivity (1950). Its remit was to investigate 'what accounting, costing and statistical information is provided for American management at different levels; by what method it is obtained and how it is used' (quoted in Stacey, 1954: 207). The team marvelled at a situation where: 'A constant flow of reports to all levels of management from the chairman to the foreman supplies vital information for the daily conduct of business' (quoted in Stacey, 1954: 207). The report was severely critical of UK cost accounting practices, but laid the fault at management's door: 'British accountants are well able to provide management with services on the American scale and according to the American pattern, but so far management, with rare exceptions, has not been concerned to require them' (quoted in Stacey, 1954: 207).

It is therefore not surprising to discover that during the 1950s accountancy firms increasingly developed costing and budgetary systems for their clients (Jones, 1981: 211). In a similar vein, the rapporteur's summary of papers entitled 'The Accountant in Industry', presented at the Sixth International Congress of Accounting in 1952, draws attention to growing work in the area of management accounting, and observes that this is increasingly encouraging the movement of accountants into business 'to perform functions on a full-time basis, which were formally carried out by professional accountants' on a consultancy basis (*Accountant*, 1952: 668).

The major growth area in management consultancy more recently, however, has been the provision of advice on the installation of computers and information technology. By 1987 it accounted for over a third of income of the Management Consultancies Association's members (*Accountancy*, Aug. 1988: 94). According to Reynolds:

Typically a major multinational would ask a consultant to offer a feasibility study on standardising and upgrading IT facilities throughout its headquarters and subsidiary locations. The consultant would bring together a team with relevant experience in the technical, sector and geographical aspects of the work. (1993: 19)

Consultancy on finance and administration earned 22% of the Management Consultancies Association's members' fees in 1987, followed by 11% from manufacturing management and technology and about the same for corporate strategy and organization development (*Accountancy*, Aug. 1988: 94). But the range of advice is vast and, at Touche Ross, has included assisting a major credit-card firm to develop a fraud detection system, designing a materials handling system for a car manufacturer, and a risk management assignment for a financial institution. Price Waterhouse gives advice on human resource management and marketing as well as manufacturing, retail, and financial services management. Ernst & Whinney carried out a study for the EEC, in the late 1980s, on the cost of not creating the single market in 1992 and of setting up a clearing bank system in Hungary (*Accountancy*, Aug. 1988: 98).

Accountancy firms expanded their consultancy work rapidly in the 1980s and, although PA Consulting remained the leader in 1987 employing 900 consultants, they were being rapidly caught by Coopers & Lybrand with 740 consultants, Peat Marwick McLintock with 630, and Arthur Andersen with 500 (*Accountancy*, Aug. 1988: 98). By 1989, Andersen were the leading accountants in the consultancy field, with a staff of 1,400, almost as big as PA Consulting with a staff of 1,600 (*Directory of Management Consultants in the U.K.*). By 1991, of the ten largest consultancies in Britain, only two were not accountants in origin (Reynolds, 1993: 19). Significantly, according to one commentator, the reason for the accountants' success was that their traditional rivals, the specialist management consultants, were less able to operate on a global scale (Reynolds, 1993: 19).

Consultancy work is, today, sufficiently sought after to produce suspicions of 'lowballing' in order to obtain access to this kind of work. For example, Price Waterhouse offered the Prudential Corporation a 40% discount on the £2.4 million audit when it went out to tender in the summer of 1990. This revelation provoked a major controversy in the profession over the 'big six' firms using audit as a loss leader to secure major clients with the objective of winning more lucrative consultancy work. Concerns re-emerged when the Prudential's 1993 accounts showed that Price Waterhouse's non-audit fees had leapt a massive 925% to £3.7 million in the period since they took over the audit (*Accountancy Age*, 12 May 1994: 1).

Work in the public sector

Consultancy work for the government has also been a continuing aspect of the British accountant's work in the post-Second World War era, indeed the amount of work undertaken accelerated. The government emerged from the war committed to a policy of full employment and this, together with the nationalization of industries and the creation of the Welfare State, caused government expenditure to rise from 39.4% of GDP in 1950 to 47.5% in 1970 (Hatton and Chrystal, 1991: 56). This huge leap in government involvement in all aspects of economic life meant that, although not directly employed by government in significant numbers, accountants were drawn in to give advice on an unprecedented scale.

The accountant's war work, discussed at the beginning of the chapter, merged seamlessly into peacetime. Sir Harold Howitt, senior partner of Peat, Marwick, Mitchell and a First World War hero who had made a dramatic escape from German captivity, became chairman of BOAC (then an adjunct of the RAF) in 1943, and then deputy chairman through until

1948 (Wise, 1982: 19; Jones, 1981: 206). After the Second World War, Howitt was usually to be found on at least one government commission. He was a friend of many prominent members of the Labour Party and this helped to bring considerable business to the firm which was, for example, heavily engaged in the nationalization of the coal and electricity industries (Wise, 1982: 17, 19). Howitt continued to be prominent in government circles, and in 1957 was one of the three original members of the Council on Prices, Productivity and Incomes (Parker, 1980*a*: n.p.). In the same year, he was appointed by the Minister of Transport to examine allegations of inefficiency in the British Transport Commission's purchasing of supplies (Gourvish, 1986: 160). Many other accountancy firms played a crucial role in the valuation of industries prior to nationalization, such as Thomson, McLintock which handled the valuations and compensations in the coal industry (Jones, 1981: 200).

Henry Benson's wartime involvement with government work continued with an array of appointments including membership of: the Royal Ordnance Factories Board 1952–5; the Wilson Committee 1959–60 on making oil from coal; and the Fleck Advisory Committee 1953–5 on the reorganization of the National Coal Board, of which he became deputy chairman (*WW*, 1993: 144; Jones, 1984*c*: 287–9). In 1960, Benson was appointed to the Special Advisory Group examining the 'structure, finance and working' of the British Transport Commission, which also included Dr Richard Beeching, the technical director of ICI (Gourvish, 1986: 309). The group was unanimously in favour of a fundamental reorganization of the Commission, but there was a major split between those, including Frank Kearton from Courtaulds, who favoured a holding company and powerful regional boards, and others, including Beeching and Benson, who advocated a stronger central railway board with functional responsibilities. The Beeching/Benson approach prevailed; Beeching was appointed chairman of the British Railway Board established in 1963, and set about making drastic cuts in services, while Coopers subsequently undertook a considerable amount of work for the Board. Benson's major 'special assignments' before and after retiring from Coopers in 1975 included investigations for the Board of Trade into John Bloom's Rolls Razor and at the time of Rolls-Royce's impending collapse (Benson, 1989: chs. 8, 12). Benson also chaired the Royal Commission on Legal Services 1976–9, which took the decision to allow lawyers to advertise, and was made a life peer in 1981.

The public sector work of William Lawson is also typical of that performed by leading accountants of this period. As partner at Binder Hamlyn, Lawson was a delegate at the Austrian Treaty Commission in Vienna in 1947, negotiating over the German assets in Austria to which the USSR laid claim as reparations. He was a member of the Transport Arbitration Tribunal from 1948 to 1957 and served on the Royal

Commission on Local Government in Greater London, 1957–60. In acknowledgement of his public work, Lawson was knighted in 1962 and, from that year to 1967, he was chairman of the agency set up to resell the steel industry to the private sector. Numerous appointments to government committees included the arbitration body for the remuneration of teachers, 1965–9, and the Review Board for Government Contracts from 1969 until his death in 1971 (*The Times*, 5 Feb. 1971; *WWW*, 1971–80: 456).

Inflation also drew the practising accountant into public roles. Ian Hay Davison of Arthur Andersen saw public service as a member of the Price Commission (1977–9), which, in common with the Monopolies Commission and the Restrictive Practices Court, was a fruitful source of work for accountants (Howitt, 1966: 126). During the 1970s, the Price Commission usually called in leading accountancy firms to collect data on industries under investigation. In order to help prepare the report on the oil industry in 1979, for example, Arthur Young McClelland Moores & Co. and Arthur Young Management Services were engaged to obtain factual information on BP, while other accountancy firms were brought in to cover the remaining oil companies (Price Commission, 1979). Inflationary wage rises also led successive governments to attempt some form of incomes policy and, again, accountants were co-opted onto the plethora of institutions involved.

Whichever way the political wind blew, of course, the accountant was involved and, when Mrs Thatcher set out to 'roll back the State' in 1979, this also meant more jobs for accountants. We might mention here the work of accountants on the denationalizations of the 1980s and 1990s. Privatizations proved extremely lucrative for Touche Ross and several other firms, whether acting as lead advisers or reporting accountants (Reynolds, 1993: 19). Indeed, the privatization schemes generated even more profitable work for accountants than had the original nationalizations (Dunkerley and Hare, 1991: 411–12). Other attempts to introduce the discipline of the market place into services previously run by the State bureaucracy also, paradoxically, brought grist to the accountants' mill. So-called market-testing in the Civil Service, the reforms in the Health Service, and even the local management of schools and colleges have each produced more public sector clients for accountants.

Ironically, one valuable source of public sector-based consultancy work has been the investigations undertaken for the Department of Trade into companies where the auditors were in some cases under fire for failure to discover irregularities. It was reported in July 1994 that top accountancy firms had received more than £20 million for Department of Trade and Industry investigations and, in the same month, it was disclosed that the 'big six' had received nearly £12 million from the Department of Transport 1989–92 for rail privatization and other work (*Accountancy Age*, 14

July 1994: 1, 11). An analysis of ministerial replies to parliamentary questions laid down by Labour MP Austin Mitchell revealed that eleven of the nineteen government departments paid £33.5 million to just five accountancy firms in 1993, and it is thought that the full figure was somewhere between £50 million and £100 million, since some of the biggest spenders 'either failed or refused to disclose information' (*Accountancy Age*, 28 July 1994: 1). As with other areas of specialization, the percentage of total fees earned from consultancy work can vary a great deal between firms. Amongst the top ten (omitting Grant Thornton who did not disclose details), Andersen was out ahead with 46% of its income from this source in 1995, while Clark Whitehill trailed in last with just 2.1%. For the top ten as a whole (other than Grant Thornton), consultancy fees totalled £786.4 million or 25.3% of all fee income (*Accountancy*, July 1995: 18–19).

We have dwelt on consultancy work undertaken for both the private and governmental sectors because it has been the major growth area for accountancy practices in the most recent past. It has helped to raise further the profile and social standing of accountants through their prominent position in successive honours lists (see, for example, *Accountancy*, July 1994: 13; Feb. 1995: 22; July 1995: 12; July 1996: 10), and has enabled accountants in public practice to develop the additional skills that have underpinned their continued appointment to top management positions. We focus on this latter, continuing, trend in the remainder of this chapter.

ROUTES TO THE TOP

The provision of a consultancy service by an accountancy firm in return for a fee is a relatively detached form of involvement of accountants in business management. Advising companies has been a constant role for accountants, stretching back, as we saw in Chapter 2, to Robert Fletcher's Bristol firm, amongst others, in the 1820s. We now turn our attention to the other side of the dichotomy within the profession—the role of accountants employed directly as business managers. In this section, we rely heavily on case-study biographies of a range of key accountants with the intention that, collectively, these will provide a meaningful, overall, indication of their background, role, and achievements as industrialists in the recent past. We return to the last matter in the final chapter, where we attempt a more broad-based assessment of the reasons underlying the rising recruitment of accountants by business.

We examine, below, the various routes through which accountants became involved in business. The taxonomy presented naturally contains a degree of overlap, and there are also some grey areas, but it provides a useful basis for further analysis.

Route 1: non-executive directors

We saw in Chapters 4 and 5 that, in the early years of the profession, almost all of the accountants who became company directors and chairmen remained in practice and were what we call today non-executives. Indeed, as late as 1951 (Table 15), over half of the ICAEW-qualified company directors remained in practice. Practising accountants who combine the two roles remain common down to the present day, but the proportion has dropped dramatically and probably no more than 10% of chartered accountant-directors are now in public practice.

We saw, in Chapter 4, that firms held different opinions on the question of whether it was appropriate for their partners to take on directorships. Focusing on the post-war period, Price Waterhouse contacted partners of all its associated firms in 1948, requesting them to retire from directorships of companies as this would disqualify them as *potential* auditors. Jones states that partners in Price Waterhouse itself had long since resigned from boards in view of the conflict of interest that might arise (1995: 236). Writing in 1989, Benson confirms that 'The partners in the bigger firms of accountants do not as a rule accept appointments as directors of public companies for the reason that there may be a conflict of interest. A large firm has among its clients many public companies, some of whom are likely to be in competition.' He further states that Coopers 'adopted the policy of not accepting directorship unless there was an exceptional reason for doing so' (Benson, 1989: 223). Exceptional circumstances clearly surfaced in his case. Benson was a director of the prestigious Hudson's Bay Company 1953–62 and was deputy governor for most of this time; he was also a director of the Finance Corporation for Industry Ltd. and successor bodies which, as we have seen, were set up to help provide large-scale funding for industry. However, these were not the normal run of commercial company, and only after retiring from Coopers in 1975 did Benson go onto the board of the Hawker Siddeley Group. We find a similar situation in the case of John Grenside (president of the ICAEW 1974–5, knighted in 1983), senior partner of Peat, Marwick, who took up non-executive directorships of Allied-Lyons and Nomura Bank only after his retirement (*WW*, 1993: 766; Cowe, 1993: 47).

An interesting first-hand insight into the role of the non-executive director in the post-war period is provided by the chartered accountant Norman Lancaster, who joined the board of Lucas in 1954: 'They [the directors] are remote, they do not have to consider bank balances and so at board meetings I am able to put in a little reminder of what it is like to go through the hoop when you need money, what it is like to suffer. In fact when I joined in 1954, Waring sent me round to every Lucas company to give a talk on those lines' (quoted in Nockolds, 1976: 388). Lancaster also made the following interesting assessment of the more general role of the non-executive director:

One of the purposes of non-executive directors was just to sit and listen—to give them somebody else to talk to apart from themselves, somebody of good business experience and intelligence who would just sit and listen. In some respects we were rather like a marriage guidance council; the very process of talking to an outsider helps to solve your problems. . . . The non-executive director does have another function—to act as an independent group on matters on which our different experiences make us specially qualified to judge (quoted in Nockolds, 1976: 389).

Route 2: entrepreneurs

The second type of commitment of accountants to business involves the relatively small, though significant, group of entrepreneurial accountants, amongst whom John Reeves Ellerman is the most outstanding early example of an accountant leaving public practice to go into business on his own account (see Chapter 4). The tradition of the dynamic accountant has continued down to the present day and, once again, a number of case histories illustrate the general pattern.

Sir Julian Hodge's career had its origins in the inter-war period but came to full flower in the post-war era. Hodge, the son of a plumber, enrolled as a student member of the Corporation of Accountants in 1925 while working in south Wales as a clerk for the Great Western Railway (Baber and Boyns, 1985: 286–90). He eventually qualified as a certified accountant in 1930 and began building up an insurance business in the Welsh valleys, also giving customers the benefit of his accountancy knowledge, and he formed companies which took control of cinemas in south Wales and the West Country. After the Second World War he bought out and redeveloped an ailing hire purchase company, while another innovation was to set up a company that acted on behalf of the small shareholders of companies subject to a takeover bid where the asking price was believed to be manifestly too low. It has been estimated that shareholders benefited by well over £20 million as the result of forcing up offer bids. Not surprisingly, Hodge made many enemies in the City of London, and his methods, based on 'probing and imaginative accountancy methods', were surrounded with controversy (Baber and Boyns, 1985: 287). Hodge was committed to the establishment of indigenous Welsh financial institutions and, indeed, constructed a huge financial empire, based in Cardiff, that included an investment trust, launched in 1963, and the Commercial Bank of Wales, founded in 1971. Hodge sold the latter to Standard Chartered for £55 million in 1973.

The growth of the conglomerate Williams Holdings provides a more recent example of accountants as successful entrepreneurs. Nigel Rudd left grammar school at 16 and was encouraged to go into accountancy by his mother, who worked for an accountancy firm, because 'she had never seen a poor accountant' (Irvine, 1991: 24). He qualified in 1968 (*WW*, 1993: 1,642) and gained early business experience as a company secretary to a small civil engineering firm that was subsequently taken over by the conglomerate London and Northern Group (Nash, 1991: 41). As divisional financial director and 'troubleshooter' with the London and Northern 1970–5, Rudd met Brian McGowan, another chartered accountant who had left school at 16. McGowan's father apparently had himself wanted to become an accountant, but his parents could not afford the premium. The McGowans were determined that their own son should have a better start in life, and Brian qualified with Edward Moores in 1967 before joining London and Northern. He moved on, building up City contacts, first with P&O as group acquisitions manager, and then with Sime Darby in Hong Kong (Nash, 1991: 41).

Rudd had already bought his way into a small building company by the time the two got together in 1982, while McGowan possessed the City connections necessary to enable them to take over an ailing foundry company, W. Williams and Sons, for £400,000. Nine years later, Williams Holdings was worth £1.2 billion and was one of the 100 largest companies in Britain (Cowe, 1993: 443). An important event in this transformation occurred in 1984 when they bought a cash-rich scrap metal dealer in exchange for their own shares, and used the cash to pay off their debts. This produced the strong balance sheet that could be used to mount further acquisitions, paid for by their own shares or cash, mainly through uncontested takeover bids (Nash, 1991: 41).

McGowan modestly ascribes much of their success to good luck and opportunism (Irvine, 1991: 24–5). He claims that they had no real strategy to begin with, other than to look for 'under-managed quality businesses' in the depressed manufacturing sector of the early 1980s. The targets were loss-making companies whose fixed assets had increased in price due to inflation, but, perhaps because accounts continued to be prepared in accordance with the historical cost concept, these values were not reflected in the stock market valuation (Irvine, 1991: 38, 41). Rudd and McGowan were not asset strippers, however, and invested heavily in their acquisitions (apparently about the same as comparable conglomerates such as BTR, but twice as much as Hanson and Tomkins) in order to upgrade the capital equipment. Their simple objective was to run their companies better than the previous management, and Rudd explains how he learned this lesson from his experience at London and Northern which 'was an appallingly run company. It was decentralised without any control whatsoever. I learned a good deal about how not to do things. For example, London and Northern used to buy businesses and leave existing management to run them' (Nash, 1991: 41). In contrast, when Williams took over a company it sent in its so-called 'hit squad'—'a group of very, very talented people who go into every business, not only to shake it around and improve its performance, but to enable us to understand the business' (Nash, 1991: 42). In 1994, McGowan left Williams Holdings to become executive chairman of the House of Fraser, leaving Rudd as chairman.

Other, less well-known, examples of chartered accountants turned entrepreneur include Martyn Arbib, who set up Perpetual, the unit trust, in 1974, of which he is at present chairman (*Sunday Times*, 26 Dec. 1993); and Ian Williams, who resigned his partnership soon after Spicer & Oppenheim's merger with Touche Ross, in 1990, and bought Smiles brewery in Bristol, raising £1.7 million from Barclays Bank and 3i and investing £300,000 himself (Grey, 1994a: 26–8). Anthony Record gave up his accountancy practice to start up in business in competition with Rentokil, the pest control company, which finally bought him out (Hawksley, 1990: 16–17). Realizing the huge growth potential of the security business, Record used the proceeds to establish Britannia, a successful burglar alarms business, in 1982.

Entrepreneurial activity is highly likely, of course, to have its failures, and this is illustrated by the story of the specialist retailer Sock Shop. Sophie Mirman, having gained experience helping to set up Tie Rack, opened her first Sock Shop in Knightsbridge Underground Station in 1983. She married the financial controller of Tie Rack, the chartered accountant Richard Ross, who also became her business partner. Three years later the company was floated on the unlisted securities market as Sock Shop International; it had 43 shops in the UK and was valued at £56.5 million (*Financial Times*, 4 July 1990). Sales rose from £613,000 in 1985 to £25.8 million in 1988 and, by 1989, their operation consisted of 103 UK shops plus 33 more in France and the USA. However, 'Mirman made a disastrous attempt to expand in the US and this combined with Sock Shop's heavy debt burden of £17 million (interest charges rose between 1987 and 1989), its administrative problems and UK transport strikes brought her management of the company to an end. Mirman and her accountant husband received nothing from their 80 per cent stake in Sock Shop—once worth nearly £60 million—when the debt-laden company was sold by administrators in August 1990 for £3 million.' (Jeremy and Tweedale, 1994: 134)

Route 3: in at the top

The third route by which accountants became involved in business decision-making is through recruitment from practice into industry full-time, at board or equivalent level. Many who followed this route were from an elite background, having attended public school and, possibly, university. At the same time the non-graduate grammar school boy (rarely girls, who, as discussed in Chapter 3, comprised an insignificant proportion of qualified accountants until relatively recently) was beginning to make his mark, such as Kenneth Bond who qualified with Cooper & Cooper in 1949 and became a partner in 1954 (*WW*, 1993: 188). Bond resigned in 1961 to become a director with Radio and Allied Industries and, in 1962 (the year before Arnold Weinstock took over as managing director), he became financial director at the parent General Electric Company. Bond was promoted to deputy managing director in 1966 and worked closely with Weinstock in the takeover of AEI in 1967 and English Electric a year later. GEC, despite employing a divisional structure, has traditionally allowed its units a large degree of operating autonomy while applying strict financial controls from a relatively small head office. It therefore functions rather like a holding company, and it is here that Bond played a key role. In 1948, GEC was the seventeenth largest manufacturing company in Britain by market value; by 1985 it had risen to third largest (Hannah, 1983: 190; Wardley, 1991: 280). Despite buoyant profits and a large accumulated cash fund, GEC's policy and performance in the 1970s and 1980s has been criticized for low growth in output, for shifting production abroad, and for a lack of new product innovation (Williams *et al.*, 1983: 133–77). GEC is also accused of inactivity and an over-reliance on defence-related business (Cowe, 1993: 285). None the less, GEC has proved one of Britain's most successful companies in the post-war period. Bond, their leading accountant, was knighted in 1977 and served as vice-chairman from 1985 until his retirement.

A member of the elite corps of accountants (that is, those who appear to come from a privileged background), who moved full-time into business late in his career, is Ian Hay Davison, who maintains that he became an accountant because his father (himself a leading chartered accountant and ICAEW council member 1961–5) told him to (Fisher, 1993: 28). Hay Davison was educated at Dulwich College and graduated from the London School of Economics—one of many leading accountants of the post-war period to study at the school where de Paula once taught. He went on to follow a Ph.D. course in Accounting, Statistics and Economics at the University of Michigan, but did not finish his thesis (*WW*, 1993: 482; Fisher, 1993: 29). Hay Davison qualified with Tansley Witt in 1956, and then worked for Price Waterhouse on Wall Street before joining the London office of Arthur Andersen, which was, in the late 1950s, still a relatively small organization in the UK. He was made managing partner of Andersen's London office in 1966, at the age of 34, and remained in that position for sixteen years, becoming heavily involved in professional affairs and government business (*Financial Times*, 17 June 1982).

In 1983, well into his fifties, Hay Davison left practice to become the first chief executive of Lloyd's of London, the insurance market. He attributes this move partly to boredom and partly to differences with the leadership of Andersen, USA. Of his time at Lloyd's, Hay Davison claims that: 'I achieved what I set out to do, I got them to publish their accounts and I caught the crooks' (Fisher, 1993: 30). He resigned after three years, however, apparently disillusioned with self-regulation: 'I was clearly getting nowhere because of the obstruction of the committee and their unwillingness to address issues like baby syndicates, their unwillingness to accept the fundamental way—corruption is too strong a word—in which self-regulation was not functioning because those who did the regulating had a direct interest in the result and did not hesitate to let that interest have an effect' (Fisher, 1993: 30). After Lloyd's, Hay Davison took on a series of non-executive directorships in the country's largest companies. He was also chairman of Crédit Lyonnais Capital Markets (1988–91) and credits himself with turning around its fortunes; whereas it made a loss of £60 million in the year he joined, it made £15 million profit three years later. Hay Davison also became non-executive chairman of Storehouse (1990–6), the retailers, after Terence Conran's resignation, and, with fellow accountant Michael Julien (see below), he set about selling off most of the company in the endeavour to achieve restored financial health. Since 1992, he has also served as chairman of the mortgage bank NMB plc and McDonnell Information Systems Group plc (*WW*, 1997: 497).

As we have seen all along, a common conduit to business, at senior level, has been from auditor to employment with a client company. There is no shortage of examples, in the post-war period, to illustrate the continuance of the pathway to the boardroom blazed by d'Arcy Cooper (see Chapter 4). Jenni Williams, finance director of ECT Cellular plc since November 1987, was no stranger to her new employer when she joined the mobile phone manufacturer. 'She already knew ECT: she was poached from its auditors, Peat Marwick McLintock, where she had been a manager, working on ECT's listing plans' (Croft, 1988: 14). Other examples include David Watson, who joined Record Holdings plc—which he had audited for Peat Marwick—as financial director in 1985 (Kelly, 1987*b*: 14), and Derek Potter, who also left Peat Marwick, this time to join the famous British football team, Tottenham Hotspur, shortly before it went public in October 1983 (Kelly, 1988: 12).

There are of course examples of situations which reflect a combination of the routes developed for our taxonomy. Ian MacDonald had been a partner with Kerr, MacLeod and Macfarlan since 1933 and, as such, had been the auditor of the Commercial Bank of Scotland, but he resigned this post to take a non-executive seat on the board (route 1) of the bank in 1947 (Munn, 1990*b*: 412). In 1953, however, he was asked to retire from public practice completely to concentrate full-time on running the bank (route 3). This he did with some success, re-forming the bank into the National Commercial Bank of Scotland in 1959 with help, and a 36% stake, from

Lloyds Bank. MacDonald then went onto the board of Lloyds, between 1961 and 1978, and, following the merger with the Royal Bank of Scotland in 1969, became chairman (Munn, 1990*b*: 413).

Route 4: working their way up

In this category are the accountants who leave accountancy firms fairly soon after qualifying and work their way up starting from a relatively low rung on the hierarchical ladder. Many of these see public practice as good business training and, from the outset, have every intention of leaving on qualification to start a career in business. Others become disillusioned with professional practice or move to obtain a sharp increase in their income. We have seen, in Chapter 5, that the career path from young qualified accountant or secretary to chief accountant and then onto the board, perhaps as managing director and finally chairman, was firmly established by the inter-war period, with accountancy already identified as the leading management training in Britain. The number of accountants in this category whose career could, and perhaps should, be recounted is substantial, but space permits us to present no more than a small sample.

We start with Basil Smallpeice, the son of a bank manager who was educated at public school (Shrewsbury) and then took an external London University B.Com. degree while working as an articled clerk in the 1920s (Mumford, 1991: 129). Following seven years with the Hoover Vacuum Cleaner Company, spent 'learning American cost-accounting principles and procedures' (Higham, 1986: 190), Smallpeice moved to Doulton & Co., the pottery firm, as chief accountant (and later also secretary) in 1937. In 1948, Smallpeice moved to the newly formed British Transport Commission as director of costs and statistics, and was recruited two years later by Sir Miles Thomas as financial controller of BOAC. There he introduced 'the modern management accounting processes of budgetary control' (Higham, 1986: 191) and is also credited with 'quietly and precisely' imposing order on the accounts of this 'nationalised and troubled concern' (Jeremy and Tweedale, 1994: 193). These changes are seen to have helped revive the company, and in 1953—the year the corporation first reported a profit—he joined the board, becoming managing director three years later. His most notable achievements were the reintroduction of the Comet (1958) and the introduction of the Boeing 707 (1959–60) (Jeremy and Tweedale, 1994: 193).

In 1963, after fundamental disagreements with the government over how the nationalized concern should be financed and run, Smallpeice and his chairman were forced to resign (Higham, 1986: 191–2). Smallpeice joined the board of the Cunard Steamship Company in the following year and served as chairman, 1965–71. The company was 'in dire trouble [in 1964] because of a fondness for tradition and a neglect of modern management concepts', and we are told that Smallpeice 'possessed precisely the right management experience and skills to deal with the situation' (Higham, 1986: 192). Smallpeice did not shirk taking the 'radical decisions which brought the company back into profit in mid-1968' (Jeremy and Tweedale, 1994: 193). Cunard was taken over by Trafalgar House in 1971 and Smallpeice went onto the main board, before taking over shortly afterwards as non-executive deputy chairman of Lonrho. He resigned from this post, in 1973, after a clash with the managing director, Tiny Rowland, and retired from business in 1979 (Jeremy and Tweedale, 1994: 193).

Another accountant to start in the accounts department and reach the top was Eric Turner whose career has been the subject of analysis and criticism in the literature. Six years after qualifying, in 1940, Turner joined the Blackburn and General Aircraft Company Ltd. as its accountant, rising to the position of managing director by 1955, before encountering considerable difficulties following his move to BSA (Smith, 1986: 570–3). Turner has aroused strong feelings on the part of Hopwood in his assessment of the decline of the British motorcycle industry. Hopwood speaks of the 'invasion of accountancy' and of Turner's 'firm non-acceptance of practising engineers and as lacking in business gumption' (quoted in Smith, 1986: 573). Specific criticism seems to have been that Turner 'refused to spend essential money on . . . models and . . . tools, preferring to spend it on flashy computerisation and dabbling in assets and diversification'. We are told that under Turner's leadership 'the board . . . concerned themselves with making money but not with the means by which to do this; the board spent its time on financial appraisal . . . and assessing results . . . rather than in making the motorcycle division function properly in all its facets' (Hopwood, quoted in Smith, 1986: 573). Turner's resignation as chairman of the BSA group in 1971 was forced by Barclays Bank's offer of additional finance subject to the following conditions: Turner leaving the company, and Cooper Brothers providing monthly reports on BSA's progress (Ryerson, 1980: 176).

Another of the accountants who left practice preferring the challenge of business is John Corrin, who was educated at Grove Park Grammar School. He decided early on that 'public practice was not for him' and, in the 1960s, left Peat's Birmingham office to work for the British Railways Board in charge of rationalizing the Eastern Region's railway system. He then spent two years with Hawker Siddeley before joining ICI (Irvine, 1993a: 22–3). When ICI decided to close fourteen factory sites in 1979, he took part in a management buyout (then still a new concept) of the one he believed should not be closed. This led to the establishment of Mayfield Holdings Ltd. in 1981. A chance meeting with Gerald Wightman, the finance director of Allied Textiles, led to merger and, within a year, Corrin had become chief executive. The *Financial Times* credits the management with 'an impressive record for picking up un-dermanaged or otherwise distressed businesses, mending them, put-ting money in and waiting for the benefits to accrue' (quoted in Irvine, 1993a: 22). In an interview in 1993 Corrin said: 'For me, it has been a golden profession—I mean gold in material terms, in intellectual terms, in terms of a challenge and in terms of the avenues it opened up' (Irvine, 1993a: 22).

Typically, though obviously not universally, the career managers who used the accountancy qualification as a management training, well into the second half of the post-war era, were non-graduate public school and grammar school boys. In this, of course, they were representative of British businessmen generally. One of the most successful of the grammar school boys was Sir Trevor Holdsworth (he was knighted in 1982), who took his articles with the Bradford firm of Rawlinson, Greaves & Mitchell (*WW*, 1993: 902). He qualified in 1950, and for two years was deeply involved in looking after his firm's biggest client, Laporte Industries, the chemical manufacturers. He is on record as saying that this provided him with a valuable education in the methods of large companies (Ritchie and Goldsmith, 1987: 108). Yet Holdsworth spoke for an increasing number of accountants from this period when he later said: 'I knew I was going into industry. I was not going to stay in practice. I didn't like that, too bitty, too disinterested, too remote.' In 1952, he went to work for Bowater, the paper manufacturers, as an accountant. There, he recalled: 'I remember I was always wanting to change things, find new ways of doing things. Bowaters was really quite primitive in those days. It didn't have budget-ary controls' (Ritchie and Goldsmith, 1987: 108). Holdsworth was the first Bowater manager ever to go on a training course—at Ashridge Manage-ment College in 1959—but is rather dismissive of its quality: 'a little bit of personnel management, a little marketing, a bit of this and a bit of that, and it did not include anything about general management and leader-ship' (Ritchie and Goldsmith, 1987: 109). The course apparently did instil a belief in developing an overall strategy for a company, however, as opposed to focusing on its internal problems. By 1959, Holdsworth was personal assistant to the finance director at Bowater and, in 1963, was made a director and controller of a paper-making subsidiary, at which point he moved to the leading engineering and steel-making company, GKN, as deputy chief accountant.

After two years at GKN, Holdsworth became chief accountant and was responsible for setting up the group's first financial control systems; he was appointed managing director of the screws and fasteners subsidiary in 1968 (Ritchie and Goldsmith, 1987: 111). By 1974, Holdsworth had become deputy chairman of the entire GKN group and was also ap-pointed managing director in 1977. It was apparently Holdsworth who, during the 1970s, formulated GKN's strategy of abandoning steel-making and concentrating on automotive components, reducing its British-based engineering output, and expanding its operations abroad. GKN also moved into military vehicles (Ritchie and Goldsmith, 1987: 112). Almost inevitably—in the light of the condition of the post-war manufacturing industry, discussed above—Holdsworth was faced with the task of managing a company in decline. In 1948, GKN were the tenth largest manufacturing company in Britain but today they are just outside the top 100 companies (Hannah, 1983: 190; *The Times 1,000 1997*, 1996: 44). The most rapid period of decline coincided with Holdsworth's chairmanship between 1980 and 1988, with the company making drastic plant closures and redundancies during and following the recession (Ritchie and Goldsmith, 1987: 115). In 1980, GKN made a loss and shed 12,000 jobs and, although profitability recovered, the 1992 profits of £122 million were the same as those of 1979 despite inflation. This does not of course mean that GKN had been badly managed; indeed the City generally rated the company as having coped fairly well with adversity. The company is also thought to have coped better with the depression of the 1990s than that of the 1980s, as a result of Holdsworth's policies, aided it is said by 'careful cash management, a cautious approach born of the disasters of the early-1980s' (Cowe, 1993: 287–9). Holdsworth was also a big supporter of long-term research and development (Ritchie and Goldsmith, 1987: 114). Holdsworth's stewardship, however, has not been without blemish. One apparent mistake was to move into the defence industry, with the production of tanks and through a stake in Westland Helicopters, in 1988. Holdsworth vacated his positions as director and chairman in the same year.

Leslie Smith, who was demobbed in 1946 and qualified as a chartered accountant in 1952, is one of many others who worked his way up to reach a top management position without the benefit of higher education. He immediately joined the Road Haulage Executive, Stowmarket Group as an accountant, moving on to British Oxygen in 1956, where he stayed for the remainder of his career (*WW*, 1993: 1,752). He became a director in 1966, managing director in 1969, and chairman and chief executive in 1972–9. As head of British Oxygen, Smith was considered 'an exceptional businessman' having pioneered the use of non-executive directors to take an active but independent role in running and planning the company's future (Ritchie and Goldsmith, 1987: 62). In the 1970s, Smith undertook an ambitious programme of diversification by acquisition and expansion abroad (Derdak, 1988: 315). Some of these moves, particularly into the food business, apparently proved unwise in more ways than one. The acquisition of Airco, the American gas company bought in 1978, resulted in its former head, Richard Giordano, joining BOC. Within a year Giordano (a lawyer who practised on Wall Street before joining Airco; Jeremy and Tweedale, 1994: 71) had replaced Smith as chief executive and soon began to reshape the company by selling off some of the concerns bought in the 1960s and 1970s (Cowe, 1993: 206). According to Ritchie and Goldsmith, 'It says a great deal for Smith's personal integrity and his underlying business acumen that he handed over executive power to a recently hostile alien, who used it to reverse many of his own initiatives' (1987: 62). Smith was knighted in 1977 and continued his commitment to BOC as chairman from 1979–85 and a director until 1992.

Despite the above examples (and there are of course many others) of accountants who achieved fame and fortune without attending university, the post-war period (particularly from about 1960) has increasingly been the era of the graduate accountant. This trend is mainly a reflection of the general rise of the graduate director and, as 94% of trainee chartered accountants are now graduates (ICAEW, 1996c: 3), degrees will inevitably become the norm among accountants who reach the top in the not too distant future. The days of the non-graduate seeking to make his or her way in the accountancy profession on the basis of a secondary school education are virtually over.

The graduate accountant does not, of course, date only from the 1960s. The ICAEW made provision in its initial charter for three years' (as opposed to five years') articles for the graduate, and we saw, in Chapter 2, that the graduate accountant was by no means uncommon in Scotland from very early times. Indeed, as noted in previous chapters, Scottish chartered accountants have figured probably disproportionately among the most successful in industry south of the border. William Hunter McFadzean is a good case in point. He was educated at Stranraer Academy and Glasgow University, qualifying with McLay, McAllister & McGibbon of Glasgow in 1927 before moving south to join the Liverpool office of Chambers, Wade & Co. (Morgan, 1985: 20). He then took the familiar route to one of the firm's major clients, British Insulated Cables Ltd., as an accountant in 1932. McFadzean played an important role in the negotiations of 1942–5, which resulted in the merger of the two dominant firms in the industry, BIC and Callender's Cables & Construction Co., to produce British Insulated Callender's Cables Ltd. He was appointed to the position of executive director in 1945, chief executive by 1950, and chairman and managing director in 1954. Under McFadzean, between 1945 and 1973 (when he retired) BICC 'became a significant multinational, with a global workforce of over 50,000 in seventeen countries and annual sales of £500 million' (Jeremy and Tweedale, 1994: 124). He has been described as 'one of the first of the new generation of accountant managers that emerged in the period following the second world war and did a great deal to bring financial control to what was a very traditional part of British industry, electric cable making' (Morgan, 1985: 20). Interestingly, McFadzean has also been noted for his 'strong belief in the value of team work, and to this end developed at BICC a management structure that brought together the skills of engineers, accountants, and other disciplines' (Morgan, 1985: 20).

Finance director stepping-stone

An increasingly important factor in the rise of the accountant through the management hierarchy has been the advent of the finance director. We argue, below, that the creation of this office in the 1950s and 1960s was not the main reason for the growing presence of accountants on British boards of directors, but it undoubtedly helped. The finance director now became a stepping-stone for the accountant in reaching the very top in management, perhaps because, 'Apart from the chief executive or managing director, he's often the only other person with a total view of the business' (quoted in Coyle, 1989: 18). In addition, according to Sir Geoffrey Mulcahy, then chief executive of Kingfishers plc, 'the finance director is the main source of information about the company for other board members, and is in a good position to take a broad strategic view' (quoted in Coyle, 1989: 18).

Harvey-Jones explains the rise of the finance director as follows: 'some functions are absolutely essential. It would be impossible for any board of directors to operate without a finance director, who deals with the complexities of the financing of the company, oversees the controller's function, and the preparation of the accounts' (1988: 266). For Mills, the finance director occupies such a central role in the company that the incumbent should be

a well-trained and widely experienced accountant who is up to date in all the intricate details which fall within the finance function. Most of the other directors are *ignorant* of these intricacies, and often a little *frightened* of them. While it can be possible to obtain this type of expertise in the form of a specialist non-executive, it can only be of practical value to the board if it is being applied daily in all corners of the company, thus ensuring that contribution in the boardroom combines theory with *detailed knowledge of the actual situation of the business encompassed.* (1985: 125—emphasis added)

The changing and more demanding role of the finance director is reflected upon by Mulcahy, who believes that during the 'past ten years [that is, the 1980s] finance directors have been forced to act more and more as strategic thinkers' (quoted in Coyle, 1989: 18), hence breaking away from the 'bean counter' stereotype. Relevant factors are seen to include: 'the 1980s takeover boom, involving finance directors in either assessing promising targets, or working to outbid defences. Another reason is the greater complexity and internationalisation of financial markets, forcing companies to assess currency risks, deal in futures and options, and choose between different sources of funds and deal with more innovative and competitive bankers and brokers' (quoted in Coyle, 1989: 18). Diane Coyle sees the finance director of the future as someone who 'has to manage the company's increasingly sophisticated portfolio of assets', with such a role involving 'choices about selling bits of the business, buying other companies, and defending his firm against takeover bids'. To discharge such responsibilities successfully, argues Coyle, requires the finance director to fulfil 'a far more active role than the old-style finance director citing accounts at board meetings, with the production of the annual report at the pinnacle of his duties' (Coyle, 1989: 18).

It is perhaps useful to continue this line of inquiry by noting a wide variety in the principal roles fulfilled by finance directors, as perceived by the incumbents of this post. Nigel Haslam, then finance director of Shell UK (he left in 1987), recounted that he divided his time 'between tricky tax and accounting problems (especially of an inter-company sort—he umpires "family" disagreements), staff development, general board duties and . . . Shell's growing portfolio of smaller companies' (Mitchell, 1985a: 9). He sees staff development as his single most important task, arguing: 'however big the business is, however much money and technology you've got, in the end it comes down to people of the right calibre' (Mitchell, 1985a: 9). Sainsbury's Rosemary Thorne sees even her day-to-day job as 'extremely varied . . . I may be overseeing the Group's internal financial accounting, budgets and corporate plans, or negotiating bank charges. I may be dealing with analysts, the City and the banks, or with one of our suppliers' (CIMA, 1996: 4). At Ford, Stanley Thomson (who left c.1990) considered his biggest task as finance director as simply 'to continue to look at ways of reducing our costs' (Mitchell, 1985b: 8), while Christopher Synge Barton, then finance director of Portsmouth and Sunderland Newspapers, described the role in the following terms:

to control central financial policy, including taxation; to steer EDP [electronic data processing] policy; to undertake acquisitions work; to identify divestment needs; to oversee systems change; to overlook important commercial contracts such as newsprint, and to input into the financial effects of the introduction of new technology. . . . [The finance director] is the nerve centre of the business, a focal point for *all* management plans: he must be objective, analytical, a *strategist*. I am a catalyst trying to co-ordinate a lot of management's thinking, and bring the overall picture into focus. (Mitchell, 1985c: 8—emphasis added)

One of the most important duties that faced Trevor Abbott, newly appointed finance director of the Virgin Group in April 1985, was 'to help arrange extended banking facilities' (Croft, 1987a: 14), while Jim Beveridge, who joined MEPC, the property company, in 1974 and has been its finance director since 1984, sees 'communicating with the City, banks and shareholders, making sure that there are no surprises and setting out clearly both the good news and, in recent years, the bad', as being one of his most important roles (Grey, 1993b: 31). This investor-relations role is also taken up by Edward Pickard, finance director of Invergordon Distillers Group, who claimed: 'I normally spend 20% of my time on investor relations' (Fisher, 1992: 26). In a similar vein, Simon Moffat, the first group finance director at Kwik Save Group, the super-market chain (1990–2), appears to have been drafted in to improve the company's standing in the City:

Autocratic, determined and with 30 years of retail experience, Mr Seabrook [man-aging director from 1988 and also chief executive from 1989] changed the face of management, putting some plump growth figures back into the accounts. How-ever, analysts report that his relations with the City were not so successful: they found him uncommunicative, and when the share price dropped after a lower than expected set of interims, a Group Finance Director was hired . . . City fears were quickly soothed by the Moffat sincerity and charm. (Grey, 1991: 23)

Turning to a fuller examination of the contributions made by finance directors, we start with two accountants whose careers cross—Allan Gormly and Eric Parker. Gormly is another Scot and a grammar school boy from Paisley, who joined Peat, Marwick, Mitchell & Co. straight from school in 1955 (*WW*, 1993: 737). He moved into industry with the Rootes Group, the motor manufacturers, in 1961, and joined John Brown, the shipbuilders and heavy engineers, in 1965. Gormly was eventually pro-moted to financial director in 1970, and spent the next seven years helping to convert huge losses into profits. Gormly became deputy chairman in 1980 and managing director in 1983. As the result of many, often unfore-seeable, problems, however, the company was near collapse when ac-quired by Trafalgar House, the construction-based conglomerate, in 1986 (Derdak, 1988: 573). It is an indication of Gormly's stature that he was retained as managing director and allowed a great deal of autonomy by Trafalgar House, under whom John Brown has fared reasonably well. Indeed, Gormly became chief executive of Trafalgar House in 1992, mov-ing over to the position of deputy chairman two years later (*WW*, 1996: 751).

The merger with Trafalgar House brings in the connection with Parker (knighted in 1991), who left grammar school to take articles with the Shrewsbury firm of Wheeler, Whittingham & Kent and qualified in 1956 (*WW*, 1993: 1,445). Following National Service in the Pay Corps, he took a job with Taylor Woodrow, the construction firm, in 1958 and moved on to Trafalgar House in 1965. There, he became finance and administrative director in 1969, deputy managing director in 1973, group managing director in 1977, chief executive in 1983, and deputy chairman in 1988. For most of his career, Parker was therefore associated with the extraordinary growth of the company created by Sir Nigel Boackes. A small company in the 1950s, Trafalgar House expanded by a series of aggressive takeovers—Trollope and Colls, 1968; Cementation, 1970; Cunard, 1971; and the Ritz,

1976. By the early 1980s, Parker had taken over from Victor Matthews as Boackes's 'right hand man' (Cowe, 1993: 427), and it was his strategy to move the group in the direction of the more profitable high-technology aspects of construction, such as the Thames Bridge at Dartford and chemical and steel plants. To this end, Trafalgar House bought Redpath Dorman Long in 1982, and Scott Lithgow and John Brown in 1986. It also bought the Ellerman Lines in 1987—the creation, as we have seen, of an illustrious accountant of bygone days.

The purchase of the ailing Davy Corporation in 1991 was Boackes and Parker's undoing, since they inherited a disastrously unprofitable contract to build a North Sea oil rig. Buying the British Rail engineering company BREL was another mistake, and these factors together conspired to produce a highly unfavourable impact on the company's balance sheet. An attempt to employ creative accounting techniques to show profits of £122.4 million for 1991 attracted the attention of the regulators, and the company was forced to issue revised accounts showing a loss of £38.5 million in order to avoid being taken to court by the Financial Reporting Review Panel (*Accountancy*, Feb. 1993: 13). These problems paved the way for the acquisition of a significant minority shareholding by a group backed by Jardine Matheson, and the removal of Boackes and Parker. Under Parker's stewardship, Trafalgar House's market valuation fell from £1.1 billion in 1985, when it was rated the 29th largest company in Britain (a situation, of course, which Parker had helped achieve), to half that value and a position outside the top 100 companies (Wardley, 1991: 280; Cowe, 1993: 425). He retired from his position as chief executive in 1992 and deputy chairman in 1993.

It is perhaps ironic that the Davy Corporation, whose takeover helped produce the low point in Parker's career, had previously been run by a chartered accountant, Harry Benson. Here was another public school nongraduate, who, after distinguishing himself in wartime service, being awarded the Military Cross in 1945, qualified with Moore Stephens. He moved into industry in 1948, and became managing director of Waring and Gillow, the furniture retailers, in the 1950s and APV Holdings, the engineering company, in the 1960s and 1970s, as well as a director of both Rolls-Royce and Vickers in the 1970s and 1980s (*WW*, 1993: 145). Benson was the chairman of Davy Corporation—'another great engineer fallen on hard times'—from 1982 to 1985, when they entered into the oil rig contract 'taken on at ridiculously low cost because the company was desperate for business and which turned out to incur [the] huge additional costs' that brought Trafalgar House to its knees (Cowe, 1993: 427).

Michael Julien is another who made his initial reputation as a finance director. Educated at St Edwards School, Oxford, he joined Price Waterhouse & Co. in 1958, aged 20, which he believes gave him 'some very good early experience' (quoted in Fisher, 1994: 25). He left Price

Waterhouse in 1967 to become the first 'chief financial officer' to be appointed at C. E. Heath, the insurance brokers, where 'they had been using the auditors to keep the books, amazingly' (quoted in Fisher, 1994: 25). The highly mobile Julien then spent eighteen months with British Leyland where he was responsible for treasury management, that is the management of: short- and long-term funds; cash and working capital; relationships with financial institutions; and foreign currency risk (Parker, 1992: 286). He later recalled: 'I was one of only two people called Treasurer in London apart from the US Oil Companies, the other being Alan Clements [at ICI]. Treasury was very much a nascent profession in those days and the two of us practically invented it' (quoted in Fisher, 1994: 25). The pair formed a treasurers' club with their US counterparts which eventually grew into the Association of Corporate Treasurers.

Julien was also the first finance director of McFadzean's company, BICC, 1976–83 and then moved to Midland Bank as executive director of finance and planning (*WW*, 1993: 1022). According to Julien, however, his ambition was always to become chief executive of a large listed company, and he was therefore keen to move out of finance and 'into a line job' (quoted in Fisher, 1994: 25). He spent a year with Guinness as managing director and, at the request of Sir Terence Conran, he joined Storehouse, the retailing group built up by Conran based around his success with Habitat, as chief executive in 1988. Theirs was a stormy relationship, since each had completely different ideas regarding the direction the group should take. Julien was accused of 'de-Conranising' Storehouse by selling off a large part of the unprofitable company including Habitat itself in 1992 (Cowe, 1993: 411). Conran later stated that appointing Michael Julien was his biggest mistake (quoted in Fisher, 1994: 26). Julien gives us a colourful insight into the range of techniques that may be employed in the endeavour to achieve a desired takeover. At a time when Storehouse was the subject of an unwanted US bid, ploys included surveillance from private investigators and an endeavour to 'entrap' Julien when 'a beautiful blonde was sent to his office under the guise of interviewing him for a book' (Fisher, 1994: 25). Not the popular image of the accountant at work! With failing health due possibly to overwork, Julien left Storehouse in 1992 just as results were improving (Cowe, 1993: 411–12), but retains a number of non-executive directorships including Guinness plc (*WW*, 1996: 1,045).

Sir Paul Girolami is perhaps the most successful example of an accountant turned industrialist, indeed one of the most successful businessmen of the post-war period. From an Italian background, Girolami came to Britain aged 2 and, in due course, took a degree at the London School of Economics. He did his articles at Chantrey & Button 1950–4 (still having at that time to pay a premium of 500 guineas) and, after qualifying, moved on to Cooper Brothers in 1956 (*WW*, 1993: 713). He later said that: 'The advice one was generally given was that if you qualified in a relatively unknown firm, before you make any decision about what way your career would take you, you should get a big name behind you' (Irvine, 1992a: 26). After nine years, mainly spent in Cooper's management consultancy arm, and at almost 40 years of age, Girolami made the move into industry. Sir Alan Wilson, the chairman of Glaxo, an audit client of Coopers, was looking for a finance director and Cooper's senior partner, John Pears, suggested Girolami.

Girolami was initially taken on as finance controller which, he later admitted, gave him time to adjust to the 'real world' (quoted in Irvine, 1992a: 27). Girolami was financial director within three years and remained in that position for a further twelve years, building up a formidable reputation within the organization. The problem with Glaxo, as Girolami saw it, was that substantial expansion through acquisition had resulted in the group consisting of a number of very powerful, independent companies, often with their own marketing, manufacturing, and research units, but 'no central management structure and no coherent strategy policy' (quoted in Irvine, 1992a: 27). Sir Alan Wilson had been brought in as chairman to rationalize the disparate group, and Girolami's 'immediate job was to create a central finance function. Glaxo had never had a group finance director—Sir Harry Jephcott [the previous chairman] had a healthy contempt for book-keepers and refused to have them anywhere near' (quoted in Irvine, 1992a: 27). Having established his reputation as finance director, Girolami became chief executive of Glaxo in 1980, chairman in 1985, and was knighted in 1988.

In 1948, Glaxo was not in the top 50 UK manufacturing companies by market value; by 1985, it was the sixth largest of all companies and the second biggest manufacturer behind ICI, and by the early 1990s it was the largest (Hannah, 1983: 190; Wardley, 1991: 280). One of Girolami's early successes was to thwart a takeover bid by Beechams: 'A brilliant pre-emptive move in 1972, masterminded by Girolami, saw off the predator by forming Glaxo Holdings, which itself took over "old" Glaxo at an 18% benefit for shareholders' (Kennedy, 1992: 106). Girolami's success has been attributed to a 'willingness to risk the known for the unknown, a comfortable performance for a potentially sensational one' (Kennedy, 1992: 108). Girolami moved Glaxo more heavily into the drug industry, which is of course highly risky and requires a huge investment in research and development that may prove valueless or alternatively produce a bonanza. The firm hit the jackpot with their ulcer cure Zantac, introduced in 1981, 'one of the blockbuster drugs of all times' (Irvine, 1992a: 27).

There were other ulcer drugs on the market, however, and it is thought to have been the development and aggressive marketing of Zantac, for which Girolami took personal responsibility, rather than any unique scientific breakthrough, which gave Glaxo the lead (Derdak, 1988: 640). The trick was to get two research teams working on the same drug, which halved development times, and to register the drug in all world markets simultaneously (Kennedy, 1992: 106). Zantac quickly achieved 36% of the world market and for years contributed half of Glaxo's world-wide turn-over—47% of group sales of £1.61 billion in 1991. According to a former colleague, Girolami 'may not have created the drug but all credit to him, he seized the opportunity. If he had left it to the usual Glaxo marketing techniques, it would have been grossly under-exploited. But he doesn't have the awful blinkered approach that British people have and he saw its potential' (quoted in Irvine, 1992*a*: 28). He also showed his aggression as an industrialist when he ruthlessly reasserted control of the company by ousting the chief executive Dr Ernest Mario in 1993 (Cowe, 1993: 61) not long before retiring as chairman in 1994, though he remained on the board of the hotel group Forte and UIS France (*WW*, 1996: 727).

Finally, among our sample of accountants who got to the top in management via the post of financial director is Ian Prosser, who went on from grammar school to study for a B.Com. degree at Birmingham University (*WW*, 1993: 1,534). He then took articles with Cooper Brothers, joined Bass Charrington immediately on qualifying, in 1969, and has stayed there ever since. He became financial director in 1978 and this provided the springboard for him to become managing director six years later. Prosser then worked under the chairmanship of Sir Derek Palmer—a fellow chartered accountant and, previously, also a finance director at Bass (*Accountant*, 28 June 1984)—before himself becoming chairman and chief executive in 1987. In estimating the likely impact of accountants at Bass, it is relevant to note that the company is viewed by the City as one of the best companies in the drinks sector (Cowe, 1993: 43–4). It is also seen as having 'maintained its conservative management policies' and has remained the least diversified of the major brewers, although it made an ill-timed move into hotels, buying Holiday Inns just ahead of the recession in 1987 (Derdak, 1988: 224). Like many other top managers, Prosser serves as a non-executive board member at other companies, in his case at Boots from 1984 and Lloyds Bank from 1988.

Many other accountants reached the top via the post of company secretary. One example is Stanley Grinstead who was educated at Strodes (grammar) School, in Egham, served in the navy during the war and then qualified with and worked for Franklin, Wild & Co. 1946–56, before joining their audit client Maxwell Joseph as company secretary, where 'His title was company secretary and his responsibilities were financial and managerial. And vague' (quoted in Ritchie and Goldsmith, 1987: 70). Grinstead became deputy chairman and group managing director of Grand Metropolitan in 1980, and chairman and chief executive in 1982. It was Grinstead who took the major strategic decisions to make Grand Metropolitan an international, more diversified, company. Speaking in

1987—a year which saw profits almost double those of five years earlier—
Grinstead described his role as follows: 'One of my responsibilities is to
ensure that the group is flourishing in twenty to thirty years' time and
therefore I have to take action and plan for that success. That means not
only nurturing and husbanding our existing businesses but also laying
down the seeds for future growth' (Ritchie and Goldsmith, 1987: 77).
Grinstead's management style was to maintain a small staff at head office,
rely heavily on close personal contact, and impose tight financial controls
on each branch of the group, with pressure on the operating companies to
be as efficient and profitable as possible (Ritchie and Goldsmith, 1987: 76).
Grinstead was knighted in 1986 and, after leaving Grand Metropolitan,
became chairman of Reed International in 1987 (he had been a director
since 1981), during the period of major restructuring and divestment of all
but its core publishing business (Cowe, 1993: 367), before moving on two
years later as director and chairman of the Harmony Leisure Group,
finally retiring in 1992 (*WW*, 1993: 774).

General management

The above case-studies provide illustrations of accountants reaching the
top via the financial or, in Grinstead's case, the secretarial function. Again,
the overall statistics provide the explanation by showing that these were
largely the areas where most accountants in corporate management
worked. Table 19 reports the fact that no more than 20% of ICAEW
members employed in business worked in general management between
1951 and 1996. Some of these also progressed to the highest rungs in
management, including the Wills brothers who are also clearly part of the
profession's elite. While in no way wishing to detract from their achievements, one might imagine that this privileged group benefited from social
and family connections, and appear to come closest to the 'clubby, gentlemanly approach' to management that Gourvish (1987: 41) detects as a
problem in British industry during this period. Colin and Nicholas Wills
were both educated at public school (Eton and Rugby) and Queen's College, Cambridge (*WW*, 1993: 2,036). Colin qualified as a chartered accountant in 1962, went to work in television, and, within four years, was deputy
general manager of ATV. He was also director or managing director of a
number of television stations (including, from 1970, Thames) owned by
the conglomerate BET—the company that his brother was destined to
head.

Nicholas qualified with Binder, Hamlyn in 1967, and immediately went
to work for Morgan Grenfell, the merchant banker (*WW*, 1993: 2,036). He
became managing director of the Birmingham and District Investment
Trust in 1970, moving to BET as director in 1975, and became its managing
director in 1982. At BET, Nicholas Wills is credited with a clear strategy

Table 19. Occupations of ICAEW members in 'business', 1951–1996

Occupation	1951 (%)	1971 (%)	1991 (%)	1983 (%)	1992 (%)	1996 (%)
Financial	35	51	56	60	60	62
Secretary	35	16	9	4	2	2
General management	20	20	20	18	13	11
Miscellaneous	10	13	15	18	25	25
Total	100	100	100	100	100	100
Total identified in sample/survey	196	246	193	29,973	29,016	36,293
Unknown	108	57	133	0	318	4,908

Notes: The 1951, 1971, and 1991 figures are based on a random sample from every tenth page of the membership lists, also used in Tables 16 and 20. The totals identified in the sample are those who gave their occupation. The unknowns are those who also revealed themselves as in 'business', i.e. gave their employer but did not give their job. The rest of the sample were in practice, worked overseas, or were retired or undesignated. The 1983, 1992, and 1996 figures are more reliable. In 1983 the ICAEW obtained a 93% response rate to their questionnaire (*ICAEW Membership Questionnaire*). However, the similarity between the results of the ICAEW questionnaires and our 1991 survey adds credibility to our earlier figures.

The occupations listed are simplifications of the ICAEW job titles. The definition of 'Financial' here includes the ICAEW titles: Corporate Accounting and Reporting; Corporate Finance; Corporate Taxation; Financial Management; Internal Audit and Treasury. 'Miscellaneous' includes: Administration; Consultancy; Human Resources and Personnel; Information Technology; Management Accounting; Marketing; Pensions; Planning; Strategy; and None of These. These definitions have been followed as far as possible in our 1951, 1971, and 1991 surveys but the differences between these and the ICAEW data are probably due to the problem of categorizing jobs. In our samples, directors have been classed under 'General Management'; finance directors under 'Financial'.

The 1983 questionnaire data are for all ICAEW members in business, it proving impossible to isolate UK members in that year. For the surveys in the latter two years, the data relate to UK members only.

Sources: For 1951, 1971, and 1991: ICAEW yearbooks; for 1983, 1992, and 1996: *ICAEW Membership Questionnaires*.

for corporate development, building a diversified service group with interests stretching from scaffolding to window frames (through the acquisition of Anglian in 1984) and laundries (following the purchase of Initial in 1985). The company was flippantly credited, during the 1980s, with buying three companies a week (Cowe, 1993: 195). This disparate spread of service-sector companies led Wills to declare BET recession-proof, but significant overspending soon created a 'debt mountain' and a dangerous level of gearing. Wills's solution was to reverse policy and disinvest—Anglian was sold in 1990 and Thames Television in 1991. Pressure from major institutional shareholders nevertheless forced Wills out of his position as chief executive in 1991, and he lasted just one more year as chairman. The new regime was reported to have found 'that financial and management controls were almost non-existent due to the previous preoccupation with acquisitions, and the philosophy of decentralisation which left individual businesses to go their own way' (Cowe, 1993: 195).

Our other example of an accountant taking the general management route to the top is George Duncan, a grammar school-educated graduate of the London School of Economics who then obtained an MBA from Wharton Business School, Pennsylvania. He qualified as a chartered accountant in 1962 and then moved into industry. By 1967, at the age of 34, Duncan was chief executive of the brewers Truman Hanbury. Following Grand Metropolitan's acquisition of Trumans and Watney Mann in 1971 and 1972, respectively, Duncan became chief executive of their combined brewery operations. In 1976, he was the chairman of a finance company, and subsequently took on a wide variety of executive and non-executive directorships, including Lloyds Bank 1982–7. Duncan's numerous appointments include chairman of ASW Holdings, the steel makers, and non-executive director of BET where he survived the departure of Nicholas Wills (*WW*, 1993: 545).

Before leaving this section, we can look briefly at the career of John Neil Clarke, who arrived in general management through the rather unusual route of tax specialist. A public schoolboy (Rugby) who gained a law degree from King's College, London, Clarke took up chartered accountancy articles 'almost as a matter of chance' on the advice of a family friend (Counsell, 1984: 8). He qualified in 1959 and went to Rowley Pemberton, a City firm of accountants, as a tax specialist, making partner in 1960. As with many accountants from this period, Clarke itched to leave practice and start 'making things happen', joining Charter Consolidated (a holding company with investments in mining and construction) as a tax consultant in 1969. He rose swiftly to become a director in 1973, managing director in 1979, and deputy chairman and chief executive in 1982. With Chartered Consolidated its major shareholder, Clarke was drawn in, as non-executive chairman, to help rescue Johnson Matthey Bank in 1984. The bank threatened to collapse taking the bullion market with it, but Clarke together with the Bank of England forced the whole board to resign and proceeded to restore the company to health. He attributes his success to the importance attached to motivating his managers, and the fact that: 'I like the challenge of a job. Adrenalin runs a little faster' (Bose, 1992: 30). He joined British Coal as chairman, in 1991, with the brief of preparing it for privatization. Clarke was described as 'the first modern troubleshooter-style of executive to arrive at British Coal' (Bose, 1992: 30). He is currently also chairman of Genchem Holdings (*WW*, 1996: 370).

Route 5: in at the bottom

The final route into top management for accountants involves those who started work in industry and qualified there. This has only recently become a possibility for members of the original chartered bodies, and the route is largely the preserve of CIMA and ACCA members. Though their combined numbers in business exceed those of the original chartered bodies, they appear to have been far less likely to reach a top management position. Table 15 shows that a relatively small proportion of non-chartered accountants become directors, and we will see below that a relatively small, though increasing, number of CIMA or ACCA members are finance directors. One example of an ACCA accountant who made it to the top is Bill Petley, described by H. G. Lazell, the accountant-chairman of the accountant-dominated Beechams, as an illustration of 'how men of great ability can be encouraged and fostered in a company' (1975: 187). Petley was appointed financial director of Beechams in 1967, and judged by Lazell to be 'the finest financial director I have ever worked with, [he] came up the hard way and qualified as a certified accountant' (Lazell, 1975: 163). Indeed, Petley became president of Beechams in 1971.

Lazell, himself a certified accountant, had an interesting career which is perhaps illustrative of the rather longer ladder to the top that even the very able accountants from outside the chartered grouping needed to climb, at least in the past. He left elementary school before his fourteenth birthday, during the First World War, to become an Inland Revenue office boy (Jeremy and Tweedale, 1994: 112). He then worked as a bookkeeper in a bookmaker's office in Regent Street, taking the examinations of the Royal Society of Arts and London Chamber of Commerce. He joined Allen and Hanburys Ltd., pharmacists, as a ledger keeper, during which time he took correspondence courses and eventually passed the examinations of one of the bodies which became the ACCA. He joined Macleans, the toothpaste makers, as an accountant in 1930, becoming a board member. Following the sale of Macleans to Beechams in 1938, he soon became Beechams' secretary and, in 1940, returned to Macleans as managing director. He was appointed managing director and chief executive of Beechams in 1951 (chairman in 1958) and 'controlled its destiny for seventeen years until my retirement in 1968' when he was succeeded by yet another certified accountant, Sir Ronald Edwards (Lazell, 1975: 1).

Lazell was convinced that companies should be led by marketing men although, by that term, he meant people with a marketing outlook rather than those necessarily trained in that area. Indeed, he had previously left Allen and Hanburys Ltd. because it was dominated by pharmacists who were determined to sell its products only to chemists (Lazell, 1975: 4). Lazell argued that even 'The chief executive must be a marketing man. He may have started life as a chemist, an engineer or an accountant, but he must think and act like a marketing man' (Lazell, 1975: 197). Lazell was also an enthusiastic promoter of research, and agreed to become joint assistant managing director in 1947 only to avoid 'losing the power to support research' (Lazell, 1975: 58–61). Following on from this commitment to a company's long-term future, Lazell was heavily critical of the pursuit of short-term objectives and profit maximization, and cites Marks and Spencer and ICI as pursuing the high principles which yield high profits long term (Lazell, 1975: 202). According to Jeremy and Tweedale 'it was Lazell's achievement to transform the group—a sprawling badly co-ordinated company tied to older proprietary products—into an international science-based pharmaceutical manufacturer. Lazell launched the firm's own research effort after 1945 and achieved brilliant success with synthetic penicillins. Beecham's turnover rose from £25 million in 1952 to £134 million in 1969; profits from £2.6 million to over £25 million' (1994: 112).

We can cite two further certified accountants with more recent prominence in British business. David Charles Jones joined Kays Mail Order Company (part of Great Universal Stores) straight from King's School, Worcester, and rose to the position of finance director in 1971, at the age of 27. He left to become managing director of BMOC in 1977, and worked in a similar capacity at Grattan plc 1980–6. Following takeover, he was appointed as chief executive of the retailers Next (*WW*, 1996: 1,031). George Simpson was educated at Morgan Academy, Dundee, and Dundee Institute of Technology. He started his ACCA examinations while working as an accountant in the gas industry 1962–9 (he was admitted in 1972), before moving into the motor industry, initially as central audit manager at BLMC. He was promoted to financial controller in 1973 and to the board three years later. A breakneck series of appointments followed as managing director of Coventry Climax Ltd. (1980–3) and Freight Rover Ltd. (1983–6), chief executive of Leyland DAF (1986–8), managing director and then chief executive of the Rover Group (1989–92), and chairman (1991–4). Simpson, who was named 'Industry Man of the Year' by *Autocar and Motor Magazine* in 1991 (ACCA, 1996: 13), was chief executive of Lucas Industries plc, 1994–6, and is currently managing director of General Electric plc. His many other appointments include deputy chief executive of British Aerospace (1992–4) and non-executive directorships at Pilkington, Northern Venture Capital, Pro Share, and ICI (*WW*, 1997: 1,788).

Allen Sheppard is one of the few cost accountants to reach the very top in management. After graduating from the London School of Economics, Sheppard made his early career in the motor industry (*WW*, 1993: 1,709).

He joined Ford in 1958, moved on to Rootes/Chrysler after ten years, and British Leyland in 1971. He joined Grand Metropolitan in 1975, moved from managing director to chief executive in 1986 and, a year later, replaced Stanley Grinstead as chairman. Under Grinstead and Sheppard's management (and another chartered accountant, Ian Martin, who joined the board in 1985 and was managing director 1991–3) Grand Metropolitan has proved a highly successful conglomerate, becoming one of the four largest wine and spirit companies in the world and more than doubling its market value between 1985 and 1993. It is also very active in buying and selling companies—acquiring the huge American Pillsbury company in 1989, and selling all its breweries to Courage in 1991 in return for control of thousands of Courage's pubs (Cowe, 1993: 51). On the negative side, one might speculate that the heavy involvement of accountants at top level explains Grand Metropolitan's high placement on Terry Smith's list of companies using creative accounting techniques (*Observer*, 23 July 1992). Sheppard was knighted in 1990 and awarded a life peerage in the 1994 birthday honours list. He retired from his position as chief executive in 1993 and chairman in 1996.

SOME NUMBERS FOR ACCOUNTANTS IN INDUSTRY

The biggest proportionate increase in the employment of accountants in industry and government took place between 1911 and 1951 (Table 16), by which time one-half of all accountants and about a third of ICAEW/SIAA members were working in that sector. The proportion then seems to have edged up slowly in the 1950s and 1960s, but gathered pace again in the 1970s and 1980s. Table 9 shows that the number of ICAEW members in business, as a proportion of the known active membership, has increased from 49% in 1983 to 55% in 1996, and this during a period when the total membership increased by 32,032. In the remainder of this section, we attempt to quantify where they worked in terms of industrial sector and size of company, what they did, the rise of the finance director, and the extent of the accountant's involvement in top management.

Where they worked

We are able to make a detailed quantification of where professional accountants worked for the period since the Second World War. Table 20 gives the breakdown of chartered accountants employed in business, analysed by the nature of the business, using the one-digit Standard Industrial Classification. It also compares these results with employment in Britain generally. The most interesting finding is the extent to which accountants were preponderant in manufacturing and construction until

Table 20. Accountants employed in 'business' analysed by sector of business, 1951–1996

Business sector	1951		1971		1983		1992		1996	
	Accountants (%)	Total employees (%)	Accountants (%)	Total employees (%)	Accountants (%)	Total employees (%)	Accountants (%)	Total employees (%)	Accountants (%)	Total employees (%)
1. Agriculture, energy, and coal extraction SIC 0–1	6	11	4	5	2	4	5	3	5	2
2. Manufacturing and construction SIC 2–5	54	45	62	44	43	30	33	27	32	22
3. Distribution, hotels, transport, and communications SIC 6–7	13	20	12	21	21	26	22	27	20	29
4. Banking, finance, and insurance SIC 8	13	9	10	18	24	10	33	12	37	17
5. Other services (mainly public sector) SIC 9	14	15	12	12	10	30	7	31	6	30
Total	100	100	100	100	100	100	100	100	100	100
Total known from surveys	248	22.2 m.	268	22.0 m.	23,083	21.1 m.	26,919	22.1 m.	21,415	21.3 m.
Unknown	56		35		8,633		2,415		1,680	

Notes: The 1951 and 1971 figures are based on a random sample from every tenth page of the membership lists, also used in Tables 16 and 19. The 'Unknown' row in 1951 and 1971 represents accountants who were identified as 'in business' but the activity of their company or organization could not be traced. The samples used in 1951 and 1971 are, of course, less reliable than the ICAEW data. The classifications used in the ICAEW surveys in 1983, 1992, and 1996 (*ICAEW Membership Questionnaires*) have been rearranged to fit the Standard Industrial Classification (SIC, one digit). In the general employment data in 1951 and 1971, 'Miscellaneous services' has been grouped under 'Other services'. The data on total employees (last column) relate to 1995. The 1992 and 1996 'Accountants' data relate to ICAEW UK members not in practice; for 1983, data cover all ICAEW members not in practice.

Sources: For 1951 and 1971: ICAEW yearbooks, *The Stock Exchange Official Year-Book*, and *Post Office Kelly's Directory*; for 1983, 1992, and 1996: ICAEW

recently, and disproportionately so compared to the overall workforce. An examination of the ACCA and the CIMA membership lists for 1991 suggests that, there also, employment in manufacturing featured strongly.

We can only speculate as to the possible reasons. It might be that manufacturing operations require tighter financial control although, on average, they are neither noticeably larger nor more complex than companies in other sectors. In addition, since manufacturing tends to be more exposed to the vagaries of the business cycle than services, the financial accountants' specialist skills might be more in demand. Related to this explanation, but a more intriguing possibility, is that the high number of accountants might be a function of the recurrent financial difficulties of the manufacturing sector. Each of these potential explanations, however, requires further research.

Even less clear-cut is the situation regarding financial services implied by Table 20. Few firm conclusions can be drawn from the data for 1951 and 1971, because of the margin of error in the sampling method and the changes in the SIC classifications between these dates with regard to total employment. It is probably safe to say, however, that accountants were not heavily represented in banking, finance, and insurance down to the 1970s. This is not true, however, of the last two decades, during which the proportion of all chartered accountants in business, working in the financial sector, rose from 24% in 1983 to 37% in 1996. Their disproportionate involvement is further reflected by the fact that there are more than twice as many professional accountants in that sector compared with employment generally, and they have very recently overtaken the numbers engaged in the still larger manufacturing sector measured by total number of employees. Explanations must remain entirely speculative at this stage but, again, it is possible that the growing problems faced by the banking and insurance sector, over the last decade, have prompted constituent companies to take on more accountants.

Table 20 also suggests that two sectors today remain relatively under-endowed with accountants. The relative lack of accountants in distribution, hotels, and catering may be causally related to the nature of trading activity. In general, this sector tends to be more sheltered from the trade cycle and foreign competition than other sectors and, for these reasons, profitability has held up far better than in, say, manufacturing. A more specific point is that, within areas such as retailing and road haulage, there are a large number of small firms whose requirements for a full-time professional accountant's skills may be somewhat limited.

The other under-represented area is the public sector (included in 'Other services' in Table 20), but the global figures naturally mask significant variations between activities and over time. In 1951, most professional accountants in the governmental sector were engaged either in local government, for example as treasurers, or in public bodies such as

the nationalized British Transport Commission. Of the chartered accountants identified in our random sample for 1951 (Table 20, row 5), only two
were in central government—a principal accountant at the Admiralty and
a tax inspector. Our sample for 1971 revealed just three ICAEW members
in central government: a chief accountant at the Inland Revenue, a senior
accountant at the Department of Trade and Industry, and a senior auditor
at the Ministry of Agriculture. The comprehensive *ICAEW Membership
Questionnaire*, for 1992, showed that 907 members were engaged in
government—3.1% of accountants 'in business'—at a time when 'Public
Administration and Defence' accounted for 7.2% of total employment in
the UK (CSO, *Annual Abstract of Statistics*). In all its aspects, around 10% of
accountants now work in the public sector (Roslender, 1992: 56).

The lack of employment of accountants in central government was
noted in the Fulton Report on the Civil Service in 1968, which went on to
call for a 'strong force of highly-qualified professional accountants'
(Sampson, 1982: 167). A senior chartered accountant was appointed as a
second permanent secretary in 1975, but there were still only 364 accountants in the Government Accountancy Service in 1979, compared to 309
when Fulton reported. The lack of accountants in government was commented on by Sampson (1982: 167), who noted that internal audits were
still carried out without the use of qualified auditors or modern techniques. This dearth of accountants was, quite obviously, attributable to
the long-established reluctance to appoint people from outside the Civil
Service to senior positions rather than promoting from within their graduate intake. We might also note the absence from the public sector, until
recently, of the competitive pressure to control finances that existed in
private industry.

The size of employing companies is of relevance to any attempt to
develop a profile of accountants in business. Recent information (there is
none available for the pre-1980s) is set out in Table 21, which reveals some
interesting results. In 1996, about 40% of accountants in business were
employed by relatively small companies—less than 500 employees; indeed, 21.8% were with companies with 50 employees or less. To explore
the matter in more detail, accountants engaged in manufacturing were
listed separately and compared with total employment in manufacturing
in the UK. This analysis shows that accountants working in manufacturing tend to be employed by larger companies compared with the distribution throughout businesses generally. Also, accountants feature less
prominently in smaller and medium-sized enterprises compared to employment in manufacturing generally in the UK. Not shown in Table 21 is
the further fact that accountants are found disproportionately in the very
large manufacturing companies—over 10,000 workers. Nevertheless, any
tendency for accountants to gravitate towards larger companies is not
perhaps as pronounced as the *a priori* significance that might be attached

Table 21. Accountants employed 'in business' by size of company

Size of company by number of employees	1996		1992
	Accountants in business (%)	Accountants in manufacturing (%)	Total employment in UK manufacturing (%)
Less than 500	39.7	32.2	44.0
500–10,000	30.0	30.9	38.3
More than 10,000	30.3	36.9	17.7
Total	100.0	100.0	100.0

Notes: For accountants in business and manufacturing, figures are for employees in the organization world-wide. Figures for total manufacturing are for employment in the UK only.

Sources: ICAEW 1996d: 8; *Business Monitor PA1002 Report on the Census of Production 1992: Summary Volume*, 1995: 268.

to an increase in scale. Moreover, observed differences may be attributable to the fact that the two sets of data are not strictly comparable (see notes to Table 21), and such discrepancies would tend to exaggerate the size of companies where accountants worked. At this stage, therefore, the main message encompassed in the data is that accountants worked in large numbers in both small and large companies. We return to this issue in the final chapter.

What they did

Our sample (Table 19) of the ICAEW membership lists, together with data from the Institute's membership questionnaires, allow us to estimate with some confidence the job descriptions of ICAEW members working in industry 1951–91. Table 19 makes it clear that chartered accountants were mainly employed to run the financial affairs of companies and public bodies, and were far less likely to be engaged in general management. This tendency has increased in recent years, and our examination of a sample of their 1991 membership list suggests that this observation also applies to certified accountants.

Using the categories 'Financial' and 'Secretary' as indicative, Table 19 suggests that, throughout the period 1951–96, about two-thirds of accountants employed in business were 'keeping the books', and we might add that the 'Miscellaneous' category contains a high proportion of accountants also using their specialist expertise in one way or another. For example, our random sample for 1951 captured, in the 'Miscellaneous' group, a counting house manager in a shop, the head of economic intelligence at a bank, a clerk to a hospital, the bursar of a university, and a brigadier in the Royal Army Pay Corps. The 1991 sample included an export controller, an implementation analyst, a projects accountant, an economic adviser, a registrar, and six lecturers.

The period 1951–91 has seen an overall reduction in the proportion of accountants serving as company secretaries. This reduction has almost certainly been relative rather than absolute, and possibly also owes something to changing job titles. The joint position of 'Accountant and Secretary' was, and to some extent still is, commonly used among the smaller companies, but was categorized for Table 19 under the title 'Financial' rather than 'Secretary'. Table 15 also shows that the proportion of *quoted* companies with an accountant as secretary increased from just over a quarter in 1951 to almost a half by 1991, with ICAEW members making headway among listed companies at the expense of members of the Institute of Chartered Secretaries and Administrators (ICSA).

The finance director

The career path for the high-achieving accountant in industry—from accountant to chief accountant and then onto the board, perhaps as managing director then chairman—that emerged during the inter-war period was firmly established by the 1950s. The sample test of the ICAEW membership lists 1951–91 used to construct Table 19 detected the increasing presence of the new function of financial controller, a position usually ranked just below board level with its incumbent being responsible for the provision of information to the board and the implementation of its policy decisions (Locke, 1984: 95). As with much management, and indeed accounting, theory and practice, the innovation occurred first in the USA, in this instance during the 1920s (Locke, 1984: 95). Chapter 5 contains a number of examples of appointments to the position of financial controller in the 1930s—A. E. Sylvester at the Gas Light & Coke Company, J. M. Sandford Smith at Metal Box, and F. R. M. de Paula at Dunlop. Our samples for later periods revealed one financial controller in 1951, thirteen by 1971, and 24 in 1991.

The apotheosis of the financial functionary within the hierarchy of British companies occurred with the creation of the board-level position of financial or finance director, with the latter term in more widespread use today. The *Accountant* had advocated the policy—'general in the United States' (11 Jan. 1930: 30)—of appointing financial directors to British boards as early as 1930. The first example we have found is J. K. Greenhalgh, who was chief accountant and finance director at Lever Brothers just prior to the First World War (Wilson, 1954: 207–9), and, as we have seen (Chapter 5), Charles Merrett was a financial director of omnibus companies in the inter-war period, but the title was clearly unusual in Britain until some time after the Second World War.

Our sample of the ICAEW membership (used in Table 19), for 1951, captured only two financial directors (at the National Coal Board, and at Ransomes, the agricultural machinery makers of Ipswich). The rate of adoption then increased; for example, the British Motor Corporation appointed their first finance director in 1965, Glaxo in 1968, and our sample for 1971 contained 27 financial directors and, for 1991, it revealed 30 (*Accountancy*, Apr. 1992: 27; Church, 1994: 82). It therefore seems fairly clear that, in the twenty years after 1951, the inclusion of a financial director on the board became common practice. Certainly, financial directors were the rule by the 1970s, and we have demonstrated, above, their importance as a route into top management.

The advent of the finance director was, of course, part and parcel of the professionalization of company boards and the growth of the salaried executive director appointed along functional lines. But the finance director was probably the first functional board seat to be created at most companies, and it remains way ahead of the other leading functional appointments at board level. The Korn/Ferry International survey of 308 large companies, for 1979, revealed that 92% had a financial director while only 45% contained a marketing director, 38% a production director, and 30% a sales or personnel director (Mills, 1981: 205–6).

A survey conducted by *Accountancy* in 1996, based on the FTSE 100 Companies concluded that 'The typical FTSE finance director earns £300,000 a year, has been in his post for four years, was appointed from outside, and is a chartered accountant. And he's overwhelmingly male' (*Accountancy*, Dec. 1996: 20). Ninety-nine companies had finance directors (with only GUS without) and 80 of these were professional accountants (of whom two held dual accounting qualifications). Membership of the original chartered bodies remained overwhelmingly the most common qualification: 54 ICAEW/ICAS, seventeen CIMA, nine ACCA, and two with CIPFA (both at privatized utilities). The number of members of the original chartered bodies in post as finance directors had, however, declined marginally from 61 in 1994 and 57 in 1995, reflecting a possible trend towards non-accountant finance directors who totalled nineteen in 1996 (up from sixteen in 1995). As with other changes, however, differences may well be attributable, as much as anything, to variations in the composition of the FTSE 100. MBAs have not filled any relative vacuum: their numbers in 1996 are nine—down from eleven in 1995 and fifteen in 1994. Indeed, amongst the nine, in only three cases is an MBA their only qualification, and five of them were also professionally qualified accountants (*Accountancy*, Dec. 1996: 20–1). The figure of 80% for accountant finance directors among the FTSE 100 compares with 74% for all companies with a turnover in excess of £125,000 in 1994 (Korn/Ferry Carre/Orban International, 1994: 26).

The business background of the finance director appears to have changed little over the years. In 1981, the finance director had typically worked his way up through budgetary control and treasury operations, but had little general management experience (*Financial Times*, 18 June 1981). This remains the case. In 1993, less than 10% of those promoted to the post of finance director had previously worked for their present company in a general managerial capacity, while just 20% had held non-financial positions in other companies (Owen and Abell, 1993: 6). The nature of the work undertaken by the finance director has, however, evolved. We reproduced, above, some of the perceptions of their job by a number of finance directors, and we can add to these the results of three surveys.

The *Financial Times* in 1981 reported a change in the role of financial directors 'to encompass more long range planning and analytical tasks, such as the impact of financial policy on overall business strategy' (18 June 1981). Inflation and the need for asset management, together with legislative changes and the need to manage currencies in multinational companies, were said to have 'forced the financial director increasingly out of the back-room into the hot seat at the board room meetings'. Whereas 80% of financial directors had been responsible for their company's internal audit four years previously, by 1981 only 60% undertook this role. The *Financial Times* expressed the opinion, however, that most finance directors had been principally trained to undertake routine accounting work and were, therefore, ill-equipped for wider responsibilities.

A 1993 survey of finance directors showed that the trend towards undertaking more general management responsibilities had continued. Finance directors still put their most important job as management accounting (81%), but this was now followed by treasury functions (50%), strategic planning (46%), information technology (40%), taxation (39%), and investor relations (30%) (Owen and Abell, 1993: 10). Most of the finance directors' time (36%) continued to be spent on internal financial reporting and control, but showed a significant decline (from 45%) compared with five years previously. Jobs on the increase in terms of the commitment of time were 'participation in strategic formulation' (15%) and dealing with brokers and analysts (9%). The survey's conclusion— that 'it is rare to find a finance director of a quoted company who is not devoting more time than he or she did five years ago to discussions with institutional investors' (Owen and Abell, 1993: 21)—is certainly borne out by Simon Moffat's experience at Kwik Save recounted above. Eighty per cent of finance directors believed that they were more and more seen as part of the management team rather than as a functional specialist; 76% that they increasingly had to understand the problems of marketing; and

74% that they were increasingly involved in problems of line management (Owen and Abell, 1993: 15). One finance director argued that: 'With the score-keeper image fading fast, the finance director is increasingly expected to lead cross-functional teams', and another that the finance director has to be 'more a pro-active commercial operator than a backroom numbers man' (Owen and Abell, 1993: 18). Sixty-six per cent thought the finance director would become more 'entrepreneurial' in the future (Owen and Abell, 1993: 30).

To obtain further insight into the role of the finance director, an open-ended questionnaire was sent to the finance directors of the top 50 companies in 1991, as detailed in Table 22. They were asked to list their five most important functions in order of importance. The response rate was disappointing, fourteen, but revealed a strong consensus of views and confirmed the above findings. The respondents classified the finance director's responsibility for overall strategy of their company as almost equal in importance to the financial function. Indeed, six respondents identified strategy as their most important role, through such phrases as 'Helping the CEO to think through strategic concepts and being party to their implementation', 'Financial strategy, planning and policy', 'Full personal participation in the strategic development of the Group', or 'Playing a lead role in the acquisition or disposal of businesses'. Trailing some way behind these two functions came the role of finance director as communicator with the City, investors, shareholders, and the press. This role is clearly related to the almost equally prominent function of ensuring adequate provision of capital for the company. Listed fifth in importance was responsibility for checking that the company complied with legal and other regulatory requirements.

Accountants in top management

The rise of the accountant in British boardrooms during the post-war period was recognized at the time. In 1946, the editor of *Financial News* announced: 'This is the age of the accountant.' The accountant had risen from being 'the humble retainer of industry' in the Dickensian era to becoming the 'family doctor of industry' in Edwardian times, but it was in the period between the two wars 'that he really came into his own, as a surgeon performing major operations. Now, in many cases, we find him installed, not as professional advisor with the board, but at the head of the table, as chairman' (quoted in *Accountant*, 21 July 1945: 37–8).

We are now in a position to quantify, relatively precisely, the importance of accountants in top management during the post-war period. As before, Table 15 charts the rapid advance of accountants in the role of managing director (latterly known as chief executive). In 1951, less than one in 20 managing directors were accountants; by 1971 the figure was

Table 22. Accountants on the boards of the top 50 UK companies listed by sales turnover in *The Times 1,000* for 1991

Company name	Financial director's accounting qualifications	Other accountant directors
Abbey National plc	ICAEW	3 (1E; 2N)
Allied Lyons plc	ICAEW	2 (1E; 1N)
Argyll Group plc	None	1 (1E)
Asda Group plc	ICAEW	1 (1N)
Barclays Bank plc	ICAEW	1 (1N)
Bass plc	ICAEW	1 (1E)
BAT Industries plc	ICAEW, ICAEW	2 (2E)
BET plc	ICAEW	3 (1E; 2N)
BOC Group plc	ICAS	3 (1E; 2N)
Boots Company plc	ICAEW	1 (1N)
British Petroleum Company plc	None	0
BTR plc	ICAEW	4 (4N)
Cable and Wireless plc	None	0
Cadbury Schweppes plc	ACCA	1 (1N)
Courtaulds plc	ACCA	0
General Electric Company plc	ICAEW	0
Glaxo Holdings plc	ICAEW	1 (1E)
Grand Metropolitan plc	ICAEW	2 (2E)
Guinness plc	ICAS	1 (1N)
Great Universal Stores	No FD	1 (1E)
Halifax Building Society	CIPFA	3 (3E)
Hanson plc	ICAEW	8 (7E; 1N)
Imperial Chemical Industries plc	ICAEW	0
Inchcape plc	ICAEW	1 (1E)
Kingfisher plc	None	0
Lonrho plc	No FD	4 (4E)
Lloyds Bank plc	No FD	1 (1N)
Lucas Industries plc	ICAEW	2 (1E; 1N)
McAlpine (Alfred) plc	ICAEW	1 (1E)
Marks and Spencer plc	None	1 (1E)
Midland Bank plc	ICAEW	1 (1N)
National Westminster Bank plc	None	3 (1E; 2N)
P&O Steam Navigation Company plc	ICAEW	2 (2E)
Pilkington plc	CIMA	1 (1E)
Prudential Corporation plc	ICAEW	3 (1E; 2N)
Rolls-Royce plc	ICAEW	1 (1N)
Royal Bank of Scotland Group plc	ICAEW	0
Royal Insurance plc	ICAEW	2 (2E)
Sainsbury (J.) plc	ICAEW	3 (1E; 2N)
Shell Transport and Trading Co. plc	No FD	1 (1E)
Standard Chartered plc	ICAEW	1 (1N)

Table 22. *Continued*

Company name	Financial director's accounting qualifications	Other accountant directors
Sun Alliance Group plc	CIMA	2 (2E)
Tarmac plc	ICAEW	0
Tate & Lyle plc	ICAEW	0
Tesco plc	ICAS	1 (1N)
Thorn EMI plc	ICAEW	0
TI Group plc	ICAEW	2 (2N)
Trafalgar House plc	ICAEW	4 (4E)
TSB Group plc	None	1 (1N)
Unilever plc	None	0

Notes: BAT had two financial directors, both of whom were members of the ICAEW. E signifies executive director; N signifies non-executive director.

Sources: The board memberships were obtained from company reports and cross-checked against the membership lists of the accountancy bodies.

one in eight, and by 1991 it was one in five. This last figure receives confirmation from the 1994 Korn/Ferry Carre/Orban International survey that showed 23% of the chief executives of companies with a turnover in excess of £1 billion as professional accountants (1994: 24). The rise of the chief executive is paralleled by the rise of accountants also as chairmen; they increased from 8% of company chairmen in 1951 to 20% by 1991. Taking all directors, almost one in ten had an accountancy qualification in 1951; by 1991 no less than a fifth to a quarter of directors were accountants. Of these, three-quarters were ICAEW members in 1951, and the figure had risen to 80% by 1991.

Finally, as demonstrated graphically in Figure 5, whereas 40% of companies had at least one accountant on the board in 1951, over 80% could claim this distinction by 1991. These data receive broad confirmation from our separate sample of the top 50 companies in 1991. We found that there were, in total, 116 professionally qualified accountants on the boards, comprising 16% of all directors serving with the companies covered (see Table 22). Forty-six (92%) of the companies had at least one professional accountant on the board. The difference in the figures, compared with the larger sample used for Table 15, is probably due to the fact that larger companies have bigger boards; 13.6 directors per company compared on average to 6.4.

A significant finding is that the high percentage of companies with accountant-directors is not principally due to the presence of a financial director possessing an accounting qualification. In other words, the rise of the accountant-director is not mainly due to the growing prevalence of the functional finance director. Of the 46 companies with an accountant on the board, in only seven cases was the finance director the only accountant; in the other 39 cases, the board contained additional accountants, presumably recruited both to augment the services supplied by the finance director and, perhaps, to bring to the board different expertise. Again, ICAEW/ICAS members predominate, accounting for 90% of the directors in our sample; 62 belonging to the former body and eight to the latter. Only 28% of accountant-directors were non-executive, however (compared to 41% in UK companies generally; Korn/Ferry International, 1991: 14), and just two companies—Lloyds Bank and the TSB Group—employed the services of professional accountants on the board only in a non-executive capacity.

Clearly companies vary greatly in the extent of the accountant's presence on the board, and it would be interesting to know (but has not been possible to find out) whether companies have a policy in the matter. At one extreme, there were companies such as Hanson Trust with five chartered accountants (four executive and one non-executive), including the deputy chairman and chief executive, Derek Bonham, on a fourteen-strong board. One might speculate that a multinational holding company such as Hanson—the creation of numerous rapid acquisitions and disposals—would need a readily available clutch of top accountants. Certainly the company has been described as 'the supreme example of the overweening role of the financial markets in the Anglo-American economies' (Cowe, 1993: 297). On acquiring a firm, Hanson introduces 'a system of centralised and strong financial controls combined with decentralised operating management' (Hast, 1991: 502) The investment criteria require that 'an investment must contribute to profits within one year and pay for itself in four years' (Hast, 1991: 503). Perhaps, as a consequence, it has been seen as guilty of 'failing to invest sufficiently, for having short-term time horizons, for using tax havens to reduce its tax bill and for leaving companies it sells in a worse state than when they were bought' (Cowe, 1993: 297).

Conglomerates generally tend to be well endowed with accountants on their boards with, in 1995, six at BTR, four at Lonhro, and three each at Trafalgar House and BAT. But there are few clear trends. Undiversified companies such as Abbey National, the Prudential, and Sainsbury had, respectively, five, four, and two accountants on their boards in 1995, while some highly diversified companies, heavily involved in reorganization, manage with no accountant-directors whatsoever. For example, d'Arcy Cooper's latter-day company—the multinational, multi-sectored Unilever—underwent a massive restructuring in the 1980s, shedding service and ancillary businesses to concentrate on core activities such as detergents and food. Between 1984 and 1992 Unilever bought 268 companies and sold 149 without, apparently, a single professionally qualified accountant on its fifteen-strong board (Derdak, 1988: 590; Cowe, 1993: 431). We have seen that leaders of Grand Metropolitan Hotels in the 1980s and early 1990s were professional accountants, but the position has changed dramatically in recent years. An eleven-strong board included accountants as chairman, managing director, and financial director in 1991 but, following the retirement of Lord Sheppard in February 1996, there were none.

Nationalized industries appear to have been as likely to employ accountants as private firms. Out of nine public corporations examined for 1951, five had accountants on the board. Of the 171 directors in these corporations, 3.5% were accountants (compared with 9% from our sample of private companies discussed above). The Metropolitan Water Board had two accountant-directors, while two corporations had chairmen who were accountants—S. J. L. Hardie at the Iron and Steel Corporation of Great Britain and Sir Arthur Edgar Sylvester (see Chapter 4) at the Gas Council. Accountants were also heavily represented on the railways. We noted above the work of Henry Benson, in a consultancy capacity, with important subsequent full-time appointments at top level being Philip H. Shirley in 1961 and his successor, Henry 'Bill' Johnson (Gourvish, 1986: 326–7, 338, 355–8, 370–9). The Labour Minister of Transport Richard Marsh seconded another accountant, Michael Bosworth, onto the board as planning member for three years from 1968. Bosworth (a partner in Peat, Marwick since 1960) was made vice-chairman in 1971 and stayed until 1983. In 1971, the British Railways Board included four accountants. Indeed, in that year, out of ten nationalized industries examined, nine had an accountant on the board—only the Port of London Authority was without. Of the chairmen of the twelve Area Gas Boards, three were accountants, as was the managing director of the British Transport Docks Board. Of the 119 directors of public corporations investigated for the year 1971, 14% were accountants, almost exactly in line with our findings for private industry.

By 1991, of course, most of the previous nationalized industries had been privatized, but we looked at nine organizations, some privatized and some still under public ownership, and found that seven had accountants on the board, again in line with our sample for private sector firms. Only Thames Water and British Gas had no accountants, while British Rail, then still publicly owned, had three accountants on their board. National Power had four accountants including the chairman, Trevor Holdsworth (discussed above), and the chief executive, John Baker, ACCA. The Port of London Authority had five accountant-directors on a board of thirteen. British Steel had two, including its chief executive, while we have seen that John Neil Clarke was the chairman of British Coal.

CONCLUDING COMMENTS

Accountancy firms have grown massively in size and been transformed into aggressive, multinational corporations during the post-war period. The four areas of their involvement with business which stretch back into the nineteenth century—audit, taxation, insolvency, and consultancy—continue down to the present day, and fee income is now conventionally presented under those four headings. Audit remains the top fee earner, but the main growth areas during the post-war period have been consultancy work and, to a lesser extent, taxation. Whatever the state of the economy or the political outlook of successive governments, the accountancy profession has generally flourished. Accountancy firms and individuals have been called in as advisers and investigators by governments which range from Clement Attlee's interventionist Labour government of the immediate post-war period to Margaret Thatcher's entrepreneurial and deregulatory Tory crusade of the 1980s. These continuing connections have helped further to raise the profile of the profession and, as we have seen, resulted in many of its members receiving public honours.

In this chapter we have developed a framework for describing, and to an extent explaining, the continued migration of professional accountants from public practice into business. Soon after the Second World War there were already about one-half of all qualified accountants working in business, and this proportion has now moved up to approximately two-thirds (Table 16). Reflecting the massive upsurge in the overall numbers of professionally qualified accountants, the figure for those 'in business' has increased approximately fivefold to well over 100,000 today (implied by Tables 8, 16). Our taxonomy of 'routes' recognizes the fact that not all accountants in top management today work there full-time or come in from outside. Route 1 focuses on the role of the non-executive director, often, but not always, a partner in public practice, who sometimes sits on the boards of numerous public companies. This arrangement has, in the 1990s, received encouragement and reinforcement from the Cadbury Report (1992), reflecting the conviction that these independent directors can play a valuable part in improving corporate governance. Route 2 comprises the important but relatively small band of accountant-entrepreneurs. This is by no means a new category but was provided with the opportunity to achieve a higher profile in the 'freewheeling' business conditions created by successive Conservative governments during the 1980s.

Turning to the large numbers transferring their expertise from public practice, routes 3 and 4 chart, respectively, the progress of those moving in at the top (which we define broadly as recruitment at board level), and those who leave soon after qualifying and work their way up from relatively junior positions. Most of these individuals qualified with the

ICAEW or ICAS, but route 5 focuses on the relatively small number of professionally qualified accountants, usually certified and management accountants, who have worked their way to the top having qualified while working in industry. A noticeable feature here was the willingness of Beechams to engage certified accountants following the achievements and promptings of H. G. Lazell. This action quite probably reflects the natural tendency to appoint people possessing qualifications which you trust. Given their early start, this kind of attitude is likely to have been of greater benefit to members of the original chartered bodies; indeed Lazell found that he had initially to fight this prejudice at Beechams itself (Lazell, 1975: 162–3). Another key factor affecting the appointment process, which we have noted throughout this book, is the tendency to move from public practice to client companies. This process continued apace during the post-war period, with the growing involvement of professional firms in consultancy work also helping many to develop the type of expertise valued by business organizations.

In the last section of the chapter, we have focused on a numbers-based analysis of accountants in business, which considers where they work, the type of work they do, the posts they fill, and the extent to which they rise to top management positions. Although it is no doubt the case that many remain career accountants, we see that they also dominate appointments to the functional position of financial/finance director, are comfortably the most numerous professional grouping at board level, where they are also heavily engaged in other capacities, and comprise nearly one-quarter of the chief executives of large quoted companies, including famous names such as Ian Hay Davison, Trevor Holdsworth, and Paul Girolami. There are some small signs that the original chartered bodies, and even professional accountants generally, are losing a little of their grip on some of the top appointments in recent years, but the variations are probably not sufficiently marked or long run to suggest that a major reassessment has been made by business of the contribution which professional accountants can make to their management.

7

Some Explanations and Conclusions

This book has focused principally on five broad themes: the rise of accountants as professionals; the numbers of accountants both in Britain, overall, and performing various functions in business; the role of the professional practice as a training ground for business managers; the routes through which accountants entered business and reached top managerial positions; and why industry and commerce have been consumers of professional accounting talent in such large numbers. In this last chapter we focus, more explicitly, on Britain's unique experience as a generator of professional accountants and, to enrich this analysis, a number of international comparisons are incorporated into the discussion. The nature of the evidence presented in this book inevitably gives us different levels of confidence regarding the conclusions which we reach in relation to the matters examined. We have been able to produce reliable measures of the numbers of accountants performing various roles, and we have devised a useful taxonomy of the different routes into business, though the precise numbers taking these pathways remain unknown. The role of the professional firms as producers of business managers has also been explored. Our explanations for the plethora of professional accountants, examined further here, are necessarily speculative and to a degree impressionistic because of the qualitative character of much of the investigation and the heavy reliance, for our evidence, on the views expressed by accountants themselves. These data, however, combined with the results of other studies and the assessments made by businessmen together with accounting and business historians, serve to build up a picture which should be sufficiently robust to withstand critical scrutiny.

A QUARTER OF A MILLION PROFESSIONAL ACCOUNTANTS

What explains the professional accountants' numerical rise to prominence in Britain? Accountants were engaged in four areas of work during the nineteenth century and they remain the same today, though in widely different proportions, namely insolvency, audit, taxation, and consultancy. There exist a range of views concerning the relative importance of these sectors of work in the period before broad-based statistics became readily available, and for explaining why particular areas gained or receded in importance (cf. Armstrong, 1987: 422–33; Jones, 1981). The central role of auditing in the history of accountancy in Britain is difficult to overstate. The prominence of the audit function is attributed, in the main, to the history of Britain's corporate development, where factors of critical importance included the funding of railway-building in the 1830s and 1840s, the liberality of Britain's company laws, the number of its joint-stock companies, and the scale of its equity market. In all these respects Britain differed markedly from other economies.

Prussia had generated only 37 joint-stock companies by 1850, whereas 755 companies were listed on the London Stock Exchange alone in 1842. Between 1890 and 1900, 1,600 companies were established in Germany while (as Table 13 shows) in just one year, 1900, 4,966 companies were set up in Britain (Milward and Saul, 1973: 423–4; Hunt, 1936: 46–7; Morgan and Thomas, 1962: 281; Cottrell, 1980: 40, 42). Regulation of companies was always closely controlled by the State in Germany; from 1852, for example, the government was given powers to examine a company's books at any time and to attend board meetings (Kitchen, 1978: 94). The German stock market was both highly regulated and underdeveloped, with industrial shares moving principally between the banks (Tilly, 1967: 164). Even today the German stock exchanges list only around 500 securities (Somers, 1991: 44). As is well known, German investment banks were the principal conduit for capital into industry (Tilly, 1967: 179). They maintained close operational links with their investments through seats on the company boards (the Deutsche Bank, for example, was represented on 221 company boards in 1913) and acted, in Kennedy's words, 'as a very large shareholders' protection agency' (Milward and Saul, 1973: 425; Cottrell, 1980: 239–44; Locke, 1984: 262; Kennedy, 1987: 130). Bank-trained auditors investigated these companies, thereby avoiding the need for an independent external audit (Locke, 1984: 126 and 261). The German Companies Act of 1931 eventually required larger companies to be audited (the auditors were to be State registered and the first German accountancy society was subsequently formed), but these numbered just 2,189 as late as 1975. An audit requirement for smaller private companies was not introduced until 1985 (Nobes and Parker, 1991: 196, 208; Mueller and Galbraith, 1976: 7).

A comparable picture emerges in other leading industrial nations both within and outside Europe. France incorporated just 599 joint-stock companies between 1819 and 1867 and, although the number of companies with limited liability grew rapidly after the law was liberalized in 1867, the banks continued to be the main source of external finance (Caron, 1979: 81; Bouvier, 1970: 360–1; Cameron, 1967: 112). It was estimated that, at the turn of the century, the London stock market traded in over twice as much corporate investment as the French and German markets combined, and this comparison did not include the huge £5 billion of foreign securities traded in England's capital city (Robb, 1992: 28). Even today there are only 400 or so companies listed on the Paris Bourse. The demand for the services of professional auditors in France, as in Germany, was low. Not until 1942 was a registered accounting body established by law in France and, as Table 11 shows, membership has remained relatively small.

The story is similar in Japan where the banks again played a major part in raising long-term capital for industry and railway building (Nakamura, 1983: 61; Patrick, 1967: 274–87; Allen, 1964: 108, 134). The Japanese capital market was also affected by the growth of the family-run *zaibatsu*, which owned their own banks and did not need to resort to public issues (Allen, 1964: 109). The result was 'a quite under-developed and unsophisticated stock market' (Hirschmeier and Yui, 1981: 156) 'with very little public participation . . . pre-eminently speculative and private in nature until after World War II' (Patrick, 1967: 274). The statutory external audit was imposed in Japan only as the result of US influence following the Second World War (and an accountants' society was established by the Certified Public Accountants Law of 1948) (Nobes and Parker, 1991: 236–8; Cooke, 1991: 262–3; Chiba, 1994: 191). The audit applied only to companies whose shares were publicly traded, however, with 1,716 companies listed today on the Tokyo Stock Exchange—approximately two-thirds the number on the London market (Takagi, 1993: 342). Therefore, partly because of the limited market for their audit skills, the numbers of European and Japanese accountants, as Table 11 shows, have remained at a modest level compared with the UK.

Far closer to British experience was the USA (and British Dominions such as Canada and Australia). Part of the reason for this is that British accountants, such as Edwin Guthrie, helped found the first US accountancy society in 1886 and played a prominent part in the transfer of this accounting technology (Kitchen and Parker, 1980: 9; Parker, 1986: 66). The US market in equities was again slow to develop, however, with the railways privately funded in the main by groups of rich individuals. Later, together with the expanding manufacturing sector, railway companies looked increasingly to investment bankers when raising new capital. Mirroring the German experience, financiers such as J. P. Morgan often took a seat on the board and became closely involved with running the companies they had helped finance. The issue of stock on Wall Street and the other exchanges was highly restricted and the number of shares traded remained limited; until 1890, only one manufacturing stock, Pullman, which was itself closely associated with the railroads, was regularly traded (Baskin, 1988: 233). In 1900, only 1,157 securities (still mainly railroads) were quoted on Wall Street, whereas the London Stock Exchange listed 3,631 securities in a wide variety of fields and, reportedly, transacted ten times more business than New York (Michie, 1987: 34, 169, 197, 264, 272; Hunt, 1936: 87–9). Indeed, even in 1992, the London market listed 2,393 companies, compared to 2,089 in New York (*The Stock Exchange Official Year-Book*, 1992: p. xxvii).

The US market in common stock grew rapidly in the 1920s and, following the Wall Street Crash of 1929, the New York Stock Exchange introduced, in 1933, an independent audit requirement for companies seeking a listing, and this received statutory support from the Securities and Exchange Act of the following year (Zeff, 1979: 209). But, again, the requirement applied to a minority of concerns, amounting even in 1989 to just 11,000 companies (Baskin, 1988: 229; Nobes and Parker, 1991: 97). The number of accountants in America has grown rapidly since the 1930s but remains, as a proportion of the labour force, less than one-half of the level of the UK (Table 11). A major driving force for the development of the US accountancy profession has been its involvement in consultancy work (Previts and Merino, 1979: 309–10); a factor which we have seen become prominent in the UK only in the last 20 years or so, reflecting a move from a professional to a commercial ethos among the leaders of the major accountancy firms.

The capital market in Britain has, therefore, always displayed important differences from that of its competitors. It started earlier, benefited from the ready availability of local finance, was granted a cheap and easy mechanism for incorporating with limited liability, and operated in a *laissez-faire* environment in which the audit was the main safeguard that the market, through contractual arrangements between investors and management, came to insist on. We saw, in Chapter 4, that a statutory audit requirement was introduced for specific categories of company, beginning with the railways in 1867, but it was not until 1900 that the Companies Act made the auditing of all limited companies compulsory. This latter provision, however, for most listed companies and many private companies, merely confirmed existing practice (Anderson et al., 1996; Howitt, 1966: 40–2, 201–2; Jones, 1981: 50–2; Worthington, 1895: 62).

While we see audit as the central factor that distinguishes Britain from other countries in terms of explaining the vast number of accountants in this country, it is by no means the only factor. Also of crucial importance has been the determination of the pioneers of this relatively new and certainly vigorous profession to chase and capture, from the outset, whatever work they could turn their hand to. In this context, the comment from the official history of the Bristol firm of Grace, Derbyshire and Todd bears repetition: 'We threw our net for business wherever we thought it would catch fish, or I should say make money' (Grace et al., 1957: ch. 2). It is certainly the case that accountants succeeded in obtaining, early on, a strong hold in insolvency work, which might have been seen as the appropriate province of lawyers, while, in the late nineteenth and early twentieth centuries, they increasingly turned their attention to internal accounting procedures, at the expense of engineers. During the twentieth century we have seen them become the acknowledged experts on tax matters (again, one might have thought that lawyers would have been better placed to deal with matters of revenue law), where the access provided by the audit to the business records on which computations are based probably proving a crucial advantage. The most recent success has been in the area of consultancy where, in the last quarter of a century, we have seen (Chapter 6) the major accountancy practices rapidly catch up and overtake many specialist management consultancy firms.

BUSINESSES' DEMAND FOR ACCOUNTANTS

Why were these professional accountants employed in increasingly large numbers by industry and commerce? Why did the proportion of quoted company secretaries who were accountants rise from less than 10% in 1911 to nearly 50% by 1991 (Table 15, row 5)? And why were only 7% of accountants employed in business in 1911 but almost two-thirds by 1991 (Table 16)? Four demand-side considerations suggest themselves— scale, corporate distress, the financial environment, and the number of companies.

The linkage between the growing scale and complexity of firms and their increased employment of accountants, noted by Armstrong (1987), has long been recognized. In the 1960s, Anthony Sampson explained the prominence of accountants on the grounds that 'They are the priest-hood of industry: the more fragmented and diversified a company becomes, the more important becomes the man who can disentangle the threads of profitability that hold it together' (1965: 521); while Jones agrees that:

larger and more complicated business organizations, such as those produced by the 1920 merger movement, in turn created a demand for more rigorous methods of financial assessment and management information. Accountants, as independent expert observers, having experience denied to most directors and possessing skills now more readily appreciated, were increasingly recruited into the ranks of management. (1981: 156)

These observations are consistent with economic theory which argues that increased scale gave more companies the need and ability to minimize their 'transactions costs' by employing their own accountants rather than buying in their services from the financial market place (Williamson, 1981). Amalgamation in Britain was accommodated increasingly during the inter-war period under the umbrella of a holding company which, it might be argued, generated new demands for the accountant's skills because of the need for head offices to monitor the performance of subsidiaries. A typical example, discussed in Chapter 5, is the regime set up by the chartered accountant James Hornby Jolly at GKN in the 1930s (Jones, 1990: 287, 369). In turn, the multi-divisional corporate structure developed in Britain, in the main since the 1950s, has also created a demand for more sophisticated finance and budgetary systems (Jones, 1981: 231). Channon (1973: 67) has estimated that, whereas only 12% of the major British manufacturers had adopted a multi-divisional structure in 1950, 72% had done so by 1970.

We have seen in Chapter 6, however, that any link between the size of British companies and the involvement of accountants does not show up strongly when subjected to quantitative analysis. This finding seems also to apply at board level. We know that, in the early years of this century, accountants could be found in the boardrooms of companies of all sizes, ranging from the Great Western Railway with an issued share capital of £73,603,578 to the James Cycle company with a capital of just £50,000 (*The Stock Exchange Official Intelligence*, 1911: 156, 730). Latterly, in 1996, at a time when most listed companies had at least one accountant on the board, a huge organization such as Grand Metropolitan had none, and the same was the case at Shell. Table 23 shows for each of the years 1911, 1951, and 1991 the proportion of companies of various sizes, as measured by authorized capital, that had accountant-directors and indicates that, from 1951 (the number of accountants on the boards identified for 1911 is too small to draw reliable implications), there has been a tendency for companies in the upper quartile to have more accountant-directors. But the effect is not that marked, and the other quartiles show no obvious pattern

Table 23. Proportion of sample companies with an accountant-director by size of company, 1911, 1951, 1991

	1911 (%)	1951 (%)	1991 (%)
Upper quartile	6.3	44.1	91.4
2nd quartile	11.7	37.1	81.5
3rd quartile	6.3	41.8	75.3
Lower quartile	6.3	33.5	76.5
Average	7.6	39.1	81.2
N =	437	340	324

Note: The size of companies' capital in the sample ranged in 1911 from £74,745,000 to £9,766, in 1951 from £47,000,000 to £15,000, and in 1991 from £913,000,000 to £73,000.

Source: As for Table 15.

between the size of company and the involvement of directors at board level. Other writers have found a more pronounced impact of scale. Florence reported that, in 1936, 53% of companies with capital in excess of £500,000 had accountants on the board, compared with 25% of companies with capital between £100,000 and £500,000 and only 14% with capital below £100,000 (Florence, 1947: 15). Similarly, an Institute of Directors survey carried out in 1965 showed that 14.6% of directors were accountants in companies with a share capital over £5 million, compared to 6.5% in all companies (Tricker, 1967: 20–1). We are unable to offer an explanation for the disparity between these results and our own.

A second argument which could explain Britain's uniqueness in the employment of accountants is based on the idea that they were drafted into British companies because of economic problems; an explanation advocated by Armstrong in relation to the inter-war period. Taking the broader picture, it could be argued that, as the long-run relative decline of the British economy became increasingly apparent during the twentieth century, more accountants were drafted in to help sort out the problems. It is certainly the case that the British accountant has frequently been referred to as the 'business doctor' in response to his involvement in corporate distress (Fea, 1957: 22). Indeed, when the trend toward appointing accountants to the board of companies became evident in the 1920s, the *Accountant* saw this action as a natural response to pressing business problems:

Every kind of company from the largest to the smallest, has in recent years been obliged to have recourse to accountants in order to straighten out such matters as reconstruction and reorganisation, or to undertake revaluation of assets or general investigation of the position. It is safe to say that in many instances of the kind the procedure would have been unnecessary if an accountant had been a member of the board. (*Accountant*, 11 Jan. 1930: 30. The first sentence of course supports our findings regarding the absence of scale effects.)

The quantitative evidence presented in Chapter 6 does not support the view that corporate distress was a major factor in the growing employment of accountants in British business, however, or in their rise to top management. Companies that were heavy employers of accountants captured in our samples included some of the most successful. Our random sample of 248 accountants in 1951 (used for Table 20), for example, included no less than seven from ICI. Moreover, the proposition, if valid, would suggest that the well-known difficulties and long-run decline in the profitability of British manufacturing would lead to a disproportionate involvement of accountants in that sector, as discussed in the last chapter. While it is true that more accountants overall were employed in manufacturing than in the other business sectors until very recently (Table 20), the likely explanation is that the manufacturing sector simply had the most companies. Indeed, the data presented in Table 24 can be used to show that neither is there a bias in the frequency of accountant-directors by sector (x^2 tests insignificant at the 5% level were found in all three years). Corporate distress was, therefore, important in drafting in accountants to top management in some cases, and it may well have led to a more general recognition of the need to employ accountants, but the numerical evidence does not establish it as a major explanatory variable.

A third element in the demand for accountants by business relates to the peculiar features of Britain's financial environment. Of importance in this context is, again, the special nature of Britain's capital market, with the major role that it plays in British corporate affairs ensuring that a company's external financial profile is of crucial importance. It is therefore plausible to argue that, just as the British capital market explains the increased demand for and rapid growth in the number of accountants serving as auditors, similarly it ensured that the auditors' training was valued by British companies keen to manage more effectively their financial affairs and relationships with investors and the City. Other factors in the financial environment also suggest themselves to be potentially important. Since the Second World War, as discussed in Chapter 6, involvement in hostile takeover activity, either as the target or the predator, has been on the increase and has been more common among British companies than elsewhere in the world. The likely consequence of this, and the continued importance of stock market rather than bank funding, is that dividend policy and the level of the company's share price are more important in Britain than elsewhere and, as a result, the accountant's skills are at a premium (see, for example, Marsh, 1990).

The rise of the financial director in the 1950s and 1960s undoubtedly reflected a growing recognition of the importance of this financial acumen, and we saw in Chapter 6 that the above (and other) factors relating to the financial environment were given specific attention by finance directors interviewed for *Accountancy* (Croft, 1987a: 14; Grey, 1991: 23; Fisher, 1992: 26; Grey, 1993b: 31). The growing complexity or competitive nature of the capital market may therefore be seen as a contributing factor in the employment of accountants, but it is possibly not the major factor. Takeovers and share flotations do not provide a substantial volume of work even the largest companies, and little or none for the very small concerns that within have nevertheless increasingly employed professional accountants. The changing financial environment should not be discounted as a significant explanatory variable, however, since small companies have also experienced an increase in the complexity of their external financial relations including the need to comply with changing company law and increasingly onerous and complex taxation requirements. Finally, on the demand side, the simple increase in the number of

Table 24. Proportion of companies with accountant-directors by nature of the business, 1911, 1951, 1991

	1911		1951		1991	
	With accountant (%)	Total sample (%)	With accountant (%)	Total sample (%)	With accountant (%)	Total sample (%)
1. Agriculture	2.9	8.0	2.3	3.2	4.6	4.0
2. Manufacturing	26.5	31.2	38.9	40.1	39.5	36.7
3. Distribution	11.9	14.8	20.6	16.2	19.0	17.9
4. Banking	14.7	7.7	16.8	15.6	25.1	29.3
5. Diversified	0.0	0.0	3.1	1.5	9.9	9.6
6. Foreign	44.1	38.3	18.3	23.3	1.9	2.5
Total	100.0	100.0	100.0	100.0	100.0	100.0
N =	34	426	131	339	263	324

Notes: The first four rows in full include: agriculture, energy, and coal extraction, SIC 0–1; manufacturing and construction, SIC 2–5; distribution, hotels, transport, and communications, SIC 6–7; banking, finance, and insurance, SIC 8. The definition of 'diversified' is a company trading in a different sector from its core activity (i.e. rows 1–4) unless this represents vertical integration. Row 6 includes all companies with a head office in Britain, but which traded exclusively abroad.

Sources: As for Table 15. The discrepancy between this table and Table 15 in terms of the number of companies in the 1911 and 1951 samples is due to the fact that the nature of their business could not be identified from *The Stock Exchange Official Year-Book*.

the small private companies (but not, as Table 13 shows, public companies) must be seen as a relevant factor in the overall increase in the numbers of accountants employed in business.

Increased scale, corporate distress, changes in the financial environment, and the large number of companies, therefore, all contributed to the growing demand from business for accountants. Turning to the supply side, the availability of professionally qualified personnel in ready numbers was the crucial factor. Unlike many other countries (see below), there was a marked absence of business or accounting graduates in Britain until relatively recently. Nor did businesses need to train accountants themselves because a huge and seemingly ever-growing pool of well-trained accountants was available to them from the auditing profession, and we have charted in detail the frequency with which companies recruited their accountants, managers, and directors from among their own auditors. The British system seems to have worked well and suited all three parties involved. Accountancy firms were happy to use a constantly renewed stream of cheap (and until the 1950s mainly free) labour to perform many of the more mundane aspects of audit work, and to release them when they qualified. In return, the articled clerk received a training that proved highly attractive to companies. Industry and commerce in their turn tapped this growing source of expertise and were able to have their financial affairs dealt with by well-qualified accountants whom they had not the expense of training themselves. The more accountants the professional practices supplied, the more they were taken on by British companies.

MANAGEMENT AND ACCOUNTING EDUCATION

The previous section discusses possible reasons why professional accountants were recruited in increasing numbers by business; evidence for which is provided in Table 16. But there is more to this story than the fact that they were recruited in large numbers by industry and commerce; the accounting qualification, and particularly the chartered accounting qualification, appears to overshadow all others as *the* appropriate preparation for a position in top management (Table 15). It therefore remains for us to explain why British accountants were able to obtain top positions in general management either having been appointed directly to such positions or having worked their way up following an initial engagement lower down, usually as accountant or company secretary.

A Marxist analysis is provided by Armstrong (1985) who attributes 'the comparative rise to pre-eminence of accountants in British management hierarchies' to an aggressive pursuit of power in the endeavour to establish their role in the extraction of surplus value by control over the labour process. Their success, Armstrong argues, was based historically on the following achievements. First, accountants had control over insolvency and later audit work. Second, accountants were helpful to the State in controlling industry 'at arm's length' during both world wars. Third, accountants were useful to industry during the depression of the inter-war period. Finally, and particularly after the Second World War, came the importance of their role in merger movements in the control of large firms, whether holding companies or multi-divisional organizations.

Much of this broad historical background to the growth in importance of the accountant is consistent with our own market-based analysis, but principally when applied to the rise of the professional accountancy firm. We have demonstrated a great deal of continuity in the broad range of services supplied by these firms, but there is no doubt that the relative importance of different areas of work has changed dramatically over time in response to market opportunities, and that emphasis on particular areas has been an important factor in drawing the attention of both business and government to the contribution that accountants can make to industrial management. Thus, Chapter 4 gives particular weight to the accountant gaining a reputation in Victorian and Edwardian Britain for disentangling the financial chaos associated with failure and fraud. In Chapter 5, we show how the accountant assisted government in administering the 'Great War' and established a reputation as the 'business doctor' in the rationalization and reorganization of major industries that occurred during the inter-war period. Chapter 6 demonstrated the fact that, post-Second World War, the involvement of accountants as government advisers continued to mushroom, while the professional firms developed enormously the scale of work undertaken in the areas of taxation and consultancy. This history has also demonstrated, throughout, the continued and fundamental importance of audit work to both the profession and industry.

These are factors which explain the rise of the accountancy profession and, we suggest, helped create the conditions for the rise of the accountant in business management. But, for us, they do not explain fully the move of accountants into industry in great numbers, much less why they have risen to the top of managerial hierarchies. Again, it could be suggested, as we argued above for the rank and file, that the increased scale of companies, and the particular travails of the British economy and its financial environment, meant that the presence of an accountant in top management was more useful to a British company than was the case in other countries. Yet, it seems clear that accountants have not reached the top in Britain primarily, or certainly only, because of their financial expertise. Of particular significance here is our survey of the boards of the 50 largest companies in 1991, discussed in Chapter 6. While confirming the high percentage of companies with accountant-directors (92%), it also shows that, of the 46 companies with an accountant on the board, in only seven cases was the finance director the only accountant. It is therefore reasonable to suggest that, in the upper echelons of British management, the 20% of company chairmen and managing directors who are accountants today, and the many other accountant board members in non-finance-oriented posts, must, of necessity, have proved capable of demonstrating a much wider range of ability than is usually associated with the narrow financial field whence, none the less, most of them sprang.

Why is it that the accountant has proved better equipped than other professional groupings to fill top managerial positions? Our evidence supports Handy et al.'s assertion that the accountants' hegemony stems from the fact that 'for many years [the accountancy qualification] has been the only serious professional preparation for would-be managers in business on offer' (1987: 12). From before the First World War, young men (and today women) joined accountancy firms and left within a year or two of qualification. This occurs for a variety of reasons which include the discovery that public practice, and sometimes particularly auditing, is not for them, because they are attracted to the challenge of a different career, or because they see it as a means of quickly increasing their income. Others always saw accounting simply as a business qualification, and enter public practice with every intention of leaving immediately on qualification, or soon afterwards. In the words of Handy et al., a high proportion of Britain's best graduates want to become qualified accountants 'because that is the most obvious, most prestigious and best-remunerated way to prepare oneself with credentials for a general career in business or in management' (1987: 171).

The many accountants today taking what we designated as 'route 4' in Chapter 6 are following in the pre-First World War footsteps of people such as Bernhard Binder (qualified in 1908 and probably left for industry the same year) and James Hornby Jolly (qualified 1909 and joined industry in 1911). Chartered accountancy's potential as a business education was also recognized early on by family-run companies. As we saw in Chapters 4 and 6, Ernest Palmer and John Benjamin Sainsbury are examples of businessmen who sent their sons to qualify with a firm of accountants before admission to the family boardroom (Corley, 1972: 184; Shaw, 1986). In more recent times, Rocco Forte (his father founded the hotel chain of which he became chairman) joined a firm of chartered accountants 'because it was a good training in business, not because he wanted to spend his life devoted to the profession' (*Accountancy Age*, 30 Nov. 1995: 3).

Some international comparisons

International comparisons are again important in illustrating the peculiar position of accountants in British business management, with its major competitors instead relying principally on varying combinations of university education and corporate training for their managers. In America, by the end of the 1920s, approximately one-third of 'executives' in the rubber, chemical, and electrical manufacturing industries were college and university graduates, while today approximately 85% of US managers have degrees (Keeble, 1992: 24 and 27). In addition, American universities led the way in business education and pioneered the establishment of business schools such as Wharton, founded in 1881 (Locke, 1984: 135; Handy et al., 1987: 30). By 1920, 65 business schools awarded over 1,500 business degrees annually in America (3.2% of all degrees) (Wheatcroft, 1970: 85; McKenna, 1989: 34). In 1949–50, 617 US institutions of higher education offered business courses attended by 370,000 students, accounting for 17% of all undergraduates; by 1989, 220,000 business degrees (24% of all degrees) were awarded (Wheatcroft, 1970: 85, 92–3; Locke, 1993: 33; McKenna, 1989: 37). The Americans also led the way in postgraduate business education, and the pioneer Harvard University produced around 400 Masters of Business Administration a year by the early 1930s (Keeble, 1992: 26). There were 4,814 students studying for MBAs in America by 1960 and 200,000 in 1993 (Locke, 1993: 34). In addition, by the inter-war period, American companies put much effort into their own management training schemes. General Motors, for example, set up its own Institute of Technology in the 1920s which offered courses, including accounting, to its executives (Keeble, 1992: 28).

In Japan, the *zaibatsu* began recruiting graduates in the 1880s and Mitsui, for example, had 731 graduates working for them in 1914 (Collins, 1989: 176; Keeble, 1992: 32). During the inter-war period, in Japan, 'it was unusual to meet an officer of the banks, industrial companies or merchant houses who had not been trained in a college or university' (Keeble, 1992: 33). Estimates indicate that 4% of company presidents in large companies in Japan were graduates in 1904; the figure was around 70% as early as 1930 and 88% by 1961. Well over 90% of all Japanese managers are graduates today (Handy et al., 1987: 81, 86; Locke, 1993: 34). Unlike the USA, university courses in Japan are not expected to be vocational—instead graduate recruits are given intensive 'in-house' training on joining a company (Collins, 1989: 182–6).

Germany also has a tradition of taking its managers from higher education (the first business school was founded in Leipzig in 1898) and, by the turn of the century, 'Engineers with doctoral degrees began to rise to the top of firms . . . They were joined at the top by trained chemists' (Keeble, 1992: 18). By 1928, 16,638 diplomas had been issued by the German business schools and, by the 1930s, German companies were taking half their graduates, frequently with accountancy-based degrees in business economics (Locke, 1984: 135, 201). By the mid-1980s, 62% of top German managers were graduates, often having completed courses of about five years' duration with an engineering or science bias, while two-thirds of the heads of large companies had doctorates (Handy et al., 1987: 45–6). In addition, recruits served an 'apprenticeship' of management training on joining a German company. These findings contrast sharply with the British experience.

British management education

Academic institutions

The above brief survey of management training abroad helps to put into perspective the role of the accountant in Britain. The primary difference is that, historically, British companies employed university graduates far less than was the case in other developed economies. Estimates tend to vary because of the flexibility of the definition of a manager, but one compilation of data by Mannari puts the proportion of university graduates among 'business leaders' at 40% in the United States in 1925, 46% in Japan in 1920, and only 19% in Britain in 1915 (1974: 198). Mannari also estimates that 94% of US chief executives, in 1970, were graduates—in France and Japan the figure was 89%, in Germany 78%, but in Britain just 40% (1974: 226). A 1956 survey showed that, in Britain, only 19% of managers above foreman level had degrees; this increased to 33% in 1980 and 52% by 1991, still significantly less than Britain's major competitors (Mansfield and Poole, 1991: 13. Handy et al., 1987: 2). Nor, in contrast with the US experience, were a significant proportion of British graduates trained in business subjects. In the 1960s, there were on average only 437 graduates annually in business or commerce, accounting for 1.2% of all graduates, and this had risen to only 4,500 or 3.6% of all graduates by 1985 (Keeble, 1992: 52). Ten years later the proportion had moved up sharply to 10.9% (Department for Education and Employment, 1997).

It was not until the end of the Second World War that significant steps were taken towards the promotion of management education on a broader basis in Britain. The Urwick Report (1945) recommended a two-stage management course to be taken at technical colleges, leading to a certificate and later a diploma. In 1947, the British Institute of Management was founded, a part-government-supported organization which provided information about managerial techniques and set about stimulating interest in management education through the provision of courses, publications, and conferences (Wheatcroft, 1970: 91). In 1949, it launched what became the postgraduate part-time Diploma in Management

Studies with 1,800 students a year enrolled on such courses between 1977 and 1985. A survey carried out in 1976 showed 36% of managers had taken the diploma, but its content was often the subject of strong criticism (Melrose-Woodman, 1976: 16; Constable and McCormick, 1986: 13; Wheatcroft, 1970: 52, 54, 124; Barry, 1989: 61).

Turning to the universities, 31 offered management options in their degree courses, by 1968/9, but only 1,681 students (1% of the total under-graduate population) were listed as studying management as their main subject (Wheatcroft, 1970: 44). In addition, at this time, there were 1,300 Council for National Academic Awards degrees awarded in business studies within the non-university higher education sector, usually by the polytechnics, and 10,000 Higher National Certificate or Higher National Diploma students (Wheatcroft, 1970: 48). By 1975, the annual output of graduates in business or management was 1,500, and this had increased to 4,500 (1.8% of all graduates) by 1985, representing the output of 23 universities and 41 polytechnics and colleges (Constable and McCormick, 1986: 12). These are clearly paltry numbers compared to the US figures noted above, even allowing for differences in the size of the population.

The slow development of business studies may be partly attributed to the fact that it conflicted with the traditions of some universities, particu-larly the more prestigious. Oxford's appointments board was 'publicly hostile to commerce and even economics education for industry as being useless' (Keeble, 1992: 121). However, some of the greatest difficulties faced by those attempting to establish accounting as a university disci-pline came from what, at the time, might have been unexpectedly close quarters. Napier has attributed the slow progress of accounting, and business administration in general, within British universities to the 'dis-dain' shown towards these subjects by theoretical economists, starting with Alfred Marshall, and this is no doubt part of the story (Napier, 1996). It must be admitted, however, that there appears to have been no pressing demand from industry for vocationally oriented academic qualifications. A frequent criticism levelled at such degrees was that they were too theoretical 'and what business wanted was men with more practical knowledge' (Keeble, 1992: 110). Nor was industry willing to help fund attempts by universities to provide management education. In 1930, for example, on the instigation of a small group of businessmen (including two practising accountants who had previously taught at the school), the London School of Economics instituted a two-year full-time post-experience course in Business Administration along Harvard lines, but it failed to attract funding or other support from business (Keeble, 1992: 115–20). The Polytechnic, Regent Street (today Westminster University), was one of the first, very few, institutions to offer part-time courses for practising managers in the inter-war period (Wheatcroft, 1970: 88).

The most significant development in postgraduate management education in Britain, as elsewhere, was to be the MBA. An important initiative was the foundation of the Cranfield Institute of Technology in 1946 to offer, among other things, a postgraduate training in management (Barry, 1989: 59). The Management Centre at Bradford University was set up in 1963, Lancaster University established its School of Business and Organizational Studies in 1964, while Oxford University, which had offered a business summer school for senior managers for some years, opened the Oxford Centre for Management Studies in 1965 (Wheatcroft, 1970: 57, 78–9). In 1960, the Foundation for Management Education was established to promote management education, while a National Economic Development Council report of 1963 highlighted the need for a trained body of skilled managers (Wheatcroft, 1970: 94, 96). This pressure led to the Franks Report in 1963 which, in turn, led to the establishment of business schools in London and Manchester in 1965; the government together with 350 companies (who subscribed £5 million) met the cost (Wheatcroft, 1970: 99–100; Barry, 1989: 62).

The number of full-time postgraduate students in management at British universities and colleges increased from 704 in 1956–7 to just 2,315 in 1969–70 (Wheatcroft, 1970: 52). About 500 students started MBA courses in 1970 (at a time when America was producing about 16,000 annually) and a similar number of British students went abroad, mainly to America, to obtain this qualification (Wheatcroft, 1970: 51, 135). Even by 1975, only about 5% of managers had a higher degree in management studies (Koudra, 1975: 23). The really explosive growth came in the 1980s when enrolment increased from 1,300 in 1980 to 9,500 (compared to about 70,000 in the USA) in 1991, by which date the number of business schools offering the degree exceeded 100 (Association of MBAs, 1992: p. ix; *Pocket MBA*, 1994: 150). The MBA programmes have also seen collaboration between business and academe: for example, Warwick with Dunlop, GEC, National Westminster Bank, Coopers & Lybrand, and others, while Shell developed an MBA programme at the Henley Management College (Barry, 1989: 64, 66).

We will see, below, that the professional accounting qualification has been the subject of censure as a business training, in some quarters, but neither have MBA graduates been without their critics. The Owen Report in 1971 accused them of being too theoretical, aggressive, and ambitious in attitude and therefore difficult to integrate within organizations (reported in Barry, 1989: 64). This scepticism is often shared in America. 'The mark of a true MBA', said Robert Buzzell of Harvard Business School, 'is that he is often wrong but seldom in doubt' (*Pocket MBA*, 1994: 150). Tom Peters, the American authority on management issues, has also gone on record as saying that 'the business schools . . . are doing more harm than good' (quoted in McKenna, 1989: 37).

In-house training

The contribution of the higher education sector to management education in Britain therefore remained negligible up until the 1960s, but this gap was rarely filled by British companies, who remained reluctant to train managers themselves. While the North Eastern Railway was handpicking graduates and grooming them as 'Traffic Apprentices' for future leadership, as early as the 1890s, such schemes were very much the exception (Keeble, 1992: 140). In his survey of thirteen large quoted companies focusing on the inter-war period, Gourvish found that most of them 'retained a cosy amateurishness' with regard to management training (1987: 34; see also Fitzgerald, 1993: 90). Even where courses were mounted, there remains the question of whether they succeeded in preparing staff for top management positions. Pilkington, the glass makers, for example, installed a training scheme in 1933 which recruited graduates, but none of their commercial trainees reached board level at St Helens (Barker, 1977: 333–4).

ICI set up its central staff department in 1927 but, according to Keeble, there was no formal training scheme until 1937 and, by 1938, only 30 commercial trainees had completed the two-year course (Keeble, 1992: 135). Moreover, it was extremely unusual for anyone working on the commercial side of the business at ICI during the inter-war period to possess a university education. Exceptions included P. C. Dickens (1888–1964), briefly secretary and then treasurer of ICI, who had been to Eton and Trinity Hall, Cambridge, but who was also a qualified accountant. In 1927, Dickens put forward a scheme whereby ICI took on about 20 to 30 boys a year, recommended by headmasters, for sponsorship through university, where most of them would be expected to read a scientific subject. The rest took an arts subject followed by a qualification in economics or accountancy. According to Dickens, one of the objects of his scheme was to enable a public schoolboy 'to appreciate the possibilities of obtaining good and well-paid work outside the so-called learned professions which are overcrowded' (Reader, 1975: 75).

United Steel ran a training scheme for its graduate recruits which numbered about a dozen a year in the early 1930s, while Tootal Broadhurst and Lee were offering a one-year training scheme for their graduates by the end of the decade (Keeble, 1992: 138). At Rowntree, where the accountant George Harris (who had married into the family) turned the company around in the 1930s (Chapter 5), a trainee scheme was also introduced. The company had apparently been pressed to set up a programme of graduate training by the Cambridge Appointments Board but, due seemingly to the company's reluctance to invest sufficiently in the scheme, it was less than a great success (Keeble, 1992: 139–40). More successful was Lever Brothers' training scheme, set up in 1928 primarily for Oxbridge graduates and underpinned by d'Arcy Cooper's appointment to the committee of the Cambridge Appointments Board (Keeble, 1992: 144). These were very much the most progressive companies, however, and a survey of 114 firms taking Cambridge graduates in 1937/8 showed only twelve to have mounted training schemes (Keeble, 1992: 141).

The greater seriousness with which companies began to view management training in the 1950s is reflected in the fact that they increasingly established their own internal training centres. It was estimated that two-thirds of the 51 large companies surveyed by the Acton Society Trust in 1956 had, by that date, organized management training (Keeble, 1992: 146). In 1968, 8% of managers, by one estimate, attended courses of at least one week's duration, about half of which were internal and the other half external (Wheatcroft, 1970: 125). By the early 1980s, at least 40 companies in Britain had their own management training centres (Handy et al., 1987: 10). Matters also improved after the Second World War as the result of a number of independent management training colleges, financed by industry, being set up as a half-way house between the State education system and 'in-house' corporate training. These included the Administrative Staff College founded in 1946, where Charles Latham, the certified accountant, was a founder member and served as deputy chairman of the board of governors until 1959 (Wheatcroft, 1970: 90; Parker, 1980a: n.p.). Similar colleges offering short courses included the Ashridge Management College started in 1959 and the Urwick Management Centre set up by the Urwick management consultancy firm in 1948. By 1960, there were about 30 such independent centres in existence (Wheatcroft, 1970: 58–60; Barry, 1989: 60).

A sample survey carried out by Rose in 1969 showed that less than half of the companies had formal management development schemes, with smaller companies even less likely to have formal arrangements. This relative lack of enthusiasm displayed by smaller companies was confirmed in a Department of Trade and Industry investigation of 2,000 companies, in 1985, which revealed that 56.1% still offered no formal management training whatsoever (Keeble, 1992: 159–60; Wheatcroft, 1970: 84). This later assessment is consistent with the Handy report which showed that, in 1986, 21% of large companies (defined as over 1,000 employees) and 75% of small companies made no provision at all for management training (Handy et al., 1987: 10).

Accounting in British universities

We have seen that the recruitment of UK-trained graduates with a business school education was rarely an option available to companies in Britain up to the 1970s. The same was the case in accounting, again in contrast with the situation in America and Germany. The ancient universities remained aloof from such matters. When Cambridge University set up an economics and politics course in 1903, accountancy was excluded on the grounds that it was merely a skill rather than a university subject (Jones, 1981: 215). The situation was of course rather different in the civic universities which saw their main purpose as serving industry and commerce 'partly through teaching and research in science and technology, partly through providing liberal arts courses for the "sons of industry" and the local professional middle classes, but also through developing courses directly relevant to the interests of commerce' (Napier, 1996: 430). Opportunities to study accounting at university were made available around the turn of the century, starting with Liverpool in 1900 (for information on this and parallel developments at Birmingham, the London School of Economics, and Manchester see: Jones, 1981: 215; Keeble, 1992: 93, 100, 103; Kitchen and Parker, 1980: 85–6; Locke, 1984: 135), but such initiatives remained very much isolated events up to the Second World War.

Compared to the business schools of America and Germany, therefore, where accountancy was a central element (Locke, 1985: 233–53; McKenna, 1989: 24), the subject was largely ignored by British universities while, for their part, the accounting associations remained entirely committed to their own pupillage and examination system of qualification. The first formal connections between the universities and the accountancy institutions south of the border occurred in 1947 when eleven universities, led by the London School of Economics, reached agreement with the professional bodies to mount accountancy degree programmes that gave students exemption from preliminary and intermediate examinations (Locke, 1984: 138; see also Stacey, 1954: 244–59). This helped establish accountancy as an academic discipline in its own right, but progress was painfully slow. In 1950–1, 350 students were taking accountancy degrees in Britain compared to 11,267 in the USA, which had a total university population of 2,160,440 compared to 85,000 in the UK (Stacey, 1954: 254). Yet, in the same year, Britain had 30,000 students registered with the accountancy societies. In 1985, still only 2,000 accountancy students graduated in Britain in a year when 6,000 accountants successfully completed their professional examinations (Constable and McCormick, 1986: 12, 14).

There were just three full chairs in accountancy in England in 1957, at Birmingham, Bristol, and the London School of Economics, while a leading civic university such as Manchester had no full professor of accountancy until 1969 (Parker, 1986: 54). There were 30 in the UK by 1976, over 50 by 1987, and 167 professors of accounting or finance in 1996, at a time when there were upwards of 1,300 full-time staff listed in *The British Accounting Review Research Register* (Gray and Hellar, 1996). The profession has gradually forged closer links with the universities, through granting a wider range of exemptions to entrants with relevant degrees (the ICAEW remains the notable exception in this process), financing public lectures and fellowships, endowing chairs, and providing tutorial support from amongst its staff. Much of this has been directed towards raising its profile within the universities in the endeavour to attract the best talent, but it has no doubt helped to strengthen the position of accounting within business schools (where accounting departments are most frequently positioned), faculties, and the universities as a whole. The first chair in accounting at Oxbridge was set up through an endowment that resulted in the appointment of Geoffrey Whittington to the Price Waterhouse Chair of Financial Accounting at Cambridge in 1988. The ICAEW, through its Research Board, is the leading private sector sponsor of accounting research in the UK, with around £400,000 available for research grants and conferences in 1996 (Gray and Hellar, 1996: n.p.). And only in the last twenty years has the number of accountancy graduates become significant, rising from a meagre 250 in 1975 to 2,000 in 1985 (Constable and McCormick, 1986: 12) and 3,704 in 1995, representing 1.6% of all first degrees awarded in the UK in that year (Higher Education Statistics Agency, 1996: 160).

The professional accounting qualification

The lack of formal education and corporate training has resulted in a third method of accumulating managerial expertise being exploited in Britain, namely a professional qualification, among which accountancy was by far the most important. The professional qualification is, of course, an arrangement which combines theoretical formal study with practical work experience, culminating in the sitting of examinations to gain entry to professional associations. Barry argues that, 'as there was no obvious route to a career in management, it is not surprising that, in a nation where professional qualifications were highly regarded large numbers of people prepared themselves for a managerial career by undertaking training in accountancy' (1989: 58). In more recent times, this route has enabled aspiring managers 'to earn while they learn', an option made available by professional firms now paying a salary rather than charging a fee to their apprentices (Handy et al., 1988: 170).

Yet there was more to the rise of accountants than the lack of an alternative; the quality of their training was probably itself a positive factor explaining their success. While it is true that railway companies, the Civil Service, the armed services, and other institutions, as well as the other professions such as law or engineering, provided elements of a management training, we will argue below that accountancy was clearly the most relevant and broadest-based preparation available.

ACCOUNTANTS IN TOP MANAGEMENT

It is the accountancy bodies, therefore, that stand at the heart of this professional management training. There are other professional bodies producing a training relevant to business and management careers, of course, including the ICSA. But whereas the ICSA had 55,000 members (23,000 in the UK) in 1996 (Henderson and Henderson, 1996: 259), there were over four times as many professionally qualified accountants (Table 8). Other relevant professions include lawyers and bankers but, as Tables 15 and 18 strongly suggest, membership of the ICAEW has, since the turn of the century, become comfortably the most important professional qualification on British boards of directors.

We therefore turn now to a consideration of the likely consequences for industrial development of the hegemony of the accountant in British management. The key question can be expressed as follows: given that accountancy was virtually the only management training available to British managers, until very recently, how appropriate was it? In answering this question, we do not attempt to assess whether accountants have been good or bad managers, but the reader can make a tentative judgement based on the numerous careers of accountant-managers presented throughout this history. Much of their performance depended on the quality of their previous education, training, and experience, however, and it is this that we explore throughout the remainder of this final chapter.

The role of the examinations

Let us consider first the theoretical, examination-based aspects of the accountant's training. The qualifying examinations for the professional accountancy bodies have always been testing, and in some cases extremely so. We saw in Chapter 3 that, throughout its history, roughly a third of all entrants have failed to complete the ICAEW's examinations. Parker makes the point that accountancy articles, in the late nineteenth century, were looked upon as an alternative to going to university (Parker, 1986: 53), and we noted earlier that the cost of articles was comparable to that of reading for a degree at Oxford or Cambridge (Napier, 1994: 5–6) Locke quotes a speaker at an SIAA assembly in 1911 who boasted: 'I think that our method of examination, subject to certain qualifications, is a far better test than even a degree in economics in Berlin University' (Locke, 1984: 131, 137). While the speaker may be guilty of hyperbole, the pretensions of the incorporated accountants' examinations before the First World War are made clear. Today, when 95% of the ICAEW student intake are graduates (ICAEW, 1996a: 3), the large accountancy firms normally insist on an upper second honours degree from new entrants, seeing it as a reasonable indication of their ability to cope with the demands of the professional examinations.

From the first, the aspiring chartered accountant also studied law (we saw that in Scotland this required him to attend university classes), and from 1922, south of the border, economics, banking, and actuarial science (Stacey, 1954: 25; Garrett, 1961: 120; Howitt, 1966: 199–200). The ICAEW, in common with the other professional bodies, have since made a series of determined attempts to ensure that the examinations have maintained their relevance to professional requirements and, in recent years, revisions of examination structures, methods of testing competency, subject descriptions, and syllabuses have come thick and fast. From the point of view of an employer, the accountancy qualification was not only a good test of accounting ability but also of intelligence and of staying power, since part-time study in the evening spread over five years (today the three-year course with much of the study undertaken during day release is of course the more common), while holding down a full-time job, was a good test of character. The rigour of the learning process, as a preparation both for examinations and for inculcating the precision required for accurate accounts keeping, must also have been a good training of the mind; every bit as much, although of a contrasting nature, as that of the classics or philosophy scholar. In addition, the accountancy training taught an analytical approach and an unemotional and dispassionate objectivity with regard to commercial problems.

The accountant's training has never been short of critics, however, which include those who might be listed among the more thoughtful members of the accountancy profession itself. A major theme has been the narrowness of the training and of the examinations syllabus. Cutforth argued for the study of political economy, in 1912, and criticized the prevailing arrangements on the grounds that 'many a student can recite the graduated percentages of Estate Duty, but does not know what Bank Rate means; he can tell you the amounts of the various penalties laid down in the Companies Act, but has hardly heard of the laws of supply and demand' (Kitchen and Parker, 1980: 71). Carr-Saunders and Wilson, writing in the 1930s, were equally disparaging. They noted that attendance at the lectures and courses of the provincial students' societies of both the ICAEW and SIAA was optional, that universities played no part (unlike Scotland where, we have seen, attendance at university courses was compulsory), and that most teaching was undertaken through correspondence courses run by private organizations. The leading professional accountant, business manager, and academic F. R. M. de Paula referred to this method of training in the following scathing terms:

in my opinion the present system of education is far from satisfactory. The practical work of the average articled clerk is mainly devoted to routine checking, which is of little educational value, and the theoretical studies of the great proportion of students are conducted by the professional 'crammers'. (Kitchen and Parker, 1980: 92)

Carr-Saunders and Wilson advocated a wider curriculum, more support from student societies, and the development of contacts with the universities. They also supported Sir Josiah Stamp's well-publicized attack on accountants, in 1921, for their lack of research effort, of any contribution to economics, or, indeed, of any theoretical study into their own art (Carr-Saunders and Wilson, 1933: 226).

Inevitably, as more accountants who qualified in public practice moved into industry, the suitability and relevance of their training became the subject of even greater concern. Keeble has maintained of the accounting societies: 'Their members gained their professional qualifications still, in business terms, semi-literate. The narrowness of the education of accountants, in terms of their own specialism as well as in the wider context of business management, was constantly pointed out to the governing bodies' (1992: 54). In 1957, the chief accountant at GKN, W. W. Fea, presented a paper to the ICAEW lamenting the fact that no specific training for industry was provided by the Institute, despite that fact that a third of articled clerks were, at that time, leaving public practice for industry on qualification. He advocated the addition of one year to articles to be spent in industry to meet the observed deficiency. 'I have yet to meet', he said, 'an accountant who has entered industry from a practitioner's office who did not freely admit, sometimes with astonishment, how much he had to learn about industry's problems and how industry is really run' (Fea, 1957: 15). There has in fact existed, since 1945, an arrangement whereby an articled clerk can 'spend periods not amounting to more than six months in all in such industrial, commercial or other suitable organisation as the Council may approve', but little use appears to have been made of this facility (Armitage, 1994). More general provision dates from 1990, when the ICAEW allowed the setting up of suitable courses for chartered accountants to train in industry. However, the Training Outside Public Practice (TOPP) scheme remains of minor importance with only about 100 or so students actually training in industry at the present time (Colquhoun, 1996: 3). The ICAS followed suit in 1991 (*Accountancy*, Feb. 1990: 201), but both trailed well behind the other early chartered body, the ICAI, which made provision for training in practice in 1983 (*Accountancy*, Oct. 1991: 12).

The accountant's articles have more recently been the subject of attack from Armstrong (1985: 129) and others for their narrowness, untheoretical approach, and general unsuitability as a preparation for general management. It is a view also held by some public accountants turned business managers, including Richard Close who was appointed chairman of the

Board for Chartered Accountants in Business in 1994. The Board, set up in 1990, assumes responsibility for looking after the 40,000 or so ICAEW members employed in commerce, finance, and industry, and its expressed functions include that of working to 'to ensure the profile of the Institute's business membership and [that] its unique contribution is recognised both by UK business and the public' (*The Ivanhoe Career Guide to Chartered Accountants 1997*, 1996: 31). Close expressed his determination to see the chartered accountancy qualification restored to its premier position as a leading business qualification:

The Institute of Chartered Accountants is my Institute and I have benefited by the training—no doubt about that. So I don't start from any kind of disaffection. But there is this perception, which I am sure is not just peculiar to me, that when people of my age qualified, it was the premier accounting qualification by a long way. And I think that this position has been eroded. (Irvine, 1994: 28–9)

Close, speaking also as managing director of finance at the Post Office, drew attention to the fact that he was the only chartered accountant in a senior position—a situation unthinkable 20 years ago:

As a big consumer of accountants, I watch these other accountancy bodies coming up the line really fast in terms of prestige and producing the kind of people we want to put in top jobs. We've also had a major input into all their training and exams yet, with my own Institute, although I am senior finance person at the Post Office, we have not even been invited to discuss ways of making the qualification more relevant. (Irvine, 1994: 29)

The Post Office sees the chartered accountancy qualification as too audit-oriented and, as a result, of the 290 qualified accountants employed in 1994, 181 were from CIMA, 45 from the ACCA, 36 were chartered accountants, and 28 were CIPFA members. Of the trainees, 250 were from CIMA, 30 from the ACCA, and just 3 from CIPFA and the ICAEW. Close confirms that 'The numbers really do reflect our preferences in terms of qualified accountants' (Irvine, 1994: 29). Close even found problems with the TOPP initiative. The Post Office applied to join the scheme in 1992, but the 'extraordinary bureaucracy'—months of forms going back and forth—nearly caused him to back out.

Concern that the chartered accountancy qualification is less relevant for the top jobs in industry and commerce than used to be the case has also surfaced recently at the institutional level. In 1993, the English Institute set up a radical review of its education and training system, partly because it felt that the business community was showing a preference for other qualifications such as the MBA, the ACMA, and the ACCA. It enlisted a market analysis from the Henley Centre for Forecasting which concluded that 'in the past the Institute's qualification attracted high quality individuals because it gave them all-round skills, a continuing choice of careers and a ladder to the top levels of business' (*Accountancy*, Jan. 1995:

18). During the 1980s, Henley claimed, the reputation of chartered accountants slumped because they were seen to react to, rather than initiate, innovative ideas, and it was further tarnished by corporate failures in the second half of the decade. Accountants, Henley said, who had once been trusted not to be reckless and were noted for their prudence, began to be viewed as 'accomplices in the process of failure' (*Accountancy*, Jan. 1995: 18).

The ICAEW subsequently appointed a working party whose investigations included a study, by questionnaire, of a random sample of 10% of ICAEW members in business. The report pointed to the possibility of too many accountants being produced by 2005, assuming past trends continue, as well as 'stiffer competition from the growing number of CIMA and ACCA members and MBA graduates, as companies look to recruit business-trained accountants and others with multi-disciplinary skills' (ICAEW Board for Chartered Accountants in Business, 1996: 18). The perceived threat to chartered accountants in the corporate sector is summed up neatly in the following segment from the report:

Another key issue is the growing divergence of the strategic and control functions within business. Historically Chartered Accountants have enjoyed fast-track careers by straddling the two areas. But that fast track is not an inalienable right and will only continue if accountants can adapt to new demands. To claim their place as senior business managers accountants must take a leading role in change management, make a major contribution to corporate strategy, and be highly efficient in their supervisory and monitoring roles. For some this will involve acquiring additional skills—perhaps by studying for an MBA or other specialist qualifications. (ICAEW Board for Chartered Accountants in Business, 1996: 32)

The question of whether the MBA itself poses a threat to the status of the professional accountant's training had previously been addressed in a 1993 survey of managing directors. The outcome was inconclusive. Whereas several respondents believed that the MBA did not contain the technical content necessary for a finance director's job, others argued that, if accountants' training was not improved, 'the high ground would be lost to MBAs' who could employ accountants to do their technical work (Owen and Abell, 1993: 27). There is little evidence, as yet, that the chartered accountant's qualification is losing its appeal. Despite increases in both the quantity and variety of management training on offer in Britain since the 1960s, noted above, and the rapid rise in the numbers of graduates engaged by industry, the popularity of the accountancy qualification, as we saw in Chapter 6, remains extremely strong. Seventy-one per cent of chief executives held a degree and 11% had MBAs by 1994, but MBAs are still comfortably outdistanced by the 23% of chief executive officers who had an accountancy qualification (Korn/Ferry Carre/Orban International, 1994: 23).

Training in a public practice

The *Accountant*, discussing the rise of the profession in general management posts in 1929, described the contribution of an accounting qualification as follows: 'general audit practice is merely the foundation of an accountant's work. It is on the wide practical experience which he derives therefrom joined to his theoretical knowledge that he attains to the capacity to fill such posts in the industrial and financial world' (19 Oct. 1929: 485). This journal, which, admittedly, could be relied on to put the best case for the profession, also quoted the City Editor of the *Observer* with approval in 1930: 'It is remarkable what an immense amount of technical knowledge is to be found in the profession. Comparisons not only of accountancy methods, but of administration and management come under their [accountants'] notice which, though confidential in detail, have general application' (11 Jan. 1930: 34). The experience gained in a public practice has not been seen by everyone, however, as an appropriate training for a career in business. Concerns have been expressed by both accountants and non-accountants.

Its significance as seen by some

The doleful impact of accountants as managers has been embraced from almost all quarters. That accountants are too cautious in their management style, are unwilling to take risks and stifle innovation, are backward looking in their outlook or foster 'short-termism', is a common viewpoint with a long pedigree. In 1945, the editor of *Financial News* argued that: 'Accountants . . . by temperament and training, must be cautious men' (quoted in *Accountant*, 21 July 1945: 37–8). While not all accountants are 'ultra-cautious, safety-first people' and many make excellent businessmen and are far-sighted, forward-looking people, none the less: ' "Chancing his arm" is the one thing which, from the signing of his articles, he has been taught to regard as the first of all the seven deadly sins' (quoted in *Accountant*, 21 July 1945: 37). *Financial News* saw two options (quoted in *Accountant*, 21 July 1945: 38): to have 'an accountant as Chief of Staff, planning everything at the highest level and doing everything for the Commander short of choosing the objective and fighting the battle'; or, if they were to become head of the firm, they should aim to 'become a kind of inverted Henry the Fifth—to forget something of the gravity and carefulness of high responsibility and taste a little of the heady wine of risk taking'. The conclusion was that 'if they could combine the two elements, we should have such a power of business direction as we have never yet seen'. Twenty years later, another journalist, Anthony Sampson, expressed his concerns with the role of accountants in the following colourful manner:

in so far as accountants are known to make decisions, they are liable to say No. To a team of engineers, no nightmare is worse than a group of men arriving to introduce realism (= pessimism), to envisage bad weather, floods and 'contingent liabilities'—that menacing accountants' phrase—to shake their heads and ask awkward questions. . . . Imagination and daring are not their [accountants] first requirements; and the business doctors are sometimes unable to diagnose the most deadly of diseases—the creeping caution and hypochondria induced by some of the doctors themselves. (1965: 525)

This view is shared by practising business leaders, and, a quarter of a century after Sampson wrote, Lord Sieff, chairman of Marks & Spencer from 1972 to 1984, argued that:

Over the last few decades many more businesses than in the past have been run by accountants. Some accountants make good administrators, and some good administrators make good chief executives. One should not generalize too freely, but it is part of an accountant's professional function to be cautious, meticulous, critical and analytical. He is there not to advise taking risks but rather to urge and advise you how to avoid them. Though there are exceptions to the rule, accountants therefore do not generally make the best principals and, though they may render great, even crucial, service in the early days of a small business, they may not be suitable to lead and energize it. (Sieff, 1990: 35)

Many academic management theorists, most prominently Charles Handy and collaborators, tell the same story: 'the accountants' proper caution, inculcated by their training, can be damaging to a spirit of enterprise and initiative in management' (1988: 173–4). Yet Earl helpfully reminds us that features that others see as vices are part of the accountant's legitimate and justifiable role: 'When they are accused of being conservative, traditional, ritualistic, above criticism, and interested only in financial numbers, they should not be overly concerned for such accusations describe the role of priest which has evolved for them' (Earl, 1983: 130–1).

Almost universally, however, the accountant, as characterized in academic analysis, is seen to possess 'skills' inimical to good management (for example, Armstrong, 1985: 129; 1987: 416, 425). The socialization process involved in the accountant's training is thought to lead to an attachment to 'caution; exactitude; anti-theoretical pragmatism; professional exclusiveness; quantification and rationality' (McKenna, 1978: 8). Tricker talks of the 'ultra cautious, historically orientated, conservative attitudes' of the accountant (1967: 9), and such ideas also find favour with some accountants. When a fellow accountant, Trevor Holdsworth (see Chapter 6), was about to become the next boss of GKN, in 1979, Norman Lancaster admitted that he would have preferred to see an engineer in the job. He lamented the fact that so many enterprises were run by accountants and, echoing the editor of *Financial News*, suggested that their training suited them only for a subordinate role: 'I always say that accountants have a very good training, in very necessary techniques, and are ideally cast as number two or three in a company.... An accountant has to be careful, exact. I'm not certain that running a business does not involve a good element of daring and risk-taking' (quoted in Mumford, 1991: 137–8).

Conservatism, enshrined in financial reporting practice as the concept of prudence, is the main focus for the attack on the accountant as manager, but there are other important areas of concern. Sir Donald Barron, then chairman of Midland Bank, was quoted, in 1983, as being worried about the rise of the accountant in management, 'not necessarily because accountants have a reputation for being over-cautious but because an accountancy qualification provides no training in marketing or production or,... in managing people' (*The Economist*, 17 Sept. 1983: 83). Indeed, while there has been criticism of the accountancy training as a route into general management, Henry McAuliffe has even questioned whether the training is sufficient to enable accountants to perform competently the duties of a finance director:

In some instances a university education followed by a chartered accountant's qualification can be the worst training of all. It concentrates too much on reading and writing; a finance director spends much of his working day talking and listening, and in these arts he has had little practice. As an auditor he has to be detached, to be very conscious of the rule book, to enjoy semi-official status with his clients. As a finance director he has colleagues and competitors rather than clients and he needs to play team games as an equal and to be involved and sympathetic. If he has never made money in his youth he can find it difficult to relate to fellow directors whose business that is. (1987: 20)

In a later article in *Accountancy*, McAuliffe argued that many accountants may struggle generally on becoming partners, chief accountants, or directors because of their deficiency in people skills. He acknowledges that accountants in public practice 'have to relate to clients and to customers and to work with colleagues, but they are less frequently in charge of staff, and then usually in a structured environment with a definite task ahead' (1988: 16).

Much of the blame for the accountant's perceived deficiencies is placed on the audit function. Mark Silver, then director of operations and finance at Aegis Group plc, who left Price Waterhouse's technical department in 1987 just two years after qualification, agrees with Fea that: 'when you come out of the profession you find you just don't know anything' (Irvine, 1992b: 24). Brian McGowan, former chief executive of Williams Holdings (see Chapter 6), states that: 'The thing I got most out of my articles was the ability to cope with boredom' (Irvine, 1991: 24). Likewise, Jim Beveridge, finance director, MEPC, reports: 'I didn't like the auditing profession, so I got out of it as quickly as I could. Quite frankly I found it boring. All the clients that I worked for were very big and I did nothing but ticking and bashing in those days' (Grey, 1993*b*: 30). Simon Moffat, as group finance director of Kwik Save, also discussed in the previous chapter, lauds the virtues of the management accountant's training. He qualified with CIMA while on Unilever's Management Trainee Scheme in the 1970s and argues that the training 'gives you immediate hands-on experience and forces you to do the original work and original thinking. The audit profession just comes along to look at what's been done' (Grey, 1991: 23).

. . . *and by others*

The above criticisms of accountants comprise a formidable list, which can be summarized as backward looking, cautious, short-term, cash and profit oriented, while lacking flair, enterprise, leadership, and communication skills. It therefore seems fairly clear that the professional accounting qualification, particularly the chartered, was, and is, not an ideal training for a career in business management. This is unsurprising, if not entirely justifiable. The principal purposes of the chartered examinations and training have been to supply the skills and to impart the knowledge necessary to work effectively as an accountant in public practice. Turning to the training itself, the position is even more clear-cut. The principal area of work continues to be audit, and so the trainee accountant will naturally spend the bulk of his or her practical training performing this function. But the value of even this 'menial' work should not be overlooked.

Audit work gave, and still gives, the accountant a wide range of experience in business, at least for those receptive to its potential. In the course of performing doubtless mainly mundane duties, the articled clerk visits companies in different industries, of all shapes and sizes, and the successful along with the less successful. This is well put by Stanley Grinstead (see Chapter 6), at the time chairman of Grand Metropolitan:

I regarded accountancy as a very good training ground. It also gave me a very good insight into a variety of businesses. You could spend two or three weeks in a company and then a month later in another, and you therefore received a very wide exposure to various aspects of business and commerce. Also you were exposed to top people, so if you had a light it was unlikely it would be concealed under a bushel. (Ritchie and Goldsmith, 1987: 70–1)

In a more recent interview, Hamilton Anstead, deputy managing director of the top nursing home, Takare plc, claimed that everything he learned in his eleven and a half years at Price Waterhouse was perfect preparation for what he had done since. He also reminds us that, particularly after the first year or so, the 'training' is not confined to 'ticking and bashing': 'As a manager in public practice you are always working at Director level with your clients and you see such a variety of organisations and ways of doing things. *I felt the experience prepared me not just for accounting responsibilities, but for business relationships and understanding what drives people and what makes organisations work'* (Grey, 1993a: 29, emphasis added).

This view is shared by some accountants, such as Richard Close (see above), who are by no means entirely enamoured with accountancy as a training for business management. He is nevertheless adamant that he has 'benefited by the training—no doubt about that'. Indeed, he admits that he has 'never regretted' the decision to move into accountancy (Irvine, 1994: 29). John Neil Clarke, of British Coal (see Chapter 6), also sees weaknesses and strengths: while insisting that he found accountancy a dull science, he acknowledges the fact that it gave him a tool to make things work (Bose, 1992: 30). Several respondents to Owen and Abell's 1993 survey of finance directors also underlined the value of auditing experience obtained in a wide range of companies. Indeed, one went so far as to disagree with the provision for chartered accountants to train outside public practice on the grounds that it 'cannot substitute for the multi-company auditing experience so early in life' (1993: 25).

It may well be also the case that the attacks mounted by some on the ultra-conservatism of accountants are misdirected. This line of argument is expressed as follows:

It is important to recognise the distinction between the man in the functional accounting role and the accountant by training and experience in another managerial post, since attributes which are commendable in one office can be a handicap if carried over into the other (Tricker, 1967: 18).

The logical proposition that the accountant takes his cautious financial training with him into general management can, in many cases, be revealed as very largely a myth. Although the model is neat, it seems clear that many accountants are well able to distinguish between their skills as accountants and the requirements of general management. At the same time, the transition may not be easy. We have seen (Chapter 6) that, in an earlier era, H. G. Lazell of Beechams insisted on the need for top managers to develop a marketing outlook. More recently, Paul Girolami, when chairman of Glaxo, was a firm believer that accountants would never make good industrialists unless they forgot about their accounting. He saw the advantages in the accounting training: 'But', he advised accountants thinking of going into business, 'don't move over as an accountant. It is not an accounting job, to run a business' (Irvine, 1992a: 26). He also pinpointed an important flaw in Morita's (the engineer-chairman of Sony) recent criticism that there are too many accountants at the head of British companies, drawing attention to the fact that Morita, himself, was not an engineer but a top manager: 'If he were to run Sony as an engineer it would be a shambles. And equally, if I were to run Glaxo as an accountant we wouldn't get started. I think there is a misconception that your early training or qualifications are branded on your personality' (Kennedy, 1992: 106).

The accountant's training does not come to an abrupt halt on qualification. Those who remain in public practice have the need and opportunity to build on existing skills and develop new areas of expertise. The idea of trainee accountants utterly weighed down with the menial tasks of auditing, unable to lift up their heads from the innumerable schedules that have to be checked and authenticated, is a severely outdated characterization. Articled clerks, today trainee accountants, who did not broaden their experience by speaking to the various levels of client staff with which they naturally came into contact, and by surveying and analysing both the accounting systems and business operations on which the financial reports are based, were simply failing to exploit the opportunities available to them, and probably performing their audit tasks less effectively than could have been the case. Once qualified, however, the public accountant's work continues to expand the experience relevant to the role of external adviser or for a full-time future career in business. When companies called in William Plender, William McLintock, or Ian Hay Davison to advise them, or employed d'Arcy Cooper, Webster Jenkinson, or Paul Girolami and numerous less well-known accountants, they acquired managers with a knowledge of the intimate and confidential workings of literally hundreds of diverse companies undertaking business in all its aspects.

On becoming employed by a company, of course, the accountant is often particularly well placed to continue to accumulate experience. Paul Girolami recently made the point that 'The accountant has to look at the whole picture. He's the only man apart from the general manager that has to look at an organisation in all its aspects' (*Business Times, Weekend Edition,* 15–16 Aug. 1992: 3). Surveys have produced a similar conclusion. The 1993 Interdisciplinary Institute of Management Report, headed by Sir Geoffrey Owen, concluded that 'the finance director has a role of central importance in the management of companies, often second only to that of the chief executive' (quoted in Bruce, 1994: 6). The 1993 survey of finance directors produced a number of comments to the effect that they, together with the chief executive, were the only board members thinking continuously about the group as a whole: 'The FD is the chief executive's right hand man; the other directors are more advocates of their own function or department.' 'The FD is not a defender of vested interests. He thinks long-term while the others tend to think short-term' was another insightful view (Owen and Abell, 1993: 20).

One of the strengths of members of the accountancy profession, therefore, in terms of their boardroom appeal, would appear to be their ingrained desire, inculcated by their training as auditors, to obtain a true and fair (impartial) view, which leads them to look at decisions in their broadest context. The accountant and finance director is also seen as someone who possesses the ability to bring a sense of realism to proposals, a point noted by Peter MacFarlane, finance director of Allied Lyons:

Strategy tends to be discussed by senior executives who are not responsible for particular decisions so that you get an unbiased view. . . . The finance director has a unique perspective. The chap who runs one division can't really criticise another whereas the finance director has had to create a dialogue with the divisional finance chiefs without dropping them in it with their managing directors. So he sometimes knows the risks and the opportunities better than the overall chief executive. . . . And anyway the finance director has an important role in that he is likely to be asked to evaluate different strategies in terms of the numbers involved. (Quoted in Bruce, 1994: 8)

The words of Anthony Sampson serve to reinforce lucidly the main thrust of these ideas concerning the utility of and potential provided by the accountant's skills: 'Few people in a vast company are *in a position to see over the tops of the trees*. An able accountant can, and from his knowledge comes power' (1965: 521, emphasis added). Owen agrees that 'finance directors are the only ones who can *look across the whole company*', and this is because they tend to have been 'more mobile in their careers and have greater experience of other companies' (quoted in Bruce, 1994: 7). The experienced accountant can, therefore, reasonably be expected to have personal knowledge of expanding companies, winding up companies, mergers and takeovers, major capital investment projects, raising capital, going public, wage disputes; in short all aspects of running a company. The fact that these relevant experiences are perceived by business as unlikely to be matched by members of other professional groupings explains the relative success of accountants in top management, as confirmed by the contents of Tables 15 and 18. Monck made the further important point, in 1952, that 'an accountant can get wider experience than the engineer without incurring the odium of changing jobs too often' (quoted in Keeble, 1992: 126). But the accountant does of course change jobs, even if only to move from public practice into industry. This may be seen as important, because one characteristic of British management historically—if less so than say the Japanese and Germans—has been their lack of mobility. A 1950s survey of 3,000 managers revealed that 61% had neither moved function nor changed department within their firms (Keeble, 1992: 56). It was estimated, in 1969, that 44% of top managers had spent all their working lives in one company (Keeble, 1992: 56–7), although the figure then fell dramatically to 14.1% in 1980 and 11.6% by 1990 (Mansfield and Poole, 1991: 14).

The 1994 Korn/Ferry study of all UK listed companies supports the notion of the accountant as mobile manager (Korn/Ferry Carre/Orban

International, 1994: 24–5). Not only are finance directors, on average, younger than other directors (63% of finance directors are aged below 50; just 33% of top executives and 48% of divisional directors can make a similar claim), but they have come to their present positions in greater numbers from outside the company (33% of finance directors were promoted from within, compared with 65% and 76% for top executives and divisional directors respectively). Also, finance directors have more recent experience of other companies than their counterparts, with 47% of finance directors having been with their present company for less than five years (for top executives and divisional directors the respective proportions were 29% and 17%).

Desirable traits

Given their training and experience, British accountants undoubtedly found themselves well placed in the market for managerial talent. Much recruitment into British management relied traditionally on informal networks, personal contacts—'the old school tie'—and patronage of various sorts until the 1950s and beyond (Keeble, 1992: 45). A survey conducted in 1951, for example, showed that 58% of a sample of 1,173 directors of large companies in Britain had been educated in public schools (Melrose-Woodman, 1976: 46). It is well known that such institutions were not 'moved to give a practical education of direct usefulness to businessmen' (Coleman, 1973: 108), so their output—what Coleman has captioned 'Gentlemen'—went into business as amateurs with little or no management training, as did Coleman's 'Players'—the often relatively uneducated, self-made, entrepreneurs who built up family firms. It is not difficult to see, therefore, why the often grammar school-educated accountants, practical men with professional 'on the job' training (often joining companies through another type of personal contact—the auditor/client relationship), should have risen to the top in management in large numbers in the post-war period. As the Gentlemen and the Players increasingly gave way to the professional in British boardrooms, therefore, there was one professional—the accountant—who was by training and experience the best placed to succeed.

The recent literature contains broad-based assessments of the desirable characteristics of a board member, and these tend to emphasize skill and judgement rather than specialist skills. Sir John Harvey-Jones, former chairman of ICI and author of the best-selling book *Making It Happen*, argues that 'directors are not chosen for their mix of skills but more particularly for their experience and judgement. It cannot be restated often enough that the job of the board is all to do with subjective judgement, based on the members' individual and collective experience' (1988: 200). Colin Coulson-Thomas, writing with experience gained at the Institute of Directors, argued that, 'being an expert, or being perceived as a professional specialist, does not usually help an individual to obtain a directorship. It is not necessary to appoint someone to the board to obtain the benefit of their expertise. A specialist can be hired to give advice as and when required' (1993: 102). Mills's normative analysis of the required attributes of a board member also downplays the importance of specialist skills, arguing that 'the board should only consider appointing those executives whose contribution can be expected to cover a wide range of boardroom topics, not just subjects within an executive's own specialist field' (1985: 124).

Numerous surveys have nevertheless been undertaken in the endeavour to pinpoint precise attributes required to make the appointment of a particular individual to board level desirable. Those reported in Hirsh and Bevan (1988: 45), Syrett (1988: 95–6), Coulson-Thomas and Wakelam (1991), and Coulson-Thomas (1990, 1993: 169) have been used to build up the following lists of the required personal attributes and specialist skills.

- *Personal attributes*: appearance, commitment, common sense, creativity, drive, humour, initiative, innovation, integrity, intelligence, interpersonal skills, judgement, leadership, loyalty, maturity, motivation, objectivity, perspective, self-discipline, team spirit, and vision.
- *Specialist skills*: broad business understanding, communication, customer focus, numeracy, organizing and planning, presentation of material, specialist knowledge, strategic awareness, and track record.

The classification of the desirable attributes is itself problematic—is communication correctly classified?—and there is clearly an interrelationship between the two groups—someone with vision is possibly better equipped to be a strategic thinker. Further, education and training may encourage certain personal attributes to blossom and, perhaps, cause others to diminish. The list is certainly consistent with Coulson-Thomas's conclusion that 'Individual qualities continue to be regarded as important in respect of appointments to boards of companies' (1993: 166). It also suggests that Hirsh's assessment that 'by and large, organisations are still predominantly interested in personal attributes rather than specific skills' (quoted in Syrett, 1988: 96; see also Coulson-Thomas, 1993: 167) may not be entirely without foundation.

Can these data help to explain the rise of the accountant in business management? If the perceived emphasis on personal attributes is valid, the implication would seem to be that the professional accountant possesses these in great abundance. H. L. Mencken's characterization of the accountant (Chapter 3) would therefore appear to be well wide of the mark. A more likely answer may be that the accountant does at least as well as other groups in terms of personal attributes and that the specialist skills tip the balance. Some would find it difficult to accept even this line of argument. One might imagine that the accountant scores rather better in some areas than others. A necessarily qualitative and impressionistic analysis may lead one to suggest that the kind of person choosing a career in accountancy, with high entry standards and the grind of (in many cases) at least a three-year training contract, would score fairly well in terms of commitment, drive, intelligence, motivation, and self-discipline. It might further be argued that the education and training programme helps develop traits such as initiative (firms will always be keen for new recruits to take on greater responsibility), integrity, interpersonal skills, judgement, leadership, objectivity, and team spirit. Leaving aside appearance and common sense (highly personal), humour (obviously), and loyalty (by definition they are going to leave), we are left with creativity, innovation, and perspective. The first two, at least, are rarely portrayed as strengths of the accountant. Indeed, it has been argued, by some, that the nature of accountants' training is more likely to stifle such attributes, if they ever existed, rather than cause them to flourish. It may be the case that this is a correct judgement; the accountant already seems to be scoring fairly well. At the same time, we have presented numerous examples of accountants who have shown considerable initiative and entrepreneurial flair, to which could be added Bruce Rattray (Kelly, 1987*a*: 15), Bernard Garbacz (Croft, 1987*b*: 14), and Timothy Brookes (Irvine, 1986: 16).

When we move to the specialist skills, accountants again at least hold their own. Moreover, in some areas one might imagine that they score very heavily in comparison with any other grouping: numeracy, specialist knowledge, and, an attribute given particular emphasis above, broad business understanding. Coulson-Thomas expresses the importance of these features in the following manner: 'In order to understand the company "as a whole" it helps to have perception, intellect, experience, and an awareness of more than one function. Cross-functional experience may be of greater value than in-depth exposure to different facets of one particular function' (1993: 115). He continues: 'the director should have an awareness of the meaning and significance of financial information. This requires an understanding of accounting and financial ratios, an appreciation of the perspective of the analyst and investor, and sensitivity to financial danger signals' (1993: 122).

CONCLUDING COMMENTS

There are widely divergent views concerning the value of the contribution made by professional accountants to British economic development. What is in no doubt is the cash value placed by society on the services supplied by these individuals, with many young men and women today drawn into this work principally because of the high remuneration that they can expect to command on qualification. Despite the large numbers now qualifying each year, the demand for their services continues to rise across all sectors, with a newly qualified chartered accountant working in industry/commerce earning a salary of around £29,000 (*Accountancy Age*, 10 Oct. 1996: 29). The chartered accountant's qualification continues to carry a premium (*Accountancy Age*, 18 Nov. 1993: 3), and much of the comment and analysis throughout this book has focused principally on that subset. The justification for this is that chartered accountants remain comfortably the most numerous and, on average, the most successful category of professional accountant. They account for approximately half of all qualified accountants in Britain and dominate the appointment of professional accountants to top management positions. At the same time, this study has endeavoured to portray a broad picture of accounting in Britain, and the role of certified and management accountants has not been ignored. Members of the Chartered Institute of Public Finance and Accountancy have naturally not figured significantly in this history due to their historical focus on, almost exclusively, the administration of activities within the governmental sector.

This history has presented some dramatic statistics which include the existence of a quarter of a million accountants professionally qualified with one or other of the six members of the Consultative Committee of Accountancy Bodies (Table 8), of whom 20% work abroad, and it must not be forgotten that there are also 170,000 students in training and an unknown number of unqualified accountants in gainful employment. The increase in numbers over the last 200 years is truly staggering. The numbers of accountants identified in the trade directories around 1800 were insubstantial (Chapter 2), and we have seen that it often proved necessary to engage in additional activities in order to make a living. The nineteenth century saw the emergence of a number of 'business' professions, with the coverage of each of them gradually being defined and delineated. Many accountants soon found it more convenient to supply services through the partnership structure and, between 1853 and 1888, we see the establishment of the original chartered bodies in Scotland, England, and Wales and Ireland. These, together with organizations subsequently formed, have done much to maintain and enhance the reputation of accountants amongst society in general, though there is an understandable concern that at least some of them may have outgrown their usefulness to today's massive, international accounting practices. It is certainly these firms that have provided the mechanism for training the vast bulk of today's professionally qualified accountants, whether subsequently developing careers in public practice, industry, or commerce. In turn, the importance of the audit function as the vehicle for developing public practices and the requirements for professional accountants is, we feel, difficult to overstate.

Auditing has a long history, of course, and we know that public accountants have been called in to perform this function for some centuries, but it was the emergence of a vigorous capital market in Britain which provided an inestimable boost for this kind of work and raised the profile of the individuals performing that function. Investigations undertaken for amateur auditors or committees of shareholders at the time of the 'railway mania' often led to more formal appointments which gained pace in line with the rise of the limited liability company following enabling Acts of 1844 and 1855. The separation of ownership from management, the need for an independent arbiter to assess the reliability of published financial information, and the increasing need to arrange for a public quotation of a company's shares provided further impetus for the development of the external audit. As a result, by the mid-1880s the vast majority of quoted companies were already subject to a professional audit. It is not possible to obtain more than anecdotal evidence concerning the extent to which professional accountants monopolized the supply of audit services to unquoted enterprises, but such evidence as does exist suggests that it was common practice by the time an external audit requirement was introduced for registered companies in 1900. The Companies Act 1948 made the appointment of a professional compulsory, of course, but, in common with many regulatory provisions relating to audit and accounts in Britain, it simply gave statutory confirmation to existing widespread practice.

The professional audit has required a growing army of personnel to undertake the work, reflecting factors which include the increasing number of companies and the expanding nature and coverage of this function, but it is only part, albeit an important part, of the story. The audit provided professional firms with opportunities to access further work that were fully exploited. Companies and individuals have turned more and more to accountants to help them cope with the growing weight of taxation that has resulted from the imposition of a wide range of new taxes over the one and a half centuries since the reintroduction of income tax in 1842, and from the usually higher rates at which individual taxes have been levied as time has gone by. In addition, the audit has provided direct access to the often more lucrative consultancy work which, although dating back at least into the nineteenth century, has grown at an unprecedented rate during the last quarter of a century.

The bulk of today's professionally qualified accountants trained within these accountancy firms, but only approximately one-half of the combined membership of even the ICAS and ICAEW now remain in public practice (Tables 9, 16). The remainder are employed in industry and commerce, principally filling the position of accountant, company secretary, finance director, or taking on a position in general management including that of chief executive. The fact that today there are one-quarter of a million British qualified professional accountants is therefore substantially attributable to the ability of business to engage their services on a massive scale. There is no mono-causal explanation for this state of affairs. We see the outcome, applying an economic determinist argument, as a combination of demand- and supply-side factors. On the demand side, we have identified and explored the importance of the growing scale, structure, and complexity of business organizations, where the accountant is called in to piece together the financial implications of activities undertaken by these increasingly diverse and often fragmented enterprises. We also produce evidence to show that accountants were often called in during times of distress and failure and, where corporate recovery proved possible, steps could be taken to ensure the appointment of a financial expert to a permanent position. A range of environmental factors, associated again with the capital market, play a part in this analysis, with the need to manage profits, dividends, and gearing, to smooth relations with the bank and institutional investors, and to handle the financial intricacies of takeovers and mergers again benefiting from the accountants' financial expertise. Finally, on the demand side, we come back to the sheer number of companies requiring 'bean counters' as being part of the explanation.

Turning to the supply side, it has been argued that, at least for much of the period under consideration, accounting has simply been the best training available. The sheer number of accountants in business reflects their ability to process efficiently the vast amount of financial and administrative work considered necessary by British business today, while their rise to prominence is attributable to the fact that accountancy was the best available training also for general management. Accountancy firms appear to have always been fairly comfortable with the situation where they train, at no cost, future recruits to industry. As a result, firms base their recruitment policy on the assumptions of continuing growth and that a given proportion of staff will leave within one or two years of qualification. When this does not happen, problems result. This was demonstrated, in 1991, when Price Waterhouse issued redundancy notices on 180 staff, including twenty just about to take their final examinations: 'The continuing recession has forced this on us' said the firm's senior partner, Ian Brindle (*Accountancy*, Aug. 1991: 12). It is of course the case that trainees were often paid nothing at all up to the 1950s, and the amounts remained nominal in all but the largest firms for about another 20 years. In more recent times, with salaries of trainees rising fairly rapidly and the training costs becoming quite heavy, particularly for some professional bodies, the willingness of accountancy firms to continue to subsidize industry appears curious. A part of the explanation is, no doubt, that industry does meet these training costs, indirectly through the higher fees paid to professional firms. Also significant is the fact that accountancy firms see benefits in releasing staff to industry on the expectation that such individuals will view their former employers favourably when involved in decisions concerning the acquisition of 'accounting' services at some future date. Certainly firms of accountants now go to considerable lengths to maintain contact with former alumni, for example through regular newsletters, though they also benefit when former leaders move on to pastures new. We saw, in Chapter 2, that the 'father' of the accountancy profession in England, Peter Harriss Abbott, later referred work to his former clerks—Quilter and Ball—when appointed Official Assignee in Bankruptcy. In more recent years, we might imagine that Lord Benson's stature with industry and government remained a valuable asset to his former firm, Coopers & Lybrand, in the decade or so following his retirement in 1975.

It has been argued that business has recruited accountants from public practice in vast numbers because of the quality of their examinations and training and their availability. The examinations appear to have provided aspiring businessmen with much of the technical knowledge and theoretical skills that they require. This is not to suggest that these examinations have proved the perfect answer to businesses' need for a management training. Indeed, the examinations have been much maligned in the past as they are today, suffering attack for their narrowness, untheoretical approach, and general unsuitability as a preparation for general management (Carr-Saunders and Wilson, 1933: 226; Fea, 1957: 15; Armstrong, 1985: 129). One apparent weakness is the simple fact that, often, they are not designed to prepare individuals for a career in business, but to equip them with the skills needed to undertake the work of the professional practice. The key factor here, however, is that the wide range of work undertaken by the British public accountancy practice is a direct reflection of business requirements rather than a response to, for example, statutory edict. We have given some attention to an analysis of the particular skills which business believes that it requires. Personal skills were seen to outnumber numerical skills, but it is of course difficult to apply any weighting to the relative importance of each of these. We have suggested that, as regards personal skills, there is no reason to suppose that professional accountants suffer by comparison with any other grouping. Turning to specialist skills, there are at least two areas of relative strength and these may be key factors in helping to explain the hegemony. Accountants are both financially literate and, following on from the fact that all aspects of business activity have financial implications, they are in a good position to develop a broad-based understanding of a company's operations. A further factor in the continued dominance of accountants may be that they are now self-perpetuating. Professional accountants who have succeeded in securing senior positions will naturally appoint people whom they know, people with whom they can communicate, and people who possess qualifications that they both know and trust.

Accountancy is not a bespoke qualification for industry, but it has proved to be the best available. There are growing concerns that the position is now changing, and we have seen that the ICAEW set up a working party that has expressed concerns regarding whether its premier position will be retained into the twenty-first century. The most obvious competitor would be the specialist management qualification, the master of business administration. We have seen that, historically, graduates were slow to obtain top management positions in Britain, compared with elsewhere, but this mainly reflected relative under-provision in that area. The position is of course now changing reflecting the rapid development of higher education since the Robins Report in the 1960s. The impact of the MBA may take a little longer to become fully apparent in view of the fact that the universities have only developed these postgraduate pro-grammes significantly over the last ten years. A parallel situation applies in the case of female accountants, where the numbers training and quali-fying have also risen to significant proportions in recent years. Given the fact the people obtaining an MBA qualification and that those women joining the professional accounting fraternity will be, in the main, at a relatively low rung on the managerial ladder, it will be a little while longer before we can assess the impact of these recent developments on the profile of top managers. In 2005 the typical finance director, for example, may no longer be 'a chartered accountant' and 'overwhelmingly male' (*Accountancy*, Dec. 1996: 20). We have already noticed a small downturn in the number of professionally qualified accountants who are finance direc-tors, and there are some signs of the MBA gaining in prominence. The changes are not major, but it may well be the case that the high point, proportionally, for accountants in top management has been reached. Certainly it would seem that saturation point must be fairly close in the case of the finance director, with about 80% having professional qualifica-tions. In other words, a relative decline in the dominance of accountants in top management may well be almost inevitable, and it is arguably desir-able, but, even if this happens, it seems unlikely that they will be displaced from their position as 'the priesthood of industry'.

APPENDIX

Family Trees of Accountancy Bodies and Firms

Sources: Boys, 1989*a–q*, 1990*a*, 1990*b*.

We reproduce in respect of the family trees also the *Notes* and *Sources* used by Boys. The *Sources* are not repeated in the References.

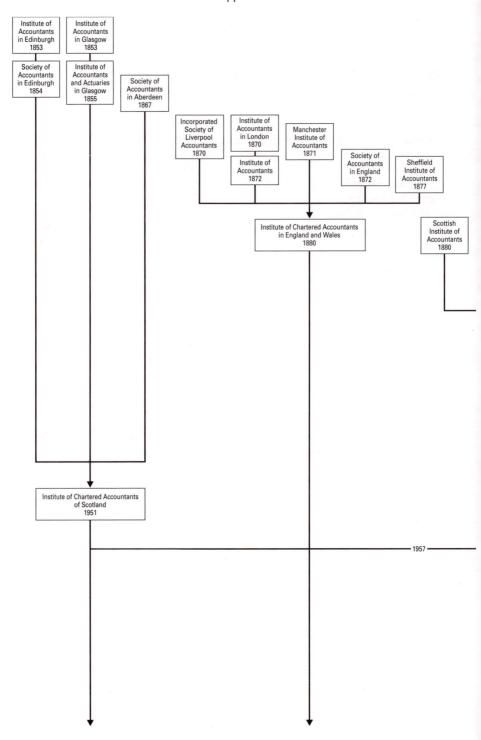

Formation and amalgamation of chartered accountancy bodies

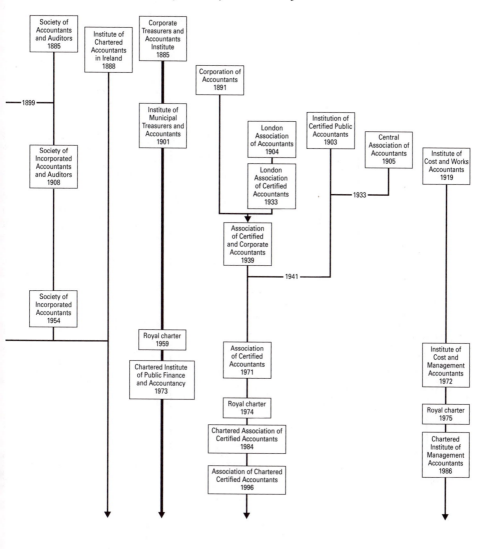

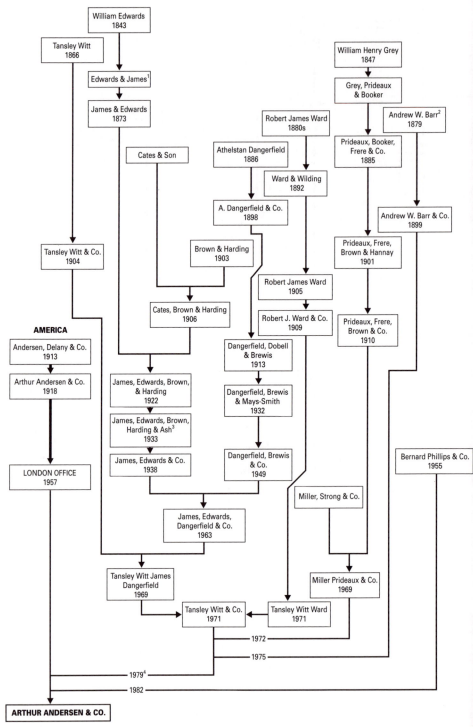

Arthur Andersen & Co.

Arthur Andersen & Co.

Additional information: From October 1994 seven BDO Binder Hamlyn offices became part of the Arthur Andersen Worldwide Organization following protracted merger discussions. The seven retain the Binder Hamlyn name, and in London continue to operate from their own offices (*Accountancy*, Nov. 1994: 13). See BDO Binder Hamlyn.

Notes:

1. Alfred Augustus James was president of the ICAEW 1902–3.
2. Andrew Wallace Barr was president of the Society of Incorporated Accountants 1898–1901.
3. Harold Garton Ash OBE MC was president of the ICAEW 1950–1.
4. The London, Bristol, Gloucester, Liverpool, Manchester, and Worcester offices amalgamated with Arthur Andersen & Co.; other offices merged with Binder Hamlyn, Arthur Young, Price Waterhouse, and Coopers & Lybrand.

Sources: *Arthur Andersen & Co: The First 60 Years 1913–1973* (1974); Leon Hopkins, *The Hundredth Year* (Macdonald & Evans, 1980); *The History of the ICAEW 1870–1965* (Heinemann, 1966); ICAEW List of Members 1881–1988; Incorporated Society List of Members 1887–1957; information supplied by Arthur Andersen & Co.

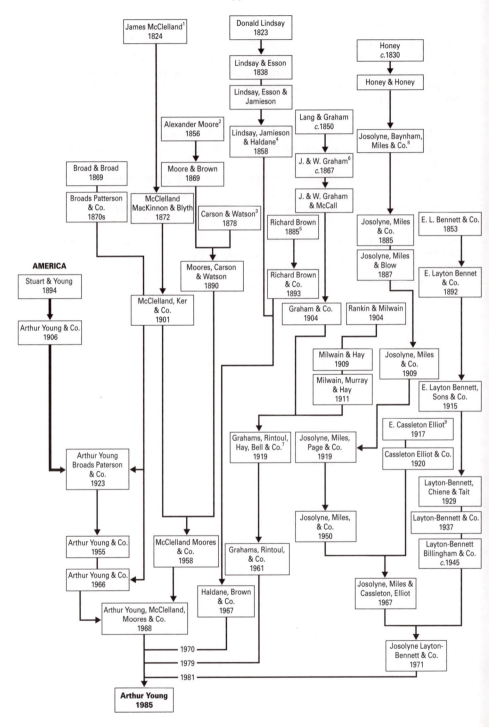

Arthur Young

Arthur Young

Additional information: Newton & Co. merged with Arthur Young & Company in 1965. Predecessor firms were: Baker & Gibson (in existence sometime before 1880); Baker, Gibson & Co. (1888); Gibson & Ashford (1895); and Newton & Co. (1945). Arthur Young merged with Ernst & Whinney in September 1989 to form Ernst & Young (*Accountancy*, Aug. 1989: 12). See Ernst and Whinney.

Notes:

1. James McClelland was the first president of the Institute of Accountants and Actuaries in Glasgow 1853–64, and his son Andrew S. McClelland was president 1900–3.
2. Alexander Moore was president of the Institute of Accountants and Actuaries in Glasgow 1884–7, and his son, also Alexander Moore, was president 1915–18.
3. D. S. Carson's son John F. Carson OBE (mil.) VD was the last president of the Institute of Accountants and Actuaries in Glasgow 1950–1.
4. James Haldane was president of the Society of Accountants in Edinburgh 1895–8, and his son H. W. Haldane was president 1934–7.
5. Richard Brown was president of the Society of Accountants in Edinburgh 1916–18.
6. John Graham was president of the Institute of Accountants and Actuaries in Glasgow 1881–4.
7. Peter Rintoul was president of the Institute of Accountants and Actuaries in Glasgow 1928–30. Sir David Allan Hay KBE was president of the Institute of Accountants and Actuaries in Glasgow 1944–6 and president of the ICAS 1952–3.
8. Algernon Osmond Miles was president of the ICAEW 1909–10.
9. Edward Cassleton Elliott CBE was president of the Society of Incorporated Accountants 1932–5.

Sources: J. C. Stewart, *Pioneers of a Profession* (ICAS, 1977); *The History of the ICAEW 1870–1965* (Heinemann, 1966); A. A. Garrett, *History of the Society of Incorporated Accountants 1885–1957* (OUP, 1961); *A History of the Chartered Accountants of Scotland from the Earliest Times to 1954* (ICAS, 1954); *Arthur Young and the Business he Founded* (1948); ICAEW List of Members 1881–1988; Incorporated Society List of Members 1887–1957; Scottish Chartered Accountants Official Directory 1896–1988; information supplied by Arthur Young.

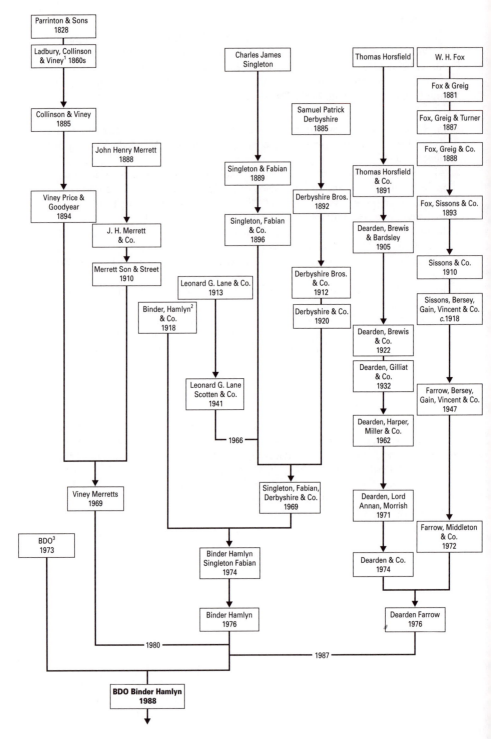

BDO Binder Hamlyn

BDO Binder Hamlyn

Additional information: The 24 offices of BDO Binder Hamlyn merged with Arthur Andersen (7), Stoy Hayward (13 and half of the Bristol office), Touche Ross (merged with Binder's Birmingham office and with half of its Bristol office), and Grant Thornton (2) (*Accountancy*, Aug. 1994: 13; Nov. 1994: 13). The Binder offices coming under the Arthur Andersen Worldwide umbrella 'will continue to use the Binder Hamlyn name' (*Accountancy*, Nov. 1994: 13). See Arthur Andersen, Grant Thornton, Stoy Hayward, and Touche Ross.

Notes:
1. George Herbert Ladbury was a member of the first council of the ICAEW.
2. Bernhard Heymann Binder was president of the ICAEW 1948–9.
3. Binder Dijker Otte (BDO) was an international group of accounting firms consisting of Binder Hamlyn (UK), Dijker en Doornbos (the Netherlands and Belgium), and Deutsche Warentreuland (Germany), whose managing partner was Hans Heinrich Otte.

Sources: *The History of the ICAEW 1870–1965* (Heinemann, 1966); *Viney Merretts: Chartered Accountants for 150 Years in the City of London*; Michael Shirley-Beavan, 'Success Story of the First Euro-accountants', *Accountancy Age* (7 Dec. 1979), 26–7; *Accountancy* (Oct. 1988), 8; ICAEW List of Members 1881–1988; information supplied by BDO Binder Hamlyn.

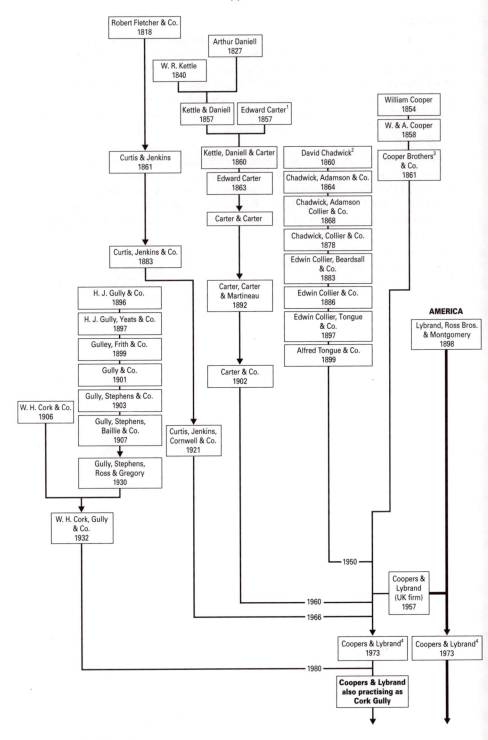

Coopers & Lybrand

Coopers & Lybrand

Additional information: Fisher, Randle, Kemp, Sendell & Co. (formed 1934) amalgamated with Carter & Co. in 1946. Predecessors of the former firm were: Walter Newton Fisher (who commenced practice sometime before 1880); Fisher & Randle (1885); and Fisher, Randle & Fisher (1893). In 1954, Francis Nicholls, White & Co. merged with W. H. Cork, Gully & Co. The firm of Nicholls & Leatherdale, in existence sometime before 1872, subsequently became Francis Nicholls & Co. (1883); and Francis Nicholls, White & Co. (1887). Coopers & Lybrand merged with the UK firm of Deloitte Haskins & Sells with effect from 29 April 1990, with the business name Coopers & Lybrand Deloitte adopted from 15 January 1990 (*Accountancy*, Mar. 1990: 132). From 1 June 1992, Coopers & Lybrand Deloitte reverted to Coopers & Lybrand, due to 'confusion in the international marketplace' between it and Deloitte & Touche (*Accountancy*, May 1992: 16). See Deloitte Haskins & Sells.

Notes:
1. Edward Carter was a member of the first council of the ICAEW.
2. David Chadwick was the first president of the Manchester Institute of Accountants 1871, and was a member of the first council of the ICAEW.
3. Arthur Cooper was a member of the first council of the ICAEW and its president 1883–4. His brother Ernest Cooper was president of the ICAEW 1899–1901.
4. McDonald, Currie & Co., Canada (founded 1910), and other firms also adopted the name Coopers & Lybrand in 1973 as members of Coopers & Lybrand (International), an international association of firms.

Sources: *A History of the Cooper Brothers & Co. 1854–1954*; *LRB & M. Journal*, 39/1 (Jan.–Mar. 1958); *The History of the ICAEW 1870–1965* (Heinemann, 1966); R. H. Parker (ed.), *British Accountants: A Biographical Sourcebook* (Arno, 1980); ICAEW List of Members 1881–1988; information supplied by Coopers & Lybrand.

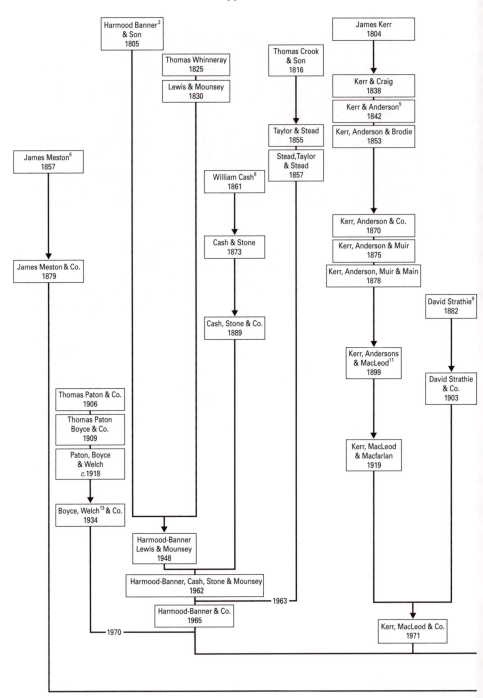

Deloitte Haskins & Sells

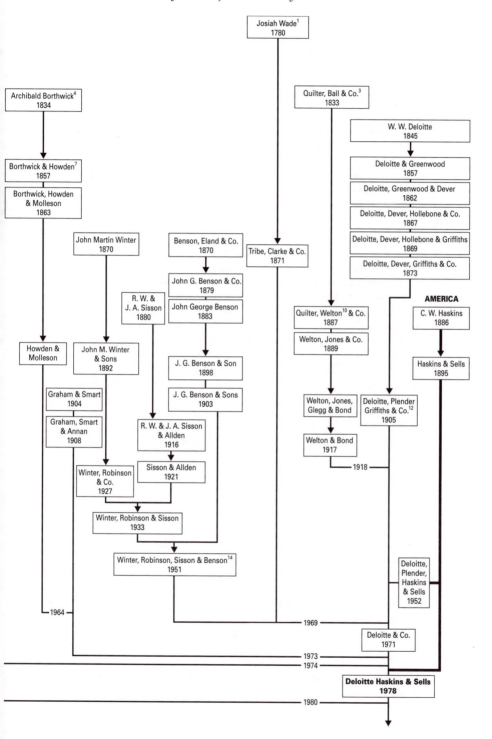

Deloitte Haskins & Sells

Additional information: Hodsoll & House (formed 1934, with predecessor firms: Payne & Henry, prior to 1880; Alfred Henry, 1887; Henry & Hodsoll, 1892; and Sydney Hodsoll, 1900) amalgamated with Lewis & Mounsey in 1941. Gilbert Shepherd, Owen & Co. amalgamated with Harmood Banner & Co. in 1973. The former firm dates back to the pre-1894 period when David Shepherd commenced practice. Subsequent name changes were: Gilbert David Shepherd (1905); Shepherd, Howell & Co. (1910); and Gilbert Shepherd, Owen & Co. (1922). The UK firm of Deloitte Haskins & Sells merged with Coopers & Lybrand with effect from 29 April 1990, to form Coopers & Lybrand Deloitte, though the Deloitte name was dropped two years later (*Accountancy*, Mar. 1990: 132; May 1992: 16). The UK practice of Touche Ross changed its name to Deloitte & Touche with effect from 1 February 1996 (*Accountancy*, Feb. 1996: 13). See Coopers & Lybrand and Touche Ross.

Notes:

1. Josiah Wade is probably the oldest firm to trace its continuous existence.
2. Harmood Banner's son H. W. Banner was a founding member and president of the Incorporated Society of Liverpool Accountants 1870, and his grandson John Sutherland Harmood-Banner was president of the ICAEW 1904–5.
3. William Quilter was a founding member of the Institute of Accountants in London (1870) and its president 1870–7. John Ball was a founding member of the Institute of Accountants in London and a member of its first council.
4. Archibald Borthwick was a founding member of the Society of Accountants in Edinburgh (1854) and a member of its first council.
5. Henry Kerr was a founding member of the Institute of Accountants and Actuaries in Glasgow (1853). William Anderson was a founding member of the Institute of Accountants and Actuaries in Glasgow, a member of its first council, and its president 1870–6.
6. James Meston was a founding member of the Society of Accountants in Aberdeen (1867) and its secretary and treasurer 1867–92.
7. James Howden FFA was secretary of the Society of Accountants in Edinburgh 1863–92 and its president 1892–5. His grandson John M. Howden DL JP was president 1922–5.
8. William Cash was a member of the first council of the ICAEW and his son, also William Cash, was president of the ICAEW 1921–3.
9. David Strathie was president of the Institute of Accountants and Actuaries in Glasgow 1918–20.
10. Thomas Abercrombie Welton was a member of the first council of the ICAEW and its president 1891–2.
11. Sir John M. MacLeod Bt. DL LLD was president of the Institute of Accountants and Actuaries in Glasgow 1926–8.
12. William Welch Deloitte was a member of the first council of the Institute of Accountants in London (1870), and of the ICAEW's first council, and president of the ICAEW 1888–9. John George Griffiths was a member of the first council of the ICAEW and president 1897–9. Sir William Plender Bt. GBE (later Lord Plender) was president of the ICAEW 1910–11, 1911–12, 1929–30.
13. Charles William Boyce CBE was president of the ICAEW 1951–2.

14. Robert Pearson Winter CBE MC TD DL was president of the ICAEW 1963–4.

Sources: James Kilpatrick, *Deloitte, Plender, Griffiths & Co.* (Wyman & Sons, 1942); *Deloitte & Co., 1845–1956* (1957); *Deloittes Newsletter*, 1 May 1974; *Haskins & Sells: The First Seventy-Five Years* (1970); *The History of the ICAEW 1870–1965* (Heinemann, 1966); J. C. Stewart, *Pioneers of a Profession* (ICAS, 1977); *A History of the Chartered Accountants of Scotland from the Earliest Times to 1954* (ICAS, 1954); *Dictionary of Business Biography* (Butterworths, 1985); ICAEW List of Members 1881–1988; ICAS Official Directory 1896–1985; information supplied by Deloitte Haskins & Sells.

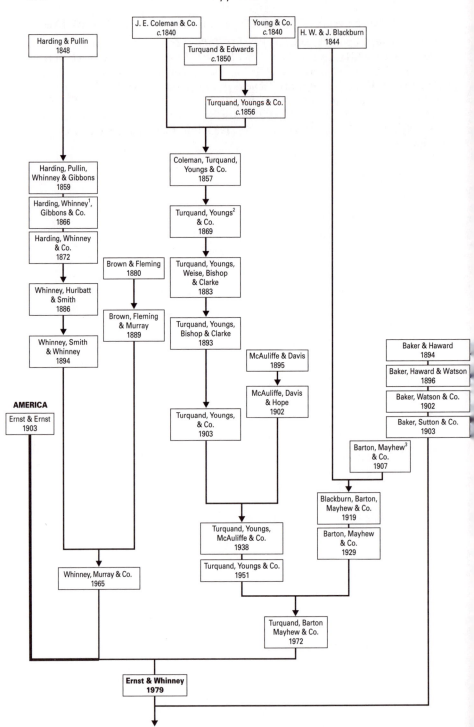

Ernst & Whinney

Ernst & Whinney

Additional information: Ernst & Whinney merged with Arthur Young in September 1989 to form Ernst & Young (*Accountancy*, Aug. 1989: 12). See Arthur Young.

Notes:

1. Robert Palmer Harding was a member of the first council of the Institute of Accountants in London (1870) and of the ICAEW's first council. He was the first vice-president of the ICAEW and its president 1882–3. Frederick Whinney was a member of the first council of the ICAEW and its president 1884–8. His son Sir Arthur Francis Whinney KBE was president 1926–7. J. B. Gibbons was a founding member of the Institute of Accountants in London and a member of its first council.

2. William Turquand was a founding member of the Institute of Accountants in London and a member of its first council. He was the first vice-president and from 1877 president of the old Institute. Turquand was a petitioner for the royal charter of the ICAEW, a member of its first council, and its first president 1880–2. John Young was a founding member of the Institute of Accountants in London and a member of its first council. He was also a member of the first council of the ICAEW.

3. Harold Montague Barton was president of the ICAEW 1944–5.

Sources: Edgar Jones, *Accountancy and the British Economy 1840–1980: The Evolution of Ernst & Whinney* (Batsford, 1981); *The Story of Baker, Sutton & Co.* (1978); *The History of the ICAEW 1870–1965* (Heinemann, 1966); ICAEW List of Members 1881–1988.

Finnie & Co.

Additional information: Prior to setting up his own accountancy practice, A. E. Woodington had worked with his father Ebenezer, who began to practise in 1866. The practice remained an independent firm once A. E. Woodington had left (*Accountancy*, Mar. 1990: 134). The name Finnie & Co. disappeared on the firm's merger with Stoy Hayward on 1 July 1992, the new firm adopting the latter designation (*Accountancy*, July 1992: 11). See Stoy Hayward.

Notes:

1. Arthur Edwin Woodington was president of the Society of Incorporated Accountants 1916–19.

2. Ebenezer Carr was president of the Society of Incorporated Accountants 1890–4.

3. Arthur Edward Green was president of the Society of Incorporated Accountants 1910–13.

4. Richard Alfred Witty was president of the Society of Incorporated Accountants 1942–5.

Sources: *A History of Pannell Fitzpatrick & Co.* (Pannell Kerr Forster, 1980); A. A. Garrett, *History of the Society of Incorporated Accountants 1885–1957* (OUP, 1961); ICAEW List of Members 1881–1988; Incorporated Society List of Members 1887–1957; ICAS Official Directory 1896–1985; information supplied by Finnie & Co.

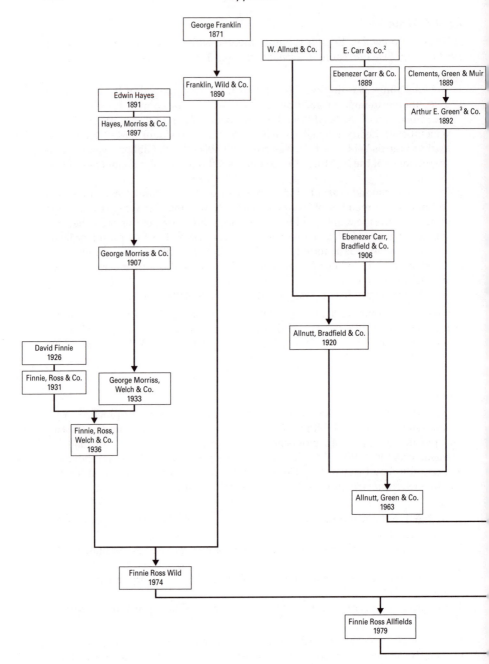

Finnie & Co.

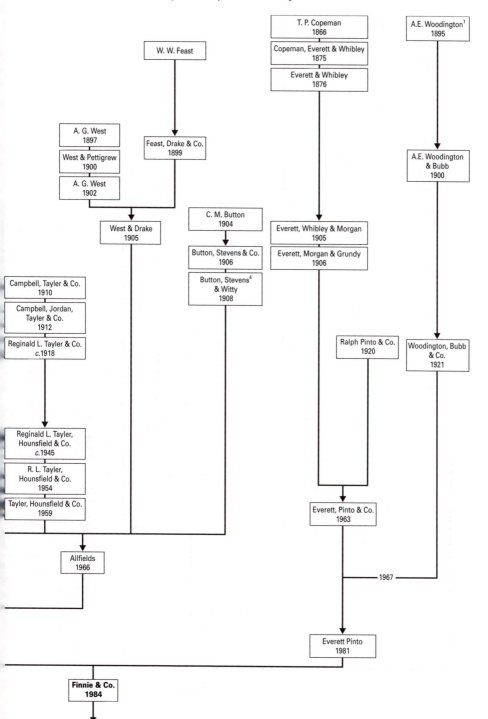

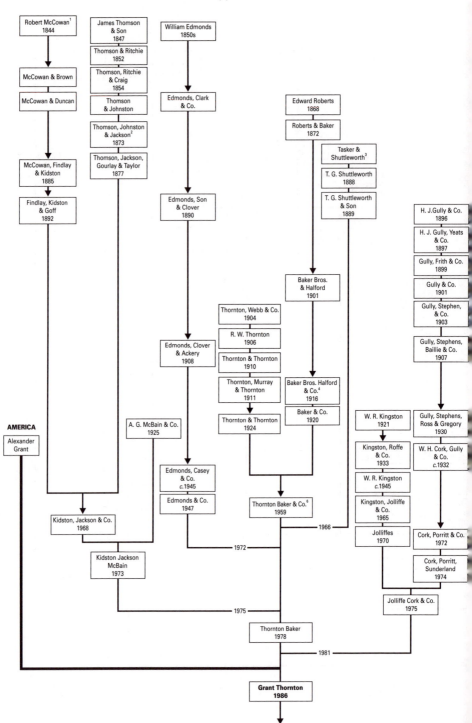

Grant Thornton

Grant Thornton

Additional information: As part of the 1994 merger of BDO Binder Hamlyn, Grant Thornton took over Binder's Northern Ireland offices in Belfast and Enniskillen (*Accountancy*, Aug. 1994: 13).

Notes:

1. Robert McCowan was active in the formation of the Institute of Accountants and Actuaries in Glasgow (1853) and was treasurer 1864–80.
2. Thomas Jackson was president of the Institute of Accountants and Actuaries in Glasgow 1903–6.
3. Thomas George Shuttleworth was a founder member of the Sheffield Institute of Accountants (1877), its first secretary, and a member of the first council of the ICAEW.
4. Baker Bros., Halford & Co. continued in practice in Leicester until 1974 when it merged with Thomson McLintock & Co.
5. The insolvency practices of W. H. Cork, Gully & Co., and Coopers & Lybrand merged in July 1980 to form Cork Gully.
6. Thornton Baker & Co. has developed somewhat differently from other large firms. As a result, some 50 practices have amalgamated with the firm since 1959. Most of these were relatively small regional practices which did not meet the criteria for inclusion in the firm's simplified family tree, although they have often had long and distinguished histories in their own areas.

Sources: *The History of the ICAEW 1870–1965* (Heinemann, 1966); J. C. Stewart, *Pioneers of a Profession* (ICAS, 1977); A. M. Hoe, *The First Hundred Years: Centenary 1877–1977* (Sheffield and District Society of Chartered Accountants, 1977); Rex Winsbury, *Thomson McLintock & Co.: The First Hundred Years* (1977); *C. & L. Journal*, 35 (Dec. 1980); Sir Kenneth Cork, *Cork on Cork* (Macmillan, 1988); ICAEW List of Members 1881–1988; ICAS Official Directory 1896–1985; information supplied by Grant Thornton.

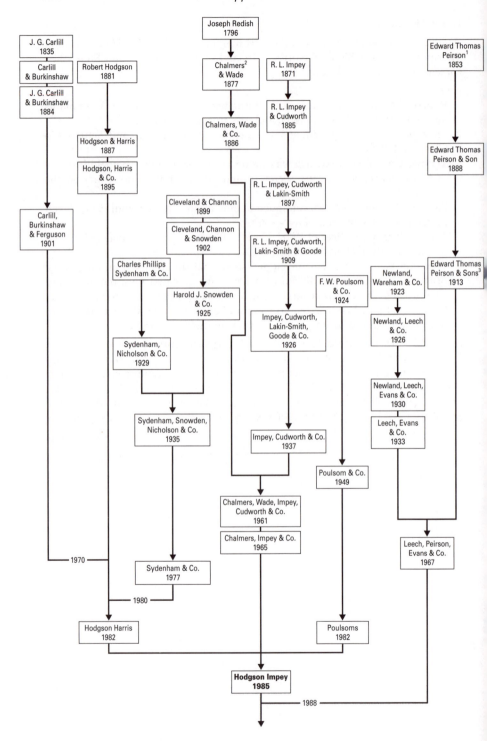

Hodgson Impey

Hodgson Impey

Additional information: Chalmers, Wade, Voisey & Co. (formed 1956, with the following predecessor firms: Joseph Davies & Co., formed sometime before 1872; Davies, Voisey & Davies, pre-1880; Lewis Voisey, 1883; Voisey & Worthington, 1895; Louis Adrian Voisey, 1898; and L. A. Voisey & Co., 1934) became part of Chalmers, Wade, Impey, Cudworth & Co. in 1961 (*Accountancy*, Mar. 1990: 134). With effect from 1 May 1990, the firms of Hodgson Impey and Kidsons merged to form Kidsons Impey (*Accountancy*, Apr. 1990: 8). Three Humberside offices of Hodgson Impey joined the Yorkshire practice of Price Waterhouse from 1 April 1990 and did not take part in the otherwise national merger with Kidsons (*Accountancy*, Mar. 1990: 10). See Kidsons and Price Waterhouse.

Notes:

1. Edward Thomas Peirson was a member of the first council of the ICAEW.
2. Anthony Wigham Chalmers was a founding member of the Incorporated Society of Liverpool Accountants, the first English body of accountants, a signatory in 1870 to its Memorandum of Incorporation, its first secretary, and the president 1878–94. He was a petitioner for the charter of the ICAEW and a member of the first council.
3. The name Edward Thomas Peirson & Sons continues as a practice in Market Harborough.

Sources: *The History of the ICAEW 1870–1965* (Heinemann, 1966); Ian Hargraves, *The Liverpool Society of Chartered Accountants Centenary 1870–1970* (1970); ICAEW List of Members 1881–1988; information supplied by Hodgson Impey.

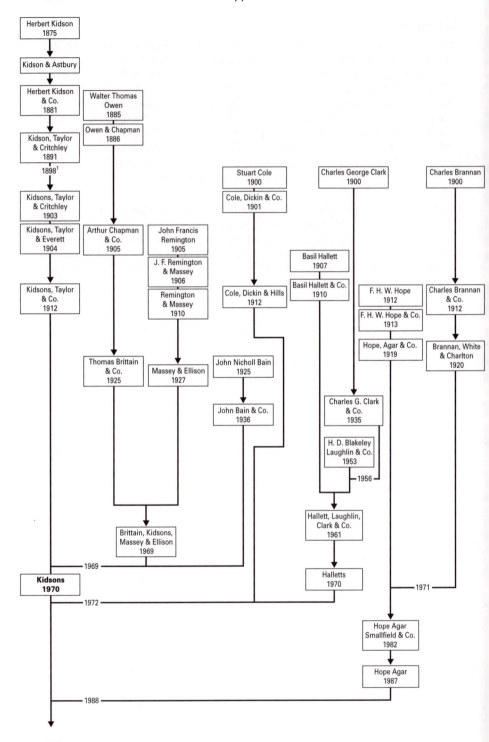

Kidsons

Kidsons

Additional information: On 1 May 1990, Kidsons Impey was formed from the merger of Kidsons with all but three Humberside offices of Hodgson Impey (*Accountancy*, Mar. 1990: 10) See Hodgson Impey.

Note:

1. The London office of Kidson, Taylor & Critchley was opened in 1898.

Sources: Jonathan Grosvenor (ed.), *The Ivanhoe Guide to Chartered Accountants 1989* (Ivanhoe, 1988); ICAEW List of Members 1881–1988; ICAS Official Directory 1896–1985; Incorporated Society List of Members 1887–1957; information supplied by Kidsons.

Pannell Kerr Forster

Additional information: The predecessor firms of Harris, Kerr, Forster & Co. (dating from 1933) were as follows: Harris, Allan & Co. (1911); Harris, Kerr & Co. (1919); and Harris, Kerr & Cook (1920) (*Accountancy*, Mar. 1990: 134).

Notes:

1. James Charles Bolton was a member of the first council of the ICAEW.
2. John Ball Ball was president of the ICAEW 1908–9.
3. John William Woodthorpe was president of the ICAEW 1919–20.
4. George Stanhope Pitt was president of the Society of Incorporated Accountants 1923–6.
5. Thomas Keens, later Sir Thomas, was president of the Society of Incorporated Accountants 1926–9.
6. Keens Shay Keens continues as the name of a practice based in Luton, Bedford, Hitchin, and Milton Keynes.
7. The Liverpool practice of Lithgow, Nelson & Co. was acquired in 1972. Bertram Nelson CBE was president of the Society of Incorporated Accountants 1954–6, and his father Charles Hewetson Nelson was president 1913–16. Lithgow, Nelson & Co. continues as the name of a practice based in London and Southport.

   The Sheffield practice of Knox, Franklin & Co. became an associated firm of Pannell Fitzpatrick & Co. in 1972. George Walter Knox, later Sir George, was a member of the first council of the Sheffield Institute of Accountants (1877), a member of the first council of the ICAEW, and its president 1896–7. The name Knox survives in the London practice of Knox Cropper.

Sources: *A History of Pannell Fitzpatrick & Co.* (Pannell Kerr Forster, 1980); R. H. Parker (ed.), *British Accountants: A Biographical Sourcebook* (Arno, 1980); *Dictionary of Business Biography* (Butterworths, 1985); Alan Hoe, 'Sheffield Scores a Century', *Accountants Weekly* (22 Apr. 1977), 23; *Accountant* (22 May 1875), 1; *Accountancy* (Feb. 1989), 10; *Accountants Weekly* (7 Nov. 1980), 3; ICAEW List of Members 1881–1988; Incorporated Society List of Members 1887–1957; information supplied by Pannell Kerr Forster and Ball Baker Leake.

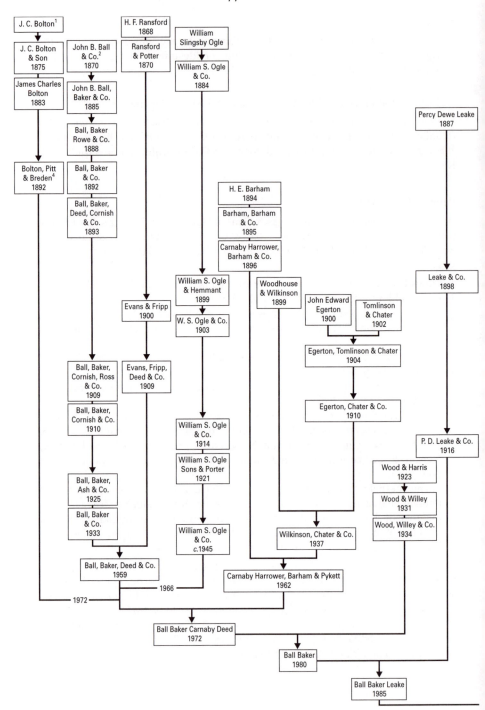

Pannell Kerr Forster

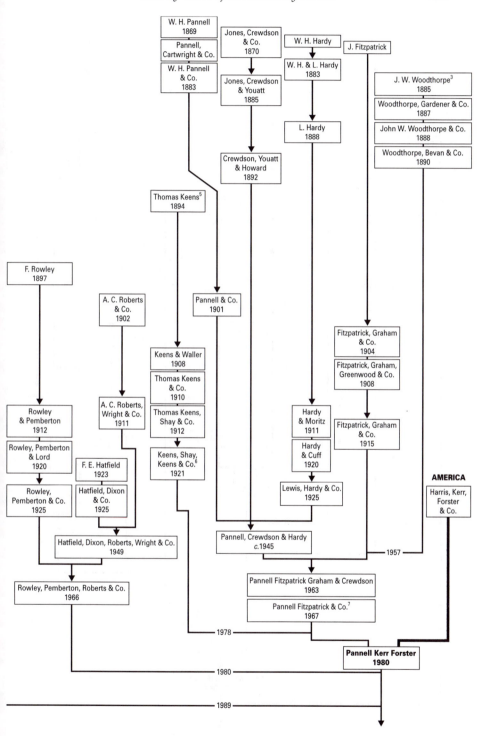

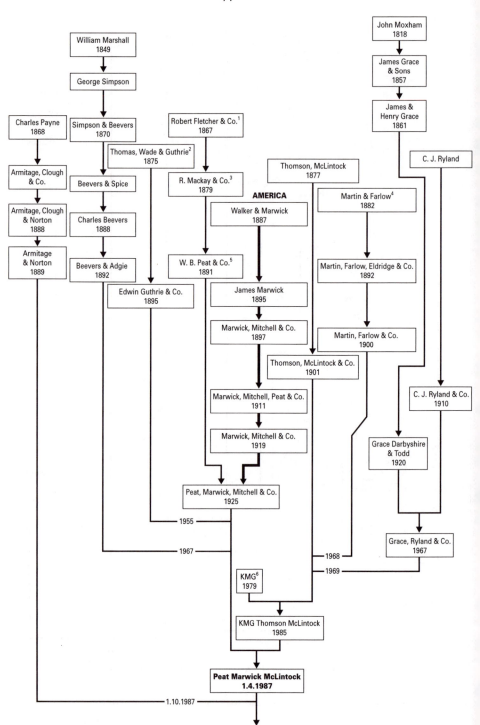

Peat Marwick McLintock

Peat Marwick McLintock

Additional information: Peat Marwick McLintock changed its name to KPMG Peat Marwick from October 1991 (Boys, 1994: 22). Since March 1995, 'on the grounds of international consistency', the designation KPMG has been adopted (*Accountancy*, Mar. 1995: 25).

Notes:

1. Robert Fletcher was one of the twelve original members of the Society of Accountants in Aberdeen (1867) and its president 1875–7.
2. Charles Henry Wade and Edwin Guthrie formed the Accountants' Incorporation Association in 1878. Both were petitioners for the charter of the ICAEW and members of its first council. Barrow, Wade, Guthrie & Co., founded in 1883, was the first British accountancy firm in New York. Guthrie was also involved in the formation of the American Association of Public Accountants, a predecessor of the AICPA.
3. Roderick Mackay was a member of the first council of the ICAEW.
4. Sir James Martin MBE was secretary of the Society of Incorporated Accountants 1886–1919, president 1922–3, and again in 1935 for the 50th anniversary celebration.
5. William Barclay Peat was president of the ICAEW 1906–8, and his son Charles Urie Peat MC MA was president 1959–60.
6. Klynveld Main Goerdeler (KMG) was an international group of accountancy firms consisting, among others, of Klynveld Kraayenhof (the Netherlands), Main Lafrentz & Co. (USA). Dr Reinhard Goerdeler, of Germany, was chairman.

Sources: Kenneth Morrison, 'PMM in the Past: The Founders', *PMM Platform* (Summer 1980), 24–5; T. A. Wise, *Peat, Marwick, Mitchell & Co.: 85 Years* (1982); Rex Winsbury, *Thomson McLintock & Co.: The First Hundred Years* (1977); *The History of the ICAEW 1870–1965* (Heinemann, 1966); J. Kitchen and R. H. Parker, *Accounting Thought and Education: Six English Pioneers* (ICAEW, 1980); R. H. Parker (ed.), *British Accountants: A Biographical Sourcebook* (Arno, 1980); *Accountancy Age*, various issues; ICAEW List of Members 1881–1988; Incorporated Society List of Members 1887–1957; information supplied by Peat Marwick McLintock.

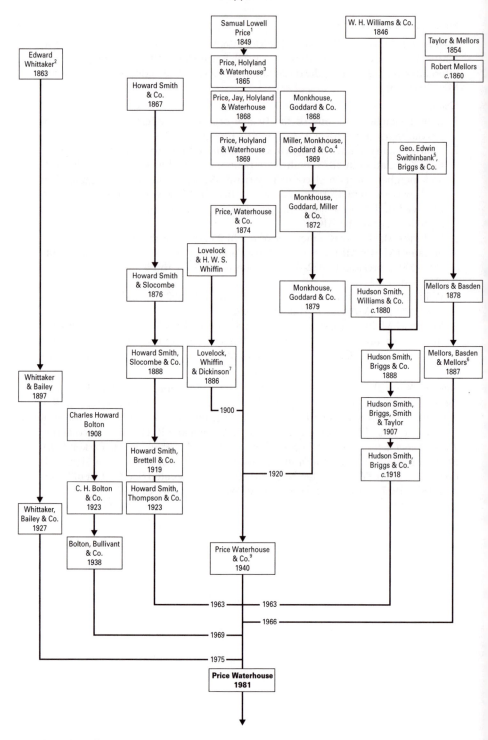

Price Waterhouse

Price Waterhouse

Additional information: The Hull, Grimsby, and Beverley offices of Hodgson Impey joined Price Waterhouse from 1 April 1990 (*Accountancy*, Mar. 1990: 10). See Hodgson Impey.

Notes:

1. Samuell Lowell Price was a founding member of the Institute of Accountants in London (1870), a member of its first council, and a member of the ICAEW's first council.
2. Edward Whittaker was a member of the first permanent general council of the Society of Incorporated Accountants.
3. Edwin Waterhouse set up in practice on his own in 1864. He was president of the ICAEW 1892–4; his son Sir Nicholas Edwin Waterhouse KBE was president 1928–9.
4. Miller, Monkhouse, Goddard & Co. petitioned the Institute of Accountants in London in 1871 to change its rules so as to admit provincial accountants. The petition was successful, and in 1872 the renamed Institute of Accountants became a national body.
5. George Edwin Swithinbank was a member of the first council of the ICAEW.
6. Thomas Galland Mellors was president of the ICAEW 1924–5.
7. Arthur Lowes Dickinson was a leading figure in the development of the American profession.
8. Clare Smith was president of the ICAEW 1932–3.
9. Comma omitted when heading redesigned to fit smaller sheet of notepaper necessitated by the war.

Sources: G. E. Richards, *History of the Firm: The First Fifty Years 1850–1900* (1950); *Reporter* (Price Waterhouse), 50 (Dec. 1987); *The First 100 Years 1867–1967: Howard Smith Thompson & Co.* (1967); *Dictionary of Business Biography* (Butterworths, 1986); *The History of the ICAEW 1870–1965* (Heinemann, 1966); S. A. Middleton, *A History of the Northern Society of Chartered Accountants* (1982); ICAEW List of Members 1881–1988; information supplied by Price Waterhouse.

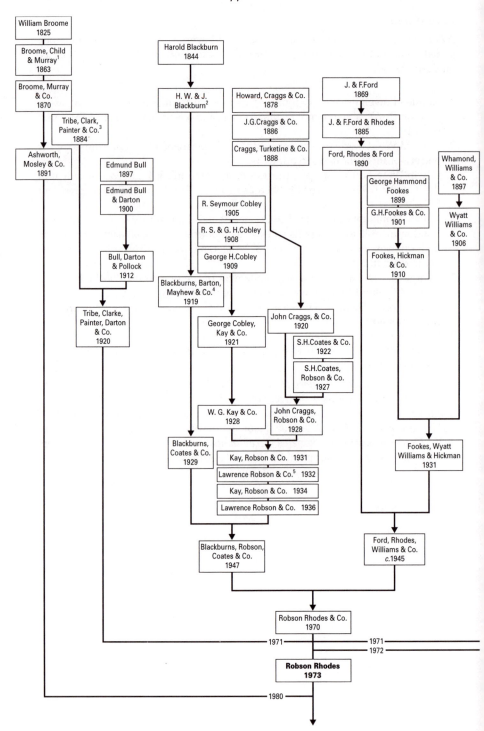

Robson Rhodes

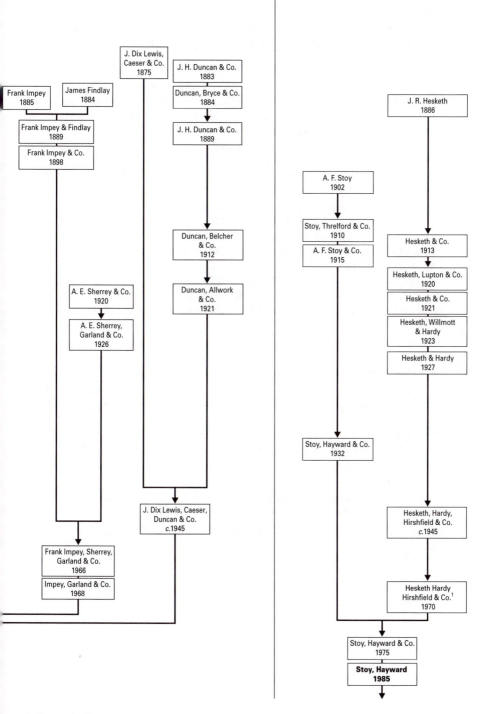

| | | J. Dix Lewis, Caeser & Co. 1875 | | | | | | J. R. Hesketh 1886 |

Robson Rhodes   *Stoy Hayward*

Robson Rhodes

Notes:

1. Adam Murray was a founding member of the Manchester Institute of Accountants in 1871. He was the joint author with Roger Carter of the first textbook on income tax.
2. John Blackburn was a member of the first council of the ICAEW. His son J. H. Blackburn was a member of council for a record 51 years.
3. Tribe, Clarke & Co. was founded in 1780 in Bristol and this office merged with Deloitte Haskins & Sells in 1969. The London office, under the style Tribe, Clarke, Painter & Co., was opened in 1884.
4. Barton, Mayhew & Co., after subsequent mergers, became part of Ernst & Whinney.
5. Lawrence Robson was president of the Institute of Cost and Management Accountants 1950–1.

Sources: David Harvey, 'Robson Rhodes: From One Client to World Prominence', *Accountants Weekly* (11 Oct. 1974), 20–1; J. Allured, 'A Short History of Ashworth, Mosley & Co., Chartered Accountants, Manchester, 1825–1980' (typescript, 1980); Edgar Jones, *Accounting and the British Economy 1840–1980: The Evolution of Ernst & Whinney* (Batsford, 1981); obituary of J. Dix Lewis, *Accountant* (4 Apr. 1914), 516; obituary of Thomas Turketine, *Accountant* (19 Sept. 1936), 390; *The History of the ICAEW 1870–1965* (Heinemann, 1966); ICAEW List of Members 1881–1988; Incorporated Society List of Members 1887–1957; information supplied by Robson Rhodes.

Stoy Hayward

Additional information: Stoy Hayward merged with Finnie & Co. on 1 July 1992, with the merged firm retaining the Stoy Hayward name (*Accountancy*, July 1992: 11). In August 1994 thirteen BDO Binder Hamlyn offices merged with Stoy Hayward to form BDO Stoy Hayward; in addition, Binder's Bristol office divided itself between Stoy Hayward and Touche Ross (*Accountancy*, Aug. 1994: 13). See BDO Binder Hamlyn and Finnie & Co.

Note:

1. Hesketh Hardy Hirshfield & Co. introduced the international connection of Horwath & Horwath to Stoy Hayward.

Sources: ICAEW List of Members 1881–1988; information supplied by Stoy Hayward.

Appendix

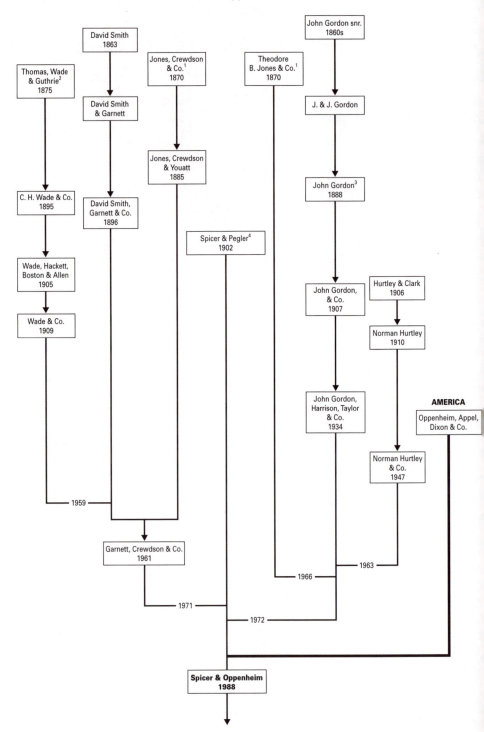

Spicer & Oppenheim

Spicer & Oppenheim

Additional information: Spicer and Oppenheim merged with Touche Ross on 1 August 1990, with the merged firm retaining the name Touche Ross (*Accountancy*, Aug. 1990: 7). See Touche Ross.

Notes:

1. Jones, Crewdson & Co. (Manchester) and Theodore B. Jones & Co. (Leeds) were both founded by Theodore Brooke Jones, the grandson of Edward Thomas Jones, who published his famous *Jones's English System of Book-keeping* in 1796.
2. Charles Henry Wade and Edwin Guthrie formed the Accountants' Incorporation Association in 1878. Both were petitioners for the charter of the ICAEW and members of its first council.
3. John Gordon was president of the ICAEW 1920–1.
4. Ernest Evan Spicer and Ernest C. Pegler are best remembered for their association with H. Foulks Lynch & Co. and in particular their textbooks.

Sources: R. H. Parker (ed.), *British Accountants: A Biographical Sourcebook* (Arno, 1980); *Accountancy* (July 1988), 7; *Dictionary of Business Biography* (Butterworths, 1985); obituary of John Gordon, *Accountant* (2 Jan. 1926), 10; *The History of the ICAEW 1870–1965* (Heinemann, 1966); ICAEW List of Members 1881–1988; information supplied by Spicer & Oppenheim.

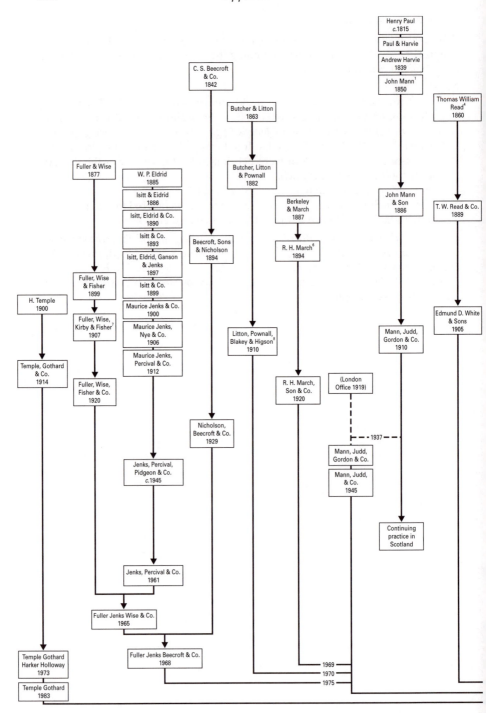

Touche Ross & Co.

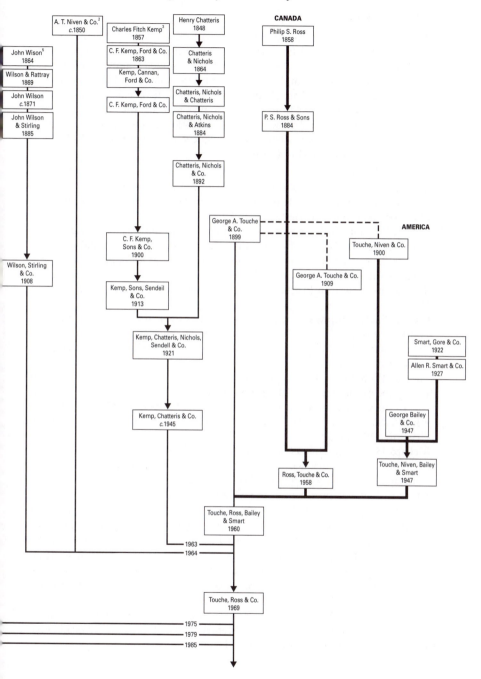

Touche Ross & Co.

Additional information: Touche Ross merged with Spicer & Oppenheim on 1 August 1990, with the merged firm retaining the Touche Ross name (*Accountancy*, Aug. 1990: 7). As part of the 1994 merger of BDO Binder Hamlyn, Touche Ross merged with Binder's Birmingham office and with half of its Bristol office (*Accountancy*, Nov. 1994: 13). The UK practice of Touche Ross changed its name to Deloitte & Touche with effect from 1 February 1996 to bring 'the firm into line with other members of the world-wide organisation, Deloitte Touche Tohmatsu International' (*Accountancy*, Feb. 1996: 13). See Spicer & Oppenheim, BDO Binder Hamlyn, and Deloitte Haskins & Sells.

Notes:
1. John Mann, Sr., was a founding member of the Institute of Accountants and Actuaries in Glasgow (1853) and its president 1906–9. He was the last survivor of the original members on his death 1910.
2. Alexander Thomas Niven was a founder member of the Society of Accountants in Edinburgh (1854), and by 1912 the sole survivor of the original members. George A. Touche was articled to Niven and in 1900 founded the American practice Touche, Niven & Co. with Niven's son John B. Niven, who was president of the American Institute of Accountants, the forerunner of the AICPA, 1924–5.
3. Charles Fitch Kemp was a founding member of the Institute of Accountants in London (1870), and a member of its first council. He was a member of the first council of the ICAEW and its president 1894–6. His son Harold Fitch Kemp was president 1930–1.
4. Thomas William Read was a prominent member of the Incorporated Society of Liverpool Accountants (1870) and its secretary 1872–83. He played an active role in the formation of the ICAEW and was a member of its first council.
5. John Wilson was president of the Institute of Accountants and Actuaries in Glasgow 1897–1900.
6. Richard Henry March was president of the ICAEW 1927–8.
7. Sir Horace Woodburn Kirby was president of the ICAEW 1913–16. Frank Lindsay Fisher CBE was president of the ICAEW 1937–8.
8. James Blakey was president of the ICAEW 1953–4.

Sources: T. Swanson, *Touche Ross: A Biography* (1972); *Touche Ross Review* (Winter 1979/80); A. B. Richards, *Touche Ross & Co. 1899–1981* (1981); *TR Times* (June 1985); *Interim Account of a Going Concern: Some Essays on the History of Mann Judd & Company* (1967); Kemp, Chatteris & Co., 1957; obituary of Thomas William Read, *Accountant* (16 Feb. 1895), 154; Ernest Reckitt, *Reminiscences of Early Days of the Accounting Profession in Illinois* (Illinois Society of Certified Public Accountants, 1953); R. H. Parker (ed.), *British Accountants: A Biographical Sourcebook* (Arno, 1980); *The History of the ICAEW 1870–1965* (Heinemann, 1965); ICAEW List of Members 1881–1988; Incorporated Society List of Members 1887–1957; ICAS Official Directory 1896–1985; information supplied by Touche Ross & Co.

REFERENCES

ACCA (1996), *A World of Opportunities: Careers in Finance*, London: ACCA.

ALDCROFT, D. H. (1992), *Education, Training and Economic Performance, 1944 to 1990*, Manchester: Manchester University Press.

ALFORD, B. W. E. (1973), *W. D. and H. O. Wills and the Development of the UK Tobacco Industry 1786–1965*, London: Methuen.

ALLEN, G. C. (1964), *A Short Economic History of Modern Japan 1867–1937*, London: Allen & Unwin.

ALLURED, J. (1980), *A Short History of Ashworth Mosley & Co., Chartered Accountants: Manchester 1825–1980*, unpublished MS.

The Alphabetical Compendium of Scotch Mercantile Sequestrations 1851 (1852), London: Longman, Brown, Green & Longmans.

ANDERSON, G. (1976), *Victorian Clerks*, Manchester: Manchester University Press.

ANDERSON, M. (1994), 'The Representation of Accountants and Other Professionals on the Boards of UK Companies, 1893–1993', unpublished M. Phil. thesis, University of Wales, College of Cardiff.

——EDWARDS, J. R., and MATTHEWS, D. (1996), 'A Study of the Quoted Company Audit Market in 1886', *Accounting, Business and Financial History*, 6 (3).

————(1997), 'Accountability in a Free Market Economy: The British Company Audit 1886', *ABACUS*, 33 (1).

ANDERSON, R. C. (1981), *A History of Crosville Motor Services*, North Pomfret: David & Charles.

ARANYA, N. (1974), 'The Influence of Pressure Groups on Financial Statements in Britain', *ABACUS*, June.

ARMITAGE, E. P. (1994), personal correspondence dated 27 July 1994 with E. P. Armitage, director, education and training, at the ICAEW.

ARMSTRONG, P. (1985), 'Changing Management Control Strategies: The Role of Competition between Accountancy and Other Organisational Professions', *Accounting, Organizations and Society*, 10 (2).

——(1987), 'The Rise of Accounting Controls in British Capitalist Enterprises', *Accounting, Organizations and Society*, 12 (5).

Association of MBAs (1992), *Guide to Business Schools*, London: Pitman.

BABER, C., and BOYNS, T. (1985), 'Sir Julian Hodge (1904–): Banker', in D. J. Jeremy (ed.), *Dictionary of Business Biography*, iii, London: Butterworths.

'Back to an Age of Falling Prices' (1974), *The Economist*, 13 July.

Baker Sutton (1978), *The Story of Baker Sutton & Co.*, London: Baker Sutton & Co.

BANYARD, C. W. (1985), *The Institute of Cost and Management Accountants: A History*, London: ICMA.

BARKER, T. C. (1960), *Pilkington Brothers and the Glass Industry*, London: Allen & Unwin.

——(1977), *The Glassmakers; Pilkington: The Rise of an International Company 1826–1976*, London: Weidenfeld & Nicolson.

BARRY, B. (1989), 'Management Education in Great Britain', in W. Byrt (ed.), *Management Education: An International Survey*, London: Routledge.

BARTY-KING, H. (1979), *Girdle round the Earth: The Story of Cable and Wireless and its Predecessors to Mark the Group's Jubilee 1929–1979*, London: Heinemann.

BASKIN, J. B. (1988), 'The Development of Corporate Financial Markets in Britain and the United States, 1600–1914: Overcoming Asymmetric Information', *Business History Review*, 62 (2).

BASSIRIAN, H. (1996), 'Six of the Best', *Accountancy Age*, 12 Sept.

BATTERSBY, T. (1878), *The Perfect Double Entry Bookkeeper and the Perfect Prime Cost and Profit Demonstrator (on the Departmental System) for Iron and Brass Founders, Machinists, Engineers, Shipbuilders, Manufacturers. &c.*, London: John Heywood.

Begbie, Robinson, Cox & Knight (1937), *A Hundred Years of Accountancy, 1837–1937*, London: Begbie, Robinson, Cox & Knight.

BELLMAN, Sir H. (1949), *Bricks and Mortals: A Study of the Building Society Movement and the Story of the Abbey National Society 1849–1949*, London: Hutchinson.

BENSON, Sir H. (1989), *Accounting for Life*, London: Kogan Page.

[BENSON, H. A.] (1954), *A History of Cooper Brothers 1854–1954*, London: Batsford.

Bolckow, Vaughan & Co. Ltd. (NERRC), British Steel Corporation, North Eastern Regional Records Centre, Skippers Lane, Middlesbrough, location no. 04603.

BOSE, M. (1992), 'Mr Clean at the Coal Face', *Director*; July.

BOSWELL, J. S. (1983), *Business Policies in the Making: Three Steel Companies Compared*, London: Allen & Unwin.

BOUGEN, P. D. (1994), 'Joking Apart: The Serious Side to the Accountant Stereotype', *Accounting, Organizations and Society*, 19 (3).

BOUVIER, J. (1970), 'The Banking Mechanism in France in the Late Nineteenth Century', in R. Cameron (ed.), *Essays in French Economic History*, Homewood, Ill.: Richard D. Irwin.

BOYNS, T., and EDWARDS, J. R. (1995), 'Accounting Systems and Decision-Making in the Mid-Victorian Period: The Case of the Consett Iron Company', *Business History*, 37 (3).

————(1996), 'Change Agents and the Dissemination of Accounting Technology: Wales' Basic Industries, c.1750–c.1870', *Accounting History*, 1 (1).

————(1997a), 'The Construction of Costing Systems in Britain to 1900: The Case of the Coal, Iron and Steel Industries', *Business History*, 39 (3).

————(1997b), 'Cost and Management Accounting in Early-Victorian Britain: A Chandleresque Analysis?', *Management Accounting Research*, 8.

BOYS, P. (1989a), 'What's in a Name—Firms' Simplified Family Trees: Arthur Andersen & Co.', *Accountancy*, Jan.

——(1989b), 'What's in a Name—Firms' Simplified Family Trees: Arthur Young', *Accountancy*, Jan.

——(1989c), 'What's in a Name—Firms' Simplified Family Trees: BDO Binder Hamlyn', *Accountancy*, Feb.

——(1989d), 'What's in a Name—Firms' Simplified Family Trees: Coopers & Lybrand', *Accountancy*, Mar.

——(1989e), 'What's in a Name—Firms' Simplified Family Trees: Deloitte Haskins & Sells', *Accountancy*, Apr.

——(1989f), 'What's in a Name—Firms' Simplified Family Trees: Ernst & Whinney', *Accountancy*, May.

——(1989g), 'What's in a Name—Firms' Simplified Family Trees: Finnie & Co.', *Accountancy*, May.

Boys, P. (1989*h*), 'What's in a Name—Firms' Simplified Family Trees: Grant Thornton', *Accountancy*, June.

——(1989*i*), 'What's in a Name—Firms' Simplified Family Trees: Hodgson Impey', *Accountancy*, June.

——(1989*j*), 'What's in a Name—Firms' Simplified Family Trees: Kidsons', *Accountancy*, July.

——(1989*k*), 'What's in a Name—Firms' Simplified Family Trees: Pannell Kerr Forster', *Accountancy*, Sept.

——(1989*l*), 'What's in a Name—Firms' Simplified Family Trees: Peat Marwick McLintock', *Accountancy*, Sept.

——(1989*m*), 'What's in a Name—Firms' Simplified Family Trees: Price Waterhouse', *Accountancy*, Oct.

——(1989*n*), 'What's in a Name—Firms' Simplified Family Trees: Robson Rhodes', *Accountancy*, Oct.

——(1989*o*), 'What's in a Name—Firms' Simplified Family Trees: Stoy Hayward', *Accountancy*, Oct.

——(1989*p*), 'What's in a Name—Firms' Simplified Family Trees: Spicer & Oppenheim', *Accountancy*, Nov.

——(1989*q*), 'What's in a Name—Firms' Simplified Family Trees: Touche Ross & Co.', *Accountancy*, Dec.

——(1990*a*), 'Not Another Merger', *Accountancy*, Jan.

——(1990*b*), 'What's in a Name: Update', *Accountancy*, Mar.

——(1994), 'The Origins and Evolution of the Accountancy Profession', in W. Habgood (ed.), *Chartered Accountants in England and Wales: A Guide to Historical Records*, Manchester: Manchester University Press.

BPP (1842), *Royal Commission on the Employment of Women and Children in Mines*, BPP, 1842, xvii.

——(1849), Monteagle Committee. House of Lords Select Committee on the Audit of Railway Accounts. First, Second, and Third Reports, Minutes of Evidence and Appendix, BPP, 1849, x.

——(1877), Lowe Committee. Select Committee on the Companies Acts of 1862 and 1867. Report and Minutes of Evidence, BPP, 1877, viii.

——(1886), *Returns of Joint Stock Companies*, BPP, 1886, lx.

——(1902), *Returns of Joint Stock Companies*, BPP, 1902, xciv.

——(1913), *Census of Population*, BPP, 1913, lxxviii.

——(1936), *Report of the Departmental Committee Appointed by the Board of Trade, Registration of Accountants*, BPP, 1936, Cmd. 3645.

Briston, R. J. (1979), 'The UK Accountancy Profession: The Move towards Monopoly Power', *Accountant's Magazine*, Nov.

—— and Kedslie, M. J. M. (1986), 'Professional Formation: The Case of Scottish Accountants—Some Corrections and Some Further Thoughts', *British Journal of Sociology*, 37 (1).

Broadbridge, S. (1970), *Studies in Railway Expansion and the Capital Market in England, 1825–1873*, London: Cass.

Brown, R. (ed.) (1905), *A History of Accounting and Accountants*, Edinburgh: T. C. & E. C. Jack; reprinted (1968), London: Frank Cass.

Brown, R. G. (1962), 'Changing Audit Objectives and Techniques', *Accounting Review*, Oct.; reprinted in M. Chatfield (ed.), *Contemporary Studies in the*

Evolution of Accounting Thought, Belmont, Calif.: Dickenson Publishing Company, 1968.

BRUCE, R. (1994), 'Been there, seen it, do it', *CA Magazine*, Jan.

BUCHANAN, R. A. (1989), *The Engineers: A History of the Engineering Profession in Britain, 1750–1914*, London: Jessica Kingsley.

Burdett's Official Intelligence, London: Spottiswoode & Co.

BURT, T. (1988), 'Management Consultancy: Troubleshooters become Agents of Change', *Accountancy*, Aug.

Business Monitor PA1002: Report on the Census of Production. Summary Volume, London: HMSO.

Business Times, Weekend Edition (1992), 15–16 Aug.

BYWATER, M. F. (1984), 'Edwin Guthrie (1841–1904): Accountant', in D. J. Jeremy (ed.), *Dictionary of Business Biography*, ii, London: Butterworths.

——(1985a), 'Sir William McLintock (1873–1947): Accountant', in D. J. Jeremy (ed.), *Dictionary of Business Biography*, iii, London: Butterworths.

——(1985b), 'William Quilter (1808–88): Accountant', in D. J. Jeremy (ed.), *Dictionary of Business Biography*, iv, London: Butterworths.

Cadbury Committee Report (1992), *Committee on the Financial Aspects of Corporate Governance*, London: Gee.

CAMERON, R. (1967), 'France, 1800–1870', in R. Cameron (ed.), *Banking in the Early Stages of Industrialization: A Study in Comparative Economic History*, Oxford: Oxford University Press.

CARON, F. (1979), *An Economic History of Modern France*, London: Methuen.

CARR-SAUNDERS, A. M., and WILSON, P. A. (1933), *The Professions*, Oxford: Oxford University Press; reprinted (1964), London: Frank Cass & Co.

CASSELL, M. (1984), *Inside Nationwide: One Hundred Years of Co-operation*, London: Nationwide Building Society.

CHANDLER, A. D. (1977), *The Visible Hand*, Cambridge, Mass.: Harvard University Press.

——(1990), *Scale and Scope: The Dynamics of Industrial Capitalism*, Cambridge, Mass.: Belknap Press of the Harvard University Press.

CHANDLER, R., and EDWARDS, J. R. (1996), 'Recurring Issues in Auditing: Back to the Future?', *Accounting, Audit and Accountability Journal*, 9 (2).

————and ANDERSON, M. (1993), 'Changing Perceptions of the Role of the Company Auditor, 1840–1940', *Accounting and Business Research*, Autumn.

CHANNON, D. F. (1973), *The Strategy and Structure of British Enterprise*, London: Macmillan.

CHAPMAN, S. (1974), *Jesse Boot of Boots the Chemist*, London: Hodder & Stoughton.

CHATFIELD, M. (1977), *A History of Accounting Thought*, New York: Krieger Publishing.

CHIBA, J. (1994), 'Kiyoshi Kurosawa 1902–90: An Intellectual Portrait', in J. R. Edwards (ed.), *Twentieth-Century Accounting Thinkers*, London: Routledge.

CHURCH, R. (1979), *Herbert Austin: The British Motor Car Industry to 1941*, London: Europa Publications Limited.

——(1994), *The Rise and Decline of the British Motor Industry*, London: Macmillan.

CIMA (1996), *A Guide to a Career as a Chartered Management Accountant*, London: CIMA.

CLARE, M. (ed.) (1720), *Youth's Introduction to Trade and Business, for the Use of Schools*; London: Symon.

COLEMAN, D. C. (1969), *Courtaulds: An Economic and Social History*, vol. ii, Oxford: Clarendon Press.

——(1973), 'Gentlemen and Players', *Economic History Review*, 2nd ser. 26 (1).

COLLINS, K. (1989), 'Management Education in Japan', in W. Byrt (ed.), *Management Education: An International Survey*, London: Routledge.

COLQUHOUN, A. (1996), 'Latest Developments in the Profession', in *The Ivanhoe Career Guide to Chartered Accountants 1997*, London: Cambridge Market Intelligence Ltd.

CONSTABLE, W. J., and McCORMICK, R. (1986), *The Making of British Managers*, London: British Institute of Management.

COOKE, T. E. (1991), 'The Evolution of Financial Reporting in Japan: A Shame Culture Perspective', *Accounting, Business and Financial History*, 1 (3).

COOMBS, H. M., and EDWARDS, J. R. (1990), 'The Evolution of the District Audit', *Financial Accountability and Management*, Autumn.

——————(1996), *Accounting Innovation: The Case of Municipal Corporations 1833–1935*, London: Garland.

COOPER, E. (1921), 'Fifty-Seven Years in an Accountant's Office', *Accountant*, 22 Oct.; reprinted (1982) New York: Garland Publishing.

Coopers & Lybrand Deloitte (1990), *Our Merger*, London: Coopers & Lybrand Deloitte.

CORINA, M. (1978), *Fine Silks and Oak Counters: Debenhams 1778–1978*, London: Hutchinson Benham.

CORLEY, T. A. B. (1972), *Quaker Enterprises in Biscuits: Huntley & Palmer of Reading 1822–1972*, London: Hutchinson.

——(1984), 'Sir Alastair Frederick Down (1914–): Oil Company Chairman', in D. J. Jeremy (ed.), *Dictionary of Business Biography*, ii, London: Butterworths.

——(1988), *A History of the Burmah Oil Company*, ii: *1924–1966*, London: Heinemann.

CORNWELL, S. V. P. (1991), *Curtis, Jenkins, Cornwell & Co.: A Study in Professional Origins 1816–1966*, New York: Garland.

——(1993), 'The Nature of a Bristol Accountancy Practice during the 1820s: Some Comments', *Accounting, Business and Financial History*, 3 (2).

COTTRELL, P. L. (1980), *Industrial Finance, 1830–1914: The Finance and Organization of English Manufacturing Industry*, London: Methuen.

——(1984), 'David Chadwick (1821–95): Company Promoter', in D. J. Jeremy (ed.), *Dictionary of Business Biography*, i, London: Butterworths.

COULSON-THOMAS, C. (1990), *Professional Development of and for the Board*, London: Institute of Directors.

——(1993), *Creating Excellence in the Boardroom: A Guide to Shaping Directorial Competence and Board Effectiveness*, London: McGraw-Hill.

——and WAKELAM, A. (1991), *The Effective Board: Current Practice, Myths and Realities*, Institute of Directors Discussion Document.

COUNSELL, G. (1984), 'Brought to Account: Neil Clarke', *Accountancy*, Nov.

COWE, R. (ed.) (1993), *The Guardian Guide to the UK's Top Companies*, London: Fourth Estate.

COYLE, D. (1989), 'Beyond Bean Counting', *Investor's Chronicle*, 28 July.

CRAFTS, N. F. R. (1991), 'Economic Growth', in N. F. R. Crafts and N. Woodward (eds.), *The British Economy Since 1945*, Oxford: Clarendon.

Crawford's Directory of City Connections (1995), London: The Economist.

CROFT, M. (1987*a*), 'Brought to Account: Trevor Abbott', *Accountancy*, Feb.

——(1987*b*), 'Brought to Account: Bernard Garbacz', *Accountancy*, Sept.

——(1988), 'Brought to Account: Jenni Williams', *Accountancy*, Apr.

CSO, *Annual Abstract of Statistics*, London: HMSO.

CURTIS, S. J. (1967), *History of Education in Great Britain*, 7th edn., London: University Tutorial Press Ltd.

CUTFORTH, A. E. (1926), *Methods of Amalgamations and the Valuation of Businesses for Amalgamation and Other Purposes*, London: G. Bell.

DAVENPORT-HINES, R. P. T. (1985*a*), 'Sir John Sutherland Harmood-Banner (1847–1927): Accountant and Steel Manufacturer', in D. J. Jeremy (ed.), *Dictionary of Business Biography*, ii, London: Butterworths.

——(1985*b*), 'Sir Mark Webster Jenkinson (1880–1935): Accountant and Industrialist', in D. J. Jeremy (ed.), *Dictionary of Business Biography*, iii, London: Butterworths.

——(1986*a*), 'Francis Vernon Willey, 2nd Lord Barnby (1884–1982): Wool Merchant and Textile Manufacturer', in D. J. Jeremy (ed.), *Dictionary of Business Biography*, v, London: Butterworths.

——(1986*b*), 'Andrew Wilson Tait (1876–1930): Accountant, Financier and Industrialist', in D. J. Jeremy (ed.), *Dictionary of Business Biography*, v, London: Butterworths.

DAVIES, P. N., and BOURN, A. M. (1972), 'Lord Kylsant and the Royal Mail', *Business History*, July.

DAVIS, L. E., and HUTTENBACK, R. A. (1988), *Mammon and the Pursuit of Empire: The Economics of British Imperialism*, Cambridge: Cambridge University Press.

DE MOND, C. W. (1951), *Price, Waterhouse & Co. in America: A History of a Public Accountancy Firm*, New York: Price Waterhouse; reprinted (1980), New York: Arno Press.

Department for Education and Employment (1997), *Education Statistics for the United Kingdom 1996 Edition*, London: The Stationery Office.

Department of Trade and Industry (1993), *Companies in 1992–93*, London: HMSO.

——(1996), *Companies in 1995–96*, London: HMSO.

DE PAULA, F. R. M. (1926), 'The Place of Accounting in Commerce', repr. in F. R. M. de Paula, *Developments in Accounting*, London: Pitman, 1948.

——(1948), '50 Years', *Accounting Research*, Nov.

DERDAK, T. (ed.) (1988), *International Directory of Company Histories*, i: *Advertising–Drugs*, Chicago: St James Press.

DE STE. CROIX, G. E. M. (1956), 'Greek and Roman Accounting', in A. C. Littleton and B. S. Yamey (eds.), *Studies in the History of Accounting*, London: Sweet & Maxwell.

DICKSEE, L. R. (1893), *Bookkeeping for Accountant Students*, London: Gee.

——(1915), *Business Methods and the War*, Cambridge: University Press.

——(1928), *The Fundamentals of Manufacturing Costs*, 2nd edn., London: Gee.

DIMSDALE, N. H. (1991), 'British Monetary Policy since 1945', in N. F. R. Crafts and N. Woodward (eds.), *The British Economy since 1945*, Oxford: Clarendon Press.

Directory of Directors, London: Thomas Skinner.

Directory of Management Consultants in the UK (1991), London: DPA.

DUNKERLEY, J., and HARE, P. G. (1991), 'Nationalised Industries', in N. F. R. Crafts and N. Woodward (eds.), *The British Economy since 1945*, Oxford: Clarendon Press.

DUNNING, J. H. (1993), *Multinational Enterprises and the Global Economy*, Wokingham: Addison-Wesley.

DUTHIE, N. W. (1927), 'The Accountant and Economics', *Accountant*, 25 June.

EARL, M. J. (1983), 'Accounting and Management', in M. J. Earl (ed.), *Perspectives on Management: A Multidisciplinary Analysis*, Oxford: Oxford University Press.

EDWARDS, J. R. (1976), 'The Accounting Profession and Disclosure in Published Reports 1925–35', *Accounting and Business Research*, Autumn.

——(1980), 'British Capital Accounting Practices and Business Finance 1852–1919: An Exemplification', *Accounting and Business Research*, 10 (38).

——(1984a), 'Sir Francis d'Arcy Cooper (1882–1941): Accountant and Industrial Manager', in D. J. Jeremy (ed.), *Dictionary of Business Biography*, i, London: Butterworths.

——(1984b), 'Sir Gilbert Francis Garnsey (1883–1932): Accountant', in D. J. Jeremy (ed.), *Dictionary of Business Biography*, ii, London: Butterworths.

——(1985), 'William Plender, Lord Plender of Sundridge, Kent (1869–1946): Accountant', in D. J. Jeremy (ed.), *Dictionary of Business Biography*, iv, London: Butterworths.

——(1986), 'Edwin Waterhouse (1841–1917): Accountant', in D. J. Jeremy (ed.), *Dictionary of Business Biography*, v, London: Butterworths.

——(1989a), *A History of Financial Accounting*, London: Routledge.

——(1989b), 'Industrial Cost Accounting Developments in Britain to 1830: A Review Article', *Accounting and Business Research*, Autumn.

——(1996), 'Financial Accounting Practice 1600–1970: Continuity and Change', in T. A. Lee, A. Bishop, and R. H. Parker (eds.), *Accounting History from the Renaissance to the Present: A Remembrance of Luca Pacioli*, London: Garland.

——and BABER, C. (1979), 'Dowlais Iron Company: Accounting Policies and Procedures for Profit Measurement and Reporting Purposes', *Accounting and Business Research*, Spring.

——and BOYNS, T. (1992), 'Industrial Organization and Accounting Innovation: Charcoal Ironmaking in England 1690–1783', *Management Accounting Research*, 3.

——and NEWELL, E. (1991), 'The Development of Industrial Cost and Management Accounting before 1850: A Survey of the Evidence', *Business History*, 33 (1).

——and WEBB, K. M. (1985), 'Use of Table A by Companies Registering under the Companies Act 1862', *Accounting and Business Research*, Summer.

——BOYNS, T., and ANDERSON, M. (1995), 'British Cost Accounting Development: Continuity and Change', *Accounting Historians Journal*, 22 (2).

————(eds.) (1996), *British Cost Accounting 1887–1952: Contemporary Essays from the Accounting Literature*, London: Garland.

EDWARDS, R. S. (1937), 'Some Notes on the Early Literature and Development of Cost Accounting in Britain', *Accountant*, 7 Aug.

ELLIOTT, P. (1972), *The Sociology of the Professions*, London: Macmillan.

ERICKSON, C. (1959), *British Industrialists: Steel and Hosiery, 1850–1950*, Cambridge: Cambridge University Press.

ESLAND, G. (1980), 'Professions and Professionalism', in G. Esland and G. Salaman (eds.), *The Politics of Work and Occupations*, Milton Keynes: Open University Press.

ETOR, J. R. (1985), 'Theodore Brooke Jones (1827–1920): Accountant', in D. J. Jeremy (ed.), *Dictionary of Business Biography*, iii, London: Butterworths.

The European Directory of Management Consultants 1995, 3rd edn. (1994), London: A. P. Information Services.

FEA, W. W. (1957), *The Future Role of the Accountant in Industry*, London: ICAEW.

FERRIER, R. W. (1984), 'Sir Arthur Eric Courtney Drake, B. A. (1910–): Petroleum Company Executive', in D. J. Jeremy (ed.), *Dictionary of Business Biography*, ii, London: Butterworths.

FISHER, E. (1992), 'Brought to Account: Edward Pickard', *Accountancy*, May.

——(1993), 'Brought to Account: Ian Hay Davison,' *Accountancy*, July.

——(1994), 'Brought to Account: Michael Julien', *Accountancy*, May.

FITZGERALD, R. (1993), 'Industrial Training and Management Education in Britain: A Missing Dimension', in N. Kawabe and E. Daito (eds.), *Education and Training in the Development of Modern Corporations*, the International Conference on Business History, 19, Proceedings of the Fuji Conference, Tokyo: University of Tokyo Press.

FLEISCHMAN, R. K., and PARKER, L. D. (1990), 'Managerial Accounting Early in the British Industrial Revolution: The Carron Company, a Case Study', *Accounting and Business Research*, Summer.

————(1991), 'British Entrepreneurs and Pre-industrial Revolution Evidence of Cost Management', *Accounting Review*, Apr.

————(1992), 'The Cost Accounting Environment in the British Industrial Revolution Iron Industry', *Accounting, Business and Financial History*, 2 (2).

————and VAMPLEW, W. (1991), 'New Cost Accounting Perspectives on Technological Change in the British Industrial Revolution', in O. F. Graves (ed.), *The Costing Heritage: Studies in Honor of S. Paul Garner*, Harrisonberg, Va.: The Academy of Accounting Historians.

FLEXNER, A. (1915), 'Is Social Work a Profession?', *Studies in Social Work*, 4, New York: New York School of Philanthropy.

FLINT, D. (1971), 'The Role of the Auditor in Modern Society: An Exploratory Essay', *Accounting and Business Research*, Autumn.

FLORENCE, P. S. (1947), 'The Statistical Analysis of Joint Stock Company Control', *Journal of the Royal Statistical Society*, 40 (1).

FOREMAN-PECK, J. (1990), 'The 1856 Companies Act and the Birth and Death of Firms', in P. Jobert and M. Moss (eds.), *The Birth and Death of Companies: An Historical Perspective*, Carnforth: Parthenon.

——(1991), 'Trade and the Balance of Payments', in N. F. R. Crafts and N. Woodward (eds.), *The British Economy since 1945*, Oxford: Clarendon Press.

Foulks Lynch (1955), *Seventy Years of Progress in Accountancy Education*, London: H. Foulks Lynch.

FRENCH, E. A. (1996), 'Northcliffe v. Plender: The Home Front', *Accounting, Business and Financial History*, 6 (3).

GARCKE, E., and FELLS, J. M. (1887), *Factory Accounts*, London: Crosby Lockwood.

GARRETT, A. A. (1961), *History of the Society of Incorporated Accountants 1885–1957*, Oxford: Oxford University Press.

GIBSON, A. H. (1887), 'Trading and Profit and Loss Accounts', *Accountant*, 18 June.

GOURVISH, T. R. (1986), *British Railways 1948–73: A Business History*, Cambridge: Cambridge University Press.

——(1987), 'British Business and the Transition to a Corporate Economy: Entrepreneurship and Management Structures', *Business History*, 29 (4).

Grace, Darbyshire and Todd (1957), *A Short History of Grace, Darbyshire and Todd, Chartered Accountants of Bristol, 1818–1957*, Bristol: Grace, Darbyshire and Todd.

GRAY, R. H., and HELLAR, C. (eds.) (1996), *The British Accounting Review Research Register*, 7th edn., London: Academic Press.

GREEN, E., and MOSS, M. (1982), *A Business of National Importance: The Royal Mail Shipping Group 1902–1937*, London: Methuen.

GREY, S. (1991), 'Brought to Account: Simon Moffat', *Accountancy*, Dec.

——(1993*a*), 'Brought to Account: Hamilton Anstead', *Accountancy*, May.

——(1993*b*), 'Brought to Account: Jim Beveridge', *Accountancy*, Nov.

——(1994*a*), 'Brought to Account: Ian Williams', *Accountancy*, Feb.

——(1994*b*), 'Brought to Account: Hilary Wild', *Accountancy*, Nov.

GRIFFITHS, A., and WALL, S. (eds.) (1993), *Applied Economics: An Introductory Course*, 5th edn., Harlow: Longman Group UK.

HALMOS, P. (1970), *The Personal Service Society*, London: Constable.

The Hambro Company Guide, August Quarter 1996 (1996), London: Hemmington Scott.

HANDY, C., GORDON, C., GOW, I., RANDLESOME, C., and MOLONEY, M. (1987), *The Making of Managers: A Report on Management Education, Training and Development in the USA, West Germany, France, Japan and the UK*, London: British Institute of Management.

——————————(1988), *Making Managers*, London: Pitman.

HANNAH, L. (1983), *The Rise of the Corporate Economy*, 2nd edn., London: Methuen.

HANS, N. A. (1951), *New Trends in Education in the Eighteenth Century*, London: Routledge & Kegan Paul.

HARPER, A. C. (ed.) (1877), *The Accountants' Directory for 1877*, London: Williams & Strahan.

HARVEY, C., and PRESS, J. (1990), 'The City and International Mining, 1870–1914', *Business History*, 32 (3).

HARVEY-JONES, J. (1988), *Making It Happen: Reflections on Leadership*, London: Collins.

HAST, A. (ed.) (1991), *International Directory of Company Histories*, iii: *Health & Personal Care Products–Materials*, Chicago: St James Press.

HASTINGS, Sir P. (1962), 'The Case of the Royal Mail', in W. T. Baxter and S. Davidson (eds.), *Studies in Accounting Theory*, London: Sweet & Maxwell.

HATTON, T. J., and CHRYSTAL, K. A. (1991), 'The Budget and Fiscal Policy', in N. F. R. Crafts and N. Woodward (eds.), *The British Economy since 1945*, Oxford: Clarendon Press.

HAWKINS, L. (1905), *Cost Accounts: An Explanation of Principles and a Guide to Practice*, London: Gee & Co.

HAWKSLEY, F. (1990), 'Brought to Account: Anthony Record', *Accountancy*, Jan.

HAYES, R. H., and ABERNATHY, W. J. (1980), 'Managing our Way to Economic Decline', *Harvard Business Review*, July–Aug.

HENDERSON, G. P., and HENDERSON, S. P. A. (eds.) (1992), *Directory of British Associations & Associations in Ireland*, 11th edn., Beckenham: CBD Research Publications.

HENDERSON, S. P. A., and HENDERSON, A. J. W. (eds.) (1996), *Directory of British Associations & Associations in Ireland*, 13th edn., Beckenham: CBD Research Ltd.

HESELTINE, M. (1993), 'Taking the Long View', Speech to Institute of Directors, Edinburgh, 5 Feb. 1993, Courtesy of Department of Trade and Industry.

HIGHAM, R. (1984), 'Sir Gerard John Regis Leo d'Erlanger (1906–62): Airline Executive', in D. J. Jeremy (ed.), *Dictionary of Business Biography*, ii, London: Butterworths.

——(1986), 'Sir Basil Smallpeice (1906–): Management Accountant and Airline and Shipping Executive', in D. J. Jeremy (ed.), *Dictionary of Business Biography*, v, London: Butterworths.

Higher Education Statistics Agency (1996), *Students in Higher Education Institutions 1994/95*, Cheltenham: HESA.

Hill Vellacott (1988), *Hill Vellacott—A Historical Account of their Development since 1788*, London: Hill Vellacott.

HIRSH, W., and BEVAN, S. (1988), *What Makes a Manager?*, Brighton: Institute of Manpower Studies.

HIRSCHMEIER, J., and YUI, T. (1981), *The Development of Japanese Business, 1600–1980*, 2nd edn., London: Allen & Unwin.

Historical Record of the Census of Production 1907–1970, (1971), London: HMSO.

HMSO (1949), *Report of a Special Committee on Education and Commerce*, London.

HOBSON, O. R. (1953), *A Hundred Years of Halifax: The History of the Halifax Building Society*, 1853–1953, London: Batsford.

Hobson's Casebook Series 1993 (1992), *The Law Casebook*, London: Hobson.

HODGKINS, P. (1979), 'Unilever—The First 21 Years', in T. A. Lee and R. H. Parker (eds.), *The Evolution of Corporate Financial Reporting*, Sunbury-on-Thames: Nelson; reprinted (1984), New York: Garland.

HOLMES, A. R., and GREEN, E. (1986), *Midland: 150 Years of Banking Business*, London: Batsford.

Howard Smith, Thompson (1967), *1867–1967: The First 100 Years*, Birmingham: Howard Smith, Thompson & Co.

HOWITT, Sir H. (1966), *The History of the Institute of Chartered Accountants in England and Wales 1880–1965, and of its Founder Accountancy Bodies 1870–1880*, London: Heinemann; reprinted (1984), New York: Garland Publishing.

HOWSON, S. (1981), 'Slump and Unemployment', in R. Floud and D. McCloskey (eds.), *The Economic History of Britain since 1700*, ii: *1860 to the 1970s*, Cambridge: Cambridge University Press.

HUBBARD, P. (1991), 'Grant Thornton: A Brief History', unpublished.

HUDSON, J. (1989), 'The Birth and Death of Firms in England and Wales during the Inter-war Years', *Business History*, 31 (3).

HUDSON, K. (1985), 'Sir John Keay (1894–1964): China Clay Industrialist', in D. J. Jeremy (ed.), *Dictionary of Business Biography*, iii, London: Butterworths.

HUGHES, E. C. (1963), 'Professions', *Daedalus*, Fall.

HUNT, B. C. (1936), *The Development of the Business Corporation in England 1800–1867*, Cambridge, Mass.: Harvard University Press.

HYDE, C. K. (1977), *Technological Change and the British Iron Industry, 1700–1870*, Princeton: Princeton University Press.

ICAEW (1994*a*), *Annual Report and Accounts 1994*, London: ICAEW.

——(1994*b*), *Members Handbook 1994*, i: *Constitutional, Ethical, Legal*, London: ICAEW.

——(1996*a*), *Education, Training and Student Salary Statistics—1994/95*, London: ICAEW.

——(1996*b*), *End of Year Membership Statistics 1995*, Milton Keynes: ICAEW.

——(1996*c*), *Statistical Circular on Members, Students and Offices as at 1 October 1996*, Milton Keynes: ICAEW.

——(1996*d*), *Questionnaire File Analysis, Reports, September 1996*, Milton Keynes: ICAEW.

——*ICAEW Membership Questionnaires*, Milton Keynes: ICAEW.

ICAEW Board for Chartered Accountants in Business (1996), *Changing Work Patterns*, London: ICAEW.

ICWA (1969), 'Institute of Cost and Works Accountants, 1919–1969: Portrait of a Profession', *Management Accounting*, Mar.

IRVINE, J. (1986), 'Brought to Account: Timothy Brookes', *Accountancy*, Oct.

——(1991), 'Brought to Account: Brian McGowan', *Accountancy*, Nov.

——(1992*a*), 'Brought to Account: Sir Paul Girolami', *Accountancy*, Apr.

——(1992*b*), 'Brought to Account: Mark Silver', *Accountancy*, June.

——(1993*a*), 'Brought to Account: John Corrin', *Accountancy*, Mar.

——(1993*b*), 'Brought to Account: Peter Davies', *Accountancy*, June.

——(1994), 'Brought to Account: Richard Close', *Accountancy*, Apr.

The Ivanhoe Career Guide to Chartered Accountants 1997 (1996), London: Cambridge Market Intelligence Ltd.

JEREMY, D. J. (ed.) (1984–6), *Dictionary of Business Biography*, i–v, London: Butterworths.

——and TWEEDALE, I. G. (1994), *Dictionary of Twentieth Century Business Leaders*, London: Bourker Saur.

JOHNSON, T. J. (1972), *Professions and Power*, London: Macmillan.

——(1980), 'Work and Power', in G. Esland and G. Salaman (eds.), *The Politics of Work and Occupations*, Milton Keynes: Open University Press.

——(1993), 'Expertise and the State', in M. Gane and T. J. Johnson (eds.), *Foucault's New Domains*, London: Routledge.

JONES, E. (1981), *Accountancy and the British Economy 1840–1980: The Evolution of Ernst & Whinney*, London: Batsford.

——(1984*a*), 'Ernest Cooper (1848–1926): Accountant', in D. J. Jeremy (ed.), *Dictionary of Business Biography*, i, London: Butterworths.

——(1984*b*), 'William Welch Deloitte (1818–1898): Accountant', in D. J. Jeremy (ed.), *Dictionary of Business Biography*, ii, London: Butterworths.

——(1984*c*), 'Henry Alexander Benson, Lord Benson (1909–). Accountant', in D. J. Jeremy (ed.), *Dictionary of Business Biography*, i, London: Butterworths.

——(1985*a*), 'Sir Basil Edgar Mayhew (1883–1966): Accountant', in D. J. Jeremy (ed.), *Dictionary of Business Biography*, iv, London: Butterworths.

——(1985*b*), 'James Hornby Jolly (1887–1972): Industrialist', in D. J. Jeremy (ed.), *Dictionary of Business Biography*, iii, London: Butterworths.

—— (1985c), 'Sir Robert Palmer Harding (1821–1893): Accountant', in D. J. Jeremy (ed.), *Dictionary of Business Biography*, iii, London: Butterworths.

Jones, E. (1986a), 'William Turquand (1818–1894): Accountant', in D. J. Jeremy (ed.), *Dictionary of Business Biography*, v, London: Butterworths.

—— (1986b), 'Frederick Whinney (1829–1916): Accountant', in D. J. Jeremy (ed.), *Dictionary of Business Biography*, v, London: Butterworths.

—— (1990), *A History of GKN*, ii: *The Growth of the Business, 1918–45*, London: Macmillan.

—— (1995), *True and Fair: A History of Price Waterhouse*, London: Hamish Hamilton.

—— (ed.) (1988), *The Memoirs of Edwin Waterhouse: A Founder of Price Waterhouse*, London: Batsford.

Jones, E. T. (1796), *Jones's English System of Bookkeeping*, Bristol; reprinted (1978), New York: Arno Press.

Jones, H. (1985), *Accounting, Costing and Cost Estimation, Welsh Industry: 1700–1830*, Cardiff: University of Wales Press.

Kaner, R. A. (1985), 'George James Harris (1895–1958): Chocolate Manufacturer', in D. J. Jeremy (ed.), *Dictionary of Business Biography*, iii, London: Butterworths.

Kedslie, M. J. M. (1990a), *Firm Foundations: The Development of Professional Accounting in Scotland*, Hull: Hull University Press.

—— (1990b), 'Mutual Self Interest—a Unifying Force: The Dominance of Societal Closure over Social Background in the Early Professional Accounting Bodies', *Accounting Historians Journal*, 17 (2).

Keeble, S. P. (1992), *The Ability to Manage: A Study of British Management, 1890–1990*, Manchester: Manchester University Press.

Kelly, M. (1987a), 'Brought to Account: Bruce Rattray', *Accountancy*, Jan.

—— (1987b), 'Brought to Account: David Watson', *Accountancy*, Nov.

—— (1988), 'Brought to Account: Derek Peter', *Accountancy*, Sept.

Kennedy, C. (1992), 'Medicine Man to the World', *Director*, Nov.

Kennedy, W. P. (1987), *Industrial Structure, Capital Markets and the Origins of British Economic Decline*, Cambridge: Cambridge University Press.

Kettle, Sir R. (1957), *Deloitte & Co. 1845–1956*, Oxford: Oxford University Press.

Kindleburger, C. P. (1984), *The Financial History of Western Europe*, London: Allen & Unwin.

Kirkham, L. (1992), 'Integrating *Herstory* and *History* in Accountancy', *Accounting, Organizations and Society*, 17 (3/4).

—— and Loft, A. (1992), 'Insiders and Outsiders: Intra-occupational Rivalry in Accountancy, 1880–1930', paper presented to the fourth Accounting, Business and Financial History Conference, Cardiff.

———— (1993), 'Gender and the Construction of the Professional Accountant', *Accounting, Organizations and Society*, 18 (6).

———— (1996), 'Census Reports and the Instruction of the Professional Accountant', paper presented at the Nineteenth Annual Congress of the European Accounting Association, Bergen.

Kitchen, J. (1979), 'The Accounts of British Holding Company Groups: Development and Attitudes to Disclosure in the Early Years', in T. A. Lee and R. H. Parker (eds.), *The Evolution of Corporate Financial Reporting*, Sunbury-on-Thames: Nelson; reprinted (1984), New York: Garland.

——(1984), 'Frederic Rudolf Mackley de Paula (1882–1954): Accountant', in D. J. Jeremy (ed.), *Dictionary of Business Biography*, ii, London: Butterworths.

KITCHEN, J. and PARKER, R. H. (1980), *Accounting Thought and Education: Six English Pioneers*, London: ICAEW.

KITCHEN, M. (1978), *The Political Economy of Germany, 1815–1914*, London: Croom Helm.

Korn/Ferry Carre/Orban International (1994), *Boards of Directors Study 1994*, London: Korn/Ferry Carre/Orban International.

Korn/Ferry International (1991), *Boards of Directors Study U. K.*, London: Korn/Ferry International.

KOUDRA, M. (1975), *Management Training, Practice and Attitude*, Management Survey Report No. 24, London: British Institute of Management.

LARSON, M. S. (1977), *The Rise of Professionalism. A Sociological Analysis*, Berkeley and Los Angeles: University of California Press.

LAZELL, H. G. (1975), *From Pills to Penicillin: The Beecham Story*, London: Heinemann.

LEE, G. A. (1977), 'The Coming of Age of Double Entry: The Giovanni Farolfi Ledger of 1299–1300', *Accounting Historians Journal*, Fall.

LEE, T. A. (1979), 'A Brief History of Company Audits', in T. A. Lee and R. H. Parker (eds.), *The Evolution of Corporate Financial Reporting*, Sunbury-on-Thames: Nelson.

LETTS, S. A. (1980), *MacIntyre Hudson, May 1880–May 1980*, London: MacIntyre Hudson.

LEWIS, R., and MAUDE, A. (1952), *Professional People*, London: Phoenix House.

LISLE, G. (1899), *Accounting in Theory and Practice: A Text-Book for the Use of Accountants*, Edinburgh: William Green.

LOCKE, R. R. (1984), *The End of the Practical Man: Entrepreneurship and Higher Education in Germany, France, and Great Britain, 1880–1940*, Greenwich, Conn.: Jai.

——(1985), 'Business Education in Germany: Past Systems and Current Practice', *Business History Review*, 59 (2).

——(1993), 'Higher Education and Management: Their Relational Changes in the Twentieth Century', in N. Kawabe and E. Daito (eds.), *Education and Training in the Development of Modern Corporations*, the International Conference on Business History, 19, Proceedings of the Fuji Conference, Tokyo: University of Tokyo Press.

LOFT, A. (1986), 'Towards a Critical Understanding of Accounting. The Case of Cost Accounting in the UK, 1914–1925', *Accounting, Organizations and Society*, 11 (2).

——(1990), *Coming into the Light: A Study of the Development of a Professional Association for Cost Accountants in Britain in the Wake of the First World War*, London: CIMA.

——(1992), 'Accountancy and the Gendered Division of Labour: A Review Essay', *Accounting, Organizations and Society*, 17 (3/4).

MCAULIFFE, H. (1987), 'Not in our Stars but in Ourselves', *Accountancy*, Oct.

——(1988), 'Accountants are People too', *Accountancy*, May.

MACDONALD, K. M. (1984), 'Professional Formation: The Case of Scottish Accountants', *British Journal of Sociology*, 35 (2).

——(1985), 'Professional Formation: Social Closure and Occupational Registration', *Sociology*, 19 (4).

MACDONALD, K. M. (1995), *The Sociology of the Professions*, London: Sage.

McDOUGALL, E. H. V. (1954), *A History of the Chartered Accountants of Scotland from the Earliest Times to 1954*, Edinburgh: Institute of Chartered Accountants of Scotland.

McKENDRICK, N. (1970), 'Josiah Wedgwood and Cost Accounting in the Industrial Revolution', *Economic History Review*, Apr.

McKENNA, C. D. (1995), 'The Origins of Modern Management Consulting', *Business and Economic History*, 24 (1).

McKENNA, E. F. (1978), *The Management Style of the Chief Accountant*, Farnborough: Saxon House.

McKENNA, J. F. (1989), 'Management Education in the United States', in W. Byrt (ed.), *Management Education: An International Survey*, London: Routledge.

McKINLAY, J. B. (1973), 'On the Professional Regulation of Change', in P. Halmos (ed.), *Professionalisation and Social Change*, Sociological Review Monograph No. 20, Keele: Keele University Press.

MACKINTOSH, M., et al. (1996), *Economics and Changing Economies*, London: International Thompson Business Press and the Open University.

MACVE, R. H. (1986), 'Some Glosses on "Greek and Roman Accounting"', *History of Political Thought*, 6.

MANNARI, H. (1974), *The Japanese Business Leaders*, Tokyo: University of Tokyo Press.

Mann Judd Gordon (1967), *[Interim Account] . . . of a Going Concern: Some Essays on the History of the Firm of Mann Judd Gordon & Company, Chartered Accountants Glasgow, circa 1817 to 1967, on the Occasion of the 150th Anniversary of its Foundation*, Glasgow: Mann Judd Gordon & Co.

MANSFIELD, R., and POOLE, M. (1991), *British Management in the Thatcher Years*, London: British Institute of Management.

MARGERISON, T. (1980), *The Making of a Profession*, London: The Institute of Chartered Accountants in England and Wales.

MARRINER, S. (1980), 'The Ministry of Munitions 1915–19 and Government Accounting Procedures', *Accounting and Business Research*, Special Accounting History Issue.

MARSH, P. R. (1990), *Short-Termism on Trial*, London: Institutional Fund Managers' Association.

MATTESSICH, R. (1994), 'Archaeology of Accounting and Schmandt-Besserat's Contribution', *Accounting, Business and Financial History*, 4 (1).

MATTHEWS, D. (1993), 'Counting the Accountants: A Trial Balance for 1911', *Accounting, Business and Financial History*, 3 (2).

MATTHEWS, D., ANDERSON, M., and EDWARDS, J. R. (1997), 'The rise of the professional accountant in British management', *The Economic History Review*, L (3).

MATTHEWS, R. C. O., FEINSTEIN, C. H., and ODLING-SMEE, J. C. (1982), *British Economic Growth 1856–1973*, Oxford: Clarendon.

MEDLAM, W. (1980), *Pannell Kerr Forster: A History of Pannell Fitzpatrick & Co. 1980*, London: Pannell Kerr Forster.

MELROSE-WOODMAN, J. (1976), *Profile of the British Manager*, London: British Institute of Management.

MICHIE, R. C. (1987), *The London and New York Stock Exchanges, 1850–1914*, London: Allen & Unwin.

MILLERSON, G. (1964), *The Qualifying Associations*, London: Routledge & Kegan Paul.

MILLS, G. (1981), *On the Board*, Aldershot: Gower.

——(1985), *On the Board*, 2nd edn., London: George Allen & Unwin.

MILLS, P. A. (1990), 'Agency, Auditing and the Unregulated Environment: Some Further Historical Evidence', *Accounting, Auditing and Accountability*, 3 (1).

MILWARD, A. S., and SAUL, S. B. (1973), *The Economic Development of Continental Europe, 1780–1870*, London: Allen & Unwin.

MITCHELL, A. (1985a), 'Brought to Account: Nigel Haslam', *Accountancy*, Mar.

——(1985b), 'Brought to Account: Stanley Thomson', *Accountancy*, July.

——(1985c), 'Brought to Account: Christopher Synge Barton', *Accountancy*, Aug.

MITCHELL, B. R. (1962), *Abstract of British Historical Statistics*, Cambridge: Cambridge University Press.

——(1988), *British Historical Statistics*, Cambridge: Cambridge University Press.

Moore and Smalley (1992), *100 Years of Moore & Smalley: A Brief History*, Preston: Moore and Smalley.

MORGAN, E. V., and THOMAS, W. A. (1962), *The Stock Exchange: Its History and Functions*, London: Elek.

MORGAN, R. M. (1985), 'William Hunter McFadzean (1903–). Cable Manufacturer', in D. J. Jeremy (ed.), *Dictionary of Business Biography*, iv, London: Butterworths.

Morris, Gregory & Co. (1953), *A History of One Hundred Years of Accounting Practice 1852–1952*, Manchester: Morris, Gregory & Co.

MUELLER, R., and GALBRAITH, E. G. (1976), *German Stock Corporation Law: The German Law on the Accounting by Major Enterprises Other than Stock Corporations*, 2nd edn., Frankfurt: Fritz Knapp.

MUMFORD, M. J. (1991), 'Chartered Accountants as Business Managers: An Oral History Perspective', *Accounting, Business and Financial History*, 1 (2).

MUNN, C. W. (1990a), 'James Ivory', in A. Slaven and S. Checkland (eds.), *Dictionary of Scottish Business Biography 1860–1960*, ii: *Processing, Distribution, Services*, Aberdeen: Aberdeen University Press.

——(1990b), 'Ian Wilson MacDonald', in A. Slaven and S. Checkland (eds.), *Dictionary of Scottish Business Biography 1860–1960*, ii: *Processing, Distribution, Services*, Aberdeen: Aberdeen University Press.

MURCH, L. (1986), 'Alexander Frederick Farquhar Young (1903–): Building Materials', in D. J. Jeremy (ed.), *Dictionary of Business Biography*, v, London: Butterworths.

MURRAY, A., and CARTER, R. N. (1895), *A Guide to Income-Tax Practice*, London: Gee.

MURRAY, D. (1930), *Chapters in the History of Bookkeeping, Accountancy & Commercial Arithmetic*, Glasgow: Jackson, Wylie; reprinted (1978), New York: Arno Press.

NAKAMURA, T. (1983), *Economic Growth in Pre-war Japan*, New Haven: Yale University Press.

NAPIER, C. J. (1994), 'The Intellectual and Professional Influence of Economics on Accounting in the United Kingdom: 1850–1950', paper presented at the Seventeenth Annual Congress of the European Accounting Association, Venice.

——(1996), 'Academic Disdain? Economists and Accounting in Britain, 1850–1950', *Accounting, Business and Financial History*, 6 (3).

——and NOKE, C. (1992), 'Accounting and Law: An Historical Overview of an Uneasy Relationship', in M. Bromwich and A. Hopwood (eds.), *Accounting and the Law*, Hemel Hempstead: Prentice Hall.

NASH, T. (1991), 'Two Men and a Hit Squad', *Director*, June.

NEWTON, F. G. (1899), 'The Auditing of Public Companies: Some Considerations Suggested by the Millwall Dock Scandal', *Accountants' Magazine*, 3 (28).

NICHOLSON, J. L., and ROHRBACH, J. F. D. (1919), *Cost Accounting*, New York: Ronald Press.

NOBES, C. W. (1994), 'The Gallerani Account Book of 1305–08', in R. H. Parker and B. S. Yamey (eds.), *Accounting History: Some British Contributions*, Oxford: Clarendon Press.

——and PARKER, R. H. (eds.) (1991), *Comparative International Accounting*, 3rd edn., London: Prentice Hall.

NOCKOLDS, H. (1976), *Lucas: The First Hundred Years*, i: *The King of the Road*, Newton Abbot: David Charles.

——(1986), 'Sir Arthur Bertram Waring (1902–74): Manufacturer of Electrical Engineering Components', in D. J. Jeremy (ed.), *Dictionary of Business Biography*, v, London: Butterworths.

NOKE, C. (1981), 'Accounting for Bailiffship in Thirteenth Century England', *Accounting and Business Research*, Spring.

NORTON, G. P. (1889), *Textile Manufacturers' Book-keeping*, Huddersfield: Alfred Jubb; reprinted (1976), New York: Arno Press.

OECD, *OECD National Accounts*, Paris.

——*OECD Quarterly Labour Force Statistics*, Paris.

OSBOURN, F. C., and BELL, R. T. (1954), *Fifty Years: The Story of the Association of Certified and Corporate Accountants 1904–54*, London: The Association of Certified and Corporate Accountants.

OWEN, G., and ABELL, P. (1993), *The Changing Role of the Finance Director*, London: ICAEW.

PARKER, R. H. (1980*a*), *British Accountants: A Biographical Sourcebook*, New York: Arno Press.

——(1980*b*), 'Those First Councillors . . . A Golden Heritage', *Accountancy*, May.

——(1984), *Macmillan Dictionary of Accounting*, London: Macmillan.

——(1985), 'Sir William Barclay Peat (1852–1936): Accountant', in D. J. Jeremy (ed.), *Dictionary of Business Biography*, iv, London: Butterworths.

——(1986), *The Development of the Accountancy Profession in Britain to the Early Twentieth Century*, n.p.: The Academy of Accounting Historians.

——(1992), *Macmillan Dictionary of Accounting*, 2nd edn., London: Macmillan.

PATRICK, H. (1967), 'Japan, 1868–1914', in R. Cameron (ed.), *Banking in the Early Stages of Industrialization: A Study in Comparative Economic History*, Oxford: Oxford University Press.

PAYNE, P. L. (1967), 'The Emergence of the Large Scale Company in Great Britain, 1870–1914', *Economic History Review*, 2nd ser. 20 (3).

——(1979), *Colvilles and the Scottish Steel Industry*, Oxford: Clarendon Press.

PERKIN, H. (1989), *The Rise of Professional Society: England since 1880*, London: Routledge.

PIMM, D. A. (1991), 'Off Balance Sheet Finance', in D. J. Tonkin and L. C. L. Skerratt (eds.), *Financial Reporting 1990–91: A Survey of UK Reporting Practice*, London: ICAEW.

PIXLEY, F. W. (1881), *Auditors: Their Duties and Responsibilities*, London: Effingham Wilson; reprinted (1976), New York: Arno Press.

——(1897), *The Profession of a Chartered Accountant*, London: Good; reprinted (1978), New York: Arno Press.

——(1908), *Accountancy*, London: Pitman.

PLUMPTON, T. (1892), 'Manufacturing Costs', *Accountant*, 26 Mar.

Pocket MBA (1994), London: The Economist Books.

POLLARD, S. (1983), *The Development of the British Economy 1914–1980*, 3rd edn., London: Arnold.

——(1989), *Britain's Prime and Britain's Decline*, London: Edward Arnold.

Post Office Kelly's Directory, London: Reed Information Services.

POYNTON, T. L. (1960), *The Institute of Municipal Treasurers and Accountants: A Short History 1885–1960*, London: The Institute of Municipal Treasurers and Accountants.

PREVITS, G. J., and MERINO, B. D. (1979), *A History of Accounting in America: An Historical Interpretation of the Cultural Significance of Accounting*, New York: Ronald Press.

Price Commission (1979), *BP Oil Ltd—Oil and Petroleum Products*.

READER, W. J. (1966), *Professional Men: The Rise of the Professional Classes in Nineteenth-Century England*, London: Weidenfeld & Nicolson.

——(1975), *Imperial Chemical Industries: A History*, ii. *The First Quarter-Century 1926–1952*, London: Oxford University Press.

——(1976), *Metal Box: A History*, London: Heinemann.

——(1981), *Bowater: A History*, Cambridge: Cambridge University Press.

REYNOLDS, B. (1993), *Excellence in Accountancy*, London: Macmillan.

RICHARDS, A. B. (1981), *Touche Ross & Co., 1899–1981: The Origins and Growth of the United Kingdom Firm*, London: Touche Ross.

——(1986), 'Sir George Alexander Touche (1861–1935): Professional Accountant', in D. J. Jeremy (ed.), *Dictionary of Business Biography*, v, London: Butterworths.

RICHARDS, G. E. (1950), *History of the First Fifty Years*, London: privately printed for Price Waterhouse.

RITCHIE, B., and GOLDSMITH, W. (1987), *The New Elite: Britain's Top Chief Executives*, London: Weidenfeld & Nicolson.

ROBB, G. (1992), *White Collar Crime in Modern England: Financial Fraud and Business Morality, 1845–1929*, Cambridge: Cambridge University Press.

Robbins Report (1963), *Report of the Royal Commission on Higher Education*, Chairman L. Robbins, Cmnd. 2154, London: HMSO.

ROBINSON, H. W. (1964), *A History of Accountants in Ireland*, Dublin: The Institute of Chartered Accountants in Ireland.

ROSLENDER, R. (1992), *Sociological Perspectives on Modern Accountancy*, London: Routledge.

RUBINSTEIN, W. D. (1984), 'Sir John Reeves Ellerman (1862–1933): Shipping Magnate and Financier', in D. J. Jeremy (ed.), *Dictionary of Business Biography*, ii, London: Butterworths.

RYERSON, B. (1980), *The Giants of Small Heath: The History of BSA*, Yeovil: Haynes.

SAMPSON, A. (1965), *Anatomy of Britain Today*, London: Hodder & Stoughton.

——(1982), *The Changing Anatomy of Britain*, London: Hodder & Stoughton.

SAYERS, R. S. (1957), *Lloyds Bank in the History of English Banking*, Oxford: Clarendon Press.

SCHMANDT-BESSERAT, D. (1992), *Before Writing*, i: *From Counting to Cuneiform*, ii: *A Catalogue of Near Eastern Tokens*, Austin: University of Texas Press.

SCHMITZ, C. (1990), 'George Auldjo Jamieson', in A. Slaven and S. Checkland (eds.), *Dictionary of Scottish Business Biography 1860–1960*, ii: *Processing, Distribution, Services*, Aberdeen: Aberdeen University Press.

SCOTT, J. D. (1962), *Vickers: A History*, London: Weidenfeld & Nicolson.

SHACKLETON, J. K., and MILNER, M. (1996), 'Alexander Sloan: A Glasgow Chartered Accountant', in T. A. Lee (ed.), *Shaping the Accountancy Profession: The Story of Three Scottish Pioneers*, London: Garland.

SHANNON, H. A. (1933), 'The Limited Companies of 1866–1883', *Economic History Review*, 4 (3); reprinted in E. M. Carus-Wilson (ed.) (1954), *Essays in Economic History*, vol. i, London: Edward Arnold.

SHAW, C. (1983), 'The Large Manufacturing Employers of 1907', *Business History*, 25 (1).

——(1986), 'Sir Robert Sainsbury (1906–): 'Grocery Chain Proprietor', in D. J. Jeremy (ed.), *Dictionary of Business Biography*, v, London: Butterworths.

Shelton Iron, Steel & Coal Co. Ltd. (NWRRC), British Steel Corporation, North Western Regional Records Centre, Shotton Works, Deeside, Clwyd, location no. 6720.

SIEFF, M. (1990), *Marcus Sieff on Management: The Marks & Spencer Way*, London: Weidenfeld & Nicolson.

SIKKA, P., PUXTY, T., WILLMOTT, H., and COOPER, C. (1992), *Eliminating the Expectations Gap?*, Certified Research Report 28, London: Certified Accountants Educational Trust.

SLAVEN, A., and CHECKLAND, S. (eds.), *Dictionary of Scottish Business Biography 1860–1960*, i–ii, Aberdeen: Aberdeen University Press.

SMITH, B. M. D. (1986), 'Eric Turner (1918–1980): Motor Cycle Company Executive', in D. J. Jeremy (ed.), *Dictionary of Business Biography*, v, London: Butterworths.

SMITH, T. (1992), *Accounting for Growth: Stripping the Camouflage from Company Accounts*, London: Century Business.

SOLOMONS, D. (1952), 'The Historical Development of Costing', in D. Solomons (ed.), *Studies in Costing*, London: Sweet & Maxwell.

SOMERS, F. J. L. (ed.) (1991), *European Economies: A Comparative Study*, London: Pitman.

South Durham Steel & Iron Co. Ltd. (NERRC), British Steel Corporation, North Eastern Regional Records Centre, Skippers Lane, Middlesbrough, location no. 04879.

SOWERBY, T. (1984), *The History of the Chartered Institute of Public Finance and Accountancy 1885–1985*, London: CIPFA.

STACEY, N. A. H. (1954), *English Accountancy: A Study in Social and Economic History 1800–1954*, London: Gee.

STAMP, E., and MARLEY, C. (1970), *Accounting Principles and the City Code: The Case for Reform*, London: Butterworths.

STAMP, Sir J. (1921), 'The Relation of Accountancy to Economics', *Incorporated Accountants' Journal*, Nov.

STEWART, J. C. (1977), *Pioneers of a Profession: Chartered Accountants to 1879*, Edinburgh: Institute of Chartered Accountants of Scotland.

The Stock Exchange Official Intelligence, London: Spottiswoode & Co.; post-1910, London: Spottiswoode, Ballantyne & Co.

The Stock Exchange Official Year-Book, London: Thomas Skinner.

STONE, W. E. (1973), 'An Early English Cotton Mill Cost Accounting System: Charlton Mills, 1810–1889', *Accounting and Business Research*, Winter.

STRACHAN, W. (1903), *Cost Accounts: The Key to Economy in Manufacture*, 2nd edn., London: Stevens & Haynes.

SULLY, A. V. (1951), *Towards the Centenary: Notes on the Origin and History of an Accountancy Practice. J. & A. W. Sully and Co.*, London.

SYRETT, M. (1988), 'So What Does Make a Manager?', *Director*, May.

TAKAGI, S. (1993), *Japanese Capital Markets: New Developments in Regulations and Institutions*, Oxford: Blackwell.

TAWNEY, R. H. (1921), *The Acquisitive Society*, London: G. Bell.

TILLY, H. T. (1967), 'Germany, 1815–1870', in R. Cameron (ed.), *Banking in the Early Stages of Industrialization: A Study in Comparative Economic History*, Oxford: Oxford University Press.

The Times 1000 1997 (1996), London: Times Books.

TRICKER, R. I. (1967), *The Accountant in Management*, London: Batsford.

Viney Merretts (1974), *At your Service*, London: Viney Merretts.

WALKER, S. P. (1988), *The Society of Accountants in Edinburgh 1854–1914: A Study of Recruitment to a New Profession*, New York: Garland.

——(1991), 'The Defence of Professional Monopoly—Scottish Chartered Accountants and Satellites in the Accountancy Firmament 1854–1914', *Accounting, Organizations and Society*, 16 (3).

——(1993), 'Anatomy of a Scottish CA Practice: Lindsay, Jamieson & Haldane 1818–1918', *Accounting, Business and Financial History*, 3 (2).

——(1995), 'The Genesis of Professional Organization in Scotland: A Contextual Analysis', *Accounting, Organizations and Society*, 20 (4).

——(1996), 'George Auldjo Jamieson—A Victorian "Man of Affairs"', in T. A. Lee (ed.), *Shaping the Accountancy Profession: The Story of Three Scottish Pioneers*, London: Garland.

——and SHACKLETON, J. K. (1995), 'Corporatism and Structural Change in the British Accountancy Profession, 1930–1957', *Accounting, Organizations and Society*, 20 (6).

————(1996), 'A Ring Fence for the Profession: Advancing the Closure of British Accountancy 1957–1970', paper presented at 7th World Congress of Accounting Historians, Kingston, Ontario.

WARDLEY, P. (1991), 'The Anatomy of Big Business: Aspects of Corporate Development in the Twentieth Century', *Business History*, 33 (2).

WATTS, R. L. (1977), 'Corporate Financial Statements, A Product of the Market and Political Process', *Australian Journal of Management*, Apr.

——and ZIMMERMAN, J. L. (1979), 'The Demand for and Supply of Accounting Theories: The Market for Excuses', *Accounting Review*, Apr.

————(1983), 'Agency Problems, Auditing and the Theory of the Firm: Some Evidence', *Journal of Law and Economics*, 26 (3).

WEBER, M. (1968), *Economy and Society: An Outline of Interpretive Sociology*, New York: Bedminster Press.

WEISS, B. (1986), *The Hell of the English: Bankruptcy and the Victorian Novel*, London: Associated University Presses.

WEST, B. P. (1996), 'The Professionalisation of Accounting: A Review of Recent Historical Research and its Implications', *Accounting History*, 1 (1).

WHEATCROFT, M. (1970), *The Revolution in British Management Education*, London: Pitman.

WHINNEY, F. (1887), 'President's Address to the Institute of Chartered Accountants in England and Wales', *Accountant*, 2 July.

WIENER, M. J. (1981), *English Culture and the Decline of the Industrial Spirit, 1850–1980*, Cambridge: Cambridge University Press.

WILENSKY, H. (1964), 'The Professionalization of Everyone', *American Journal of Sociology*, 69.

WILKINS, M. (1988), 'The Free Standing Company, 1870–1914: An Important Type of British Foreign Direct Investment', *Economic History Review*, 2nd ser. 41 (2).

WILLIAMS, I. A. (1931), *The Firm of Cadbury, 1831–1931*, London: Constable.

WILLIAMS, K., WILLIAMS, J., and THOMAS, D. (1983), *Why are the British Bad at Manufacturing?*, London: Routledge & Kegan Paul.

WILLIAMSON, O. (1981), 'Modern Corporation: Origins, Evolution and Attributes', *Journal of Economic Literature*, 19.

WILLMOTT, H. (1986), 'Organising the Profession: A Theoretical and Historical Examination of the Development of the Major Accountancy Bodies in the UK', *Accounting, Organizations and Society*, 11 (6).

——COOPER, D., and PUXTY, T. (1993), 'Maintaining Self-Regulation: Making "Interests" Coincide in Discourses on the Governance of the ICAEW', *Accounting, Auditing and Accountability Journal*, 4 (4).

WILSON, C. (1954), *A History of Unilever: A Study in Economic Growth and Social Change* (2 vols.), London: Cassell.

——(1977), 'Management and Policy in Large-Scale Enterprise: Lever Brothers and Unilever, 1918–1938', in B. Supple (ed.), *Essays in British Business History*, Oxford: Clarendon Press.

WILSON, J. F. (1988), *Ferranti and the British Electrical Industry, 1864–1930*, Manchester: Manchester University Press.

——(1995), *British Business History, 1720–1994*, Manchester: Manchester University Press.

WINSBURY, R. (1977), *Thomson McLintock & Co.: The First Hundred Years*, London: privately published.

WISE, T. A. (1982), *Peat, Marwick, Mitchell and Co.: 85 Years*, New York: privately printed for Peat, Marwick, Mitchell and Co.

WITTY, R. A. (1906), *How to Become a Qualified Accountant*, London: Pitman.

WOOLF, A. E. (1912), *A Short History of Accountants and Accountancy*, London: Gee; reprinted (1986), New York: Garland.

WORKMAN, E. W. (1929), *Costing Organisation for Engineers*, 2nd edn., London: Pitman.

World Trade Organization (1996), *Annual Report*.

WORTHINGTON, B. (1895), *Professional Accountants: An Historical Sketch*, London: Gee; reprinted (1978), New York: Arno Press.

WW—*Who's Who: An Annual Biographical Dictionary*, London: Adam and Charles Black.

WWW—*Who Was Who*, London: A. & C. Black.

YAMEY, B. S. (1956), 'Edward Jones and the Reform of Book-keeping, 1795–1810', in A. C. Littleton and B. S. Yamey (eds.), *Studies in the History of Accounting*, London: Sweet & Maxwell; reprinted (1978), New York: Arno Press.

ZEFF, S. A. (1979), 'Chronology: Significant Developments in the Establishment of Accounting Principles in the United States, 1926–1978', in T. A. Lee and R. H. Parker (eds.), *The Evolution of Corporate Financial Reporting*, Sunbury-on-Thames: Nelson.

INDEX